History Making and Present Day Politics
The Meaning of Collective Memory in South Africa

Edited by
Hans Erik Stolten

NORDISKA AFRIKAINSTITUTET, UPPSALA 2007

Indexing terms:

History
Political history
Political development
Social change
Nation-building
Post-apartheid
Historiography
South Africa

Language checking: Elaine Almén

Index: Rohan Bolton

Cover photo by Aleksander Gamme

ISBN 978-91-7106-581-0

© the authors and Nordiska Afrikainstitutet 2007

Printed in Sweden by Elanders Gotab AB, Stockholm 2007

Contents

CHAPTER 1

History in the new South Africa:

An introduction

Hans Erik Stolten

South Africa is a country that continues to fascinate the rest of the world. In addition to being part of the Third World, the country is a micro-cosmos that serves to illustrate many of the global problems we all face. In a spirit of optimistic activism, through self-mobilising popular movements with ties to solidarity organisations in northern countries, the people of South Africa became master of their own destiny. For many years, the whole of southern Africa was dominated by South Africa. Its future course will have great impact on the region and its foreign relations could potentially develop into an exemplar of South-South co-operation. Seen from the North, South Africa has a growing middle class market for sophisticated products and the country could function as a gateway to the rest of Africa. It also has a competitive academic environment with highly qualified scholars engaged in structural and social studies.

More than ten years have now elapsed since the fall of apartheid and the dissolution of its last white minority government. During this time, South Africa has developed from Rainbowism to African Renaissance and New Patriotism.[1] Since 1994, South Africa has gone through different phases in the attempt to create a new kind of historical dynamic driven by the aspiration of equal rights and better living conditions.[2] Therefore, one might expect to find a profound interest in the historiography of that country, but the study

---

1. Mbeki, Thabo, *Africa Define Yourself,* Cape Town, Tafelberg, 2002; Roger Southall, "ANC and Black Capitalism in South Africa", *Review of African Political Economy,* Vol. 31, No. 100, 2004, pp. 313–328.

2. Bond, Patrick, "From Racial to Class Apartheid: South Africa's Frustrating Decade of Freedom", *Monthly Review,* March 2004.

of history in South Africa has in fact experienced serious decline.[3] After 1994, the number of history students has decreased at most institutions. At many universities, history options were transformed into feeder courses for other subjects. Most universities had to cut the number of history lecturers or even to abolish entire departments. Mergers with neighbouring departments and the formation of multi-disciplinary "schools" have endangered the institutional independence of history as a discipline. In some provincial areas, history as an institutionally based discipline is threatened with extinction.[4] In the last few years, however, the situation seems to have stabilised and some history departments have succeeded in attracting students by broad introductory courses linking history to heritage or to film and art history.[5]

Several explanations for the local "crisis of history" have been suggested.[6] The many years of apartheid education discredited institutionalised history and even if liberal, radical, and nationalist groups used history in their struggle for democracy, many black South Africans came to see history as a type of knowledge with which they could not identify. A more controversial explanation could be that while the use of history at a certain stage helped people in an instrumental way to meet their most important need, that is, to get rid of apartheid, the main priority for most people today is to pursue an individual career in a free market.

Knowledge of history helps to shape qualities of imagination, sensitivity, balance, accuracy, and discriminating judgment and provides multiple perspectives on how various elements have come together to create a society or to build a nation. History writing is an important part of a nation state's

---

3. Kader Asmal (then Minister of Education) "Making hope and history rhyme" in Gurney, Christabel (ed.), *The Anti-Apartheid Movement: A 40-year Perspective*, Conference Report, London, AAM Archives Committee, 2000.

4. Patrick Harries, "Zero Hour and Beyond: History in a Time of Change", paper from ICS/SOAS Conference, University of London, 10–12 September 2004.

5. At Rhodes University and the University of Cape Town, for example. It should be noted, however, that many of these new students are not black South Africans, but overseas students.

6. See also Kros, Cynthia, "Curriculum 2005 and the end of History", History Curriculum Research Project, Report No. 3, Cambridge University Press & History Workshop, University of the Witwatersrand, Johannesburg, 1998; Sieborger, Rob," History and the Emerging Nation: The South African Experience", *International Journal of Historical Learning Teaching and Research*, Vol. 1, No. 1, 2000; papers from the South African History Project's conference of 2002 on "History, Memory and Human Progress – Know the Past, Anticipate the Future".

collective memory and history is not simply a product of the past, but often an answer to demands of the present.[7]

During segregation and apartheid, historical research was used extensively to seek solutions for problems of contemporary importance. Most of the great debates on South African history have had hidden agendas mirroring vital contemporary problems rather than the ones actually described. The discussion around the frontier theory outlining the self-identification of the Boers on the isolated border, the formulation by early liberals of "protective" segregation, the later liberal critique of dysfunctional elements in the apartheid policy, and the construction of a working class tradition by radical historians provide illustrative examples of history used for ideological mobilisation by some of the most distinguished South African and international scholars.[8]

How was the idea of a South African nation constructed? In what ways have racialised identities been ascribed to South Africans over time? From what concepts did the various schools of history assign different pasts to different South Africans? Can history help people regain their pride or give them back their land? Should understanding, critique, or guidance for action be prioritised in the practice of history?

This collection will deal with different patterns of use and abuse of history during the formation of group identity and national unity. The importance of history and historians for the transformation of the South African society will be discussed from several different angles.

In August 2002, The Nordic Africa Institute convened an extended workshop of historians, Africanists and development researchers at the Centre of African Studies, the University of Copenhagen. This Danish institute, situated in the old inner city, functioned as an efficient co-organiser of the event that gathered more than fifty participants under the heading: Collective Memory and Present Day Politics in South Africa and the Nordic Countries. The NAI/CAS workshop provided for an exchange of views between veteran historians involved in the international debate over many years, historians from the new South Africa, and concerned Nordic researchers, as well as

---

7. Hofstadter, Richard, *The Progressive Historians: Turner, Beard, Parrington*, New York, 1969, p. 3; Kader Asmal, "Speech by the Minister of Education", Department of Education, August 2001.

8. Beinart, William and Dubow, Saul, "The historiography of segregation and apartheid" in Beinart and Dubow (eds), *Segregation and Apartheid in Twentieth Century South Africa*, New York, Routledge, 1995.

NGOs and individuals from the aid sector.[9] The workshop also served as a conclusion of my research project at NAI.[10]

The passionate discussion about the use of history for freedom and democracy during the years of struggle was partly inspired by international solidarity and exiled academics. In this spirit, the leading thought behind the workshop was to make a transnational attempt to renew the debate over the most important concepts in South African historiography and to add to a revival of the once lively exchange of ideas between progressive academics and the surrounding society.

The tradition of progressive history writing

The changing patterns of research dealing with contemporary history in South Africa reflect deep conflicts external to academia. As a result of the unequal access to education, the historiographical tradition is characterised by the absence of black historians, and the education in and communication of history at the university level have been distinguished by the English liberal tradition's long-standing predominance, although this was challenged by Afrikanerdom during the creation of apartheid and by Marxist tendencies during late apartheid.

For at least 25 years, from the end of the 1960s to the early 1990s, there were in South African historiography two fairly clear, mutually diverging viewpoints on the relationship between capitalism and apartheid, and their presence can still be sensed in new influential works of history.[11] The radical-revisionist viewpoint claimed that apartheid was created by and served capitalist interests that, because of the system, enjoyed access to great quantities of forced, cheap labour and state subsidies. In the view of the radical historians, the rapid growth in the South African economy during most of last century showed that segregation and apartheid were intentional and rational forms

---

9. Unpublished papers from the conference can be viewed on this website: http://www.jakobsgaardstolten.dk. Choose the path: History Conference | Links to unpublished papers.

10. For a short description of my research, see my former website at NAI: http://www.nai.uu.se/research/areas/archive/historical_research.

11. For example, Neville Alexander, *An Ordinary Country: Issues in the Transition from Apartheid to Democracy in South Africa*, Approaches to Cultural History Series, New York, Berghahn Books, 2002; Louw, P. Eric, *The Rise, Fall, and Legacy of Apartheid*, Westport Connecticut, Praeger, 2004.

of government.[12] The liberal viewpoint has assumed that apartheid was the result of the racist sentiments of Afrikaner nationalists, who dominated political power at least after the Pact government of 1924, and that, contrary to the opinion of revisionists, the system has slowed down economic growth.[13]

The contrasting historical interpretations of the relationship between capitalism and apartheid raised questions about the relative importance of race and class in the development of the South African society, as well as questions about the nature of the relationship between business and government, including the extent to which the government ought to be viewed as a tool of capital, or as an autonomous actor depending only on more indeterminable group interests, such as those of a privileged electorate. These questions were not only of theoretical interest for South Africa, but also important for the development of political strategies. If fractions of capital were opposed to apartheid, they were potential allies in the battle against the system. If, on the other hand, separation of workers according to race supported capitalism, or was perhaps even a condition for the existence of capitalism in South Africa in a certain historical period, then the struggle against the prevailing form of capitalist exploitation might have been an important ingredient in the battle against racial discrimination.[14] As lessons of the struggle showed, these two strategic lines were not totally incompatible.[15]

The liberal-radical history debate which culminated in the late 1980s was on the whole very stimulating for both productivity and quality in South African historical research, and it would, as I see it, be a loss, if this discussion and the related interaction between academia and society should just fade away in favour of some kind of more or less static consensus in the area of basic approaches.

This complex of problems is, despite great societal changes, still relevant at a time when the South African government's policy for economic growth

12. Deacon, Roger, "Structure and Agency: The Historical Development and Theoretical Articulation of South African Marxist Historiography", B.A. Hons. Thesis, Political Science and History, University of Natal, 1986.

13. Thompson, Leonard M., *A History of South Africa*, New Haven, Yale University Press, 1990/2000.

14. Luckhardt, Ken and Wall, Brenda, *Working for Freedom. Black Trade Union Development in South Africa throughout the 1970s*, World Council of Churches, Geneva, ca. 1981.

15. Marx, Anthony W., *Lessons of Struggle: South African Internal Opposition, 1960–1990*, New York, Oxford University Press, 1992.

seems to include the reluctant acceptance of increasing social stratification and poverty.[16] The question of to what extent capitalism was the main reason for brutal social repression along race lines for most of last century, or to what extent capitalism in fact liberated South Africa from outdated political apartheid, still has implications for strategies for social struggle, economic policy choices, possibilities of reconciliation, etc., at least if the preferred course includes the deepening of democracy, the broadening of equality, and the revival of human solidarity.

The end of the Cold War has led to revisions of post-World War II history writing in many countries, also in the western world, in some cases with the purpose of relieving history of its ideological burdens, making it more "objective", or, as in other instances, with the intent to ascribe guilt and shame to old opponents in a continuation of the ideological strife.[17] In a comparative way, the time may have come for the South Africans to take another look at the images and myths of their era of repression in the new light of the fact that their liberation has turned out to be more of a neo-liberal victory than the national democratic revolution that many had expected.[18]

The fall of the Berlin Wall brought political freedom to the peoples of Eastern Europe, but it also resulted in changes in balances of social power worldwide. For many social movements, the outcome has had weakening effects, such as the loss of alternative power bases, organisational discipline, and political education.[19] With the withdrawal of the stakes deployed by the

16. *Economic and Social Rights Report*, 5th, 2002/2003, South African Human Rights Commission, http://www.sahrc.org.za/economic_and%20_social_rights.htm; David Everatt, "The politics of poverty", *Development Update*, 2004, http://www.polity.org.za/pdf/PoliticsOfPoverty.pdf.

17. In the case of my native country, Denmark, for instance, Steen Andersen, *Danmark i det tyske storrum. Dansk økonomisk tilpasning til Tysklands nyordning af Europa*, Lindhardt og Ringhof, 2003; Dansk Institut for Internationale Studier, *Danmark under den kolde krig*, København, DIIS, 2005.

18. Friedman, Steven, "South Africa's reluctant transition", *Journal of Democracy*, Vol. 4, No. 2, pp. 56–69, 1993; Ginsburg, David, "The Democratisation of South Africa: Transition Theory Tested", *Transformation, Critical Perspectives on Southern Africa*, No. 29, pp. 74–102, University of Natal, Durban, Dept. of Economic History, 1996; Bond, Patrick, *Elite Transformation: From Apartheid to Neoliberalism in South Africa*, London, Pluto and University of Natal Press, 2000.

19. "Die Zukunft der Solidaritätsbewegung: Tema, Internationale Solidarität", *Blätter Des Iz3*, No. 201, pp. 23–46, 1994; Noreena Hertz, *The silent takeover*, The Free Press, 2001; Eddy Maloka, *The South African Communist Party in Exile, 1965–1990*, The Africa Institute of South Africa, 2003, Ch. 6, 7. A Danish social democratic histo-

superpowers in their competition over Africa, most of the continent became more isolated from globalisation.[20] The dwindling faith in socialist solutions has also affected the ideological self-consciousness of left-wing intellectuals.[21] It could be argued that, simultaneously, the objective need for "social defence" has in fact been growing, partly due to the enforcement of neo-liberal policies.[22] Dominant groups, rather than those who are in subaltern positions, stand to gain, if people are conditioned to perceive the basic structures of their world as unchangeable.[23] Against this background, the historical dispute between liberal and Marxist-inspired views is surely still relevant,[24] unless history has in fact ended and social struggle inside nation states has become obsolete.[25]

The modern liberal tradition, sceptical of segregation, had its breakthrough in South Africa with the writings of William Macmillan, Professor of History at the University of the Witwatersrand and was developed further

rian, Søren Mørch, has expressed it this way: "The price of insurance against social upheavals has gone down". Mørch, Søren, *Den sidste Danmarkshistorie. 57 fortællinger af fædrelandets historie*, Cph., Gyldendal, 1996, pp. 434–435.

20. Mark Huband, *The Skull beneath the Skin: Africa after the Cold War*, Boulder, Westview Press, 2001, p. xi.

21. Paul Tiyambe Zeleza, *Rethinking Africa's Globalization, Volume I: The Intellectual Challenges*, Trenton, NJ and Asmara, Eritrea, Africa World Press, 2003, p. 59.

22. Ashwin Desai, *We Are the Poors: Community Struggles in Post-Apartheid South Africa*, Monthly Review Press, 2002.

23. Neville Alexander, *An Ordinary Country: Issues in the Transition from Apartheid to Democracy in South Africa*, Approaches to Cultural History Series, New York: Berghahn Books, 2002, p. 26.

24. On the question of the relevance of this debate, see Rich, Paul, "Is South African Radical Social History Becoming Irrelevant?", *South African Historical Journal*, Vol. 31, 1994, p. 191; Legassick, Martin (interviewed by Alex Lichtenstein), "The Past and Present of Marxist Historiography in South Africa", *Radical History Review*, Issue 82, 2002 pp. 111–130, 2002. Also Cobley, Alan, "Does Social History Have a Future? The Ending of Apartheid and Recent Trends in South African Historiography", *Journal of Southern African Studies*, September 2001.

25. For international debates on this topic, see Fukuyama, Francis, *The End of History and the Last Man*, London: Hamish Hamilton, 1992; Mark Poster, *Cultural History and Postmodernity: Disciplinary Readings and Challenges*, New York, Columbia University Press, 1997, pp. 38, 59; Jean Comaroff, "The End of History Again? Pursuing the Past in the Postcolony", Lecture 29 March 2004, Koninklijke Academie voor Nederlandse Taal- en Letterkunde, Gent.

by his student C.W. De Kiewiet among others.[26] Writing mainly in the 1920s and 1930s, their accounts of the history of white conquest and African dispossession were self-consciously critical of Theal's earlier settler version of South African history.[27] The development of black poverty alongside and in competition with white poverty, the resurgence of Afrikaner nationalism, and the gradual political awakening of blacks, became major foci of attention. The liberal school of historians was part of the wider community of liberal economists, anthropologists, and sociologists who came into prominence between the two world wars, and whose intellectual foundations were those of classical liberalism.[28] Their work dealt with social issues and economic unification processes and gave greater prominence to the role of blacks in South African history. They evinced a great concern for black welfare, but they did not do in-depth research on black societies themselves.[29]

From the early 1960s, a small group of English-speaking liberal scholars, influenced by the decolonisation of tropical Africa, the civil rights movement in America, and other tendencies, became engaged in professional studies of the history of the black majority in South Africa. For John Omer-Cooper, Leonard Thompson, and the anthropologist Monica Wilson, the history of African societies was "the forgotten factor" in South African history.[30] This new stream of liberal Africanist historical writing also had an anti-apartheid purpose behind it. Wilson and Thompson returned to the key idea in the writings of Macmillan and De Kiewiet: that interaction between all of South

---

26. Macmillan, William M., *The Cape Colour Question*, London, Faber and Gwyer, 1927; De Kiewiet, C.W., *The Anatomy of the South African Misery*, The Whidden Lectures, Oxford University Press, 1956. Some have retrospectively seen Macmillan as a social democrat, or simply as an economic historian, and no doubt, he was to the left of the main stream of liberals. Others have seen him and especially De Kiewiet more as British imperial historians and Theal as a more genuine South African historian.

27. Theal, George McCall, *Compendium of South African History and Geography*, Vol. 1–2, Lovedale, South Africa, Printed at the Institution Press, 1873, 2. ed. 1876, 3. ed. 1877.

28. Wessel Visser, "Trends in South African Historiography and the Present State of Historical Research", paper presented at the Nordic Africa Institute, Uppsala, Sweden, 23 September 2004.

29. Smith, Kenneth Wyndham, *The Changing Past: Trends in South African Historical Writing*, Johannesburg, Southern Book Publishers, 1988, p. 86.

30. Du Bruyn, J., "The Forgotten Factor Sixteen Years Later: Some Trends in Historical Writing on Precolonial South Africa", *Kleio, Journal of the Department of History*, University of South Africa, Pretoria, Vol. 16, pp. 34–45, 1984.

Africa's people was the main theme in its history. This was a central assertion in their editing of the seminal *Oxford History of South Africa*,[31] a multi-disciplinary work which sought to show both that the history of blacks had to be integrated into the totality of South African history, and that besides conflict, there had been much inter-racial co-operation before the social engineers of the apartheid era took steps to end it.[32]

Nevertheless, the liberal school has been severely criticised. Some researchers have argued that the liberal way of historical thinking has included a built-in market determinism, which deliberately placed the political realisation of a predicted future on the agenda.[33] After disappointing results of early liberal efforts to make segregation work in an acceptable way,[34] main figures of the liberal school claimed from the late 1920s that race prejudice and race separation as such were outdated and irrelevant and were bound to be gradually weakened due to the logic of modern economic rationality. The free market was colour-blind and would, in time, help to liberate suppressed race-groups, so that the close connection between racial and class affiliation would be broken.[35] As it turned out however, the South African reality de-

31. Wilson, Monica and Thompson, Leonard M. (eds), *The Oxford History of South Africa*, Oxford, Clarendon Press, 1969–71.

32. Saunders, Christopher, "History Writing and Apartheid: Some Threads", in Prah, Kwesi Kwaa, *Knowledge in Black and White. The Impact of Apartheid on the Production and Reproduction of Knowledge*, Cape Town, Centre for Advanced Studies of African Society (CASAS), 1999.

33. Hirsch, Alan, "Capitalism and Apartheid: South Africa, 1910–1984", review of Merle Lipton's book, *Journal of African History*, Vol. 28, No. 3, pp. 450–51, Cambridge University Press, 1987; Lundahl, Mats, *Apartheid in theory and practice: An economic analysis*, Boulder, Westview Press, 1992, p. 155.

34. Trapido, Stanley, "The friends of the natives: Merchants, peasants and the political and ideological structures of liberalism in Cape, 1854–1910" in Marks, Shula and Atmore, Anthony (eds), *Economy and Society in Pre-Industrial South Africa*, Longman, 1980/85, p. 247; Legassick, Martin C., "The frontier tradition in South African historiography", *Collected Seminar Papers on the Societies of Southern Africa*, Vol. II, pp. 1–33, University of London, Institute of Commonwealth Studies, 1971; Legassick, Martin C., *The making of South African 'Native Policy' 1913–23: The origins of segregation*, Institute of Commonwealth Studies Postgraduate Seminar, 5/2–1972, University of London, 1972. Neither Macmillan nor De Kiewiet were part of the liberal involvement in early segregation, which could be defined as segregation initiatives before the Pact government of 1924. Key liberal figures, like Rheinallt Jones, R.F. Alfred Hoernlé, Edgar H. Brookes, Charles T. Loram, and J.H. Pim, were however involved.

35. Frankel, Sally Herbert, "The Position of the Native as a Factor in the Economic

veloped in a somewhat different direction that included an all-embracing legislation meant to maintain racial divisions.

Many would probably argue that, seen in a long-term perspective, history proved the liberals right. However, in the South African situation, their unambiguous connection between economic growth and liberal reforms proved to be highly problematic. Throughout the period of segregation and at least for the first two decades of apartheid, race discrimination did not hamper growth at all.[36] Moreover, at the political level, the liberal thesis had pacifying effects. International solidarity and the activities of the national freedom movements could be considered less important, compared to market forces – if these were just allowed to work.[37]

The liberal doctrine that capitalism in all its stages played a progressive role in undermining racial discrimination seemed shameless to many in the light of the total suppression of the 1960s. Inspired by the growing domestic democratic movement and by international solidarity, radical historians started attacking the liberal view. Many radical academics felt it necessary to distance themselves from the relaxed evolutionary beliefs and more or less

Welfare of the European Population in South Africa", *Journal of the Economic Society of South Africa*, Vol. 2, No. 1, 1928, p. 24; De Kiewiet, C.W., *A History of South Africa: Social and Economic*, Oxford, Clarendon, 1941; O'Dowd, Michael C., "The stages of economic growth and the future of South Africa" in Schlemmer, Lawrence and Webster, Eddie (eds), *Chance, Reform, and Economic Growth in South Africa*, Johannesburg, Centre for Applied Social Sciences and Ravan Press, 1978. Based on original paper from 1966.

36. Houghton, Hobart, D. and Dagut, Jenifer (eds), *Source Material on the South African Economy*, 1860–1970, Vol. 1–3, Cape Town: Oxford University Press, 1972–73; Wolpe, Harold, "Capitalism and Cheap Labour Power in South Africa: From Segregation to Apartheid", *Economy and Society*, Vol. 1, No. 4, pp. 425–56, London, 1972; Moll, Terence, "From Booster to Brake? Apartheid and Economic Growth in Comparative Perspective", in Nattrass, Nicoli and Ardington, Elisabeth (eds), *The Political Economy of South Africa*, Cape Town: Oxford University Press, 1990; Seekings, Jeremy and Nicoli Nattrass, "Apartheid Revisited: Analysing Apartheid as a Distributional Regime", Graduate School of Humanities with the Centre for African Studies Seminar, University of Cape Town, 2000.

37. Vale, Peter and Ungar. S., "South Africa: Why Constructive Engagement Failed", *Foreign Affairs*, Vol. 64, No. 2, 1986; Rhoodie, N.J. and Couper, M.P., "South Africa's Perceptions of Political Reform", in Van Vuuren, Rhoodie, Wiehanh, and Wiechers (eds), *South Africa: The Challenge of Reform*, Human Sciences Research Council, Pretoria, 1988; Merle, Lipton, "The Challenge of Sanctions", *The South African Journal of Economics*, Vol. 57, No. 2, 1989.

collaborative attitudes towards the apartheid state common to some liberals.[38]

The liberal tradition in South Africa contains many moral qualities, but also many unanswered questions, above all concerning the relationship between capitalism and racial discrimination. In a situation clouded by widening social gaps,[39] which could eventually lead African workers and unemployed to challenge fundamental economic assumptions and norms, proponents of liberalism in South Africa can hardly afford to leave these questions unanswered.[40]

An important condition for those radical and Marxist-inspired historical interpretations, which, from the beginning of the 1970s, challenged both the official apartheid ideology and liberal academic dominance, was the recurrence of popular political struggle in apartheid South Africa itself. After the Soweto Uprising in 1976, a growing respect for the militant black resistance influenced the historians. In the last half of the 1980s, the situation in South Africa was characterised by repeated waves of widespread popular protests and the brutal attempts to suppress them. At the same time, the economy moved into a real crisis.[41]

This situation affected the choice of subject matter researched by progressive historians, so that new issues were brought into focus. The process of pro-

38. For example, Houghton, Hobart D., *The South African Economy*, Cape Town: Oxford University Press, 1964, accepting separate development in the last chapters, p. 212; Bromberger, Norman, "An Assessment of Change. Economic Growth and Political Changes in South Africa: A Reassessment" in Schlemmer, Lawrence and Webster, Eddie (eds), *Chance, Reform, and Economic Growth in South Africa*, Centre for Applied Social Sciences and Ravan Press, 1978, defending the system at p. 58. On the other hand as Merle Lipton has made me aware of during our discussions, many progressive political liberals like John Harris, Hugh Lewin, Eddie Daniels, and Patrick Duncan suffered as victims of apartheid.

39. Charles Simkins, "What happened to the distribution of income in South Africa between 1995 and 2001?", University of Witwatersrand, 2004. Published on the Internet by Southern Africa Poverty Reduction Network.

40. Some attempts have been made to keep the critical liberal tradition alive, even if the project of political liberalism has been less than convincing in the post-apartheid setting: Vigne, Randolph, *Liberals against Apartheid. A History of the Liberal Party of South Africa*, 1953–68, London, Macmillan, 1997; Adam, Heribert, Slabbert, Frederik van Zyl, and Moodley, Kogila, *Comrades in Business: Post-Liberation Politics in South Africa*, International Books, 1998.

41. Murray, Martin, *South Africa. Time of Agony, Time of Destiny*, Verso, London, 1987; Gelb, Stephen, *South Africa's Economic Crisis*, Cape Town, David Philip, 1991.

letarianisation, the social effects of industrialisation, the organisations and the culture of the black working class, the strength and flaws of the popular movements, the development of self-consciousness among blacks, and the forgotten struggles in rural areas, became popular fields of research.[42] The trade unions, the ANC, and the Communist Party, were now seen as key agents of radical change and the importance of their historical achievements for the identity of black South Africans grew correspondingly.[43] Studies of popular movements improved the understanding of structural conflicts in South African history. Tom Lodge's overview of black resistance after 1945 and Helen Bradford's comprehensive examination of the Industrial and Commercial Workers Union, ICU, represent this tendency.[44] Some studies looked into popular culture, such as music and dance, sports and literature. Studies like these broadened the understanding of everyday life for township residents and migrant workers.[45]

A feminist critique also emerged. Jacklyn Cock's *Maids and Madams* was an interview-based social history that revealed the conditions of domestic

---

42. For example, Van Onselen, Charles, "Worker Consciousness in Black Miners 1900–1920", *Journal of African History*, Vol. 14, No. 2, Cambridge University Press, 1973; Webster, Eddie (ed.), *Essays in Southern African Labour History*, Ravan Press, Johannesburg, 1978; Bozzoli, Belinda (compiled by), *Labour, Townships and Protest. Studies in the social history of the Witwatersrand*, Ravan Press and History Workshop, Johannesburg, 1979; Beinart, William and Colin Bundy, *Hidden Struggles in Rural South Africa. Politics & Popular Movements in the Transkei & Eastern Cape* 1890–1930, London, James Currey & University of California Press, 1987.

43. Karis, T., Carter, G.M. and Gerhart, G.M. (eds), *From Protest to Challenge. A Documentary History of African Politics in South Africa* 1882–1964, Standford University, 1972–1977; O'Meara, Dan, "The 1946 African Mineworkers Strike and the Political Economy of South Africa", *The Journal of Commonwealth and Comparative Politics*, Vol. 13, No. 2, London, 1975; Lodge, Tom, "The Creation of a Mass Movement: Strikes and Defiance 1950–52", in Hindson (ed.), *Working Papers in South African Studies*, Vol. 3, Ravan Press, Johannesburg, 1983; Bradford, Helen, *A Taste of Freedom: The ICU in Rural South Africa, 1924–30*, New Haven, Yale University Press, 1987.

44. Lodge, Tom, *Black politics in South Africa since 1945*, Longman, London, 1983; Bradford, Helen, *A taste of freedom: The ICU in rural South Africa, 1924–30*, Yale University Press, New Haven, 1987. Also, Lodge, Tom and Nasson, Bill (Mufson, Shubane, Sithole), *All here, and now: Black politics in South Africa in the 1980s*, South Africa Update Series, London, Hurst and Cape Town, David Philip, 1992.

45. Coplan, David, *In Township Tonight! South Africa's Black City Music and the Theatre*, London, Longman, 1979/85; Mutloatse, Mothobi (ed.), *Umhlaba Wethu*, Johannesburg, Skotaville Publishers 1987.

servants, who were subjected to the threefold suppression of race, class and gender. Cock became the object of both death threats and an attempted dynamite assassination after the publication of her book.[46] Walker, Bozzoli, Unterhalter, Marks and others, also made impressive feminist studies.[47]

Resistance to the ideology of Afrikanerdom became an important part of radical historical studies. Dan O'Meara's book, *Volkskapitalisme*, contributed to the dismantling of more than half a century's idealisation and romanticisation of Afrikaner history and struck a blow against apartheid dogma.[48] O'Meara's investigation persuasively challenged the Boer claim that Afrikanerdom represented an undifferentiated, timeless, ethnic-cultural "Volks unity". He argued that it was primarily economic processes and social interests, not ethnic conflicts, which formed the historical basis of Afrikaner nationalism. Even if some of the early structuralist analyses were quite schematic, this was largely rectified in later works from the radical school.[49]

It should be emphasised that the radical tradition did not come out of nothing. As Magubane demonstrates in his contribution to this collection, socialism and non-racialism have a long history in South Africa, even if some of the Neo-Marxists had difficulties committing to that legacy.[50]

The many passionate interpretations add fascinating dimensions to historical research on South Africa. Grassroots activists across the entire political spectrum have used history as a resource for political engagement. It is therefore not surprising that popular history was disseminated far and wide

46. Cock, Jacklyn, *Maids and Madams*, Johannesburg, Ravan Press, 1980.

47. Walker, Cheryl, *Women and Resistance in South Africa*, London, Onyx Press, 1982; Bozzoli, Belinda, "Marxism, Feminism and South African Studies", *Journal of Southern African Studies*, Vol. 9, No. 2, Oxford University Press, 1983; Unterhalter, Elaine, "Class, Race and Gender", from Lonsdale (ed.), *South Africa in Question*, London, 1988; Marks, Shula, *Not Either an Experimental Doll*, The Women's Press, London, 1988.

48. O'Meara, Dan, *Volkskapitalisme: Class, Capital and Ideology in the Afrikaner Nationalism, 1934–48*, Johannesburg, Ravan Press, 1983.

49. Dan O'Meara acknowledges this in his later book, *Forty Lost Years: The Apartheid State and the Politics of the National Party, 1948–1994*, Ravan Press / Ohio University Press, 1996.

50. Walker, Ivan L. and Weinbren, Ben, 2000 *Casualties. A History of the Trade Unions and the Labour Movement in the Union of South Africa*, Johannesburg, 1961; Bunting, Brian, *The Rise of the South African Reich*, Penguin African Library, 1964; Simons, H.J. and Simons, R.E., *Class and Colour in South Africa 1850–1950*, Penguin, Harmondsworth, 1969; La Guma, Alex (ed.), *Apartheid. A Collection of Writings on South African Racism by South Africans*, International Publishers, New York, 1971.

during the last 25 years of the anti-apartheid struggle. At the University of the Witwatersrand, academic engagement with popular history developed within the History Workshop, which explored and published "counter-histories". Committed "people's history" and "history from below" distinguish these works, which moved the boundaries of historical materialism.[51] Luli Callinicos' books, for example, can be seen as expressions of a development that many radical historians underwent during the 1980s. The first volume, *Gold and Workers*, is an undisguised, class-based counter-history. The second, *Working Life*, analyses social structures by means of an in-depth, experience-based methodology without forgetting the class point of view. These and later volumes were used as alternative teaching material by local union education committees, amateur history writers, and teachers in need of meaningful and relevant learning material in the classroom.[52]

Radical history changed considerably during late apartheid, partly because of the influence from modern social history. Social history, on the other hand, was transformed through the increased interest in the history of working class organisations, as Murray has established.[53] The fact, that South African labour history soon developed a broader understanding, can be seen as a realisation of the close relationship between economy and politics: the black trade unions were forced to operate within a broader social framework and were frequently organised outside the workplaces in order to survive. Social history, with its emphasis on popular culture and group solidarity across class and race barriers, was, in some ways, more in harmony with the growing political mobilisation.

It is still debatable to what extent the historians of the radical-revisionist school have managed to put over their original ideas successfully. It was Bozzoli's opinion that large scale syntheses, which, taken together, could constitute a new South African historiography, would require many in-depth,

51. Saunders, Christopher, "Radical History – the Wits Workshop Version – Reviewed", *South African Historical Journal*, Vol. 24, 1991, pp. 160–166.

52. Callinicos, Luli, *Gold and Workers, 1886–1924. A People's History of South Africa*, Vol. 1, Johannesburg, Ravan Press, 1981; Callinicos, Luli, *A People's History of South Africa*, Vol. 2. *Working Life 1886–1940. Factories, Townships and Popular Culture*, Johannesburg, Ravan Press, 1987; Callinicos, Luli, *A Place in the City. Rand on the eve of apartheid. A People's History of South Africa*, Vol. 3, Johannesburg, Ravan Press, 1993.

53. Murray, Martin, "The Triumph of Marxist Approaches in South African Social and Labor History", *Journal of Asian and African Studies*, Vol. 23, 1988.

detailed studies of the same type as Van Onselen's.[54] That sort of thorough source study is extremely time-consuming and perhaps did not appeal much to the exile community of younger radical scholars or to the international solidarity community trying to achieve visible, practically applicable results in the 1980s.

Despite numerous well-defined analyses, the radical-revisionist school have never presented a complete alternative synthesis of South African history. Examples of partial syntheses can be found in the introductory chapters of the three collective works Shula Marks has edited together with Tony Atmore, Richard Rathbone and Stanley Trapido respectively.[55] Even though the radical school fulfilled a need for corrections to earlier historical writing, the call for a new synthesis, a general history, which, under a progressive government, could have the same potency as Walker's and Davenport's general history works had under prior liberal academic dominance,[56] has not disappeared.[57]

Developments in society, government changes of policy, and new global tendencies have challenged the ideological relevance of both Afrikaner nationalist and liberal historiography.[58] First and foremost, however, Marxist-

---

54. Bozzoli, Belinda and Delius, Peter, "Radical History and South African Society", *Radical History Review*, Vol. 46, No. 7, pp. 14–45, 1990. For example, Van Onselen, Charles, *Chibaro. African Mine Labour in Southern Rhodesia 1900–1933*, London, 1976; Van Onselen, Charles, *Studies in the Social and Economic History of the Witwatersrand 1886–1914*, *New Babylon*, Vol. 1, *New Nineveh*, Vol. 2, Longmans, 1982. As well as the more recent work: Van Onselen, Charles, *The Seed Is Mine: The Life of Kas Maine, A South African Sharecropper, 1894–1985*, Johannesburg, David Philip, 1996.

55. Marks, Shula and Anthony Atmore (eds), *Economy and Society in Pre-Industrial South Africa*, Longman, 1980/85; Marks, Shula and Richard Rathbone (eds), *Industrialisation and Social Change in South Africa. African class formation, culture and consciousness 1870–1930*, London, Longman, 1982/1985; Marks, Shula and Stanley Trapido (eds), *The Politics of Race, Class and Nationalism in Twentieth-Century South Africa*, London, Longman, 1988.

56. Walker, Eric A., *A History of South Africa*, London, Longman, Green and Co., 1928; Davenport, T.R.H., *South Africa. A Modern History*, London, Macmillan, 1977. Later version with Chris Saunders: Davenport, Rodney and Christopher Saunders, *South Africa. A Modern History*, Fifth Edition, London, Macmillan, 2000.

57. Some attempts inspired by the progressive tradition have been published recently, for example, Glaser, Daryl, *Politics and Society in South Africa: A critical introduction*, SAGE Publications, 2001; Maylam, Paul, *South Africa's racial past the history and historiography of racism, segregation, and apartheid*, Research in migration and ethnic relations series, Aldershot, Ashgate Publishing Limited, 2001.

58. Mark Sanders, *Complicities: The Intellectual and Apartheid*, Philosophy and Post-

inspired historians need to do some painful soul-searching, and while several of the radical-revisionists were engaged in that practice some years ago,[59] these attempts seem to have faded out. Left intellectuals will have to develop new convincing analyses to explain why popular black activism should focus on socialist oriented reforms. If capitalist exploitation and racist oppression are not inseparable in Africa, then South African socialism's most important rationale will have to be based on something other than basic anti-racism.

Growing historiographical consensus

The debate between historians has been quite heated at times and liberal allegations that engaged radicals have often adopted a warlike tone in their attempts to mobilise the anti-apartheid opinion are probably justified. To the extent that this hostility was directed against de facto supporters of apartheid, it is perhaps defensible, but in the light of the victory over apartheid, it is of course easier to acknowledge that this attitude was sometimes unfair to progressive political liberals. It is however interesting in this connection that only few liberal researchers have made an effort to distinguish between early liberal segregationists, well meaning political liberals (or social democrats), economic liberalists, etc. Actually, one could argue that the most enlightened liberals have been used to give credibility to liberalism as such.[60] Then again, left liberals were occasionally criticised heavily by right-wing liberals for not defending apartheid reforms.[61]

Was liberal pragmatism harmful? Some of the social conflicts in South Africa, which the liberals wanted to avoid during late apartheid, were clearly

coloniality Series, Durham and London, Duke University Press, 2002.

59. Jewsiewicki, Bogumil, "African Historical Studies: Academic Knowledge as 'Usable Past' and Radical Scholarship", *African Studies Review*, Vol. 32, No. 3, 1989; Freund, Bill, "Radical History Writing and the South African Context", *South African Historical Journal*, Vol. 24, pp. 154–160, 1990; Deacon, Roger A., "Hegemony, Essentialism and Radical History in South Africa", *South African Historical Journal*, Vol. 24, pp. 166–184.

60. Adam, Heribert, "Predicaments and Options of Critical Intellectuals at South African Universities", in van den Berghe (ed.), *The Liberal Dilemma in South Africa*, New York, 1979; Rainer Erkens, F. van Zyl Slabbert, and Donald Woods, "South Africa, a Change for Liberalism?", papers presented during a seminar of the Friedrich Naumann Foundation in December 1983, Liberal Verlag, Sankt Augustin, 1985.

61. Wentzel, Jill, *The Liberal Slideaway*, South African Institute of Race Relations, Johannesburg, 1995. Also, John Kane-Berman's late writings.

necessary and unavoidable. Moreover, some of them still are – which is exactly why this debate is still topical.

The socialist expectations of the 1980s suffered severe setbacks in the 1990s, despite the victory over apartheid. Over time, there has been a growing consensus between progressive liberals and compromising radicals, and it must be conceded that in the work of many post-radicals, one can trace developments of converging views, where, in the analyses, form of production or class is no longer regarded as decisive for human relations.[62]

Attempts to amalgamate liberal and radical views, concerning the relationship between racism and its social background, into broader and more generally formulated statements within South African historiography will however have a difficult time getting very far, as I see it. Racism always appears as part of a more extensive complex of motives and views,[63] and it will only be possible to agree on a common view on, for instance, the effects of socio-economic changes, if this view is based on a somewhat concordant analysis of the relationship between racism and the underlying interests of the various sections of the population. In the same manner, it is only possible to find common agreement on the effects of economic growth on income distribution, or similar central factors, if the analysis is based on shared understandings of the mechanisms that determine the division of income and welfare in society. This in itself presupposes a certain agreement on the role of the economy, government power, and ideology in communal or societal processes.[64] Any attempt to ignore the nature of the liberal-radical controversy will therefore run into some general problems.[65] The judgments of historians in cases of existing or past reality depend to a certain degree on their ideas of an alternative society. Despite a great deal of new thinking focused on general values, ethics, religion, culture and ecology, for example, new visions will probably in the final instance still have to relate to more or less clearly formulated liberal or socialist welfare-oriented, ideological models.[66]

---

62. Some saw this tendency very early. Lonsdale, John, "From Colony to Industrial State: South African Historiography as Seen from England", *Social Dynamics*, Vol. 9, No. 1, 1983, p. 71.

63. Richard Delgado and Jean Stefancic (eds), *Critical Race Theory: The Cutting Edge*, Philadelphia, Temple University Press, 1999.

64. Simon Clarke, *Social Theory, Psychoanalysis and Racism*, Macmillan, 2003.

65. Bobbio, Noberto, *Destra e sinistra*, Danish version, *Højre og venstre. Årsager til og betydning af en politisk skelnen*, Hans Reitzels Forlag, 1995.

66. Bond, Patrick, "From Racial to Class Apartheid: South Africa's Frustrating Decade

Could it be that the disappearance of a concrete socialist developmental model, however incomplete, has made the radical intellectuals less radical and their ideology less conspicuous?[67] It seems that the places and forums where the more fundamental questions are left open and the debate has been focused on narrow historical problems, and pedagogical and practical solutions, are – unfortunately, as I see it – also the places where some kind of research debate has developed despite the less prominent role the history profession now plays.[68] Even where "values in education" are in the centre of discussions, the genuine ideological debate is often marginalised.[69] In some parts of the world, clashes over what, on the surface, appear to be religious and cultural issues have produced a backlash against rational social movements theory in public and expert discussions, but so far South African academics have largely avoided that development.

However, the present situation holds both contradictions and possibilities. There is evidence that undogmatic, post-structuralist historians are increasing their influence at the English-speaking universities in some kind of symbiosis with open-minded liberals and it can perhaps be argued that the practical influence of former radicals is actually greater now than in their celebrated heyday of the 1970s and '80s.[70] A parallel development can also be traced, however: a mounting liberal self-confidence increasing from a modest level in the late apartheid era, where some liberals adopted an almost socialist rhetoric.[71] Now, we are approaching an almost reversed situation where many post-radical intellectuals have apparently forgotten Marxist notions altogether. Concurrent with the consolidation of South Africa's democracy,

of Freedom", *Monthly Review*, March 2004.

67. Lazar, David, "Competing Economic Ideologies in South Africa's Economic Debate", *The British Journal of Sociology*, Vol. 47, No. 4, 1996.

68. "History and Archaeology Report", Department of Education, updated version, 2002.

69. The Report of the Working Group on Values in Education, The Values in Education Initiative, Department of Education, 2001.

70. Through representation in institutions of history and heritage, work in government departments, and taking part in the regional network of SADET (www.sadet.co.za), for example.

71. Butler, Jeffrey, Richard Elphick and David Welsh (eds), *Democratic Liberalism in South Africa. Its History and Prospect*, Wesleyan University Press, Middeltown, Connecticut, 1987, pp. 188, 258, 399, 409; Villa-Vicencio, Charles, *Trapped in Apartheid: A Socio-Theological History of English-Speaking Churches*, New York, Orbis Books, 1988, p. 131.

there has been a growing disarticulation between progressive scholarship and social movements.[72]

Dogged radical scholarship, including what is now officially called the "ultra-left",[73] will still exist in university milieus, as will probably a few Afrikaner nationalist, hedgehog positions, but perhaps the immediate future for South African historical research will appear as a symbiotic hegemony consisting of all the progressive streams from liberal Africanism and radical social history to ANC-informed strategic thinking. This would certainly appear quite natural in the wake of the national compromises of the reconciliation period.

The severe social inequalities that South Africa faces makes it, nevertheless, difficult to believe that a paradigmatic harmony between essentially different ideologies can endure for very long. The discussion about South Africa's controversial past, and its significance for policy choices in the new South Africa, will most likely arise again in a way that resembles previous controversies between liberal and radical scholars.[74]

Black history writing

During segregation and apartheid, the writing of South African history was marked by the absence of black historians. With a political climate that did not exactly invite critical intellectual questioning and an official regime ideology based on a view of history, which saw the white man as destined to superiority, it is not surprising that the great majority of South Africans, already excluded from parliamentarian political life, were also denied access to their

---

72. Blade Nzimande, "Articulation and disarticulation between progressive intellectuals, the state and progressive mass and worker organizations: A case for 'Public Sociology?'", speech at the Congress of the American Sociological Association, 15 August 2004.

73. Thabo Mbeki, *Statement,* ANC Policy Conference, Kempton Park, 27 September 2002.

74. At this point in time, a limited number of historians are keeping the liberal-radical history debate alive with new works, including Hein Marais, *South Africa – Limits to Change: The Political Economy of Transition,* Zed Books, New York, 2001; Bond, Patrick, *Cities of Gold, Townships of Coal,* Africa World Press, 2000; Terry Bell and Dumisa Ntsebeza, *Unfinished Business: South Africa, Apartheid and Truth,* Verso, 2003; Seekings, Jeremy and Nattrass, Nicoli, *Class, race, and inequality in South Africa,* Yale University Press, 2006.

own history. The whites had colonised history and their restricted education did not give black people any feeling of a past they could identify with.[75]

It will be a problematic task for the historiographers to outline in greater detail in what way, and with what effects, white apartheid history was forced on black students and academics, but it goes without saying that the devaluated image of history has contributed to the fact that so few blacks have been attracted to the study of history at universities.

Even if there are examples of outstanding black history writers,[76] they have been almost invisible in the institutional communication of history, as they largely still are, despite governmental initiatives,[77] idealistic programmes in history departments,[78] and a rising interest from white authors of history.[79]

---

75. As stated by Majeke, Nosipho, *The Role of the Missionaries in Conquest*, Cape Town, Johannesburg, Society of Young Africa, 1952, Introduction (according to Jay Naidoo, Majeke was a pseudonym for Dora Taylor); Wilson, Monica (ed.), *Freedom for My People. The Autobiography of Z.K. Matthews: Southern Africa 1901–1968*, Cape Town, David Philip, 1981.

76. Molema, S.M., *Chief Moroka. His Life, His Times, His Country and His People*, Cape Town: Methodist Publishing House and Book Depot, 1951; Luthuli, Albert, *Let My People Go: An Autobiography*, London, Collins, 1962; Mbeki, Govan, *South Africa: The Peasants Revolt*, England, Penguin, 1964; Mokgethi, Motlhabi, *The Theory and Practice of Black Resistance to Apartheid: A Social-Ethical Analysis*, Skotaville history series, Johannesburg, Skotaville Press, 1984; Gebhard, Wolfgang, *Shades of Reality: Black Perceptions on South African History*, Die Blaue Eule, Englischsprachige Litteraturen Afrika, 3, Essen, 1991; Modisane, Bloke, *Blame Me on History*, London, Penguin Books, 1990; Plaatje, Sol T. (Comaroff, Willan and Reed (eds), *Mafeking Diary: A Black Man's View of a White Man's War*, Cambridge, Meridor, 1990; February, Vernon, *The Afrikaners of South Africa*, Monographs from the African Studies Centre, Leiden, 1991; Mbeki, Govan, *The Struggle for Liberation in South Africa: A short history*, Mayibuye History and Literature Series, No. 13, Cape Town, David Philip, 1992.

77. For instance Rob Sieborger et al., *Turning Points in History*, Textbook series commissioned by the Department of Education, STE Publishers, 2004; several works from South African Democracy Education Trust, www.sadet.co.za and Human Sciences Research Council (HSRC), www.hsrc.ac.za.

78. For example Guy, Jeff, *Creating History. An introduction to historical studies: A resource book*, Durban, University of Natal, 1996; History Department at UND http://www.history.und.ac.za; Department of History at UWC http://www.uwc.ac.za/arts/history/index.htm.

79. Just to mention a few: Van Onselen, Charles, *The Seed Is Mine: The Life of Kas Maine, a South African Sharecropper, 1894–1985*, Johannesburg, David Philip, 1996; Jeff Guy, *The View across the River: Harriette Colenso and the Zulu Struggle against Imperialism*, Reconsiderations in Southern African History, University Press of Virginia,

White history writers have narrated the history of Africans in South Africa from the very first encounters.[80] There is nothing new in that and anything else would actually have been strange. Theal wrote more about Africans than most historians since have done.[81] Macmillan, De Kiewiet, Monica Wilson,[82] Marxist-inspired historians,[83] and ANC-friendly scholars,[84] have all shown a keen interest in "the native question" as it was called in the early days. The question remains, however: How many of these writings have been genuine "black" history serving the underprivileged majority of the population?[85] It has been said, for instance, that much of the social history produced in South Africa draws its strength from moving evocations of the pain and suffering

2002; Karel Schoeman, *The Griqua Captaincy of Philippolis, 1826–1861*, Protea Book House, 2002; Maureen Rall, *Peaceable Warrior: The Life and Times of Sol T. Plaatje*, Kimberley, Sol Plaatje Educational Trust, 2003.

80. Gordon, Ruth E. and Talbot, Clive J. (compiled by), *From Dias to Vorster: Source Materials on South African History 1488–1975*, Goodwood, Nasou, 1977; Revd., Dr. John Philip, *Researches in South Africa: Illustrating the civil, moral and religious condition of the native tribes*, 2 vols, London, James Duncan, 1828.

81. Theal, George McCall, *The Yellow and Dark-Skinned People of Africa South of the Zambezi. A Description of the Bushmen, the Hottentots, and Particularly the Bantu, with Fifteen Plates and Numerous Folklore Tales of These Different People*, New York, Negro University Press, 1969, originally published 1910.

82. Macmillan, William Miller, *Bantu, Boer and Britton: The Making of the South African Native Problem*, London, Faber and Gwyer, 1929; Monica Hunter, *Reaction to Conquest: Effects of Contact with Europeans on the Pondo of South Africa*, Oxford University Press, 1936; De Kiewiet, C.W., "Social and Economic Developments in Native Tribal Life", in Menians, E.A. (ed.), *Cambridge History of the British Empire*, Vol. VIII, Cambridge University Press, 1959.

83. Innes, Duncan and O'Meara, Dan, "Class Formation and Ideology: The Transkei region", *Review of African Political Economy*, Vol. 7, pp. 69–86,1976; Peires, J.B, "Suicide or Genocide? Xhosa Perceptions of the Nongqawuse Catastrophe", *Radical History Review*, Vol. 46, No. 7, 1990; Onselen, Charles van, "Race and Class in the South African Countryside: Cultural Relations in the Sharecropping Economy of Transvaal, 1900–1950", *The American Historical Review*, Vol. 95, 1990, pp. 99–123.

84. Carter, Gwendolen M., Karis, T. and Stultz, N.M., *South Africa's Transkei: The Politics of Domestic Colonialism*, London, Heinemann, 1967; Marx, Anthony W., *Lessons of Struggle: South African Internal Opposition, 1960–1990*, New York, Oxford University Press, 1992.

85. "Black" in the inclusive meaning of the word expressed by Steve Biko in *I Write What I Like. A Selection of His Writings*, Stubbs, Aelred (ed.), London, Heinemann Educational, 1979, p. 48. See also Taylor, Rupert, "Is Radical History 'White'?" *South African Historical Journal*, Vol. 27, 1992, in a discussion started by William Worger.

experienced by ordinary people, treating blacks mostly as victims.[86] What is needed is for African historians to write history arising from African agency on a scholarly level.[87] This is necessary if the research community under democratic majority rule is not to appear as an exclusive white island, a colonial remnant from the apartheid period. Such a situation would be an irony of fate considering that the English-speaking university communities over many years have advocated for racial integration in principle.

After more than 10 years of freedom, the situation in this field has changed less than expected.[88] Specialist literature written by black historians does not take up much space on the shelves of the university libraries. This is the most serious weakness of all in South African historiography, and a great responsibility rests on the institutionalised historical science as well as on the government and the popular movements. There are, however, positive signs of a new beginning,[89] even if neighbouring branches of social science seem to have come further than history.[90]

86. Elof, Callie, "'History from Below': 'n Oorsig, *South African Historical Journal*, Vol. 25, p. 199; Eddy Maloka, "Haul the historians before the TRC", *The Sowetan*, 23 August 2003; some of the literature surrounding the TRC, including an interview with H.E. Stolten for the Danish weekly *Weekendavisen*, 30 October 1998. The French historian Alan Corbin calls this kind of social history "dolorisme".

87. Such as Magubane, Bernard M., *The Political Economy of Race and Class in South Africa*, Monthly Review Press, New York, 1979; Nxumal, Jabulani 'Mzala', *The National Question in the Writing of South African History: A critical survey of some major tendencies*, DDP Working Technologies, No. 22, the Open University, 1992; Archie Sibeko (Zola Zembe) with Joyce Leeson, *Freedom in Our Lifetime*, Indicator Press, University of Natal, 1996.

88. Nico Cloete and Ian Bunting, *Higher Education Transformation*, Centre for Higher Education Transformation (CHET), Cape Town, 2000; Jonathan Jansen, "The State of Higher Education in South Africa: From Massification to Mergers", in Adam Habib, John Daniel and Roger Southall (eds), *State of the Nation*, HSRC Press, 2003; Hans Erik Stolten, "History writing and history education in post-apartheid South Africa", in *Disseminating and Using Research Results from the South*, Report No. 3, 2004, edited by Greta Bjørk Gudmundsdottir, Institute for Educational Research, University of Oslo.

89. Switzer, Les and Mohamed Adhikari (eds), *South Africa's Resistance Press. Alternative Voices in the Last Generation under Apartheid*, Ohio University Center for International Studies, Africa Series No. 74, 2000; Eddy Maloka, *Basotho and the Mines: A Social History of Labour Migrancy in Lesotho and South Africa, c. 1890–1940*, Dakar, CODESRIA, 2004.

90. For example, Olufemi, Olusola, "Feminisation of poverty among the street homeless women in South Africa", *Development Southern Africa*, Vol. 17, No. 2, 2000, pp. 221–

History on South Africa has great potential and, despite a complicated and paradoxical situation, there is sufficient information to sustain positive expectations. A significant tendency is that universities abroad are reaching out for collaboration with institutions in the new South Africa. South African based historians now write in greater numbers for international journals and participate in more international conferences than ever before. Some of the well-known universities attract considerable numbers of undergraduates from the best universities in the world. The isolation of the apartheid period is definitely over.

The articles

The editorial work on this collection has been an arduous task. However, it has also been extremely rewarding and entertaining, and a learning process in itself. Some of the contributions to this book are quite controversial. Social scientists are humans. They disagree. They become committed. They have different political attitudes. Many of them are activists in one form or another. At the conference in Copenhagen, and in this book, we have tried to make room for divergent views and temperaments to give a broad and inclusive picture of South African historiography.

The contributions on history and nation-building

Saul Dubow's article "Thoughts on South Africa" serves as a general introduction to South African historiography in this anthology. The problem of what the South African nation is and who the South Africans are, as defined by history, remains fundamental. The questions Dubow asks are central for our historical understanding: How was South Africa conceived and imagined? What form did ideas about South Africans and South African societies take, and how was the South African "problem" defined over time?

Dubow reminds us that the endeavour for national unification is not exactly new in South Africa. His article offers a concentrated overview with focus on the creation of national identity, which was of course not an obvious process for the native peoples of South Africa, since they were excluded from,

234; Sakhela Buhlungu, "The state of trade unionism in post-apartheid South Africa", in Adam Habib, John Daniel and Roger Southall (eds), *State of the Nation. South Africa 2003–2004*, Ch. 8, pp. 184–203, Human Sciences Research Council, 2003.

not included in, that nation.[91] He writes with impressive intuition about early black history-related writing and shows how social anthropology, from the beginning of the twentieth century, discovered the dynamics of African societies, but at the same time, developed a tendency to focus on particular tribal groups in a messy interplay with emerging concepts of segregation.

Dubow uncovers the extent to which the history of the black majority has been absent in the works of white historians. He outlines the emerging Africanism in early black historical literature and describes the 1940s as a point of intersection when it comes to blacks identifying themselves as South Africans. He also presents the dilemma of non-racialist denying of the existence of racial and ethnic groupings, on the one hand, and the de facto acceptance of multi-racialism as in the different branches of the Congress Alliance and in the idea of a "Rainbow Nation", on the other.

Dubow makes an important point when he demands more openness around the identity of the author and his/her motivation in the writing of history. His paper convincingly explains ideas and concepts of history and provokes the question whether Africanist views deserve more attention from historians.

Colin Bundy's contribution to the collection "New nation, new history" supports the view that history in the 1970s and 1980s became the master tool of intellectual resistance, partly because South African historians had sought a praxis extending beyond the university world, translating historical knowledge into popular, accessible expressions.[92]

Bundy traces the first post-apartheid warnings of inter-disciplinary anxiety to the very year of 1994.[93] The political project of the new ANC-led government shifted quite rapidly in a direction that confused left-of-centre academics. A growing gap between what the academy had to offer and what the state wanted is identified by Bundy. Apparently, many South African his-

---

91. Hamilton, Carolyn, "Historiography and the Politics of Identity in South Africa", paper presented at the conference on "Problematising History and Agency: From Nationalism to Subalternity", Centre for African Studies, University of Cape Town, 1997, pp. 17–18.

92. Also, Etherington, Norman, "Edward Palmer Thompson", *Southern African Review of Books*, Vol. 5, No. 6, 1993, p. 5.

93. Etherington, Norman, "Fissures in the Post-Apartheid Academy", *South African Historical Journal*, Vol. 31, 1994, pp. 206–7; Freund, Bill, "The Art of Writing History", *Southern African Review of Books*, Sep/Oct 1994, p. 24; Maylam, Paul "Tensions within the Practice of History", *South African Historical Journal*, Vol. 33, 1995, pp. 3–12.

torians have been caught up in different types of "struggle history" and now remain stranded in some kind of limbo.

Bundy registers the demoralising effects of postmodern critiques in South Africa, as elsewhere, and the turn to issues like ethnicity, nationality and nationhood. He also has relevant reservations about individualised and narrow identity history. The primary enquiry in his analysis remains the "National Question" and he considers it a serious problem to find out what political, economic, or moral bridge can span the contradiction between a juridical assertion of common citizenship and the reality of difference, separateness, and inequality in the new South Africa.

Bundy discovers three major discursive attempts to narrate the new nation, namely the "Rainbow Nation", the "African Renaissance", and "Ethnic Particularism" and he observes the optimistic multiculturalism of the rainbow nation fading out from the mid-1990s, when many black intellectuals and editors began to distance themselves from the language of reconciliation and instead adopted notions of more or less outspoken African nationalism.

Elaine Unterhalter's article "Truth rather than justice" debates the craftsmanship of the historians in their work with gender relations and with the Truth Commission. The article points to the relatively low priority of women's human rights in the work of the TRC as well as in the history writing of the democratic movement in general. The author's equating of lifetime with political time and her focus on the concept of space represent refreshing new angles. From a literary perspective, Unterhalter seeks to distinguish between autobiographical writing, reflecting the meaning of history, and historical scholarship conducted by professional historians.

Her focus on mentality, changing identity, and personal experience as factors in the creation of historical consciousness adds new qualities to the debate and raises questions such as: How does identity become linked to ideas? How do you take on an identity?

The Swedish anthropologist Anna Bohlin's contribution "Claiming land and making memory" examines how the notion of heritage is employed within a specific political initiative: the Land Restitution Programme. Within this programme, dispossessed or displaced communities are encouraged to mobilise their local histories in order to obtain compensation for lost land. Bohlin explores the contradictory role of heritage as a political resource in a nation-building project, as well as a social, cultural, and economic resource for the local communities involved. While she was researching the memories of forced removals from a small community in Kalk Bay in the Western

Cape, Bohlin became directly involved in the land claim process. Partly as a result of her fieldwork, former residents, who had been forced to leave Kalk Bay after it was declared a white Group Area in 1967, decided to participate in the programme of land restitution and submit claims for the homes they left behind. The paper illustrates the extent to which people "on the ground" can engage with official projects, and thereby partly shape the outcome of the process.

This study also brings up the differences between the TRC and the Land Restitution Programme. In contrast to the TRC, the role of memory in the Land Commission was mainly instrumental. However, despite not being explicitly designed as such, the Land Restitution Programme can also be seen as a site of production of new collective memory. The nation-wide collection of land claims forms a unique memory bank of cases of displacement and dispossession. While the TRC was event-oriented, the land claim documents highlight structural injustices experienced by ordinary South Africans.[94] Bohlin argues that because the restitution programme was not explicitly designed to produce new histories, the memories that emerged out of the land claim process escaped some of the constraints posed by more institutionalised attempts at shaping history in present day South Africa.

In his article "Reflections on practising applied history", Martin Legassick outlines a concept for contemporary historical research, which he calls "applied history". This approach illustrates how ordinary people's history connects to present day conflicts in administration and politics. It is a kind of history that will bring historians out of the "ivory tower" of academia. In the cases mentioned by Legassick, historians have worked together with communities of "claimants", people with a specific and instrumental interest in history. In this way, research in historical injustices can be used practically to satisfy the wronged, proving the usefulness of history in present practical matters.

Legassick's emphasis on personal experiences relating to museum history, his inside description of the progressing work in the South African Democracy Education Trust and the South African History Project, together with his account of the problems surrounding the school history curriculum provide a vibrant picture of some of the most important South African historical

---

94. On the debate on the Truth Commission, see Ann Langwadt, "Healing history, narrating trauma. History and the TRC", paper presented at the conference "Collective Memory and Present-Day Politics in South Africa and the Nordic Countries", Copenhagen, 22–23 August 2002.

activities together with some principal considerations on how to use oneself as a historian.[95]

Thiven Reddy's contribution "From apartheid to democracy" presents a theoretical overview of the analytic discourses, parameters, categories, and criteria relevant for analysing the history of the transition process.

In some studies of democratic transition, the South African case is viewed as a primary example of a "transition by transplacement". Reddy's paper challenges this representation as one-sided and argues that the dominant discourse very often organises the story of the South African transition in a particular way by relying on a familiar narrative structure. Reddy criticises standard transitology theory for its narrow definition of democracy, its reliance on conventional metaphors to frame its study of democratisation, and its overemphasis on political institutions.[96] He also explores two notions that usually occupy a subordinate position in the dominant narrative of change: first the notion of "the masses", particularly its role in both regime and opposition elite discourses, and secondly the association between violence and elite negotiations.[97]

The chapters dealing with memory and heritage

Gary Baines' contribution "The politics of public history" forms a bridge between those chapters dealing with history and nation-building and those dealing with heritage. He views the recasting of history and public memory in post-apartheid South Africa as an explicitly political process. In his analysis,

95. On the curriculum debate, see also Seleti, Yonah, "Changing the Landscape of School History Education in Post-Apartheid South Africa: Prospects and Challenges, 2000–2002", paper presented at the conference "Collective Memory and Present-Day Politics in South Africa and the Nordic Countries", Copenhagen, 22–23 August 2002.

96. A discussion of Reddy's paper can be found in Strandsbjerg, Jeppe, "Criticism and Knowledge Production of the Transition from Apartheid to Democracy in South Africa – a Reaction to Thiven Reddy", paper presented at the conference "Collective Memory and Present-Day Politics in South Africa and the Nordic Countries", Copenhagen, 22–23 August 2002.

97. A different angle to this discussion can be found in Gunnarsen, Gorm, "Leaders or Organizers against Apartheid: Cape Town 1976–1984", a PhD thesis from University of Copenhagen, 2002, which was summarised in a paper for the NAI/CAS conference "Collective Memory and Present-Day Politics in South Africa and the Nordic Countries", Copenhagen 22–23 August, 2002: "The tricameral boycott of 1984 and the democratization of South Africa".

the shift in political power in 1994 has gradually been followed by attempts to renegotiate the meaning of the South African past, so that it will reflect both the experiences of the black majority and the new elite's demand for stability. The heritage industry has become particularly involved in the process of reconciliation as it often seeks to promote a common history, which glosses over struggles of a conflict-ridden past. At the same time, the emergence of new kinds of identity politics has nevertheless resulted in competing claims to the ownership of that past. Baines' article examines how certain heritage projects and museum displays reflect the tensions that exist between an official history that validates nation-building and the public memories of groups that seek to preserve their own identities. Through case studies on museums in Port Elizabeth and Denmark, Baines argues for the acknowledgment of a principal difference between history and memory.

Christopher Saunders' first article in this collection "The transformation of heritage" offers an overview of developments in the field of heritage sites and museums. This area has seen expansion in the use of history with the establishment of a number of new museums. This development could be viewed as an extension of progressive popular history or as an advance of New Patriotism. In some cases, it can also be interpreted more negatively as tourist propaganda or as the privatisation of history.

Saunders follows this process of restructuring from the time of the transfer of political power in 1994. The relations between historians and other heritage practitioners are discussed. Principled and political considerations around historical naming are problematised and disputes over exhibits of indigenous people are observed. The construction of new, and the removal of old, public monuments is debated. Saunders argues that historians provide a broad understanding of what happened in the past, while those involved with heritage are mostly concerned with specific aspects of that past. His critique of the Freedom Park project stands as a defence of pluralism and his appraisal of the District Six Museum challenges new national myth building. The dangers of streamlining official history are stressed in this article.

The South African War of 1899–1902 had a significant and enduring impact both on society and on history writing. It assumed a central place in Afrikaner historical consciousness and fed into the rise of Afrikaner nationalism during the first part of the last century.

With majority rule in the new South Africa, the cultural meaning of the war became more of a contested terrain than before. Several competing groups have tried to reshape the significance of the war along different lines and the aim of Albert Grundlingh's article "Reframing remembrance" is to disaggregate these permutations and to elucidate their purpose.

It seems that at least in some areas, history in South Africa is very much alive. Heritage and various kinds of popular history arouse as much interest as ever, as can be seen from the great number of books published to mark the centenary of the Boer War. Heritage studies have also been a growth area at South African universities, and not only for antiquarian reasons.[98] "The Heritage Industry invokes a sentimentalised past which makes bearable a sordid and painful present", as Jeff Guy has put it.[99]

According to Grundlingh, the ANC-government had some problems developing its view on the historical conflict between Afrikaners and English-speaking whites in a direction that is relevant for blacks. As it turned out, some of the high profile events during the centenary celebration were actually used by black communities to address pressing issues of poverty alleviation. Grundlingh enumerates several different cases of present use and misuse of the history of the South African War, including the white fear that the counting of black war graves could make the Afrikaner history of suffering seem less important, and, as another case in contrast to this, how some Afrikaners have used the construction of a shared anti-imperialist past as a basis from where the old white elite could speak to the new black elite. Statements from President Mbeki show that he is open to this approach.[100] The use of battlefield tourism is also discussed. The killing fields of yesteryear are analysed as the potential money-spinners of today.

In his article "Apartheid in the museum", Georgi Verbeeck critically analyses the newly established Apartheid Museum in Johannesburg. This museum is destined to serve as a mirror for the new South Africa trying to come to terms with its past. It has provoked both admiration and criticism. To some degree, it meets the actual needs of the majority to identify with the past. Critics like Verbeeck, however, point at a growing tendency to create a new nationalistic discourse. In their eyes, the museum constitutes a controversial attempt to close the history dialogue by locking away the memory of apartheid. Verbeeck also draws attention to problematic connections between

---

98. Also Nuttall, Tim and Wright, John, "Probing the Predicaments of Academic History in Contemporary South Africa", *South African Historical Journal*, Vol. 42, May 2000, pp. 29, 30, 34.

99. Guy, Jeff, "Battling with Banality", *Journal of Natal and Zulu History*, Vol. 18, pp. 156–193.

100. President Mbeki, "Address at the ceremony to hand over the garden of remembrance Freedom Park", 8 March 2004.

the funding of heritage sites and certain people from the business world in need of absolution for their earlier de facto apartheid support.

Martin Murray's article "Urban space, architectural design, and the disruption of historical memory" is a piece of penetrating research in present South African city architecture seen from a historical viewpoint.

In the aftermath of the 1994 change of power, propertied urban residents have in ever-increasing numbers retreated behind fortifications, barriers, and walls. Fortified enclaves of all sorts have resulted in the privatisation of public space. The creation of themed entertainment destinations, like heritage theme parks, has produced new kinds of congregating, social spaces that are, in the classical liberal sense, neither fully public nor private. Whereas the historical lines of cleavage during the apartheid era typically crystallised around the extremes of white affluence and black impoverishment, the new divisions go hand in hand with a post-apartheid rhetoric that in Murray's view has been transformed into a defence of privilege and social status despite the egalitarian discourses of non-racialist nation-building and rainbowism. Taken together, these practices have led to new forms of exclusion, and separation. Murray's paper reveals the social functions of enclosed institutions like the Waterfront that are made apparently inclusive by the use of cultural heritage. The article unmasks how the use of invented traditions in styled cocooned areas can disguise the meaning of class stratification.

Conflicting views of history

As the first contribution in Part Three of this book, dealing with differing interpretations of South African history, Bernhard Magubane's article "Whose memory – whose history" argues that colonial history writing was deliberately constructed to justify genocidal wars.[101] After 1910, when the fact of conquest had been firmly established, new methods were, in Magubane's view, used to reduce black people to objects. The crude racism of Theal was replaced by a liberal discourse that used much energy to explore whether the policies of segregation were compatible with capitalist growth.[102] After the Second World

---

101. This could be true for writings like: Theal, George M., *South Africa,* London, George Allen & Unwin Ltd; Theal, George McCall, *Records of the Cape Colony,* 36 vol., printed for the Government of the Cape Colony, London, 1897–1905.

102. Even if it is debatable if Macmillan was a classical liberal, his work should be viewed as important for this approach. Macmillan, William M., *Complex South Africa. An Economic Footnote to History,* London, Faber and Faber, 1930.

War, as the process of decolonisation swept the world, the early, partly segregationist, liberal view gave way to the renewed liberal Africanist discourse of the *Oxford History* and the subsequent Neo-Marxist historiography.[103]

What in Magubane's opinion is striking about even the two latter paradigms is the absence of the African as an active participant in history despite the long record of national struggles. In Magubane's view, very little of what has been written from both liberal and Neo-Marxist perspectives about the African experience has taken into full account the African memory. The author's central argument, therefore, is that any historical discourse in South Africa should of necessity focus on African agency.

The methodology that Magubane brings with him from historical anthropology attempts to raise the levels of abstraction and understanding through the use of historical parallels; a possibility often ignored by conventional historians in favour of the search for the unique and individual.[104] Magubane asks the important question: Did the events of 1994 make everything written by liberal historians nonsense? A question just as important seems to be where 1994 – or rather, global pragmatism towards neo-liberal solutions – has left the radical historians.

In some respects, Christopher Saunders' second contribution to this book "Four decades of South African historical writing" stands in contrast to Magubane's article. One of the key observations in Saunders' paper is that the transfer of power in South Africa in the 1990s was not accompanied by any major new trend in historical writing. He argues that a major reason for this is that South African historiography had already undergone a fundamental change since the 1960s, when the liberal Africanist work came into existence. In Saunders' view, previous interpretations of twentieth century South African historiography, including those in his own work,[105] have laid too much emphasis on the distinction between liberal and radical historiography. While he recognises that there were fierce battles between the two schools of thought, he argues that the more important historiographical development was the one in which both liberal and radical historians were involved: placing black Africans at the centre of the story of the South African past.

---

103. Wilson, Monica and Thompson, Leonard M. (eds), *The Oxford History of South Africa*, Oxford, Clarendon Press, 1969–71.

104. See also, Bernhard Magubane, *The Making of a Racist State: British Imperialism and the Union of South Africa 1875–1910*, Trenton, New Jersey, Africa World Press, 1996.

105. For instance, Saunders, Christopher C., *The making of the South African past: Major historians on race and class*, Cape Town, David Philip, 1988.

Saunders conclusion is that the demands on the history profession as part of the nation-building process have been surprisingly mild.

Merle Lipton's article "The role of business under apartheid: Revisiting the debate" aims to review and evaluate a debate central to the liberal-radical dispute inside South African historiography. She continues to explore the question whether or not business interests and pressures contributed to the erosion of apartheid.[106] Lipton's argument for a continued historical debate is built on the understanding that not all conflicts have disappeared and that the social structure behind the liberal/radical terminology still exists.

Certain parts of Lipton's paper draw on testimony presented to the Truth and Reconciliation Commission. She discusses the relevance of this material to the liberal-radical debate and to post-apartheid relations between the ANC, the business world, and white liberals in South Africa.[107] Lipton seeks to show that the Marxist argument has been continuously crumbling and that even the trade union movement now admits to the changing historical role of capital under late apartheid. She recognises that there are still disagreements between working class and liberal historical views, but now more over interpretations than over facts, it seems. Lipton denies that the "classical" phase of the debate on the relationship between capitalism and apartheid, which began around 1970, constitutes an exceptional intellectual breakthrough by the Neo-Marxists, as is often claimed. She argues that it was essentially a continuation of a longstanding debate in which many liberal, Marxist, Africanist, and conservative scholars were already engaged.

In the appendix to her article, Lipton defends herself against allegations about her work raised at earlier stages of this impassioned ideological debate.[108]

During the 20th century, a whole corpus of anti-communist literature was produced in South Africa, to a large degree by Afrikaners. Wessel Visser's article "Afrikaner anti-communist history production" investigates the rationale behind this part of Afrikanerdom.

---

106. A logical continuation of her work in Lipton, Merle, *Capitalism and Apartheid. South Africa*, 1910–1984, London, Gower, Temple Smith, 1985. Also as paperback: *Capitalism and Apartheid. South Africa*, 1910–1986, London, Wildwood House, 1986.

107. On this issue, see also Terry Bell and Dumisa Ntsebeza, *Unfinished Business: South Africa, Apartheid and Truth*, Verso, 2003.

108. For a comment on Lipton's work, see Stolten, Hans Erik, "The discussion of the relationship between capitalism and apartheid: Elaborations over Lipton's position", paper presented at the conference "Collective Memory and Present-Day Politics in South Africa and the Nordic Countries", Copenhagen, 22–23 August 2002.

Visser's analysis explains the tensions between proletarian and religious factors among poor Afrikaner workers and describes the ideological offensive of the Afrikaner churches against communism in the trade unions. Even liberalism was condemned by certain Afrikaner ideologists as a so-called "fifth column" of communism. With the establishment of the Institute for the Study of Marxism at the University of Stellenbosch in 1980, communism as a historical factor also drew serious academic interest.

Many Afrikaners are in the process of coming to terms with their past and Afrikaans-speaking historians are at present trying to assess the historical role of Afrikaners in South African history. Visser's account provides a unique insight into the creation of the ideology of apartheid throughout the twentieth century. The article concludes that Afrikaner anti-communism has come to a halt, but also suggests that a new kind of anti-Marxism could emerge from government and certain ANC leaders' critique of the so-called "ultra-left".

Allison Drew's contribution "1922 and all that" examines the construction of facts in history writing, while using the early history of the Communist Party of South Africa as a case study. Drew finds a paucity of political history writing in South Africa as compared to other types of history, and with an impressive source collecting work behind her,[109] she defends the importance of written sources.

As an expert in the history of the early communist party, CPSA, Drew is aware that the party, during the white workers' "Rand revolt" in 1922, had a problem recognising the position of the black workers, but she reasons that the CPSA was not responsible for the notorious slogan "Workers of the World Fight and Unite for a White S.A.", and that many communists argued strongly for the need to organise black workers. The aim of Drew's article is not so much to clear the early South African socialists of all accusations of racism. The focus is on the way a myth has been institutionalised by recognised historians.

Drew feels that the challenge in the post-apartheid era is to develop an intellectually autonomous practice of history. At the same time, her article can also be seen as a reaction to the subjectivism and relativism of certain postmodernists. She emphasises the need for more workers' history and feminist history, but how should this be furthered? In professional autonomy, by

---

109. Drew, Allison (ed.), *South Africa's Radical Tradition, A Documentary History*, Vol. 1–2, UCT Press / Buchu Books / Mayibuye Books, 1996–97; Drew, Allison, *Discordant Comrades. Identities and Loyalties on the South African Left*, Aldershot, Ashgate, 2000.

external popular pressure, or by a progressive governmental programme for the profession of history?

The last article in this collection, Catherine Burn's "A useable past", can be read as a critical engagement with the claim that South African historical research is suffering from a deep "post-crisis". Examining the demands and expectations being placed on history specialists by gender activists, educationalists, development specialists, and others, Burns' paper argues that historians are being called on with just as much urgency as in the 1980s, but to answer very different questions. Against this background, Burns explains why it could appear as if history as a genre is under siege. The optimistic argument of her paper is, however, that this appearance disguises important key openings and potentials for the profession.

Burns throws light on the importance of activist use of history inside the Aids Campaign and advocates for more focus on health related history. She predicts that "the study of desire, disease, delight and death" will provide new ground for historical research. Young South Africans face a world of global complexity and Burns identifies with their needs to communicate, be understood, and change. That is where she believes the teaching of history has its mission.

The historians' contribution to the construction of a new South Africa

The question of how to develop a practice that can enable a constructive combination of scholarly work and political engagement remains a central issue in South African historiography. Can, for instance, the traditions and ideals of the former national liberation movement continue to inspire professional historical research in a meaningful way? What significance could partiality resulting from this have, now that the movement's leading organisation constitutes the ruling party? To see the importance of this question, one just has to read a few examples from the new (more or less) official history writing.[110] Relationships between research and political priorities, sanctioned by decision-makers from the former freedom movement during the prolonged

---

110. Bam, June and Pippa Visser, *A New History for a New South Africa*, Cape Town and Johannesburg, Kagiso Publishers, 1996; Rob Sieborger et al., *Turning Points in History*, Textbook series commissioned by SA Department of Education, STE Publishers, 2004; Michael Morris (Bill Nasson historical adviser), *Every Step of the Way: The Journey to Freedom in South Africa*, HSRC Press and Ministry of Education, 2004.

transitional period, could influence the educational system for a long time to come.[111]

Even if the historian has an obligation to use a representative choice of sources in a fair and comprehensive way, to seek the truth, and construct an accurate picture of the historical reality based on facts, the nature of history writing remains essentially selective and often ideological. While most historians have largely abandoned Rankean aspirations,[112] there is still a widespread tendency for historical work to be written in a style that appears to remove the author's voice from the text, creating a false impression that he or she is a seemingly neutral observer presenting authoritative accounts and explanations. As Maylam has stated, the claims of historians to be objective are, however, always a mere pretence.[113] History writing, memories, and stories, can never be "free". They will always be laden with meaning.[114]

The intellectuals' self-defence against demands of socialisation, whether such demands have been expressed by an official authority or put forward by an alternative party, has often been the traditional, apparently unproblematic argument for autonomy. In this argument for legitimacy and respectability, research is often viewed as ethically and politically neutral, a value-free, objective practice that develops within its own rationale and logic.[115] Harold

---

111. Bam, June, "Making history the South African way: Allowing the pieces to fall together", paper written in connection with the NAI/CAS conference on "Collective Memory and Present-Day Politics in South Africa and The Nordic Countries", Copenhagen 22–23 August, 2002; Asmal, Kader and James Wilmot, *Spirit of the Nation, Reflections on South Africa's Educational Ethos*, NAE, HSRC, and the Department of Education, 2002.

112. Georg G. Iggers and James M. Powell (eds), *Leopold von Ranke and the shaping of the historical discipline*, New York, Syracuse University Press, 1990.

113. Maylam, Paul, *South Africa's racial past: The history and historiography of racism, segregation, and apartheid*, Research in migration and ethnic relations series, Aldershot, Ashgate Publishing Limited, 2001, p. 3. See also Vincent L., "What's love got to do with it? The effect of affect in the academy", *Politikon, South African Journal of Political Studies*, Vol. 31, No. 1, 2004, pp. 105–115.

114. Sarah Nuttall, "Telling 'free stories'? Memory and democracy in South African autobiography since 1994" in Nuttall, Sarah and Carli Coetzee (eds), *Negotiating the Past: The Making of Memory in South Africa*, Cape Town, Oxford University Press, 1998, p. 88.

115. Norvick, Peter, *That noble dream: The 'objectivity question' and the American historical profession*, Cambridge University Press, 1988; Appleby, Joyce, Hunt, Lynn and Jacob, Margaret, *Telling the Truth about History*, W.W. Norton & Company Ltd, 1995; Dahl, Ottar, "Om 'sannhet' i historien", *Historisk Tidsskrift*, Vol. 3, pp. 365–73, 1999.

Wolpe articulated an alternative ideal. Deeply engaged in South African liberatory history, he maintained that the goal of progressive historians occupied with the creation of a more just future could best be achieved, if the priorities of the freedom movement were kept in mind, without this leading to a simple reliance on the ideology and policy of the movement. In his opinion, this would be the best compromise between the idealistic notion of complete research autonomy on the one hand and reduction of research to a purely ideological function on the other.[116] Norman Etherington applies a comparable approach, although from a different (some would say almost opposite) angle, when he promotes reconciliation history:

> What I am arguing here is that historians will tell their stories better if they hold the ideal of a shared history constantly in mind.[117]

In most modern societies, it has been the mission of state-funded history to provide people with a meaning of life in accordance with the interest of the state, serving as a substitute for the obsolete ideological use of religion, culture, and ethnocentrism; and in this, it differs at least in the degree of its directness from natural science.[118] The practice of history can almost never be fully autonomous. In reality, it is nearly impossible to disconnect education policy interests, professional values, and personal career improvement from research results. It is a fact of life that demands as much openness as possible about the interests behind the research, especially when this research deals with ideologically controversial matters.

For the average reader, there will always be hidden agendas, but it should be a priority for the responsible researcher to reveal them. Although many scholars might regard such a measure as rather ingenuous and unsophisticated, it might be an idea to establish in the ethical code of the profession

---

116. Wolpe, H., "The Liberation Struggle and Research", *Review of African Political Economy*, Vol. 32, 1985, p. 74. Some of the same viewpoints can be found in Saul, S. John, *Socialist Ideology and the Struggle for Southern Africa*, Trenton, New Jersey, Africa World Press, 1990, p. 6. Wolpe's approach has been criticised by Belinda Bozzoli in, "Marxism, Feminism and South African Studies", *Journal of Southern African Studies*, Vol. 9, No. 2, Oxford University Press, 1983.

117. Norman Etherington, *The Great Treks: The Transformation of Southern Africa, 1815–1854*, London and New York, Pearson Longman, 2001, p. xi, xii, xviii.

118. Ferro, Marc, *The Use and Abuse of History*, London, Routledge & Kegan Paul, 1981; Tosh, John (ed.), *Historians on History: An Anthology*, Pearson Education, Harlow, Longman, 2000, Ch. 7, 8, 9.

the proviso that every history book ought to start with a paragraph openly revealing the author's background, present employment, organisational affiliation, networks, additional material interests, and ideological convictions, together with the priorities of the publishing house. These aspects may often be more important for the outcome of the research than the scientific methodology used. This could then be followed by a subsection loyally presenting alternative angles, together with relevant themes and events not discussed in the book. All source-critical historians are aware of this problematic, but even though it is a logical response to the impact of postmodernism, few authors take it seriously.

Some of the contributors to this book have noticed a narrowing of ideological differences between South African historians. There are several possible explanations for this beside the obvious ones: the crisis of socialism and the ANC's move to the right. Part of the reason might be ascribed to a general decline in present-day use of history for policymaking, or to white English-speaking historians' aversion to participating in President Mbeki's New Patriotism – an aversion shared by many of the old Neo-Marxists. Another possible explanation may actually lie in the opportunism inside the profession. Why should former left-wing academics stick to socialist ideals that, for the time being, seem to have no penetrating-power and could be counterproductive to their careers? It is perhaps typical, that only COSATU workers, still with few possibilities for individual career moves, find that assigning historical guilt to business will help their bargaining position, as Merle Lipton touches on in her analysis.

The tendency among historians to escape into individualised concerns and more or less exotic subjects may undermine the use of history to sustain progressive movements in favour of social reforms. Empathy and insight into the feelings and needs of ordinary people often arise directly from progressive political organisations. Structural analyses, on the other hand, do not come spontaneously and ought to be a priority for historians and other researchers, who wish to contribute to the continued process of social emancipation and democratic build-up in South Africa.

Of course, there are reasons to be cautious of the dangers of this route. Even the former liberation movement does not own its own history. New history projects, such as those included in the South African Democracy Education Trust, would certainly benefit from an overall inclusive approach. That does not mean, however, that the research evolving from such projects should necessarily be "neutral" or mainstream.

Writing the history of the South African nation

Several of the articles in this collection refer to government approaches to history making. Some of them also deal with "the national question" in one form or another.

Immediately after 1994, many initial post-apartheid efforts were aimed at using the past to mobilise collective enthusiasm for fundamental changes.[119] Concentrating on the common future of all South Africans, however, was the way the South African government chose early in Nelson Mandela's presidency.[120] Mandela actually called on South Africans to "forget the past".[121] As social inequalities continued to develop,[122] this picture changed slightly. Under Thabo Mbeki's leadership, the past has been used to unify and regain pride for the black majority, but more in the shape of heritage projects than in the form of history writing.[123] As in many European nations in the era before the developed welfare state, some kind of patriotic mobilisation seems to be desirable for social stability.[124] In this scenario, full of contradictions, the notion of the "Rainbow Nation" may have been toned down, because it failed to assist in the emergence of a "New African Nation" and "New Patriotism".[125]

---

119. Freund, William M., "The Weight of History and the Prospect for Democratisation in the Republic of South Africa", *Afrika Zamani*, Camerun, 1994. Greenstein, Ran, "The Study of South African Society: Towards a New Agenda for Comparative Historical Inquiry", *Journal of Southern African Studies*, Vol. 20, No. 4, pp. 641–652, 1994; Maharaj, Gitanjali, "The limit of historical knowledge: The subaltern and South African historiography", *Current Writing*, Vol. 8, No. 2, p. 1–12, 1996.

120. Kiguwa, S.N.W., "National Reconciliation and Nation Building: Reflections on the TRC in Post-Apartheid South Africa", paper presented at the conference "The TRC: Commissioning the Past", University of the Witwatersrand, June 1999.

121. Among other events: October 6 1994, Online News Hour, Public Broadcasting Service. It could be said though that Mandela has expressed the opposite view on other occasions.

122. Hendricks, Fred, *Fault-Lines in South African Democracy. Continuing Crisis of Inequality and Injustice,* Discussion Paper, No. 22, The Nordic Africa Institute, 2003; Leibbrandt, Murray, "Incomes in South Africa since the fall of apartheid", *NBER working paper series*, 11384, Cambridge, Mass., 2005.

123. See for instance, Thabo Mbeki, "Address at the occasion of the launch of Freedom Park", 16 June 2002.

124. Lettre d'un Franc, à son ami, "Upon the necessity of patriotism and unity for the public welfare", Paris, 1789, (BL: R.187.15.); Toyin, *Nationalism and African Intellectuals*, University of Rochester Press, 2001.

125. On these notions: Closing Address by President Nelson Mandela, Debate on State of

Notwithstanding this, the present nation-building exercise is increasingly carried out by cultivating the skills needed in an economic and market-based context as well as in an ever more globalised environment as Ray observes.[126] A present-minded generation, interested mostly in the market and its utilitarian values, demonstrates an impatience with history.[127] As a result, history is often seen as peripheral. Even if official South African rhetoric still promotes the idea that the past has to be dealt with in order to cope with the present, the real interest in this past seems to be limited.[128] The overall development since 1994 has been characterised by a growing "non-use" of history as well as by the declining prestige of the discipline.[129]

Even if President Mbeki's claim, that historians have ignored Africans in their writings, might not be very accurate, it is too easy for the historians just to blame the South African government for their situation. Some historians still seem to be relatively unconcerned with the legitimate feelings of black communities and their need for counter-histories of the freedom struggle, even if it is necessary to recognise that there were in fact victims and heroes in that struggle. It was hardly possible to avoid the emergence of identity politics in post-apartheid South Africa, and the idea of a common past that all South Africans can gather around is probably something of an illusion. The question may rather be *how* group identities and a plurality of histories are defined and used in this new situation.[130]

the Nation Address, Cape Town, 15 February 1996; "New Patriotism Must Cut across Class and Colour", statement issued by the African National Congress 18 August 1997.

126. Giulia Ray, "Creating the Future – Post-Apartheid Use of History Education for Nation Building Purposes", paper presented at the NAI/CAS conference "Collective Memory and Present-Day Politics in South Africa and the Nordic Countries", Copenhagen, 22–23 August 2002.

127. Address by Professor Kader Asmal, (then) Minister of Education for South Africa, to the Closing Session of the symposium organised by the Anti-Apartheid Movement Archives Committee to mark the 40th Anniversary of the establishment of the Anti-Apartheid Movement, South Africa House, London, 26 June 1999.

128. Address of the President of South Africa, Thabo Mbeki, on the occasion of the Heritage Day celebrations, Taung, North West Province, 24 September 2005.

129. The notion of "non-use" of history has been defined by Johanna Åfreds in *History and Nation-Building – The Political Uses of History in Post-Colonial Namibia*, MFS-reports 2000, 2, Department of Economic History, Uppsala University, 2000.

130. Glaser, Daryl, *Politics and Society in South Africa: A critical introduction*, SAGE Publications, 2001, p. 156.

The majority of South Africans may have a past they can at least partly identify with; namely, the resistance against colonisation and the freedom struggle, but that is not the past of most whites, and having conflicting pasts is not necessarily very conducive to the building of a common, harmonious nation. Kadar Asmal has expressed it this way:

> We need to build an inclusive memory where the heroes and heroines of the past belong not only to certain sectors, but to us all ... Memory is identity and we cannot have a divided identity.[131]

An analogous explanation for the limited official interest in contemporary history may lie in the fact that social protests were an important part of the liberation struggle.[132] To stress that today, however, could lead to the realisation that, at least from a structural point of view, the historical conflict is not over. That might help explain why neutral, present-day symbolism is often preferred to signify shared citizenship.

The future of African historiography

During the first 20 years following the decolonisation of tropical Africa, African nationalism, the traditions and roots of the independence movements, and anti-imperialism were the main themes for African historians north of South Africa. They sought continuity between pre- and post-colonial phenomena to show that original African values had survived despite white supremacy and that these values could provide the new states with an African character, for instance in the form of "African socialism".[133]

---

131. Kader Asmal in his speech at the launch of the series, *Turning Points*, quoted from *Daily News*, April 2, 2004.

132. Marks, Shula and Trapido, Stanley (eds), "Social History of Resistance in South Africa", special issue of *Journal of Southern African Studies*, Vol. 18, No. 1, Oxford University Press, 1992.

133. William H. Friedland and Carl G. Rosberg, Jr. (eds), *African Socialism*, Hoover Institution on War, Revolution, and Peace, Stanford University Press, 1964/65/67; Langley, J. Ayo, *Ideologies of Liberation in Black Africa, 1856–1970: Documents on modern African political thought from colonial times to present*, London, 1979; McCracken, Scott (ed.), *After Fanon: A Journal of Culture, Theory and Politics*, No. 47, Lawrence & Wishart, 2002, containing four articles which examine the intellectual legacy of Franz Fanon.

African historians have shown that Africa had old kingdoms, mining and trading centres, and a well-functioning infrastructure before the arrival of the Europeans.[134] Some researchers have even suggested that the genuine values in Africa's history are to be found in stateless societies based on local autonomy, cooperation and cooptation, rather than on discipline and competition.[135] Perhaps a new generation of black South African historians could learn from these experiences without entirely renouncing universal, theoretical understandings.[136]

A growing demand for a closer connection to the rest of Africa is about to be added to the agenda of the South African historians. If South Africa wants to become a genuine African country, a stronger engagement with general African history will prove to be necessary.[137] The South African government recognises that such a change of mentality is required, but so far, only approximately 10 per cent of South Africa's university researchers concentrate a significant part of their work on other African countries.[138] As a minor, but not unimportant, initiative, the former Minister of Education secured copyright permission to UNESCO's General History of Africa, so it can be distributed to schools.

It is not easy to predict what direction black South African historiography will take in the years to come. Even if South African society develops in the best way possible, towards a reasonably stable, pluralistic system, the black population will have to continue its struggle for rights and opportunities. This also applies to the academic world.

---

134. Falola, Toyin (ed.), *African Historiography. Essays in Honour of Jacob Ade Ajayi*, Harlow, Longman, 1993.

135. Curtin, P., "Recent trends in African historiography and their contribution to history in general", from Ki-Zerbo (ed.), *General history of Africa*, Vol. 1, UNESCO, London, 1981, p. 58.

136. Newbury, David (ed.), "African History Research Trends and Perspectives on the Future", *The African Studies Review*, Vol. 30, No. 2, The African Studies Association, Emory University, Atlanta, 1987; in same volume, Felix Ekechi, "The Future of the History of Ideas in Africa", p. 67; Mkandawire, Thandika (ed.), *African Intellectuals: Rethinking Politics, Language, Gender and Development*, Zed Books, 2005.

137. On this debate, see works of John Illiffe, John Lonsdale, and Mahmood Mamdani among others.

138. Bam, June, "Making history the South African way: Allowing the pieces to fall together", paper written in connection with the NAI/CAS conference "Collective Memory and Present-Day Politics in South Africa and the Nordic Countries", Copenhagen 22–23 August, 2002.

A development foreseen by some, which has not fully materialised, was the elevation of the history of the liberation movement to honour and dignity. Even if the history of the ANC has been advanced lately,[139] it is hardly possible to interpret this as the emergence of a new nationalist history writing, in line with what occurred in other African countries in the aftermath of decolonisation. It could be argued that if South Africa really had been liberated from white supremacy and unchained from neo-colonial dominance, it would have been only natural if a school of Africanist history writing had matured and prevailed. However, after more than 10 years of democracy, there are only weak tendencies in this direction. A few African intellectuals have raised the demand that African values be given priority in African universities,[140] but the transfer of political power has not yet been matched by any significant transformation of the content of historical research. The fears of Afrocentrism and state centralism, expressed by some white academics as a response to affirmative action and student demands,[141] have not really materialised and the traditional values of the historically white universities have not been seriously threatened.

There are a number of possible reasons for this. Some researchers have pointed to the nature of the negotiated settlement, which, in the eyes of many, diminished the victory.[142] Liberal historians have given a partly con-

139. For instance in Dubow, Saul, *The African National Congress*, Sutton Pocket Histories Series, Stroud, Gloucestershire, Sutton Publishing, 2000; Shubin, Vladimir, "Historiography of the ANC: Conflicting views", paper written in connection with the conference "Collective Memory and Present-Day Politics in South Africa and the Nordic Countries", Copenhagen 22–23 August 2002; Ray Alexander Simons (Raymond Suttner (ed.)), *All my life and all my strength*, STE publishers, 2004; Ben Turok, *Nothing but the Truth: Behind the ANC's Struggle Politics*, Jonathan Ball Publishers, 2003; Luli Callinicos, *Oliver Tambo: Beyond the Engeni Mountains*, David Philip, 2005.

140. Makgoba, W., "Africanise or Perish", *Frontiers of Freedom*, South African Institute of Race Relations, Johannesburg, 1996, pp. 17–18; Murove, M.F., "The Dominance of the Spirit of Neo-Liberal Capitalism in Contemporary Higher Education Practices in Post-Colonial Africa: A Reconstruction of an African Ethic of Indigenisation", paper from the conference "The African University in the 21st Century", June 27th–June 29th 2005, University of KwaZulu-Natal, Durban http://www.interaction.nu.ac.za/SAARDHE2005/.

141. Hugo, Pierre, "Transformation: The Changing Context of Academia in Post-Apartheid South Africa", *African Affairs: The Journal of the Royal African Society*, Vol. 97, No. 386, January 1998, p. 19, 22, 26.

142. Adam, Heribert and Kogila Moodley, *The Negotiated Revolution: Society and Politics in Post-Apartheid South Africa*, Johannesburg, Jonathan Ball, 1993; M. Legassick and

flicting explanation to account for the absence of a new direction in South African historiography: that South African history writing was decolonised long before the political decolonisation of 1994 – referring to the wave of liberal Africanism spearheaded by the *Oxford History* around 1970.[143] In 1976, Belinda Bozzoli, nevertheless, called for the decolonisation of South African history; a task that she considered had largely been achieved, when she wrote, fourteen years later, that radical historians had rewritten the history of South Africa.[144] A couple of other rather obvious reasons for the current shortage of dynamism may be suggested: first, that so few African researchers have entered into the profession; second, that radical liberatory history became less relevant during what many saw as the ANC-government's social demobilisation. There is no "wave to ride" as Nuttall and Wright have expressed it.[145] For a non-South African researcher, who was involved in anti-apartheid solidarity for many years, it feels appropriate to ask: To what extent was South African historical writing actually liberated with the fall of apartheid?[146]

G. Minkley, "Current Trends in the Production of South African History", *Alternation: International Journal for the Study of Southern African Literature and Languages*, Vol. 5, No. 1, 1998.

143. Saunders Christopher, "History and the 'Nation': South African Aspects", draft overview article, University of Cape Town, 2001.

144. Bozzoli, Belinda, "Intellectuals, Audiences and Histories: South African Experiences 1978–1988", *Radical History Review*, Issue 46/47, pp. 237–263, 1990.

145. Nuttall, Tim and John Wright, "Probing the Predicaments of Academic History in Contemporary South Africa", *South African Historical Journal*, Vol. 42, p. 47.

146. For a post-modernist discussion of mental aspects of the apartheid legacy, see Norval, Aletta J., "Social Ambiguity and the Crisis of Apartheid", in Laclau, Ernesto (ed.), *The Making of Political Identities*, pp. 115–34, London, Verso, 1994.

PART I

THE ROLE OF HISTORY
IN THE CREATION OF
A NEW SOUTH AFRICA

— CHAPTER 2 —

Thoughts on South Africa:
Some preliminary ideas

Saul Dubow

Historians and identity

Writing in 1996 Norman Etherington suggested future South Africans might look back to the period 1960 to 1990 as "a golden age of historical writing".[1]

That the study of history has lost much of its excitement and appeal in South Africa in the years since 1996 cannot be seriously in doubt.[2] There are many reasons for this decline, amongst which structural, political and intellectual factors invite examination.[3]

In the first place it may have been wrong to assume, as so many professional historians of various intellectual persuasions appear to have done in the apartheid era, that history really matters. Paradoxically, it may be that the "miracle" of the South African transition was able to take place in part because of the country's fragmented history and fragmentary historical consciousness. In other comparable societies characterised by endemic racial and ethnic conflict (Israel/Palestine and Northern Ireland for example) historical events continue to be routinely evoked in order to block or frustrate processes of political transition. In South Africa, by contrast, it appears that politicians and populace alike largely agreed to forget (if not to forgive) the past and to concentrate instead on building a future.

---

1. N. Etherington, "Post-Modernism and South African History", *Southern African Review of Books,* Vol. 44, 1996.

2. It is not at all clear that South Africa is following world trends in this respect. In Britain, for example, history has recently become a vogue subject commanding vast television audiences: it is, as some say, "the new gardening".

3. This contribution is a preliminary sketch of a considerably longer paper intended for a new Cambridge History of South Africa.

Secondly, it may be mistaken to assume that the reflective, argumentative and critical modes of engaging with the past that are intrinsic to the practice of academic history *ought* to find a receptive audience amongst "new" South Africans, at least in the short term. Nor should one presume that Western traditions of historiography command universal appeal; in a post-modern age it is difficult to claim that the academic study of history is more than a culturally specific means of engaging the present with the past. Even in Etherington's "golden age" it is not clear that the exciting revelations and discoveries made by South Africa's social historians reached far beyond the academy. Notwithstanding the genuine desire of groups like the Wits History Workshop to disseminate the lessons of history to trade unionists and community activists, the major accomplishment of the social or "popular" history-writing tradition in South Africa may turn out to have been its role in altering the apartheid-mindset of the receptive white liberal middle classes and in helping them to understand – or engage with – the wider liberation struggle.[4]

Whether or not there is merit in this argument, if the task of revitalising South African history is to be achieved it will be essential to get away from the perception that history writers – whatever their political or intellectual affiliation – are predominantly drawn from, or dominated by, the white intellectual elite. This task is made more difficult because of the disinclination on the part of many liberal as well as Marxist historians to reflect on issues of identity, including their own authorial positions. Master narratives about "class", "nation", "race" or even "the struggle" have, at least until recently, allowed historians to avoid complex questions of subjectivity, not least because they deal with abstract historical forces, structures and movements. The absence of authorial identity has been reinforced by an unconscious disposition on the part of English-speaking South Africans, refined over generations, to define everyone else in the country as either racially or ethnically "other" – while blithely assuming their own identity to be somehow "normal" and therefore not suitable for deep investigation. In the case of white radicals, a similar measure of invisibility (or opacity) has been achieved by adhering to the colour-blind universalism of class analysis.

South African historiography provides a good case-example of such insularity, an inward-looking attitude that betrayed itself in overheated tones of scholastic controversy. A preoccupation with the great "liberal-radical" debate of the 1970s and 80s obscured many assumptions that were shared by both in-

---

4. I argued this point at greater length in a review of P. Bonner et al., *Apartheid's Genesis*, Johannesburg, 1993, in *Journal of Southern African Studies*, Vol. 22, No. 2, 1996.

tellectual camps. Take, for example, the widely shared if largely unexamined conceptualisation of South Africa and its peoples. For all the outstanding work on the invention of tradition and the creation of spurious ethnic and tribal entities, it is remarkable that South Africa has so often been analysed as a unitary category; the presumption that all its peoples were and are South Africans has likewise been taken for granted. Some twenty years after the publication of seminal works like Benedict Anderson's *Imagined Communities* and Hobsbawm and Ranger's *Invented Traditions*, it must surely be surprising that the history of South African nation-building has been so little explored.

The creation of South Africa

It is well to remember that, before becoming a political entity in 1910, "South Africa" was little more than a figurative expression. The term "South Africa" was current from as early as the 1830s but until the beginning of the twentieth century it referred principally to a region extending northwards from the Cape peninsula to the Zambezi. Only the constituent elements of the subcontinent – African territories and societies, British colonies, and Boer republics – had any definite meaning and even then the make-up and boundaries of these states and societies were often vague.

It was during the last quarter of the 19th century that the modern idea of South Africa began to acquire meaning and attract interest. Within just ten years of the start of diamond mining at Kimberley in 1871, the Cape was granted responsible government; Carnarvon's hubristic scheme of South African political confederation was floated; decisive wars of colonial conquest were conducted against the Pedi, Xhosa, Sotho and Zulu; and the imperial government first annexed and then lost control of the South African Republic. These tumultuous events served to bring South Africa into focus as never before, both within the region and without.

The early process of imagining South Africa may usefully be seen in terms of a developing imperial and colonial dialogue, which saw outside observers engage in discussion with locally-based intellectuals and experts. Amongst the most influential overseas observers were the celebrated English historian, James Anthony Froude, who toured South Africa in 1874 and 1875 and played an important role as a protagonist of confederation, and the renowned novelist and the traveller, Anthony Trollope, whose two volume *South Africa* (1878) soon superseded Livingstone's *Missionary Travels and Researches* as a standard work of reference.[5]

The discovery of South Africa by Froude and Trollope in the 1870s was paralleled by the initiatives of locally-based intellectuals who likewise sought to make sense of the country, its history and its peoples. In the field of history, important examples include G.M. Theal's *Compendium of South African History and Geography* (1873, 1876, 1877), John Noble's *South Africa. Past and Present* (1877), Wilmot and Chase's *History of the Cape Colony* (1869), Wilmot's *History of the Zulu War* (1880) and F.R. Statham's *Blacks, Boers & British. A three-cornered problem* (London, 1881). This cluster of books, all published within a decade of each other, represent a definitive departure from the familiar genre of almanac-like compendia aimed principally at prospective immigrants, in which brief historical digests were randomly mixed with statistical information, geographical description and economic and social data. Considered as a body of literature, we see the emergence at this time of a distinctive and competing use of historical narrative and interpretation to define, survey and explain the South African predicament. Noble and Theal, as well as Wilmot and Chase, all attempt to narrate a continuous story starting with the period of first European settlement; their interpretations differed in important respects, but in all cases the history of discovery and the discovery of history were used to inscribe Europeans as a permanent fixture of the African continent.

Growing intellectual awareness of and interest in African societies was also a marked feature of the 1870s, unsurprisingly so given the colonial wars of conquest at this time and the assumption underlying Carnarvon's confederal strategy that a comprehensive solution to the problem of native labour was urgently required. Developing concerns with African societies – who they were, how they were governed, their ability to attain civilisation, whether they would diminish and die out in the face of colonialism, how they evolved, and so on – were initially provoked by the antiquarian interests and spirit of curiosity that so strongly animated the Victorian mindset. Answers to such questions had practical implications as High Commissioner Frere, and Governor Grey before him, well understood. But knowledge of South Africa's indigenous peoples was not only generated to satisfy immediate instrumental needs. It was stimulated as much by the desire to achieve cognitive mastery as the need to achieve physical control over the sub-continent.

---

5. Introduction by J.H. Davidson to Anthony Trollope's *South Africa*, Cape Town, 1973, p. 18; John Hall, *Trollope: A biography*, Oxford, 1991.

Scientific and intellectual developments played an important part in the process of familiarisation, acquaintance and control that full-fledged British settler colonialism sought to establish. And, as always in the study of indigenous peoples, questions about the collective "other" were simultaneously questions about the collective "self", in particular about European understandings of their own place in history, their status in respect of other peoples, and their own national destiny. These problems were closely associated with efforts to develop a collective sense of settler colonial national identity. Indeed, it is from the 1860s and 70s that one might begin to talk meaningfully about the inauguration of a locally-based tradition of African Studies in South Africa.[6]

The conception of the native question

The mineral revolution of the 1870s and 80s significantly changed geographical and conceptual understandings of the country as "the interior" became the focus of economic activity and came to exert a massive centripetal influence on the subcontinent as a whole. These events were abetted and reinforced by the external agency of imperialism which sought, even after the failure of confederation, to create a more or less unified South African dominion directly shaped and controlled from the metropolis. With historical hindsight it is clear that the nationalist forces – African as well as Afrikaner – that emerged clearly in the early twentieth century, were coalescing in embryonic form at this time too. The first explicitly political organisation to represent Africans, the *Imbumba Yama Nyama*, was formed in 1882 to fight for "national rights". Directly modelled on, and partly inspired by the newly-created *Afrikaner Bond,* the *Imbumba* was expressly opposed to the *Bond's* political objectives to the extent that it questioned whether Boers rather than blacks were the true "Afrikaners".[7]

The British annexation of the Transvaal in 1877, and the ensuing war of retrocession in 1880–1, did much to facilitate the emergence of an Afrikaner nationalism that was pan-South African in scope, though the process was

---

6. See, for example, my paper "Earth history, natural history and prehistory at the Cape, 1860–75", presented to seminars at School of Oriental and African Studies, London and Basle, Switzerland.

7. André Odendaal, *Vukani Bantu! The Beginnings of Black Protest Politics in South Africa to 1912,* Cape Town, 1984, pp. 8, 12.

much more fragmented than many conventional accounts admit.[8] But, until the 1895 Jameson Raid, which caused enduring damage to Anglo-Dutch relations and unleashed a new phase of rampant imperialist sentiment in the sub-continent, many political leaders anticipated the possibility of a common white South African identity that would permit loyalty to the empire to coexist with Afrikaner and English colonial patriotism. In 1879 the mercurial founder of the Afrikaner Bond, S.J. Du Toit, declared that, "the ultimate object of our national development must be a united South Africa under its own flag", but this apparent expression of Afrikaner nationalism did not necessarily mean a rejection of British authority and nor did it imply a commitment to republicanism. English-speaking politicians who abhorred imperialist ascendancy and felt personally betrayed by Rhodes for abusing Cape colonial nationalism in the service of wider imperial designs on Southern Africa, continued to resist the bifurcation of complex affiliations and loyalties, even after 1895, albeit in tones that were out of keeping with the demand for making simple choices. As W.P. Schreiner informed the House of Commons in 1897: "I am South African first, but I think I am English after that." [9]

Amongst those who grappled with the prospects for future South African unity, a fascinating and dissonant voice was articulated by Olive Schreiner. As she wrote in *Thoughts on South Africa* in a manner that anticipates the multicultural rainbowist language of a century later:

> ... there is a subtle but a very real bond, which unites all South Africans, and differentiates us from all other peoples in this world. This bond is our mixture of races itself. It is this which divides South Africans from all other peoples in the world, and makes us one.[10]

By the late-nineteenth century it was almost conventional for commentators and politicians to identify the native question as the country's real unanswered problem, echoing Trollope's well-known dictum that "South Africa is a country of black men, – and not of white men. It has been so; it is so; and it will continue to be so."[11] But the political salience of Africans was occluded by the growing crisis within white politics and the temptation to defer the

---

8. See e.g. M. Tamarkin, *Cecil Rhodes and the Cape Afrikaners*, London, 1996.

9. *Second Report from the Select Committee on British South Africa* (HMSO, 1897), questions 4134, 4175; Garson, "English-Speaking South Africans", p. 28.

10. Olive Schreiner, *Thoughts on South Africa*, London, 1923, p. 61.

11. Trollope, *South Africa*, Cape Town, 1973, J.H. Davison, pp. 454–5.

"native question" to the future was therefore always tempting. Even the wide-ly-travelled James Bryce, an astute observer of the South African predicament and an advocate of racial tolerance, found it hard to conceive of the "colour problem" as a pressing political issue in the 1890s.[12]

Africans or black South Africans

The experience and aftermath of the South African war helped to clarify the basis upon which South African nationhood would develop in the twentieth century. Viewed as a cathartic civil war, involving all the inhabitants of the country, the conflagration bears the distinction of being South Africa's first national political event.

The inclusive white nation that was practically realised at Union in 1910 was predicated on the exclusion of Africans, coloureds and Indians as full citizens of the new nation state. Discussions about the moral and intellec-tual status of Africans, their capacity to absorb European civilisation and, indeed, the desirability of their being encouraged to do so, acquired urgency and focus in the process of constituting the "Native Question" – a unitary problem clearly requiring a national solution. This was the clear message of the landmark 1903–5 *South African Native Affairs Commission* whose terms of reference explicitly stated the need for comprehensive agreement on "affairs relating to the Natives and Native administration" in light of "the coming Federation of South African Colonies".[13]

Although the formative history of African nationalism has been well re-searched, the question of how Africans saw themselves as South Africans or, indeed, how they viewed white claimants to that status, has scarcely been addressed.[14] Important clues are, however, provided in the literary output of Africans writing in the segregationist era. Sol Plaatje's *Native Life in South Africa* (1916) is an obvious point of departure, not only in view of Plaatje's pre-eminence as political activist and man of letters, but also in virtue of the book's title which situates the predicament of black victims of segregation in a national context. The author's insistence that the terms "South African" and "white" should not be regarded as coterminous is borne out by the book's

---

12. J. Bryce, *Impressions of South Africa*, 3rd edition, London, 1899, pp. 365–7.

13. *Report of the South African Native Affairs Commission* 1903–1905 (Cd.2399, 1905).

14. In order to do so, evidence contained in missionary records, government commissions of enquiry, political organisations, private papers, newspapers, etc., will have to be scoured.

famous opening sentence which declares that on the day of the passage of the 1913 Land Act "the South African native found himself, not actually a slave, but a pariah in the land of his birth". This message is further reinforced by Plaatje's early use of the term "black South Africans", his self-description in the prologue as a "South African native workingman", and his challenging of the authority of a journal named *South Africa* to proclaim views about the country regardless of African voice or opinion.[15]

Further insights into Africans' sense of collective self and national identity at this time are provided in works of literary narrative and historical chronicle such as those by Thomas Mofolo (1925), John Dube (1932) Rolfes Dhlomo (1936) and B.W. Vilakazi. Magema Fuze's *The Black People and Whence They Came*, first published in Zulu as *Abantu Abamnyama* (1922), illustrates especially well the equivocal negotiation of boundaries and cultural worlds that characterise works such as these.[16] The author speaks simultaneously in the voices of oral tribal chronicler and literate historian-ethnographer; he retains affiliations to the world of Christian mission as well as the sphere of tradition and custom; and, although the primary focus of his interest is on Zulu history, there are ample hints of his desire to cultivate a wider sense of African identity and unity. Fuze's statement that Nguni-speakers "sprang from a common source, and there is no doubt that we were one in ancient times" provides an implicitly nationalist twist to standard colonial accounts of Bantu southward migration. Mofolo's *Chaka* is similarly suggestive of an Afro-centric perspective. Its opening sentence describes South Africa as "a large headland situated between two oceans" and goes on to describe the different black nations who inhabit the subcontinent. Though reminiscent of colonial accounts which commonly mix geographical with ethnographic descriptions, the effect is to situate South Africa as a southern extension of the African landmass rather than as the gateway to colonisation from the sea.[17]

If ambiguity and complex subjectivity characterise the work of African writers like Fuze and Mofolo a contrary tendency is evident on the part of white observers and self-appointed "experts" who strove, from the early years

---

15. T. Plaatje, *Native Life in South Africa*, London, 1916.

16. For more on this theme see C. Hamilton, *Terrific Majesty. The Powers of Shaka Zulu and the Limits of Historical Invention*, Harvard, 1998.

17. M. Fuze, *The Black People and Whence They Came*, trans. H.C. Lugg (ed.) A.T. Cope, Pietermaritzburg, 1979, p. vi. and also p. 1, "Our forebears tell us that all we black people originally came from the north"; T. Mofolo, *Chaka*, trans. D.P. Kunene, London, 1981, p. 1.

of the century, to pronounce on the "native question" with increasing technical precision and scientific detachment. Influential attempts to frame the native question resulted from presentations and discussions associated with the Fortnightly Club in Johannesburg at this time. From a scholarly perspective a key intervention was the address given by Alfred Haddon, to the 1905 joint meeting of the British and South African Associations of Science on the state of anthropological knowledge. The quest for theoretical and applied anthropological knowledge was henceforth closely interlinked and a dialogue between segregation and anthropology was established as a result.[18] One might even argue that the sociological concept of South African society – or societies – was born out of this dialogue.

The modern discipline of social anthropology that emerged from the 1920s revealed much about the indigenous peoples of South Africa and challenged many of the crude stereotypes and ethnocentric assumptions of the day. Relativist understandings of culture cautioned against drawing societal comparisons based on the supposed universality and superiority of European "civilisation" and downplayed – or displaced altogether – evolutionist assumptions based on the primacy of biological race. The founding generation of liberal anthropologists who were trained in the traditions of structural-functionalism (Winifred Hoernlé, Monica Hunter (Wilson) and Isaac Schapera) presumed that African societies were dynamic entities, the inference being that any attempt to freeze Africans into static or distinct tribes was contrived or unsustainable.[19] Herein lay the basis of a potentially powerful liberal critique of segregation, but it was often left implicit.

The integrative potential of this liberal message was, however, undermined by the tendency of anthropologists to develop specialist knowledge about particular tribal groups and to stress variation and difference over similarity and commonality – a tendency that was enthusiastically adopted by conservative anthropologists for whom segregation and, later, tribally-based apartheid, was a distinctly desirable outcome. The historian W.M. Macmillan, whose major conceptual contribution consisted of his insight that South Africa could only be understood as an economic and social unity, was a strong contemporary critic of social anthropology and he fulminated against its "paralysing conservatism" and its fixation on "decaying cultures".[20] This criticism may be

18. Howard Pim outlined his call for segregation at the same 1905 meeting.

19. W.D. Hammond-Tooke, *Imperfect Interpreters. South Africa's anthropologists 1920–1990*, Johannesburg, 1997, pp. 50–2.

20. W.M. Macmillan, *My South African Years*, Cape Town, 1975, p. 215.

unfair in the case of anthropologists like Schapera, Hunter or Hellman, but it was undoubtedly applicable to segregationist-inclined social reformers and educationists like C.T. Loram who were dazzled by the promise of social anthropology as a practical science in the 1920s and 30s.

Whatever one's view about the ideological direction of anthropological research – and in spite of calls by anthropologists for greater awareness and understanding of African problems – the growing bifurcation of South African society into black and white was not seriously challenged by their findings; indeed, it may be that anthropologists' professional impulse to define the study of Africans as a special intellectual domain contributed to the process of racial "othering", whether or not this was their intention. The fiction that the "native question" somehow existed at a remove from national politics was given endorsement by segregationist demands to strip Africans of their political rights and civic status. Thus, even as Hertzog's clutch of "Native Bills" came to dominate his legislative agenda, the major white political parties regularly upbraided each other for treating segregation as a "political football"; until well into the 1920s, if not the 1930s, it was assumed that "race" referred to English and Afrikaner.

White ignorance and emerging Africanism

Efforts to excise the African presence from national politics were given practical reinforcement by the Native Affairs Department which strove to achieve sole dominion over Africans and regarded the governance of blacks as essentially a technical and administrative exercise. Sarah Gertrude Millin captured this duality well in *The South Africans* (1926), written as a deliberate reprise to Trollope and rendered in a similar aphoristic style. In sketching the country's races and ethnic groups she discussed "Boers", "English", "Jews" "Asiatics" and "Half-Castes" in one section – while relegating "The Kaffir" to another. To Trollope's question whether South Africa was to be a land of white or of black men, Millin could not provide a definite answer. Instead, she portrayed blacks as a menacing, subterranean presence, largely invisible to whites, but nonetheless exerting a palpable influence on all key aspects of national life.[21]

This characterisation is borne out in the historiography of the time. Although blacks figured in historical accounts of the nineteenth century (prin-

21. S.G. Millin, *The South Africans,* London, 1926.

cipally as a foil to the story of conquest and pacification) interwar historians largely failed to grasp the idea of black, coloured or Indian political agency, whether expressed through individuals or by means of collective organisation. Eric Walker's standard *History of South Africa* (1928 and 1935) made virtually no mention of any late-nineteenth or twentieth-century political figure or organisation that was not white (Gandhi is the exception); J.S. Marais' brief coverage of the same period in his *Cape Coloured People 1652–1937* (1939) relegates Dr. Abdurahman to two footnotes; and, for all its appreciation of the underlying unity of South African society, De Kiewiet's elegant social and economic *History of South Africa* (1941) treats blacks as an abstraction. The same is largely true of Macmillan's writings. It goes almost without saying that blacks were virtually entirely absent from Afrikaner nationalist historiography whose major themes in the 1920s and 30s concentrated on the trek, the political and constitutional history of the Boer republics, and the experience of the two Anglo-Boer wars; if Africans feature at all it as warlike tribes, cattle thieves and as obstacles to civilisation.[22] The contrast with black efforts at self-definition and self-projection – an exemplar being T.D. Mweli Skota's *African Yearly Register* (which, tellingly, was conceived of as a "national biographical dictionary") – is striking.[23]

Closer readings of individual texts by recognised white scholars are required to make the argument with more subtlety but the general point that blacks intrude into national politics only as a generalised problem or menace is difficult to refute.[24] Against this, Edward Roux's study of black resistance *Time Longer than Rope* (1948) seems all the more remarkable. In his foreword, Roux argues that despite the considerable literature on "the so-called "Native problem" up to now there has been no general account of the political history of the black man in South Africa, the battles he has waged, the organisations he has built and the personalities that have taken part in the struggle." Roux

---

22. Ken Smith, *The Changing Past. Trends in South African Historical Writing*, Cape Town, 1988, pp. 69 and ff. 87.

23. T.D. Mweli Skota (ed.), *The African Yearly Register. Being an illustrated national biographical dictionary (who's who) of black folks in Africa*, Johannesburg, 1930; T. Couzens in his *The New African. A study of the life and work of H.I.E. Dhlomo*, Johannesburg, 1985, p. 17 points out that Skota deliberately eschewed tribalism or ethnicity in compiling the dictionary's entries.

24. An interesting exception is the two volume study by the American scholar Raymond Leslie Buell, *The Native Problem in Africa*, Harvard, Mass., 1928, which deals in some detail with contemporary African resistance movements in South Africa, including the I.C.U., the Israelites, ANC and Bantu Union.

went on to observe that "The phrase 'South African' almost always implies 'white South African'", a point made even more forcibly some twenty years later by an American visitor commenting on white South African perceptions.[25]

African responses to their political effacement and denial of citizenship took different forms. To those who projected the privileges and freedoms of the nineteenth century Cape onto a common South African future, the hope of inclusion in the body politic on the basis of common humanity and individual achievement became increasingly remote after 1910. But the credibility of this ambition was eroded both by the African elite's signal failure to reverse segregationist measures in the 1920s and 30s and also because the aspirations of middle class Africans were increasingly challenged by constituencies with a more radical and popular social base.

A different response was to opt out of the idea of a unitary inclusive South Africa and to stress instead a common African or black identity. This reaction had roots in the rise of independent African churches during the second half of the nineteenth century. It was exemplified by the separatist "Ethiopian" movement and the growth of the African Methodist Episcopal Church which rejected white paternalism and black "progressivism", emphasising instead the virtues of self-reliance and autonomy.[26] Expressed in the notion of "Africa for the Africans" such ideas were not always easily contained in the civic and political boundaries of South Africa and, indeed, were incommensurable with liberal notions of gradual advancement. They were pan-African in scope and often looked elsewhere – black America in particular – for inspiration and guidance. In the political ferment of the 1920s, the impact of Garveyism and the emergence of movements led by charismatic leaders like Wellington Butelezi stressed deliverance from, rather than inclusion in, a white-dominated state.

Another variant of Africanism focused more closely on national politics and stressed the need for unity in opposing white supremacy. Amongst its

---

25. Eddie Roux, *Time Longer than Rope. A history of the black man's struggle for freedom in South Africa*, London, 1948, pp. 7, 16. See also Douglas Brown, *Against the World. Attitudes of White South Africans*, New York, 1968, p. 80: "Take the country's very name, South Africa. In common parlance, when used emotively rather than geographically, this means white South Africa. It is only by swallowing hard, either apologetically or defiantly, that most whites can bring themselves to refer to their black fellow-citizens as South Africans."

26. J.T. Campbell, *Songs of Zion. The African Methodist Episcopal Church in the United States and South Africa*, New York, 1995.

most prominent proponents were the African National Congress presidents John Dube and Pixley ka Isaka Seme. The central themes were expressed in Seme's 1911 call for a "Native Union" (a term he evidently preferred to the "pretentious title" of the SANNC) and also in his 1906 statement on "The Regeneration of Africa" which sounded a lyrical note of race pride and looked forward to the emergence of a uniquely African civilisation.[27] Although held in check by more pragmatic and constitutionally-oriented liberal approaches, this form of prophetic cultural nationalism later re-emerged in the Africanism of the Youth League; it is surely not coincidental that one of its chief exponents, Anton Lembede, was directly influenced by Seme. In the intervening decades Africanism coexisted with, and sometimes reinforced, other forms of social radicalism, including the rural populism of the Industrial and Commercial Workers Union in the 1920s and Josiah Gumede's presidency of the ANC (1927–30). Gumede's dual sympathies towards Garveyism and communism found an echo in the 1928 decision of the Communist Party of South Africa to adopt the slogan of the "Native Republic" – a formulation which, however painful and problematic, signalled an awareness that South Africa's destiny would henceforth be shaped by the needs and claims of its majority black population. Prior to this controversial decision, even communists assumed that the coming revolution would be led by white workers.

South Africanism and black radicalism

When did blacks begin to see themselves as South Africans? The question is perhaps unanswerable, but it is nonetheless worth putting. Although there are clear expressions of a pan-South African identity in the post-Union decade the experience of the Second World War proved to be a transforming moment in this regard, as in so many others. Certainly, by the 1940s, the rhetoric of African nationalism began to focus fully on the illegitimacy – rather than the unfairness – of white power and on the means of replacing minority with

---

27. T. Karis and G.M. Carter (eds), *From Protest to Challenge, Vol. 1*, Stanford, 1972, documents 20 and 21. See also document 21, "The African National Congress – Is It Dead?", 1932, where Seme says: "The African National Congress will teach us 'Race pride,', and this 'Race Pride' will teach us how to become a nation and to be self dependent". Jordan Ngubane's *An African Explains Apartheid*, London, 1963, pp. 69 and ff., draws a useful distinction between the liberalism of Jabavu, the Africanism of Seme and Dube, and the militant rejection of white authority represented by Bambatha.

majority rule. The emergence of mass-based politics, a growing international discourse of democratic rights and freedoms, and a developing anti-colonial sentiment in Africa and Asia, all helped to entrench the idea that to be an African was *ipso facto* to be a South African. But this was not yet generally recognised.

In the case of white politics the expansive South Africanism of Smuts and Hofmeyr reached its apogee as English and Afrikaner conscripts joined battle in the fight against fascism. Wartime conditions proved conducive to extensive schemes of social welfare and scientific planning and the role of the state as an agent of positive change was considerably enhanced. Vigorous publications with a strong South Africanist flavour like *The Democrat, Trek* and *The Forum* provided new avenues for liberal and radical thought. The extensive programme of army education devised by E.G. Malherbe, R.F.A. Hoernlé and Leo and Nell Marquard, exposed many receptive soldiers to liberal-democratic ideas and caused them to reflect on South African society in novel ways.[28] An important statement of left-wing thinking was Leo Marquard's *The Black Man's Burden* (1943) which mixed historical and contemporary analysis to produce a powerful indictment of racial and capitalist exploitation.[29]

This forward-looking and confident vision of South Africa was not, however, deeply rooted in the white electorate as a whole. In 1941 G.H. Calpin, a conservative English-speaking journalist wrote a best-selling book entitled *There are no South Africans* in which he lamented the lack of any shared national sentiment and dismissed spurious attempts to cultivate a common South Africanism. Divisions between English and Afrikaners meant that there were "two flags, two languages, two policies towards the Native, two ideas of economic advance...". Far from bringing the country together, participation in the war was causing the "two streams" of national life to "diverge to polar limits".[30]

Consumed by the absence of a common white identity, Calpin had nothing whatsoever to say about black South Africans for whom the war had a transforming effect, in political, social and intellectual terms. A newly confident and assertive generation of urban-based intellectuals pressed for inclusion in South African society, not as a privilege, but as a right. In the paint-

---

28. See e.g., S. Dubow, "Scientism, social research and the limits of South Africanism: The case of E.G. Malherbe", *South African Historical Journal*, Vol. 44, 2001.

29. John Burger, *The Black Man's Burden*, London, 1943.

30. G.G. Calpin, *There are no South Africans*, London, 1941, pp. 25, 32.

ings of George Pemba and Gerard Sekoto, in the proletarian "marabi" music of the streets and shebeens, or the more sophisticated American-influenced swing rhythms of big bands such as the Jazz Maniacs, township life acquired vibrant and tumultuous cultural forms which embraced modernity even while drawing on older African motifs and traditions. Middle-class African educators attempted to steer this exuberant creativity into "a model African National Culture" suitable "for all classes of African townsmen".[31]

The gradualism and deferential attitudes of mission-educated Africans and the paternalism of well-meaning white liberals was dismissed with amused disdain by the writer Herbert Dhlomo who proclaimed the emergence of the progressive and forward-looking "New African". To the journalist Jordan Ngubane, writing in 1941, Dhlomo's writing moved "beyond tribalism and tutelage" to a "truly national spirit" which affirmed that "it will be the African himself who shall rise to fight to reach his goal". His poems were, Ngubane felt, "an encouragement to fight with greater confidence to become a citizen of the country of [our] birth".[32]

The African National Congress re-emerged during the war years as the leading force in black oppositional politics, its character newly reshaped by a growing mass base and an infusion of trade union, communist and Africanist ideas. In documents such as *African Claims* and *The Atlantic Charter from the Standpoint of Africans*, adopted as official policy by the ANC in 1943, a new rhetoric of democratic rights, citizenship, and national self-determination is conspicuously evident. The Congress Youth League and its leading intellectuals, Anton Lembede and Peter Mda, proclaimed the philosophy of Africanism in uncompromising tones of national assertion and racial pride. Whereas earlier emanations of Africanist ideas frequently countenanced avoidance of white authority (and flourished in the countryside where white authority was dispersed and separatist dreams could take hold) the Africanism of the 1940s was overwhelmingly urban in orientation and was addressed directly to the institutions of state. It focused on the need for African unity, was fulsome in its rejection of "tribalism", and had as its primary objective the removal of white domination and the attainment of full citizenship under African leadership. As if in answer to Trollope and Millin, Lembede pronounced

---

31. D.B. Coplan, *In Township Tonight. South Africa's Black City Music and Theatre*, Johannesburg, 1985, pp. 132, 138.

32. N. Visser and T. Couzens (eds), "Introduction" to *H.I.E. Dhlomo. Collected Works*, Johannesburg, 1985, p. xv. See also Couzens, *The New African*.

African nationalism's first cardinal principle with a blunt assertion: "Africa is a blackman's country".[33]

Variants of socialist and Marxist analysis acted as a counterpart to the Africanist-inspired radicalism of the Youth League and sought to explain South African history in terms of colonial dispossession, social class and economic exploitation. The Communist Party benefited from a large increase in its membership during the 1940s and served as an important source of radical ideas; so, too, did the small Cape-based Trotskyite Non-European Unity Movement, whose leadership was predominantly drawn from coloured teachers and intellectuals. Several works, typically published in pamphlet form, sought to analyse South African history from the perspective of the indigenous peoples' experience of colonial conquest.[34] These examples of politically-engaged history can be seen as forerunners of the Marxisant popular history approach which flourished in South African liberal universities from the mid-1970s, but they remained almost unknown and unread beyond narrow circles of political activists before their rediscovery by left-wing academic historians. Until the publication of Jack and Ray Simons' *Class and Colour in South Africa* in 1969 – a major work which mixed scholarly research with Communist Party discipline – only Leo Marquard's *Black Man's Burden* and Eddie Roux's *Time Longer than Rope* were available to a broader audience.[35] Nevertheless, the ephemeral writings and intense debates of Unity Movement and Communist intellectuals during the 1950s (whose participants also included Kenny Jordaan, Ben Kies, A.C. Jordan, Thomas Ngwenya, Michael Harmel, Ruth First and Joe Matthews) were important in raising theoretical questions such as the nature of capitalist exploitation, the relationship between race and class, and approaches to the "national question".[36] In so doing, the essence of the South African problem was being thoroughly reconceived.

33. A.M. Lembede, "Policy of the Congress Youth League" in *Inkundla ya Bantu*, May, 1946, cited in T. Karis and G.M. Carter (eds), *From Protest to Challenge,* Vol. 2, Stanford, 1973, p. 317.

34. C.C. Saunders, *The Making of the South African Past. Major historians on race and class,* Cape Town, 1988, pp. 136–7; Bill Nasson, "The Unity Movement: Its legacy in historical consciousness", in *Radical History Review*, Vol. 46, No. 7, 1990.

35. The circulation of *Class and Colour in South Africa* and *Time Longer than Rope* was restricted in South Africa by official censorship. Both *Time Longer than Rope* and *The Black Man's Burden* were published in London by Victor Gollancz.

36. Lionel Forman, *A Trumpet from the Housetops,* S. Forman and A. Odendaal (eds), Cape Town, 1992.

Black nationalism and multi-racialism

The 1950s saw a new awareness of South Africa as a multi-cultural or multi-ethnic society, a perception shared – though by no means acknowledged – across the political spectrum from the National Party to the Congress Alliance. This is evident in the emphasis placed by theorists of apartheid on ethnic or tribal sub-divisions which represented a significant departure from the old *idée fixe* which conceived of Africans as a homogenous mass, save for the difference between "westernised" or "detribalised" individuals on the one hand and tribal traditionalists on the other. Government use of the term "Bantu" in preference to "natives" dates from this period and indicates official efforts to clothe apartheid policies in the enabling language of *volks* anthropology. One option for opponents of apartheid was simply to deny the existence of racial and ethnic groupings – often signalled by a refusal to deal in its linguistic coinage. But this strategy of principled non-racialism, favoured by many liberals as well as by Marxists, failed to take account of practical politics. For the ANC the problem was all the more acute because the increasingly assertive "Africanist" constituency within its ranks was deeply suspicious of the participation of non-Africans in Congress affairs.

At the historic Congress of the People in 1955 the ANC was confirmed as first among equals within a liberation movement now structured as a parallel organisational alliance comprised of interest groups (trade unionists and women) and peoples (African, coloured, Indian and white). Notably, every constituent organisation bore the name "South African" in its title, thus re-inforcing the idea that the Congress movement's goal was a unitary state in which "national" and "cultural" differences would be accorded recognition, celebrated even, though never at the cost of achieving a common or supra-South African nationality. This was made clear by Congress' strong disdain of "tribalism". It was powerfully reiterated by the Freedom Charter's declaration that "South Africa belongs to all who live in it, Black and White" and the promise that "all national groups shall have equal rights". But, despite this inclusive rhetoric, it was evident that the inter-racial configuration of the Congress movement mirrored the official racial categories of the apartheid state in uncomfortable ways. The "four nation" make-up of Congress was attacked by principled proponents of non-racialism such as the Unity movement as well as by members of the ANC Youth League and pan-Africanists who resented the formal equivalence of African and non-African groupings.[37]

---

37. See Karis and Carter, Vol. 3, pp. 63, 65, 94.

The disquieting similarity in the discourse of government and liberation movement around issues like "groups" and "peoples" was a reflection of the growing acceptance of the politics of "multi-racialism". The term seems to have been first used by the liberal philosopher Alfred Hoernlé in 1939 to define the South African condition, but it was only a decade later that it came into vogue.[38] In the 1950s South Africa multi-racialism came to be closely associated with moderate Christian and liberal bridge-building initiatives.[39] Albert Luthuli welcomed the Congress of the People as the embodiment of "our multi-racial nation" (to the disquiet of Youth Leaguers) and the Progressive Party, formed in 1959, made much of the idea that multi-racialism was an undeniable fact.[40]

With backing like this, it is hardly surprising that apartheid ideologues disparaged multi-racialism as a left-liberal concept that wrongly presumed different groups could co-exist peacefully within a single political framework.[41] In their view only total separation between black and white – coupled with a recognition that the "Bantu" were a heterogeneous collection of different "ethnic groups", each of whom should enjoy a measure of "self-determination" – would suffice. The bristling rejection of "multi-racialism" by apartheid intellectuals like Werner Eiselen nonetheless concealed tacit acceptance of its underlying assumptions; thus, when the hubristic plans of apartheid's engineers began to falter in the 1970s, apartheid would duly be reclothed in terms of multi-racial or multi-national partnership.[42] Later, still,

---

38. See Hoernlé's influential Phelps-Stokes lectures, published as *South African Native Policy and the Liberal Spirit*, Lovedale, 1939, p. viii. One source of its reintroduction was the shift from empire to commonwealth in debates around federation in the Rhodesias, for example, multi-racialism was recommended as a means of reconciling settler political interests with those of the indigenous majority.

39. For instances of both, see e.g. N. Manseragh, *Multi-Racial Commonwealth*, 1955; *The Christian Citizen in a Multi-racial Society*, Strand, 1949; *God's Kingdom in Multi-Racial South Africa. A report on the inter-racial conference of church leaders*, Johannesburg, 1955.

40. A. Norval, *Deconstructing Apartheid Discourse*, p. 152; A. Luthuli, "The Christian and Political Issues", in *The Christian Citizen in a Multi-Racial Society*; M. Wilson and L. Thompson (eds) *Oxford History of South Africa*, Vol. 2, Oxford, 1971, p. 490; Ngubane, *An African Explains Apartheid*, pp. 100–1.

41. A. Norval, *Deconstructing Apartheid Discourse,* London, 1996, pp. 73, 142, 148.

42. H.A. Fagan made this point somewhat earlier: "Whether we like it or not, the Republic of South Africa therefore has to be dealt with as a multi-racial state. A policy based on any other approach would be so false and unrealistic that it must lead to ultimate disaster", in *Coexistence in South Africa*, Cape Town, 1963, p. 64.

the idea would re-emerge in the more fluid and inclusive language of the "rainbow nation".

From plural society to black consciousness

A new generation of liberal historians of the 1960s invested complexity and time-depth to the idea of South Africa as multi-racial. These Africanists, as they styled themselves (in a pre-Saidian age of innocence) stressed themes of interaction and mutual dependence between the "peoples" of Southern Africa and placed special emphasis on instances of African agency and initiative. The defining statement of liberal Africanism was the two volume *Oxford History of South Africa*, edited by the anthropologist Monica Wilson and the historian Leonard Thompson. Its opening words declared:

> This work derives from our belief that the central theme of South African history is interaction between peoples of diverse origins, languages, technologies, ideologies, and social systems, meeting on South African soil.[43]

It is a measure of the division that existed between English liberals and Afrikaner nationalists at this time that the Wilson/Thompson and Muller histories occupied separate intellectual spheres,[44] neither of which felt the need to take more than passing account of each other. Indeed, the real challenge to the *Oxford History* came nearer to home from a new generation of scholars, strongly influenced by historical materialist analysis. For the so-called "Neo-Marxist revisionists" the conceptual assumptions of the Oxford History – in particular, its lack of attention to structural economic determinants – were a fatal weakness. As the "liberal-radical" historiographical debate gathered momentum, in an environment of acrimonious disagreement, argument centred on the importance or otherwise of social class to South Africa's formation of its past and the making of its future.[45]

The *Societies of Southern Africa* seminar at the University of London, inaugurated in the same year that the Oxford and Muller histories were published, was a vital forum for the production and dissemination of radical

---

43. Preface to *A History of South Africa*, Vol. 1, (ed.) M. Wilson and L. Thompson, Oxford, 1969. The term "multi-racial".

44. C.F.J. Muller (ed.), *Five Hundred Years: A history of South Africa*, first English edition, Pretoria, 1969, originally published in Afrikaans in 1968.

45. For an early expression of this debate see H. Wright, *The Burden of the Present: Liberal-Radical Controversy over Southern African History*, Cape Town, 1977.

history. Guided by Shula Marks, the innovative seminar had a political as well as an intellectual agenda and in its early years many of its participants launched powerful attacks on liberal presuppositions. Viewed in retrospect, however, the paradigmatic differences in approach that divided liberals and radicals occluded significant underlying similarities in approach. It is worth noting, for example, that the name of the seminar could equally have been adopted by Wilson and Thompson. Many (though by no means all) revisionists shared with liberal Africanists a concern with pre-colonial African history, a sensitivity to anthropological approaches, and an engagement with wider Africanist scholarship.[46] Both groups were, moreover, indebted to the earlier insights of Macmillan and De Kiewiet and both viewed South Africa as a zone of interaction and conflict between different peoples, all of whom had legitimate claim to a common citizenship.

A further similarity between liberal Africanist and radical historians lay in their determination to avoid apartheid-imposed labels and tribal categories. This often manifested itself in punctilious efforts to produce correct African orthographies (it soon became a convention for books to begin with a critical note on racial terminology and nomenclature). Important as these emendations undoubtedly were within the world of scholarship, their impact was, necessarily, limited. Indeed, a more powerful and politically ambitious challenge to apartheid habits of mind and linguistic conventions was arising at the same time, though from a very different direction. This was expressed by intellectuals of the black consciousness movement whose thinking was sharply opposed to liberal Africanists as well as Marxists.[47]

Black consciousness intellectuals rejected racial categorisations that divided the "oppressed", arguing instead for a common black identity encompassing the shared experience of Africans, "coloureds" and Indians. In denouncing the patronising and studied "non-racialism" of liberals they argued that white South Africans, regardless of political outlook or sympathies, were beneficiaries of the apartheid system. The objectives of the black consciousness movement were considerably more wide-ranging and radical than the Afri-

---

46. See, for example, L. Thompson (ed.), *African Societies in Southern Africa*, UCLA, 1969, whose contributors include Marks and Legassick as well as Thompson and Wilson. Disciplinary differences between radical historians and anthropologists on the one hand, and theoretically-minded Neo-Marxists on the other (such as Davies, Kaplan and Morris), now seem more striking than the apparent gulf between liberals and radicals.

47. The South African Students Organisation under the leadership of Steve Biko was formed in the same year as the publication of the *Oxford History*, 1969.

canism of Lembede and Mda that preceded it by a generation or more. True liberation required a transformation in black self-image. The word "black" was therefore infused with powerful new resonance, becoming a synonym for the oppressed as well as a byword for freedom.[48] By embracing Africa as a whole and rejecting extraneous "European" influences, black consciousness laid claim to a sense of national identity and self-realisation that transcended the country's borders and extended the idea of liberation beyond the realms of tangible political power.[49]

The black consciousness movement's determination to confront white supremacy by challenging the hegemony of colonial linguistic constructions was signalled by the frequent usage of "Azania" in preference to "South Africa". Terms bearing negative connotations such as "non-white" or "non-European" were dismissed with due contempt; conversely, "blackness" was invested with positive spiritual and moral qualities and divested of biophysical connotations. Steve Biko's courtroom exchange in the 1976 SASO/BPC trial, when he mocked the anomalous character of the judge-inquisitor's "whiteness", is a famous example of this strategy of linguistic inversion and destabilisation.[50] The rebuff delivered to white liberal students in 1969 when SASO denounced NUSAS hypocrisy in 1969 was another sharp reminder – this time directed to an ostensibly sympathetic white political constituency – that the very status of whites as South Africans was deeply problematic. It underlined the message that blacks had to be the agents of their liberation and that white sympathisers should only aspire to play a supportive part in the struggle for freedom; hence the iconic black consciousness slogan enunciated by Barney Pityana in 1971: "Black man, you are on your own".

The effect of black consciousness on young white South Africans who sought to identify with the liberation movement was profound, in some cases traumatic: no longer could whites presume to speak on behalf of others or to take their South Africanness for granted. Rick Turner's influential *Eye of the Needle* was an especially important and timely intervention because of

48. B. Pityana et al., *Bounds of Possibility. The legacy of Steve Biko and Black Consciousness,* Cape Town, 1991, pp. 9, 24, 104–5.

49. See e.g. SASO Policy Manifesto, July 1971, "The basic tenet of Black Consciousness is that the Blackman must reject all value systems that seek to make him a foreigner in the country of his birth and reduce his basic human dignity." Karis et al., *From Protest to Challenge,* Vol. 5, p. 482.

50. S. Biko, *I Write what I Like. A Selection of his Writings,* Stubbs, Aelred (ed.), Harmondsworth, Penguin, 1978, pp. 103–6.

the fundamental ways in which he posed questions about white South African assumptions and self-perceptions.[51] In the post-1976 era, the onus was increasingly upon white sympathisers to prove themselves white Africans, to eschew European cultural dominance, and to engage in a process of personal and institutional "Africanisation".[52] In the 1980s and 90s this process was visibly apparent in dress, style, food and also in the way the country projected itself externally. The apartheid vision of a "constellation of states" yielded to the ANC's 1994 electoral slogan of "One Nation, Many Cultures". In the "New South Africa", Bishop Tutu's compelling metaphor of the "rainbow nation" – nowhere symbolised more poignantly than when Nelson Mandela donned Francois Pienaar's jersey in the 1995 rugby world cup – came to symbolise reconciliation and freedom.

In his recent concise history of the country Robert Ross observes:

> ... even if the essential unity of South Africa and the identity of South Africans are beyond dispute, there remains the question of what is, and what is not, South Africa. Who are, and who are not, South Africans.

William Beinart's comparable historical introduction turns around the idea of a "state without a nation".[53]

Such questions would probably have been more familiar to observers of the first "new South Africa" in 1910 than they were to subsequent generations of professional historians for whom the basic unit of analysis – the nation-state – was obviously contentious. A century later, in the era of the second "new South Africa", these questions have returned in fresh and troubling ways. One purpose of this contribution is to suggest that there is nothing self-evident or natural about South Africa or South Africans. It is surely time, therefore, for historians to formulate detailed questions about how South Africa has been conceived and imagined, to analyse the different forms in which ideas about South Africans and South African societies have developed over time, and to trace the ways in which the South African "problem" or predicament has been conceptualised. In order to do so we should remember that struggle *for* South Africa has long been, and continues to be, a struggle to *become* South African.

51. R. Turner, *The Eye of the Needle,* Sprocas, Johannesburg, 1972.

52. NUSAS gave important leads to this process. See e.g. Discussion documents by Patrick Fitzgerald and Rai Turton to NUSAS annual congress, 1976, in Karis et al., *From Protest to Challenge,* Vol. 5, pp. 444–6.

53. R. Ross, *A Concise History of South Africa,* Cambridge, 1999, p. 3; Beinart, *Twentieth Century South Africa,* Oxford, 1994.

— CHAPTER 3 —

New nation, new history?
Constructing the past in post-apartheid South Africa

Colin Bundy

In 1992, one of South Africa's most incisive intellectuals addressed an audience of some 150 history teachers and academics.[1] "We are not in the period of transition as passive spectators" said Neville Alexander, and went on:

> We are part of this transition – we can shape it. In shaping and fashioning the history curriculum we are ourselves making history. We are giving shape both to the history of the present and the future.[2]

His confidence is understandable. South African history writing and teaching, when he spoke, had for twenty years been a fertile field. Its practitioners had pioneered new topics, revised existing interpretations, and honed their critical edge through a series of intense debates with one another. The various components of what was known as "radical" or "revisionist" historical scholarship had become the most influential body of work shaping the understanding of the South African past. Nor was their influence restricted to the academy. In South Africa, remarked a leading imperial historian, "history in the 1970s and 1980s became the master tool of intellectual resistance" to apartheid.[3] Numbers of South African historians had also sought a praxis extending beyond the academy, translating historical knowledge into popu-

---

1. In 1992, three history curriculum conferences were held in Durban, Johannesburg and Cape Town "to give teachers and interested academics an opportunity to contribute in a democratic way" to forming a new history curriculum for schools, History Education Group, *History Matters: Debates about a new history curriculum for South Africa,* Heinemann-Centaur, Johannesburg, 1993, p. 1.

2. History Education Group, *History Matters: Debates about a new history curriculum for South Africa,* Heinemann-Centaur, Johannesburg, 1993, p. 13.

3. Etherington, Norman, "Edward Palmer Thompson", *Southern African Review of Books*, Vol. 5, No. 6, 1993, p. 5.

lar, accessible and "relevant" registers; working with publishers to update and improve school teaching texts; or with teachers to improve pedagogy and classroom practice.

Constructing the past – which past?

Yet today the mood is very different. The last decade has been disquieting – even demoralising – for South African historians. The confidence of 1992 now looks like hubris. In its place are anxiety and uncertainty about the academic standing and social function of the discipline. The production and practice of history have been called sharply into question and leading members of the profession fear that they have lost "both influence and, to a large extent, a sense of direction".[4] Early intimations of disciplinary *angst* were voiced by several scholars in 1994 – the very year of the first democratic election, the highwater mark of political transition – and in the following year Paul Maylam's presidential address to the South African Historical Society was a sober and thoughtful warning entitled *Tensions within the Practice of History.*[5]

More recently, this precipitate slide from confidence through questioning to crisis has been charted in a pair of probing and reflective articles by Tim Nuttall and John Wright; and their analysis has been amplified in various ways by others.[6] What follows here is essentially an attempt to knit these

---

4. Nuttall, Tim and Wright, John, "Exploring History with a Capital 'H'", *Current Writing*, Vol. 10, No. 2, 1998, pp. 38–61, p. 38.

5. Rich, Paul, "Is South African Radical Social History Becoming Irrelevant?", *South African Historical Journal*, Vol. 31, 1994, p. 191; Etherington, Norman, "Fissures in the Post-Apartheid Academy", *South African Historical Journal*, Vol. 31, 1994, pp. 206–7; Freund, Bill, "The Art of Writing History", *Southern African Review of Books*, Sep/Oct 1994, p. 24; Peires, Jeff, "The Art of Writing History", *Southern African Review of Books*, 1994, p. 24; Maylam, Paul, "Tensions within the Practice of History", *South African Historical Journal*, Vol. 33, 1995, pp. 3–12.

6. Nuttall and Wright, op. cit, 1998, Nuttall, Tim and Wright, John, "Probing the Predicaments of Academic History in Contemporary South Africa", *South African Historical Journal*, Vol. 42, 2000, pp. 26–48; Cobley, Alan, "Does Social History Have a Future? The Ending of Apartheid and Recent Trends in South African Historiography", *Journal of Southern African Studies*, Vol. 27, No. 3, 2001, pp. 613–26; Comaroff, Jean, "The End of History, Again? Pursuing the Past in the Postcolony", lecture delivered at the Anglo-American Historians Conference, July 2002; Polakow-Suransky, Sasha, "Reviving South African History: Academics debate how to represent and teach the nation's past", *The Chronicle of Higher Education*, 14 June 2002, http://chronicle.com.weekly/v48/i40.40a03601.htm.

strands into a description and explanation of the crisis of contemporary South African historical scholarship.[7]

It is clear that the dilemmas of the discipline and perils of the profession are multi-causal in origin. They are the result of pressures that were local and international, contingent and structural, practical and philosophical.

At the immediate and institutional level, the 1990s saw history as a field of study increasingly unable to attract students, teachers, or inter-institutional resources; and as a subject that was unexpectedly a major casualty of curriculum and syllabus review. It was not just that history was not "useful", nor that it failed to lead to obvious employment; it was also experienced by many students as a "source of discomfort and embarrassment".[8] Pupils in Cape Town schools believed that "history is a wrong subject ... because ... we must make peace in our land" that "it makes pain for other people and their families" and that "we must forget history and think of the future".[9] Sentiments of this kind translated rapidly into falling enrolments for history at high school and at university alike.[10] South African universities in the 1990s were late but zealous converts to the creed of affordability, efficiency, and rational resource allocation. History departments were renamed, restructured and downsized.[11]

History departments became adept at proffering their expertise as interdisciplinary or "service" courses: history for lawyers, history for medical students, history in film courses, and history for accountants.

The other shock that was registered at the immediate or institutional level was the brusque treatment meted to history as a subject in the school syllabus (with obvious implications for its study at tertiary level) under the new ANC government between 1994 and 1999. Excellent, and anguished, accounts exist of the discrepancy between the expectations of history educationists in the early 1990s and the outcome of Curriculum 2005.[12] Under Minister of Edu-

---

7. If "crisis" seems too strong, then by all means refer instead to "uncertainty and confusion" (Nuttall and Wright, op. cit., 1998, p. 38) or "predicaments" (Nuttall and Wright, op. cit., 2000) or "parlous state" (Comaroff, op. cit., 2002, p. 7) or "erosion of history as an academic discipline" (Cobley, op. cit., 2001, p. 624).

8. Nuttall and Wright, op. cit., 2000. p. 28.

9. Sieborger, Rob, "Reconceptualising South African School History Textbooks", *South African Historical Journal,* Vol. 30, 1994, pp. 98–108.

10. Nuttall and Wright, op. cit., 2000, p. 27.

11. Cobley, op. cit., 2001, p. 624.

12. Bam, June, "Negotiating history, truth and reconciliation and globalisation", *Mots*

cation Sibusiso Bengu (1994–99) a flurry of curriculum-planning-cum-negotiations under the National Education and Training Forum, "comprising education departments, with business, parent, teacher and student organisations" with minimal input by academic historians resulted in an unsatisfactory "interim" history syllabus for schools which evidenced no attempts at reconceptualising the past nor asking first principle questions.[13] This was bad enough: but Curriculum 2005, promulgated in 1996, defining the compulsory school syllabus for the next decade, was even worse. It removed all reference to history from the curriculum; its rigid model of "outcomes-based education" was patently inimical to any considered evaluation of the past. Nor was this simply oversight. Successive meetings were sought by delegations of "progressive" historians with officials from Bengu's department in 1996 and June 1998.[14]

Historians registered their alarm and disapproval of Curriculum 2005 and its indifference to the study of the past.[15] They were fortunate to find an audience, in the person of the (from June 1999 to April 2004) Minister of Education, Kader Asmal. Asmal, unmistakably, demonstrated a personal appreciation of the discipline and moved to take steps to reverse the more egregious consequences of Curriculum 2005. He appointed a series of review committees and panels. In 1999 a ministerial review committee chaired by Linda Chisholm revisited Curriculum 2005 and insisted that the teaching of history was vital to the school syllabus. It threw a "lifeline to history" and this was handed on to a Working Group on Values in Education, and especially

---

pluriels, No. 13, 2000; Kros, Cynthia, *Trusting to the Process: Reflections on the flaws in the negotiating of the history curriculum in South Africa*, History Curriculum Research Project, Report No. 1, Cambridge University Press & History Workshop, University of the Witwatersrand, Johannesburg, 1996; Sieborger, Rob, "History and the Emerging Nation: The South African Experience", *International Journal of Historical Learning Teaching and Research*, Vol. 1, No. 1, 2000.

13. Sieborger, op. cit., 2000, p. 2; Kros, op. cit., 1996, p. 10.

14. Bam, op. cit., 2000, p. 3; Polakow-Suransky, op. cit., 2002, p. 3.

15. Kros, Cynthia, *Curriculum 2005 and the End of History*, History Curriculum Research Project, Report No. 3, Cambridge University Press & History Workshop, University of the Witwatersrand, Johannesburg, 1998; South African Historical Society, "Statement on the Implications of Curriculum 2005 for History Teaching in the Schools", *South African Historical Journal*, Vol. 38, 1998, pp. 200–04; Sieborger, Rob, "'How the outcomes came out. A personal account of and reflections on the initial process of Curriculum 2005" in Bak, Nelleke (ed.), *Going for the Gap*, Juta, Cape Town, 1998; Taylor and Vinjevold 1999.

to a History/Archaeology Panel as a sub-structure.[16] The Report of the Panel, backed by the Working Group, then – crucially – led to the appointment, almost exactly a year ago, of the members of the South African History Project, and the eloquent commitment by Asmal at its launch to "the relevance of the past ... [to] the creation of a more liberated present".[17]

At the proximate or societal level, professional history was affected by developments in the political/public realm in South Africa in a number of linked ways. South African historians who had been in various ways "caught up in the deep and narrow groove of 'struggle history'" now found themselves at a loss.[18]

The difficulty in coming up with any straightforward answer to "what sort of new history?" was compounded by the fact that the political project of the new government shifted quite rapidly in a direction that perplexed and discomfited left-of-centre academics.[19] Norman Etherington, perceptively, identified a growing gap between what the academy had to offer and what the state wanted as early as 1994:

> Not so long ago ... it was taken for granted that new insights into the construction of knowledge, historical experience and economic policy would have a direct bearing on the practical questions of government, poverty and racial oppression. That sense of praxis has largely been lost. Economists speak of markets and macro-economic policy settings in a language far removed from the discourses of historians and literary theorists.[20]

But in the years to follow it was not merely two vocabularies that were at variance. Increasingly the overall trajectory of post-1994 macro-economic policy jettisoned the broadly social democratic approach of the RDP for the neoliberal orthodoxies of GEAR: fiscal conservatism, deficit reduction, deregulated competition, privatised state assets, and a reliance on "trickle-down"

---

16. Sieborger, op. cit., 2000, p. 4.

17. The report of the History/Archaeology Panel, the brief of the History Project, and Asmal's speech at its launch on 31 August 2001 are available at http://education.pwv. gov.za; Polakow-Suransky, op. cit., 2002, p. 1.

18. Nuttall and Wright, op. cit., 1998, pp. 40–41.

19. Cobley, op. cit., 2001, p. 618.

20. Etherington, Norman, "Fissures in the Post-Apartheid Academy", *South African Historical Journal*, Vol. 31, 1994, p. 207.

benefits to address poverty and inequality.[21] As Heribert Adam provocatively averred:

> When former activists turn into instant millionaires, they not only bury their own history but confirm the triumph of non-racial capitalism.[22]

The gravy train left the chariots of struggle far behind. It undoubtedly helped shape the "mixed agenda of the post-apartheid state in the promulgation of national history" – an agenda experienced by some historians as a de-commissioning of history: "The past is now far less important than the immediate future".

The diminished value placed in the public sphere on history concerned with conflict was matched by a new premium upon history as state-sponsored and commercial "heritage" and "legacy projects".[23] Heritage studies – "that ultimate commodification of history in pursuit of the tourist dollar" [24] – has been a growth area in South African universities, and in Guy's words:

> ... the Heritage Industry invokes a sentimentalised past which makes bearable a sordid and painful present.[25]

History, as interpreter of the past, cohabits uneasily with its common-law partners, "heritage" and "commemoration".

Finally, at the level of underlying or embedded change, South African history as a scholarly pursuit has experienced an intellectual crisis that was international in its origins and scope. The South African academy was shielded to some extent from international currents by the pressing local agenda before 1990; but throughout the 1990s the humanities and social sciences buckled

---

21. I have argued this case more fully in Bundy, Colin, "The long shadow of history: Reflections on post-apartheid South Africa", unpublished paper, delivered at Imperial History seminar, Kings College London, 2002. The most important work developing and illustrating it is Marais, Hein, *South Africa: Limits to Change: The political economy of transformation,* 2nd edition, Zed Books, London & New York / UCT Press, Cape Town, 2001.

22. Quoted from Bertelsen, Eve, "Ads and amnesia: Black advertising in the new South Africa", in S. Nuttall and C. Coetzee (eds), *Negotiating the Past: The making of memory in South Africa*, Oxford University Press, Cape Town, 1998, p. 222.

23. Nuttall and Wright, op. cit., 2000, pp. 29, 30, 34; Carruthers, op. cit., 2000, p. 1, 5.

24. Cobley, op. cit., 2001, p. 618.

25. Guy, Jeff, "Battling with Banality", *Journal of Natal and Zulu History, Vol.* 18, 1998, pp. 156–193.

under the impact of theoretical perspectives assailing basic epistemological and methodological precepts. Postmodern, post-structuralist and post-colonial critiques rendered the unquestioned suddenly untenable; what had been central, decentred; what was fixed, fluid. History was particularly vulnerable to the textual turn: evidence, objectivity, truth, the nature of historical enquiry itself were all listed as casualties by some reporters of the postmodernist wars.[26] In South Africa, as elsewhere, many historians were unnerved by the theoretical challenges to the validity of their subject.

Building a nation – whose nation?

Simultaneously, another set of exchanges took place in South Africa on a larger stage with higher stakes, and with a corresponding intensity. Its focus swivelled and switched over a set of related issues: social identity, ethnicity, race, citizenship, nationality and nationhood.

In the political catechism of the New South Africa, the primary enquiry remains the National Question. What is the post-apartheid nation? Who belongs or is excluded, and on what basis? How does a "national identity gain its salience and power to transcend the particularities of ethnicity and race?" [27] How should those resilient abstract nouns – class, gender, region, language – be defined in a national dictionary? What political or economic or moral bridge can span the contradiction between a juridical assertion of common citizenship and the experiential reality of difference, separateness and inequality? How in short is nation to be imagined, let alone realised?

Attempts to imagine the nation in post-apartheid South Africa have been heavily freighted with "the burden of race".[28] There is an overwhelming awareness that the deep structures of South African society – power, class, place, distribution of goods – are drawn along racial axes; and that South African history in the "longue durée" established discrimination, segregation, difference and a pervasive sense of "the Other" as ruling coordinates. There

---

26. A good guide to the literature sustaining the postmodernist critique of history is provided in the "Further reading" section in Evans, 1997, especially pp. 288–301.

27. Pieterse, Edgar, "In Search of a Nation: Nation Building in the New South Africa", *Safundi*, Issue 8, 2002, p. 1.

28. In July 2001 the University of the Witwatersrand hosted a conference entitled The Burden of Race? "Whiteness" and "Blackness" in Modern South Africa. Some of the conference papers appear in a special issue, also called "Burden of Race?", in *Transformation*, No. 47, 2001.

is also a growing realisation that over the decades of apartheid, modes of racial reasoning were constituted as commonsensical, insinuated into habits of thought and reflexes, and that "race thinking" shaped the perceptions and experiences of all South Africans, even to the extent of excluding alternative ways of thinking.[29]

Unsurprisingly, then, discursive projects in nation-building since 1994 have also been exercises in weight-lifting, grappling with the burdens of race and history. At the risk of drastic over-simplification, it is proposed here that there have been three major discursive projects, three over-arching attempts to narrate the nation. In shorthand, these may be thought of as the rainbow nation (or "unity and diversity"); as the African Renaissance (or "African hegemony in the context of a multi-cultural and non-racial society"); and as ethnic particularism (or the assertion of sub-national identities as primary).

The origins of symbolism and rhetoric of the Rainbow Nation (or rainbow notion!) have been usefully sketched elsewhere.[30] "Rainbowism" essentially claimed the possibility of a harmonious, common identity even while its imagery signalled that such identity was constituted by different colours (or races or cultures or communities). It was:

> ... a successful albeit romanticised representation of the Charterist interpretation of a South African nation.[31]

As an ideological and political project it was associated particularly with Mandela and Tutu, and imbued briefly with all the moral authority and urgency that this remarkable pair could muster. Their championing of the rainbow concept overlapped with their commitment to the Truth and Reconciliation Commission (TRC).[32] The TRC posited a society of diverse but shared culture, with tolerance and acceptance of "the Other" underpinned

---

29. Posel, Deborah, 2001, p. 51; Maré, Gerhard, "Race counts in contemporary South Africa: 'An illusion of ordinariness'", *Transformation,* No. 47, 2001, p. 79.

30. Baines, Gary, "The rainbow nation? Identity and nation building in post-apartheid South Africa", *Mots pluriels,* No. 7, 1998.

31. Filatova, Irena, "The Rainbow against the African Sky or African Hegemony in a Multi-Cultural Context", *Transformation,* 34, 1997, p. 50.

32. There is by now a large literature on the TRC: apart from the five volume Report and other documents at www.trc.org.za there are important participant memoirs, a number of full-length academic monographs and edited collections, as well as journal articles by historians, political scientists, jurists, literary theorists, etc.

by disclosure, confession, remorse and forgiveness. As Sitas, memorably, said of the TRC:

> It was to be the grand, sorrowful performance and ritual of a society re-making itself. It was to be one of the most compromised, yet most significant pieces of nation-building ever imagined.[33]

While the discourse of rainbow undoubtedly found a popular resonance in 1995/96, its multi-hued appeal dulled quite rapidly; its optimistic multiculturalism suddenly seemed naive rather than noble. Sitas attributes the rainbow's fading to white indifference to the TRC. Their collective "refusal to own the past" disappointed Tutu, angered Mandela, outraged the African intelligentsia, and strengthened the hand of Africanists within the ANC.[34] Black intellectuals and editors distanced themselves from the language of reconciliation and pluralism and adopted instead a notion that spoke to the African Renaissance:

> ... the discovery of "Africanness" ... the re-invention and revision of a black legacy in search of a new, a particularly African way forward.[35]

The concept had been aired by Deputy President Thabo Mbeki a few times since 1994, but became prominent after its formal unveiling by Mbeki as the basis for South Africa's policy towards Africa in April 1997. It soon assumed a meaning broader than the foreign policy one.

The African Renaissance is notoriously difficult to define with any precision. At its most rhetorical (here by Mbeki) it is a conflation of pan-Africanism with conventional desiderata of progress:

> The new African world which the African renaissance seeks to build is one of democracy, peace and stability, sustainable development and a better life for all

---

33. Sitas, Ari, "Madiba Magic: The Mandela Decade", *Indicator SA*, Vol. 18, No. 1, 2001, p. 17–18.

34. Africanism has meant different things in South African politics at different times. Here, reference to the Africanists in the ANC, or Africanism in that body, describes a political culture or mood rather than organised tendency: it involves: "...the re-assertion of pride, the invention and re-invention of black identity, styles and fashions, culture ... revision of a black legacy in search of a new, a particularly African way forward" (Filatova, op. cit, 1997, p. 52). Or, as the ANC puts it: "...truly an African nation on the African continent ... in the style and content of its media, in its cultural expression, in its food, in the language accents of its children, and so forth", ANC 1999, p. 4.

35. Filatova, op. cit., 1997, p. 52

people, nonracism and nonsexism, equality among the nations and a just and democratic system of international governance.[36]

A carefully considered formulation links ways of thought with social outcomes:

> It means the centering of the majority experience in the national life of South Africa. This kind of understanding is the foundation of any kind of reawakening ... The 'African Renaissance' in South Africa is about how we can make the diverse instruments of the state serve the interests of the newly liberated ... It is not a program of action but a social process.[37]

The linkage between renaissance and nation-building is sometimes explicit: the African Renaissance conference held in September 1998:

> ... was about strategy and repositioning ourselves as a people, particularly in South Africa where contestation around the broad national agenda [remains constant].[38]

More often, it operates as politically inflected metaphor, as a rallying cry for advancement, solidarity and Africanism. An important moment in translating metaphor into party politics occurred in the closing months of 1997. The ANC produced a position paper, *Nation-Formation and Nation-Building* and its general approach was endorsed in a *Resolution on the National Question* at the ANC's 50th National Conference at Mafeking in December 1997. The document defines the National Democratic Revolution (NDR) as "an act of addressing the national question: to create a united, non-racial, non-sexist and democratic society." While the main thrust of the NDR is "to encourage the emergence of a common South African identity", what is required is "a continuing battle to assert African hegemony in the context of a multicultural and non-racial society." The rainbow notion is repudiated: it fails to assist in "the emergence of a new African nation" and New Patriotism. In a sentence prickly with racial suspicion, the rainbow concept is judged "prob-

---

36. Makgoba, Malegapuru William (ed.), *African Renaissance*, Mafube, Tafelberg, Johannesburg and Cape Town, 1999, p. xviii.

37. Ndebele, Njabulo, "African Renaissance", in *Beyond Racism: Embracing an interdependent future*, Southern Education Foundation, Atlanta, 2000, p. 21.

38. Makgoba, Malegapuru, Shope, Thaninga and Mazwai, Thami, "Introduction", *African Renaissance*, in Makgoba (ed.), Mafube, Tafelberg, Johannesburg and Cape Town, 1999, p. vii.

lematic" if it includes "whites who pay allegiance to Europe, Indians who pay allegiance to India and, Coloureds somewhere in the undefined middle of the rainbow".[39]

Several scholars have noted that the ANC's racialised view of the society compromises its formal commitment to "non-racism".[40] The phenomena of heightened ethnicity and identity politics are defining features of the postmodern world: a sardonic cosmic joke at the expense of the twentieth century.

In South Africa, the CODESA moment (the negotiations between May 1990 and December 1993) was particularly concerned with the assertive and separatist claims of the Afrikaner right and Buthelezi's Inkatha. But while these primordialist, ethnonationalist versions of alternity – with their rumblings of secession and self-determination – were placated or contained by negotiated concessions, few at that time anticipated the volume or variety of claims to ethnic particularism that were to be staked so vigorously in the period after the 1994 election.

John Comaroff's depiction of ethnic identities as typically rooted in relations of inequality – "caught up in equations of power at once material, political, symbolic" – is as suggestive as it has been influential.[41] During the second half of the 1990s, savage inequalities persisted; programmes of affirmative action and black economic empowerment ignited new anxieties. This was fertile ground for popular and manipulated ethnic resentment. Indians and Coloureds, "particularly the unskilled and poor among them", experienced the government's affirmative action measures as "deeply unsettling".[42] The most quotidian and parochial politics saw "countless examples" of tensions associated with inequality or with racialised redress pitting ethnicised Havenots against ethnicised Haves:

---

39. ANC, 1997, pp. 2–5.

40. Boyce, Brendan P., "Nation-Building Discourse in a Democracy", in Palmberg, Mai (ed.), *National Identity and Democracy in Africa*, Human Sciences Research Council / Mayibuye Centre at the University of the Western Cape / Nordic Africa Institute, Pretoria, 1997, p. 235; Maré, Gerhard, "The Notion of 'Nation' and the Practice of 'Nation-Building' in Post-Apartheid South Africa", in Palmberg, op. cit., 1999, p. 248.

41. Comaroff, John L., "Ethnicity, Nation and the Politics of Difference in an Age of Revolution" in Comaroff, J. and Stern P. (eds), *Perspectives on Nationalism and War*, Gordon & Breach, Amsterdam, p. 249; Comaroff, op. cit., 2002, p. 9.

42. Pieterse, op. cit., 2002, p. 5.

At this level nation-building competes against impossibly deep and complex identity formations and racialised material interests.[43]

Adapting a typology proposed by Mattes we might identify three major approaches to the question of what prospects there are for attaining "state nationalism" in South Africa.[44] For the first of these:

> ... the development of a South African nationalism is impossible almost by definition since they operate along a largely ethnic notion of nation.[45]

Drawing on theorists like Horowitz and Lijphart, Herman Giliomee, Van Zyl Slabbert and David Welsh typify this approach. They call for political and constitutional systems specifically engineered to accommodate ethnic or group differences.

A second approach is associated especially with the writings of Johan Degenaar, a prominent and thoughtful political philosopher. Degenaar is critical of nation-building qua nation-building: the entire project is part of "a modernist discourse in a post-modernist age". He advocates instead the creation of "civic nationalism":

> ... a constitutional pluralist democracy based on a sense of common citizenship with mutual respect for different cultural levels.

Protecting and nurturing the sense of national belonging is realized through the hard work of making and maintaining democracy through "... the praxis of citizens who actively exercise their civil rights".[46] Interestingly, this view can be traced back to de Tocqueville's explanation for the cohesion of American national identity.[47]

The third approach is a variant of "civic nationalism", but draws on theorists such as Bottomore and Miliband to advocate "a wide notion of democracy" as the sine qua non for a nation-building project in a deeply

43. Maré, op. cit., 1999, p. 255.

44. Mattes, Robert, "Do Diverse Social Identities Inhibit Nationhood and Democracy? Initial Considerations from South Africa" in Palmberg, op. cit., 1999, pp. 268–71.

45. Mattes, op. cit, 1999, p. 270.

46. Quoted in Pieterse, op. cit., 2002, p. 7, which is a useful summary of Degenaar's writings on the nation.

47. Quoted in Boyce, Brendan, P., "Nation-building Discourse in a Democracy", in Palmberg, op. cit., 1999, p. 239.

divided society. In a series of articles this case has been made by Gerhard Maré.[48] He is concerned not so much with formal or electoral democracy as with participatory democracy, the "deepening of democracy" à la Laclau, and "the possibility of a united effort towards social justice".[49] Such an approach, he proposes, will build a horizontal comradeship from the societal and not from the political realm; it will focus debate and measures to address the gender inequalities, class inequalities, etc.[50] I return to this notion of nation-through-democracy in the closing section of this chapter.

The nation and its history

The modern nation-state, nationalism and the discipline of history have had an intense, complex relationship. During the nineteenth century, the great wave of European nationalism was accompanied by the rise of history as a distinct, professional and pivotal discipline in universities. New nation-states in nineteenth century Europe actively promoted historical research: a "powerful alliance was forged between historical scholarship and officially approved nationalism".[51]

Many have warned of dangers inherent in the relationship between history and nation. History written within the force-field of nationalism easily lapses into selective myth-making, heroic teleology, or romantic anachronism.[52] Nationalism relies on irrational and self-aggrandizing modes of explication that are (or should be) at odds with the objectivity valued for so long by historians as a disciplinary ideal. Not only this: nationalism regards history as its ideological armoury, and raids the past for legitimacy and justification.

While they do not overlook the baneful potential of the links between the nation and its histories, Joyce Appleby and her colleagues suggest a more positive view of the relationship. They posit the historian as critic, and the discipline as corrective, to official attempts to forge identity, to control collec-

---

48. Maré, Gerhard, "Swimming against many currents: Nation-building in South Africa", in de la Gorgendière, L., King, K. and Vaughan, S. (eds), *Ethnicity in Africa: Roots, meanings and implications,* Centre for African Studies, University of Edinburgh, Edinburgh 1996; Maré, op. cit., 1999; Maré, op. cit. 2001.

49. Maré, op. cit., 1999, p. 256.

50. Maré, op. cit., 1999, p. 257.

51. Tosh, John, *The Pursuit of History,* 2nd edition, London, Longman, 1991.

52. In the South African case, of course, Afrikaner nationalist historians provide a classic instance of these generalisations.

tive memory and to promote a self-congratulatory image of the nation. They proceed from the observation that nations need to control national memory, because nations keep their shape by shaping their citizens' understanding of the past. However, in practice it is the historians who do research on the past, write the histories, and teach the nation's youth.[53]

This chapter proposes that the predicaments of academic history in contemporary South Africa are compounded by the unsettled and unsettling debates over the nation and how it might be imagined.[54] This again prompts some large questions. What role, if any, can historians play in providing solutions to the National Question? What are the possible and appropriate scholarly responses by historians of South Africa to the implosion of identity politics? To what extent are both debates (about history and about the nation) affected by the historical moment – by economic, technological and cultural developments (inadequately) characterised as "globalisation" and "neo-liberalism"? What are the implications of that historical moment for the ways in which history is produced and consumed? What are the implications of that historical moment for the ways in which the nation is constructed and deconstructed?

To answer such questions systematically would require a different and much longer article. Here, I approach them obliquely by posing a question of a different order: What kind of textbooks should be produced for teaching history in the schools and universities of South Africa in the years immediately ahead? I hope that this exercise may yield some provisional and tentative answers to the questions in the previous paragraph. What the post-apartheid textbook should be is an issue that has preoccupied South African scholars for years.[55] It is revisited here in the light of the two debates already summarised – about academic history and about national identity.

---

53. Appleby, Joyce, Hunt, Lynn and Jacob, Margaret, *Telling the Truth about History*, New York, Norton, 1994, pp. 154–156.

54. See also Nuttall and Wright, op. cit., 2000.

55. Bam, op. cit., 2000; Bundy, Colin, "What makes a nation happy? Historiographical changes and the implications for text-books", unpublished paper, delivered at Sparkling Waters Colloquium on History Textbooks, 1993; Bundy, Colin, "The future of our past: Understanding South African history", unpublished paper, delivered at Grahamstown Festival Winter School, 1999; History/Archaeology Panel, *Report of the History/Archaeology Panel to the Minister of Education*, 2nd ed., Department of Education, Pretoria, 2000/1; History Education Group, *History Matters: Debates about a new history curriculum for South Africa*, Heinemann-Centaur, Johannesburg, 1993; Kros, op. cit., 1996, Kros, op. cit., 1998; Kros, Cynthia and Grebe, Shelley,

Between about 1992 and 1994, there was – as outlined at the outset of this chapter – a swirl of activity – involving academics, teachers, publishers and civil servants – seeking to tackle just this issue as a matter of pedagogic and political urgency. There was effectively a common point of departure: that textbooks of the kind that had served apartheid education (at primary, secondary and tertiary level) had to go. They would not be much lamented: the affable, unthinking racism of Boyce and Smit, the crude apologia for apartheid policies peddled by Joubert and Britz, and the complacent narrowness of Muller's *Five Hundred Years* attracted their share of critics but very few defenders during the final years of apartheid.[56] But what would replace them?

One model promoted quite strenuously in the late 1980s and early 1990s might be called conservative pluralism. Floris Van Jaarsveld, doyen of Afrikaans-language historical scholarship, had for two decades warned his colleagues of the vulnerability of the class Afrikaner nationalist paradigm; he called for a present-minded approach sensitive to the demands of a "new", "industrialised" and "modernised" South Africa. What was needed was a "general" history of South Africa which found a place for all politically legitimated "groups". In 1982 he wrote:

> Along with an individual historical image which can account for an own existence and the identity of a cultural or national group, we need a general South African image of the past which does justice to the totality of the people, regardless of colour or class, giving them a feeling of belonging to one South African nation and one fatherland – the RSA.[57]

In 1990 Van Jaarsveld went further:

> In revised curricula more room will have to be made for Black history in its own right, and a balance must be struck between Black and White history ... There

---

The Rainbow Nation vs Healing Old Wounds, History Curriculum Research Project, Report No. 2, Cambridge University Press & History Workshop, University of the Witwatersrand, Johannesburg, 1997; Sieborger, op. cit., 1994; Sieborger, op. cit., 1998; Sieborger, op. cit., 2000; Sieborger, Rob and Reid, Janet, "Textbooks and the School History Curriculum", *South African Historical Journal*, Vol. 33, 1995.

56. The references are, respectively, to a primary school text used in "white" schools, to a secondary "history" textbook used in African schools run by the Department of Education and Training, and to a widely prescribed and albocentric general text for university use first published in 1969.

57. Quoted in Van Jaarsveld, Floris, "Controversial South African History", *Internationale Schulbuchforschung*, Vol. 12, 1990, p. 137.

must be an awareness ... that in the historical unity of South African society there is a spectrum of diverse and contra-distinctive groups, each with its own historical origin ... the syllabus content must be presented with emphasis on the diversity ... [syllabi] will have to be based on consensus among the groups involved, Black, Brown and White.[58]

An intervention designed to produce just such a syllabus was the Human Sciences Research Council abridged report on *The Teaching of History in Secondary Schools in the RSA* produced in 1991.[59] Like Van Jaarsveld, its authors' point of departure was the existence of ethnically defined groups or communities:

Every community has its own unique historical roots and identity and can rightly demand that the teaching of its children will acknowledge and respect this.

It held out some hope for a more inclusive history: "the core themes presented in the syllabus should be themes involving all South Africans" and envisaged syllabi that should "therefore be neither eurocentric nor afrocentric, but historically balanced".[60] The writers of this Report were worried that there were some areas of South African history where commonality of experience was tenuous at best, or characterized by conflict, at worst. Their solution was "a perspectivistic approach, to state all sides of the experience".[61]

A textbook designed on this conservative pluralist/multi-cultural model might have produced a bland, sanitised negotiated history based on consensus. "Content may be reached by means of intergroup conferences", hazarded Van Jaarsveld.[62] Or it might have pursued the logic of one-community-one-chapter and provide an "eie sake" history,[63] regionalised and compartmentalised, buttressing ethnic identities, and surrendering in advance any possibility of an interpretative overview.

A second model sought a more explicitly corrective version of the past, and was unapologetic about its political project: we might call this nation-build-

58. Van Jaarsveld, *Controversial South African School History,* 1990, p. 136.

59. The quotations from it are those I used in earlier commentaries in Bundy, op. cit., 1993; Bundy, op. cit., 1999.

60. Quoted in Bundy, op. cit., 1993, p. 5.

61. Bundy, op. cit., 1993.

62. Jaarsveld, op. cit., 1990, p. 136.

63. The expression "own affairs" is apartheid-speak for limited forms of devolution during the 1980s.

ing pluralism. One of its clearest expressions is to be found in a short survey, published in 1993, of Debates about a new history curriculum.[64] Perhaps the most cautious register was that sounded by P.T. Govender, who called for a new history syllabus based on three goals: national reconstruction, reconciliation and the recognition of cultural and geographical diversity.[65] The language echoed that of the Codesa talks being held at the time. Ismail Vadi made the analogy explicit:

> The whole exercise [curriculum reconstruction] ... is fundamentally a political exercise ... Just as the political future of this country is going through a complicated route of negotiations, similarly, curriculum development must involve all the major participants.[66]

Vadi also called for a curriculum based on the "principle" of a national history:

> ... [one] which can begin to generate a sense of a single nation ... a central mechanism which can generate a sense of national consciousness and identity.[67]

John Pampallis, similarly, said the big question was:

> ... how a history curriculum can promote national reconciliation while redressing past imbalances and without glossing over the gross injustices and struggles of our conflict-ridden past.[68]

At the time the members of the HSRC task team and those of the History Education Group represented opposing political positions: broadly supportive, respectively, of de Klerk's reformism and the Mass Democratic Movement/ANC. Yet in retrospect what is striking is how similar their "solutions" to the textbook question were. Although the HEG was committed to a unitary, democratic state and to a version of the past that sought to redress the "neglect and vilification" of the African majority, like the HSRC report they also relied on a somewhat simplistic process of making texts more inclusive – as though "what we put in or leave out of the syllabus is seen as the vital

---

64. History Education Group (HEG), op. cit., 1993.

65. History Education Group (HEG), op. cit., 1993, p. 16.

66. History Education Group (HEG), op. cit., 1993, p. 26.

67. History Education Group (HEG), op. cit., 1993, p. 27.

68. History Education Group (HEG), op. cit., 1993, p. 21.

issue".[69] Although inflected in more progressive tones, the HEG proponents also looked to a negotiated, or consensus, version of the past.

But the HEG commentators formulated their ideas during meetings held in 1992. How has the project of an inclusive and nation-building history been advanced since then? Shortly after *History Matters* was published, two colloquia on Writing School History Textbooks were held. "Some participants advanced nation-building as being at the core, others were less convinced.[70] One participant warned of a considerable tension between the political objective of nation-building and the educational project of equipping young South Africans with the ability to think historically about themselves and their society. The problem of a history syllabus designed to "generate a sense of national consciousness and identity" is that it all too easily becomes hortatory, didactic and teleological.[71] A statement generated by the colloquia emphasised democracy rather than nationalism:

> The approach to the past should be inclusive and democratic: it should explore the past of ordinary men and women as well as leaders and heroes.

And it expressly advised an approach that:

> ... seeks to reconcile national unity and cultural diversity by making it clear that nationalism, ethnicity, culture and identity have been constructed over time.[72]

The TRC process (the hearings, its Report, and the public debates that these generated) posed some major issues for the project of nation-building pluralism. The TRC itself – as James Campbell put it – saw a society "going through a very public ritual about confronting the past" and the Commission was charged with producing as full an historical record as possible of gross human rights abuses over a thirty year period. But were historians to respond to its calls for reconciliation, or to its data on violence and horror? Many of the official "public history" commemorations and monuments sought the former approach. Others found an entirely different lesson. One warned that:

---

69. Cuthbertson, Greg and Grundlingh, Albert, "Some Problematical Issues in the Restructuring of History Education in South African Schools", *South African Historical Journal*, Vol. 26, 1992, p. 161.

70. Sieborger, op. cit., 1994, pp. 102–103.

71. Bundy, op. cit., 1993, p. 7.

72. Sieborger, op. cit., 1994, pp. 100, 101.

Those intent on promoting reconciliation at all costs see those who wish to pre-serve the history of the past as spoilers at best, revenge merchants at worst.[73]

Moodley and Adam even hope that that an unsavoury past might serve as a unifying bond:

One axis along which a new nation may be built is through grappling with a shared horrendous history with a new national identity emerging from the ashes of the past.[74]

Perhaps the most significant attempt actually to write a narrative history of South Africa as a counterpart to the TRC is Norman Etherington's impor-tant synthesis of scholarship on the period 1815–1854, which seeks to treat the Great Trek and the events associated with the mfecane with "equal atten-tion", integrating them "into a single narrative".[75] He clarifies his project:

How might the task of writing 'truth and reconciliation history' be expressed in a revisionist account of early nineteenth century South Africa?

He acknowledges that the idea of a past that all South Africans can share is chimerical:

Pursuing such a goal will not, of course, produce a single agreed version of his-tory. There will always be many points of view, many stories to be told. What I am arguing here is that historians will tell their stories better if they hold the ideal of a shared history constantly in mind.[76]

Etherington's strategy links with a third version of post-apartheid history.[77] For want of a better label, I call it the new model textbook approach. In essence, while it remains concerned with the content and interpretation of

---

73. De Kok, 1998, p. 71.

74. Moodley, Kogila and Adam, Heriber, "Race and Nation in Post-Apartheid South Africa", *Current Sociology*, Vol. 48, No. 3, 2000, p. 66.

75. This is my shorthand: Etherington, following Cobbing, rejects the concept and the term "mfecane" and speaks more generally of chiefdoms, state-builders and leaders, diasporas and population movements, etc.

76. Etherington, Norman, *The Great Treks: The Transformation of Southern Africa 1815–1854*, Pearson, Harlow, 2001, p. xi, xii, xviii.

77. There is not space here to do justice to the subtlety with which Etherington decon-structs and reconstructs conventional histories of the period, devising a new vocabu-lary for familiar issues, a different set of geographical terms, and consciously seeking

South African history, its main emphasis is that the curriculum should "reflect advances in the discipline of history". That is: school texts should reflect recent and current debates about the past; the approach to the past should be inclusive and democratic; the approach to historical knowledge should be analytical and explanatory; skills and content should be inseparable so that the curriculum conveys a sense of how knowledge is produced and history not presented as a set of given facts. Historical education should develop "empathetic understanding, emotional and moral commitment with the past" and an awareness of the constant interrelationship of the past and the present. South African history should reflect the diversity of its population, while also accounting for processes that have created a single society; and should locate the country's history within regional, continental and global events and processes.[78]

The new model textbook is an attractive concept and has been consciously pursued in the production of "progressive" textbooks by several publishers. Reflecting the epistemological debates of the 1990s, the new model textbook has in some cases incorporated "postmodern" emphases. A 1998 new school and college text covering the apartheid years emphasises that it offers but one of many other kinds of possible accounts of apartheid; reflects on the particular interests and background of its authors; points to the existence of alternative approaches and stresses the importance of debate and independent enquiry.[79] A critique of Curriculum 2005 advocates an approach to school history that questions established categories, argues for multiple identities, calls for the disruption of boundaries and celebrates "the loss of certainty".[80] A slightly different inflection of the new model textbook invoked the left-wing American scholar Harvey Kaye and called for an approach that honoured "the powers of the past" – perspective, critique, consciousness, remembrance and imagination.[81]

Most importantly, the value of historical knowledge was restated by a Panel reporting to the then Minister of Education, Kader Asmal. It is similar

a distinctive perspective from which to write "a fair and democratic history" (Etherington, op. cit., 2001, p. 4).

78. Sieborger, op. cit., 1994, pp. 100–101.

79. Nuttall and Wright, op. cit., 1998, pp. 53–54.

80. Kros, op. cit., 1998, pp. 8–16.

81. Bundy, op. cit., 1999.

to the 1994 statement in avoiding any direct reference to nation-building, but argues that:

> A study of the past can serve a range of important and enriching social, political, cultural and environmental functions. Its general potential is particularly pronounced in our own society, which is consciously undergoing change ... we are living in a country which is currently attempting to remake itself in time. In these conditions, the study of history is especially urgent as it helps to prevent amnesia, checks triumphalism, opposes the manipulative or instrumental use of the past, and provides an educational buffer against a. 'dumbing down' of our citizens.[82]

It specifies further that the study of history encourages civic responsibility and critical thinking; fosters discriminating judgement; is important in the construction of identity; helps a society to hear formerly subjugated and marginalized voices, and is a vital ingredient in promoting democratic values.

Some observations in lieu of a conclusion

Firstly, it is clear that the inconclusive and rancorous exchanges over the National Question since 1994 have resolved very little. They produced no National Answer. The Rainbow Nation sought to finesse the historical legacy of racialised inequality through reconciliation. The African Renaissance sought to unmake, to invert, that legacy through social and psychological engineering. Ethnic essentialism accepted the legacy of racialised difference – indeed insisted on it – but tried to write self-serving codicils.

None of these discursive endeavours has succeeded in narrating a persuasive alternative future to a society still fractured by its past. None has provided a coherent, unifying, ideological and political framework which might make possible some shared popular understanding or some meaningful programme of action in the public sphere. This failure is in large part explicable by the extent to which all three discourses operate with racial identity as an unquestioned given. They all sustain the "illusion of ordinariness" of race thinking.[83]

Secondly, although little remarked, it seems to me that the crisis within academic history in South Africa has been compounded by the broader failure in recent years to achieve any semblance of the "horizontal solidarity"

---

82. History/Archaeology Panel, op. cit., 2000, p. 6.

83. Maré, op. cit, 2001.

of Anderson's imagined community. The institutional base of historians was weakened, their professional status and social function questioned, and their epistemological foundations gave way underfoot – these were the accurately reported symptoms of decline – but all these insecurities were intensified by a fundamental uncertainty as to their audience, their script or their role in the drama of the post-apartheid 1990s.

Thirdly, I had not previously been aware of the convergence between those political theorists who favour democracy as the keystone of nation-building and those historians whose "new model textbook" places a premium on the democratic possibilities of their discipline. There may be scope here for important interdisciplinary social science projects that challenge the racial thinking of so much that passes for analysis, and provides a potential framework for new history texts. I have in mind Herbert Gutman's not-so-long-ago vision of a "new national synthesis" for American history that would use the findings of social history to reformulate older versions; it materialised in the two hefty volumes of *Who Built America*, a college textbook produced by the American Social History Project. Its editors explained that it surveyed:

> … the nation's past from the perspective of the ordinary men and women and the role they played in the making of modern America.

Which they claimed permitted:

> … the integration of the history of community, family, gender, race and ethnicity into the more familiar history of political and economic development. [84]

While recognising that this pre-dated the "textual turn" and the insistent claims of cultural history, it does raise questions as to the echoing silence, today, of the claims made in the 1980s for a scholarly "People's History" of South Africa.

Fourthly, one should acknowledge the strong countervailing undertow of contemporary currents which would complicate such a project. The South African tendency to accept racial/ethnic identities as banal or natural has already been remarked. Nor do I find much reassurance in some claims made elsewhere for history in the new millennium. Richard Evans (writing of the United Kingdom) is confident:

> History as it is written and researched, and above all as it is presented to a popular audience at the beginning of the twenty-first century, is about identity, about

---

84. Quoted in Bundy, op. cit., 1993, p. 8.

who we are and where we came from. At a time when other sources of identity such as class and region have declined, history is stepping in to fill the gap.[85]

His embrace of "history-as-identity" seems to me uncritical. It hardly takes into account the concerns of Appleby and her colleagues about the reactionary content of extreme forms of multiculturalism:

> History for them has become an adjunct to 'identity politics' inimical to any comprehensive national history.[86]

Nor does it provide any intellectual purchase to issues raised by Jean Comaroff. On the one hand, she sees:

> ... ordinary South Africans ... avidly reclaiming their rights to the past, pressing it into the service of a host of identities, new and old, majestic and banal.

On the other hand, she asks:

> But what kind of 'community' can this kind of history be said to be building, given that 'community' itself is being invoked ever more vacuously, ever more as a beguiling linguistic fiction whose referent remains vague and elusive? Is History being privatised, dissolved into 'his story' and 'her story'?

Should critical scholars not be on guard when these new forms of history are:

> ... part of a mercenary impetus toward an ever more plural, private and ultimately alienating vision, a dispossession of the past?[87]

Fifthly, and finally, I suspect that more work needs to be done on the history of South African statehood and national integration as a corollary to theorising the nation and national identity. Historical disapproval of successive forms of white minority rule may have blurred the political significance of the relative maturity of the South African state. One does not need to be a supporter of segregation or apartheid to note that the South African state has occupied its present borders since 1910 as a single politico-juridical entity.

---

85. Evans, Richard, "Prologue: What Is History? – Now", in Cannadine, D. (ed.), *What Is History Now?*, Palgrave Macmillan, Basingstoke, 2002, p. 12.

86. Appleby et al., op. cit., 1994, pp. 292, 295.

87. Comaroff, op. cit., 2002, pp. 7, 18.

Jakes Gerwel has recently argued that there is an "amplified sense of post-1910 South Africa as a nation" and even that "a binding awareness of nationhood ... stretches back at least to the 1910 state".[88]

Similarly, whether one explains it as "interaction between people of diverse origins" or as "the meshing of conquered and colonised communities into a single capitalist system", both liberal and Marxist historians have for several decades highlighted the rapidity with which a common society and economy emerged in the nineteenth century. There are large areas of research that have hardly been broached for twentieth century South Africa: what aspects of material culture, what patterns of consumption, what forms of social behaviour, became generalised? Even allowing for the "remnant identities and particularisms" that have shaped the ways diverse communities experience and explain their lives, in what ways were these overlaid with an emerging "varied hybrid, and distinctive national culture"?[89]

Robert Mattes has analysed five major surveys measuring social identity between 1994 and 1997. Unsurprisingly, these all indicated that majorities of South Africans actively use constructs of race and ethnicity to define themselves. However, and less frequently realised, the same survey data shows that over 90 per cent of the legal citizens of South Africa (i) accept the appropriateness of the demarcated territory known as South Africa; (ii) see themselves as members of that community; and (iii) are proud of that membership. In comparison with multiethnic states like the Soviet Union or Yugoslavia, South Africa exhibits relatively high cohesion.[90]

Such survey findings are suggestive rather than conclusive. But do we have a firm enough historical grasp on the consciousness they sketch? It is not my intention to disparage the innovative and finely textured forms of cultural history that are currently in vogue in South Africa, as elsewhere. But while they serve to illuminate difference and alternity, we also need to think more systematically about those dimensions of social existence, of historical interdependence, that may provide the basis of a South African identity alongside or plaited into the myriad sub-national identities of the post-colonial moment. For in that moment, Jean Comaroff reminds us that:

---

88. Gerwel, Jakes, untitled: The Bram Fischer Lecture, delivered in Oxford, June 2002, p. 3.

89. Beinart, William, *Twentieth Century South Africa*, 2d edition, Oxford University Press, 2001, p. 6.

90. Mattes, op. cit., 1999, pp. 271, 272, 275, 279, 280.

... history is endangered less by its appropriation by the powerful than by its unrestrained indulgence, its diffusion to everywhere and hence to nowhere in particular. An infinite regress of assertive voices threatens to postpone, indefinitely, the process of shared re-collection, the subsuming of difference into an overarching totality ... against which claims can be relativized and difference measured.

In South Africa, that process of shared recollection should remain an aspiration for academic historians. It is also crucial to imagining the nation.

— CHAPTER 4 —

Truth rather than justice?

Historical narratives, gender, and public education in South Africa

Elaine Unterhalter

For some years I have been working on a project concerning gender and South African autobiographical writings of the anti-apartheid struggle.[1] A key concern has been the ways in which this rich resource, which amounts to close to eighty published texts uses lifetime to narrate historical time and comment on its meaning.[2] Another focus has been the ways in which these autobiographical writings exhibit features of the making and taking of gendered identities. Many of these texts work powerfully to overcome the racialised

1. This chapter has developed from papers presented at the African Studies Association Conference, Cambridge September 2000 and the workshop on narrative and education organised by the University of East London, April 2002. I am grateful to all those who contributed to the discussion at both events. Debbie Gaitskell initially encouraged me to undertake a comparison of the work of Tutu and Krog. The paper has developed from ongoing discussions with Melanie Walker that are always stimulating, insightful and rewarding. My thanks to Joe Crawford and Hans Erik Stolten for very useful comments on drafts, and to Margot Levy for research assistance in tracing the publication histories of the two books.

2. For some published work from this project see Unterhalter, E., "The schooling of South African girls: Statistics, Stories, and Strategies" in Bunwaree, S. and Heward, C., *Gender, Education and Development*, London, Zed, 1999, pp. 49–64; Unterhalter, E., "The work of the nation: Heroic masculinity in South African autobiographical writing of the Anti-Apartheid Struggle", *The European Journal of Development Research*, Vol. 12, 2000, No. 2, 2000, pp. 157–178; Unterhalter, E., "Remembering and forgetting: Constructions of education gender reform in autobiography and policy texts of the South African transition", *History of Education*, Vol. 29, No. 5, 2000, pp. 457–472; Unterhalter, E., "Gendered diaspora identities: South African women, exile and migration, c. 1960–1995", in Ali, S., Coates, K. and Wa Goro, W. (eds), *Global Feminist Politics. Identities in a changing world*, London, Routledge, 2000, pp. 107–125; Unterhalter, E., "Gender, race and different lives: South African women teachers' autobiographies and the analysis of education change" in Kallaway, P. (ed.), *The History of Education under Apartheid*, New York, Peter Lang, 2002.

divisions of South Africa yet contribute to a reinscription of gender divisions and the subordination of women. In this chapter I want to build from some of these earlier papers to look at autobiographical writings concerned with narrating not so much the struggle against apartheid as the vision of a new nation. I am interested in the ways in which works of public education such as these address, as C. Wright Mills enjoined, the connection between private sorrow and public policy.[3] Mills highlighted the importance of analysing the intersections of biography, social structure and history. How much do works that stitch together biography and history afford insight into social structure, and more particularly what clues do they give for social justice projects concerned with gender, race, class and other elements of inequality?

The first part of the paper links these concerns to debates regarding the scholarship and professional craft of historians, the ethical framing of their work, and the relationship of history to memory. It also surveys some writings on the South African Truth and Reconciliation Commission (TRC) and attempts to situate autobiographical writings linked to the TRC in relation to other commentaries.

The second part examines two books that use elements of autobiography to comment on the meaning of history through reflection on the Truth and Reconciliation Commission: Desmond Tutu's *No Future without Forgiveness* and Antjie Krog's *Country of my Skull*.[4] Both books attracted significant publicity inside and outside South Africa on publication; both were published in hardback and in paperback at prices aimed at a popular market.[5] They are both significant examples of public education and in both a major theme is that through a personal process of engaging with truth and taking moral decisions, a national project of the truth of the past can be laid bare, and a new future imbued with better values constructed. The particular process of equating lifetime and historical time is thus portrayed as redemptive.

In reflecting on these works as examples of contributions to public education concerning the Truth and Reconciliation Commission (TRC) three questions are addressed. Firstly how do the two texts render the relationship between life-time and historical time? Secondly what constructions of gender are evident in the texts and the meanings they make concerning history? Lastly to what extent do these narratives link to a new project for the nation

---

3. Mills, C.W., *The sociological imagination*, London, Penguin Books, 1959.

4. Tutu, D., *No Future without Forgiveness*, London, Rider/Random House, 1999; Krog, A., *Country of my Skull*, London, Jonathan Cape, 1998.

5. The publishers of both books were unable to divulge sales figures.

concerning social justice and what issues does this raise for thinking about the connections between history and memory in South Africa?

The argument I am making seeks to distinguish between autobiographical writings, which reflect on the meaning of history, and historical scholarship conducted by professional historians.

History, social responsibility, and the Truth and Reconciliation Commission

The history of the South African TRC, from its inception in 1995 to its report in 1998, has been extensively documented and analysed using a wide range of disciplinary perspectives.[6] The Commission was a key enterprise of the government of national unity reflecting both its important aspirations for uniting a divided country and also some of its shameful accommodations with the past and the perpetrators of violence. Moments of high drama during the TRC hearings were broadcast widely in South Africa and abroad. The material collected by the TRC on gross violations of human rights was extensive; only a fraction of this has been published. The Commission itself acknowledged it had worked with a limited definition of gender and that the way gross violations of human rights were defined in the legislation that established the Commission underplayed the ways in which women's human rights had been violated.[7] A special hearing on women did take place, along with other special hearings on 'sections' like business and medicine.

The published volumes of the TRC Report are both a form of historical scholarship reporting on the extensive documentation exercise, and a particular political statement linked to the project of national reconciliation associated with South Africa's political and religious elite. Posel and Simpson have highlighted how the Commission report moves problematically between the

---

6. The report of the Commission is published as Truth and Reconciliation Commission, *South African Truth and Reconciliation Commission, Vols.* 1–5, London, Macmillan, 1999. For some critical analysis of the significance of the TRC see Mamdani, M., "The truth according to the TRC", in Amadiume, I. and An-Na, *The politics of memory,* London, Zed Books, 2000, pp. 176–183; James, W. and Van de Vijver, L. (eds), *After the TRC: Reflections on Truth and Reconciliation in South Africa,* Cape Town, David Philip, 2000; Boraine, A., *A country unmasked,* Oxford University Press, 2000; Wilson, R., *The politics of truth and reconciliation in South Africa: Legitimizing the post-apartheid state,* Cambridge University Press, 2001; Posel, D. and Simpson, G., *Commissioning the past,* Johannesburg, Witwatersrand University Press, 2002.

7. TRC, 1999.

disciplines of positivist social science and law, intended to establish facts, and the drama of individual testimony based on memory, rather than facts, intended to form part of a healing process. The general significance of the Commission was seen by its leadership to rest more on the second dimension than the first.[8]

A number of commentators, writing after the publication of the TRC report, have emphasised that the testimony to the Commission was not always healing.[9] Historians and anthropologists who have looked in detail at the contexts of events reported to the Commission have concluded how the reports made obscured the complexity of local social contexts and thus considerably over-simplified the interpretation of specific incidents.[10] The failure of the TRC to take seriously issues of individual or socially situated action has been the focus of a number of critical accounts.[11] Feminist scholars have highlighted how the terms of reference of the Act which established the TRC were used as a reason not to extend its remit and engage critically with the gender order of South African society.[12] Only limited attention was paid to the gendered dimensions of gross violations of human rights, usually on terms

---

8. Posel, D. and Simpson, G., "The power of truth: South Africa's Truth and Reconciliation Commission" in Posel and Simpson, *Commissioning*, 2002, pp. 4–7.

9. Dube, P.S., "The story of Thandi Shezi" in Posel and Simpson, *Commissioning*, 2002, pp. 117–130; Matshoba, M., "Nothing but the truth: The ordeal of Duma Khumalo", in Posel and Simpson, *Commissioning*, 2002, pp. 131–146; Slovo, G., "Making history: South Africa's Truth and Reconciliation Commission", 2002. Contribution to a debate on the politics of apology. Open democracy website on line http://www.opendemocracy.net/debates/article.jsp?id=3&debateId=76&articleId=818.

10. See for example Bonner, P. and Nieftagodien, N., "The Truth and Reconciliation Commission and the pursuit of 'social truth': The case of Kathorus", in Posel and Simpson, *Commissioning*, 2002, pp. 173–203; Wilson, *Legitimizing*.

11. See for example Holiday, A., "Forgiving and forgetting: The Truth and Reconciliation Commission", in S. Nuttall and C. Coetzee (eds), *Negotiating the Past. The making of memory in South Africa*, Oxford University Press, 1998, pp. 43–56; Slovo, *History*; Mamdani, *The truth*.

12. Meintjes, S., Pillay, A. and Turshen, M. (eds), *The aftermath: Women in post conflict transformation*, London, Zed, 2002; Epstein, D. and Unterhalter, E., "Gendering education for reconciliation: Femininity, memory and silence in the South African Truth and Reconciliation Commission Report", paper presented at second international Gender and Education conference, University of Warwick, 1999; Walker, M. and Unterhalter, E., "Knowledge, narrative and national reconciliation: Storied reflections on the South African Truth and Reconciliation Commission", *Discourse*, 2003.

that reinforced aspects of women's subordination. There was little examination of aspects of masculinity.

The accounts by prominent figures associated with the TRC, like Kader Asmal and Alex Boraine, on the whole fail to engage with these commentaries. Their works draw out the overall political significance of the Commission.[13] This has generally been the approach taken by many non-South African commentators who have set some of the achievements of the TRC in a comparative context.[14]

A number of historians and philosophers have pointed out the importance of distinguishing the professional work of history from unmediated acts of memory.[15] Proponents of narrative in history, while highlighting how individual human action might take a narrative form, do not advocate the collapse of history into "simple" narration.[16] Thus one approach to understanding differing perspectives on the history of the TRC is to distinguish between the work of professional historical scholars and the works that are largely based on memory, even if sometimes, as in the work of Boraine, memory is intercut with reflections on a range of legal and philosophical writers.[17]

However this solution poses particular challenges for feminist historians. The evidence to be sifted, the interpretations to be made, even the narrative form to be appropriated are generally those associated with groups who have access to political, economic and cultural resources. Can the history of those who have been silenced or made invisible be apprehended by a disinterested craft? Surely it is only by political struggles to formulate alternative ways of looking at the world that orthodoxies of gendered power, in history, as elsewhere can be challenged. This is not what historians would do "just because the evidence was there".

13. Boraine, *Unmasked;* Asmal, K., Asmal, L. and Roberts, R.S., *Reconciliation through Truth* Cape Town, David Philip, 1996.

14. Hayner, P.B., *Unspeakable truths: Confronting state terror and atrocity*, New York, Routledge, 2001; Ignatieff, M., "Something happened", *Guardian Weekend*, 2002. On line at http://www.guardian.co.uk/weekend/story/0,3605,567500,00.html.

15. See for example Evans, R., *In defence of history*, Cambridge, 2001; Grant, A., Leerssen, J. and Rigney, A., *Historians and social values*, Amsterdam University Press, 2000; Williams, B., *Truth and truthfulness*, Princeton University Press, 2002.

16. Carr, D., "Getting the story straight: Narrative and historical knowledge" in G. Roberts (ed.), *The history and narrative reader*, London, Routledge, 2001, pp. 197–208.

17. Boraine, *Unmasked*.

In considering the social justice implications of much mainstream history, a number of feminist historians have examined the significance of autobiography as a form through which silenced voices can narrate history.[18] What are the implications of eliding history and autobiography in this way in the context of aspirations for social justice in South Africa? In order to examine this issue further I want to look at the autobiographies of Desmond Tutu and Antjie Krog, which draw on their memories of the TRC in order to shape a new vision for South Africa.

Lifeworlds and the meaning of history: Narrating personal and national truths

Tutu's and Krog's autobiographies are both centrally concerned with the connection between personal narration and the project of nation-building. Desmond Tutu was appointed Chair of the Truth and Reconciliation Commission (TRC) in 1995 and travelled the length and breadth of South Africa attending hearings. The book is primarily about his work in the TRC, but uses the personal voice of autobiography. It begins with Tutu's experience of voting for the first time in the elections of 1994, and draws on elements of his personal history reaching back to childhood. The dust cover of the first UK edition of *No future without forgiveness* has a picture of Desmond Tutu in his robes as Archbishop, flanked by an excerpt from a comment by Nelson Mandela, underlining the significance of the book and the connection between these two key male figures of the South African transition.

Antjie Krog is a poet and journalist. From 1996 she began reporting on the TRC hearings for the South African Broadcasting Corporation. *Country of my Skull* is her account of the impact of those hearings on her, as a white Afrikaans speaking South African woman, and her attempt to examine through this the implications of the TRC in general and the reframing of white identities in particular. She too uses her personal history to interpret the significance of the TRC period. The dust cover of the first UK edition of her book, unlike Tutu's, does not highlight her political power, but instead presents a compelling photograph of Joyce Mtimkulu, who gave evidence to the TRC concerning the murder of her son, Sipho, and the dismemberment of his body by the security forces. Inside the back cover we are informed that

---

18. Smith, S. and Watson, J., (eds), *Women, autobiography, theory*, Madison, University of Wisconsin Press, 1998.

in the photograph Joyce Mtimkulu is holding a portion of her son's hair. The resonance between Sipho Mtimkulu's hair and Antjie Krog's skull (the title of the book) is powerful. Once again there are gendered elisions, but here this does not relate, as in the Tutu cover, to binding up a common whole, but to crossing over through a process of fragmentation into another part of the fractured society.[19]

Both Tutu and Krog use the device I have noted in other South African autobiographical writings of equating lifetime with political time.[20] In both books a major theme is one of awareness dawning, of personal change – both physical and emotional- taking place as South Africa moves towards democracy. For example Tutu describes himself as personally transformed by the election of 1994, literally seeing and being in the world differently:

> The moment for which I had waited for so long came and I folded my ballot paper and cast my vote. Wow! I shouted, 'Yippee'. It was giddy stuff, like falling in love. The sky looked more blue and beautiful. I saw the people in a new light. They were beautiful. They were transfigured. I too was transfigured.[21]

It is worth noting the significance of bodily transformation and transfiguration in this passage.

While Tutu's book is not particularly theological in tone, it nonetheless works with powerful ideas from Christianity. Indeed Tutu's work in the Truth Commission can be read as leading the nation in confession, purgation and forgiveness. Inherent in this task is a notion of history as redemptive. The lifeworld becomes a frame for the historical world and the significance of personal time is its link to historical time.

Krog does not make quite the same transcriptions but uses the device of her *observing* self to highlight how she (and white South Africans like her) moves from a position of outsider to the concerns of the TRC to a new identity as deeply involved participant. The book arcs between two scenes. In its opening paragraph Krog is literally outside the building in which the TRC legislation is being finalised, running haphazardly towards this new endeavour, her gaze fixed on the 'past-in-the-present' the men who oppose the establishment of the TRC:

---

19. For a further discussion of the photograph of Joyce Mtimkulu see Epstein, and Unterhalter, "Gendering education", 1999.

20. Unterhalter, *Heroic Masculinity*, 2000.

21. Tutu, *No Future*, p. 3.

Sunk low on their springs, three weathered white Sierras roar past the wrought-iron gates of Parliament. Heavy, ham-like forearms bulge through the open windows – honking, waving old Free State and Transvaal flags. Hairy fists in the air.[22]

She portrays herself here as vulnerable, protected only by her role as reporter "clutching notepad and recorder", located neither inside the TRC hearings nor with the men in the white cars.

However, by the end of the book, her body has taken on the rhythm of the TRC and its historic task. In the last few pages she describes herself literally "in the same boat" sailing with the TRC commissioners on a trip to Robben Island.

In a wild arch of air I rock with the Commissioners in the boat back to the mainland. I am filled with an indescribable tenderness towards this Commission. With all its mistakes, its arrogance, its racism, its sanctimony, its incompetence, the lying, the failure to get an interim reparation policy off the ground after two years, the showing off – with all of this – it has been so brave, so naively brave in the winds of deceit, rancour and hate. Against a flood crashing with the weight of a brutalizing past on to a new usurping politics, the Commission has kept alive the idea of a common humanity. Painstakingly it has chiselled a way beyond racism and made space for all of our voices. For all of its failures, it carries a flame of hope that makes me proud to be from here, of here. But I want to put it more simply. I want this hand of mine to write it. For all; all voices; all victims. [23]

Here, like Tutu, her body feels with the Commissioners, is "rocked" by the same "flood" of the seas outside Cape Town and the events from the past. The Commission gives her a voice (essential for a recorder, as essential as feeling the sickness of the country is for Tutu), and she insists on her embodiment, her hand inscribing the insight of the way she has become one with the country and its past.

The personal changes both writers record in their states of mind and body equate neatly with the moment of transition in South Africa. For both authors that transition for all its complexity is rooted in a particular space with a particular relationship to time. Although the writers each have a different relationship to space, both suggest how space is given a particular meaning by historical time. Space is not just a backdrop to the historical events they have

---

22. Krog, *Country*, p. 1.

23. Krog, *Country*, p. 278.

been part of, but carries significant meanings, elucidated through the process of autobiographical reflection.

For Tutu the space of his lifeworld and of historical time is unambiguously a place, South Africa, which remains for him the "land of our birth". The word "land" with its slightly archaic resonance has overtones of deep processes of belonging that contrast with the more neutral "country". In Tutu's autobiographical text one of the major motifs is of spaces denied under apartheid to him (and to South Africa as the two are often intertwined). These forbidden spaces open up as part of the process of forming a new nation. Thus historical time makes new spaces, which are peopled by the "reborn". In a long passage in the opening chapter of the book, Tutu describes driving away from his official residence, Bishopscourt, and "the leafy up-market suburb surrounding it" so that he can vote for the first time in Gugulethu "a black township with typical matchbox houses in row after monotonous row".[24] He describes the camaraderie of people waiting in queues to vote, and how in that space, people discovered each other, and learned to tolerate each other.

> Hardly any of them wanted to drive the whites into the sea. They just wanted their place in the sun.[25]

While apartheid divided people and space, people living out history overcome those divisions.

There are many moving passages in the book where physical space, bodily space, emotional space and redemptive historical space cross-cut each other building up a picture of new openings and new meanings. Here is one of many such passages describing Nomonde Calata giving evidence to the TRC about the death of her husband:

> At this point in her evidence Mrs. Calata broke down, uttering a piercing wail which in many ways was the defining sound that characterised the Truth and Reconciliation Commission – as a place where people could come to cry, to open their hearts, to expose the anguish that had remained locked up for so long, unacknowledged, ignored and denied. I adjourned the proceedings so that she could recover her composure and when we restarted, I led the gathering in singing 'Senzenina?' (What have we done?)[26]

---

24. Tutu, *No future*, p. 2–3.

25. Tutu, *No future*, p. 4.

26. Tutu, *No future*, p. 114.

Private anguish is given a new meaning located in space and time defined through Tutu's work with the TRC. Spatial metaphors are key to this process. Lifetime gives meaning to historical time and historical time re-interprets the pain of lifetime. Thus in this passage the TRC is portrayed as a place, the heart as a prison, like the country had been, and the space of voices singing together stands for the re-formation of people through self-reflection together.

Krog also gives an account of this searing moment and Nomonde Calata's grief-stricken cry which reached out across time:

> For me, this crying is the beginning of the Truth Commission – the signature tune, the definitive moment, the ultimate sound of what the process is about. She was wearing this vivid orange-red dress, and she threw herself backwards and that sound... that sound...it will haunt me for ever and ever.[27]

Krog's writing here, as in much of the book, breaks up and fragments the narrative, juxtaposing a seemingly insignificant detail –the colour of a dress– with the significance of tears for the Commission. The sound of weeping for her escapes beyond the bounds of the place of the Commission. [28]

Krog's portrayal of space is more complex and more fragmented than Tutu's. Space, for her is not simply recontextualised and given meaning through its association with historical time. A major theme in her book is how the land and the space it represents often threaten to overwhelm the meanings about a new society she is struggling to make. In the book she portrays herself as often assailed by the weather, for example torrential downpours of rain, or by her childhood memories of her parents' farm and her connection to the land read through their identities. Her feelings of horror engulf her when she thinks of places of torture and terror and she highlights their meaning by juxtaposing passages where she describes these with passages which recount everyday spaces of her work as a journalist, her everyday tasks with her children.

Krog's response to South Africa's space is to set its overwhelming beauty or prosaic comfort *against* the truths revealed to the TRC. The meaning of

---

27. Krog, *Country*, p. 42.

28. There is a very striking contrast between the meanings assigned by Tutu and Krog to this moment and that implicit in the account given by Alex Boraine. Boraine describes Nomonde Calata chiefly in terms of her relationships as a wife and a mother, and remarks that the significance of her cry, which was broadcast on the radio, was that many people had to turn it off. Boraine, *Country*, p. 103.

history is achieved *despite* the beauties of the landscape, the pull of everyday achievements. This is the moral purpose of her work of observing and making sense of history. While for Tutu biography and history confirm each other, for Krog history requires a special effort beyond biography. This heterodox history, woven of observation and poetry and feeling enables biography to go beyond the givens of stone and sun and work with seed.

While Tutu imposes his identity and meanings on space and time, Krog struggles to assert her identity and the meaning of time, despite space. What they have in common is that for both time has meaning and this compels a particular relationship to space. For neither can the lifeworld stand distinct from a historic purpose of understanding and taking responsibility. But the lifeworlds of the two authors, which they place centrally in their narratives, are very different. To what extent does gender shape their identities and the ways that they interpret history?

Gendered identities and the meaning of truth

The gendered identities taken by each author are signalled on the covers of their books. Tutu takes an identity given by his moral and political leadership; he invests masculinity with a teleological and historical significance that is partly created through action as head of the Truth Commission and partly created through faith. This is a version of what I have termed "heroic masculinity."[29] However, it is a version of heroic masculinity that is somewhat less patriarchal, and somewhat more aware of the aspect of gender, than that taken by some other male South African leaders working in this genre. The contrast comes out strongly when Tutu's account of the TRC is set side-by-side with that of Alex Boraine or Piers Pigou, both of whom recount administrative details and very distanced versions of their experiences.[30]

Krog, by contrast, takes on a fragmented identity, in which her complex and overlapping positions as journalist, poet, mother, wife, lover, sister, daughter, friend allow her to move between different spaces and in this dispersal and fracturing of her self to apprehend the dismemberment of the nation, like the body of Sipho Mtimkulu, and its attempts to hold together all the bleeding elements.

29. Unterhalter, "Heroic masculinity".

30. Boraine, *Country*; Pigou, P., "False promises and wasted opportunities?", in Posel and Simpson, *Commissioning*, pp. 37–65.

Is this fragmented identity feminised? Although Krog draws on aspects of her identity as a woman, I would argue that there is nothing particularly "male" about heroic masculinity, as this form of autobiography as *bildungsroman* has also been written by South African women, while there is nothing particularly "female" about portrayals of the self as fractured, although admittedly this form of writing has been much more associated with the autobiographies of South African women, rather than men.[31]

The form of identity each takes on is linked to their ideas concerning truth. Thus for Tutu truth entails forgiveness, and the meaning of history is recognising the past in order that it should be forgiven and thus not repeated.[32] He quotes a distinction made by Albie Sachs, a judge in the South African Constitutional Court, concerning orders of truth: forensic factual truth, the social truth of experience established through discussion and the personal truth of "wounded memories" healed through public therapeutic acts. According to Sachs these three do not exclude each other, but Tutu, in accepting the distinction, implies that the last is the most important.[33] These distinctions were used to frame the methodology of the Commission.[34]

Krog, by contrast, suggests there is no single truth, and much of her book concerns how difficult and porous the notion of truth is. Truth undoes a single notion of personhood it tears apart, and generates tears. This is not simply healing, but carries two meanings (tears and tears). But in its undoing it also carries out a work of morality. Her vantage point for this morality inhabits not the space of the Archbishop or the judge, but the space of a woman on the margin:

> I see my mother coming back from the chicken-run with her two youngest grandchildren, each swinging a basket of eggs. She seems frail, but the scene is so peaceful, we are so lucky, so privileged…But whereas this privilege used to upset me in the past, now I can hold it against a truth that we are all aware of. No longer an unaware privilege, but one that we know the price and mortality of. [35]

---

31. Unterhalter, "Schooling"; Unterhalter, "Remembering".

32. Unterhalter, E., "Reworking the nation: Changing masculinities in South Africa", Paper presented to Gender Forum, Jesus College, University of Cambridge, November 2002.

33. Tutu, *Future*, p. 33.

34. For a discussion of some of the epistemological difficulties with this approach see Posel, "What kind of history?"

35. Krog, *Country*, p. 272.

Through torn fragments and apprehensions of mortality and unknowability she affirms a morality. Here she stands closer to feminist theorists of autobiography, while still asserting the significant social responsibility entailed in her form of knowing truth.

The works of Tutu and Krog both entail translations of history into personal narrative and from personal narrative into the meaning of history. Both use their differently gendered identities to construct a single meaning of truth linked to a collective purpose. However in connecting biography and history in this way they occlude concern with social structure.

This is evident in the ways both deal with gender relations, but similar points could be made about class. Neither challenges the gender order of the society beyond noting how there had been some neglect of women's contribution to the struggle. Tutu comments but does not substantiate that gender was an additional burden placed on women on top of the discrimination they suffered as black South Africans. In describing his own family he speaks with fatherly outrage at the prospect of his wife and daughters being searched at the roadside.[36] In certain passages he is surprised by the "extraordinary resilience and courage of women" and confesses that it was not until he learned how women had their identities as mothers or lovers used against them by their torturers, that he appreciated their contribution to the struggle.[37] But acknowledging women as honorary, but different, comrades in arms is not an engagement with features of gender discrimination or the failures to distribute even the honours of the struggle fairly. It is not at all clear how celebrating women's contribution opens a way to gender equality in a new society.

Krog wrestles more openly with the question of gender inequality. She suggests, but does not clarify beyond allusion, that gendered difference is residual, mythic and formative in the language and the society, with black femininity always signalling deficit or lack.[38] But through writing and recording, she, partly through her feminised identity, makes a different sense beyond this untruth. She quotes both the courageous testimony of women and the extraordinary difficulties women had to tell their stories; as so many identities, particularly identities as political activists, were denied to them.[39] The ways in which a particular feminised identity linked to sexuality was

---

36. Tutu, *Future*, p. 15.

37. Tutu, *Future*, p. 182–3.

38. Krog, *Country*, p. 190.

39. Krog, *Country*, p. 177–190.

intertwined with the kinds of evidence women were able to give to the Truth Commission is not a difficulty for Krog. The fragmentary identities women expressed through sexuality resonate for her with truth telling as a processing of tearing/tearing up, seeping into the unknown. The chapter that touches questions of gender and the TRC is called *Truth is a woman.*

But for all the ontological and epistemological sleights of hand Krog does not deal with the social structures of gendered oppression. Indeed the socially constructed gendered nature of truth in the end disappears into her narrative. We learn nothing of the gendered inequalities of South African society from her. Her overall insight is very like Tutu's, concerning the moral truth of recognition and forgiveness.

Personal truth, history and public education for social justice

The argument thus far has shown how, through translating autobiography into history, Tutu and Krog write powerful works of public education that expand our understanding of the formation of a democratic South Africa. But they do this without recourse to any analysis of social structure. The assumption runs that through the epiphanies of spirituality or poetry, both resonating with reality, public insight and education is achieved and from this social justice effects will follow. In work I have co-authored with Melanie Walker, which draws on an analysis of *Country of my Skull* we have shown some of the ways in which this happens.[40] However, side-by-side with these pedagogic processes of learning through individual truths, I want to raise a number of questions concerning dimensions of social justice.

Nancy Fraser identifies gender and race as bivalent categories requiring both distributional and recognitional remedies.[41] With regard to redistribution, gender and race have to lose significance, thus for example gender should become irrelevant in hiring and firing. With regard to recognitional remedies gender and race need to gain significance, for example women's neglected and frequently fragmentary ways of describing the world in diaries, say, or personal letters, should become recognised as special and worthy of notice. Distributional remedies tend to engage with the domain of political economy, while recognitional remedies engage the domains of culture and symbolic forms.

---

40. Walker and Unterhalter, "Knowledge".

41. Fraser, N., *Justice interruptus,* London/New York, Routledge, 1997.

Social structure is an important means of understanding political econo-my. It is much less significant, but not irrelevant, in addressing issues relating to the symbolic sphere. Much history writing, concerned with social struc-ture, has paid scant attention to gender inequalities. Despite some significant work in this area, this has been a muted theme in South African history. Tutu and Krog do not engage with political economy, but undertake im-portant work in the symbolic realm. One of their key devices for doing this is to refuse a public-private division between lifeworlds and history. Much feminist scholarship has engaged with a similar issue, highlighting how the personal realm of the family or the body is highly political, a terrain for strug-gles over power and meaning, and a place where pain is inflicted as much as pleasure encountered.

But Tutu and Krog's accomplishment, though significant, is partial. Neither addresses political economy in ways that help us advance questions regarding inequalities and redistribution. They do not engage in the profes-sional work of history, which gives a particular perspective and depth to the compelling contemporary questions of social justice. History requires partic-ular skills that are neither spiritual nor poetic. History entails an assessment of the balance of evidence. Knowledge cannot be endlessly plastic, although many historians accept that it is partial. Partly because Tutu and Krog are not historians or political philosophers or social scientists they are not able to address in any depth the distributional questions of social justice. In one sense this does not matter because they seek to define a moment of rebirth for South Africa. But in another sense it does matter because beyond that moment there is a new terrain of history in which issues beside the collective consciousness of the nation must be addressed.

The Truth Commission and the autobiographical writings, of which Tutu and Krog are examples, are necessary, but not sufficient for social justice. They have created a new language through which forms of recognitional jus-tice, particularly concerning race, can be acknowledged. They suggest a form of ethics through remembering. This form of recognitional justice might be a crucial step that prefigures redistributional justice. In recognising a common humanity, a new society, a new orientation beyond the fragments, conditions may begin to be established that allow gender, race and class inequalities to be addressed.

But recognition alone cannot do the work of redistributing opportunities and shaping outcomes. This requires attention to principles for redistribution and to the forms of public participation through which this redistribution is decided. Truth or recognitional justice is interlinked with distributional justice, but cannot in and of itself transform into distributional justice or generate the disciplinary or political philosophical insights that can engage with questions of distributional justice. However a theory of justice that does not attend to the ways we narrate our different and common truths through memory and history would be a thin theory. Truth without justice cannot sustain new ways of living in a more equal society. But bringing social justice into being through policy and practice requires meticulous and skilful attention to what we know and do not yet know and the forms our knowledge takes. Attending to the truths others tell in words that may be framed by memory, and in formats that are sometimes unsettling because they are not the "master narratives" is part of that task. But it is not the whole task. In making these distinctions we need the accumulated insights of many disciplines, including history, which needs to stand separate from, but attentive to, personal and collective memory.

— CHAPTER 5 —

Claiming land and making memory:
Engaging with the past in land restitution

Anna Bohlin

Established after the transition to democracy in 1994, the Truth and Reconciliation Commission (TRC) aimed to create a broad, collective record of the past, a "repository of South African memory."[1] Much attention has focused on the creation of this memory bank, and the debate on its benefits and shortcomings is likely to continue for years to come.[2]

The programme of land restitution, driven by the Commission on Restitution of Land Rights (CRLR), is another key political initiative of the post-apartheid era. Compared with the TRC, however, surprisingly little academic work has examined how the CRLR has generated new forms of memory and history.[3] The explicit aim of the programme is to restore rights

1. Nuttal, S, and C. Coetzee (eds), *Negotiating the Past: The Making of Memory in South Africa*, Cape Town, Oxford University Press, 1998, p. 1.

2. See for example Bozzoli, B., "Public Ritual and Private Transition: The Truth Commission in Alexandra Township, South Africa 1996", *African Studies*, Vol. 57, pp. 167–195, 1998; Jeffery, A., *The Truth about the Truth Commission*, Johannesburg, South African Institute of Race Relations, 1999; Krog, A., *Country of my Skull*, Johannesburg: Random House, (1998) 2002; Posel, D. and G. Simpson (eds), *Commissioning the Past: Understanding South Africa's Truth and Reconciliation Commission*, Johannesburg, Witwatersrand University Press, 2002; Wilson, R.A., *The Politics of Truth and Reconciliation in South Africa: Legitimizing the Post-Apartheid State*, Cambridge, Cambridge University Press, 2001.

3. Exceptions are two Master theses by Broadbridge, H., "Relevant, Important and Credible: Reflections on Applying Anthropology in the South African Land Restitution Process", Masters thesis, University of Cape Town, 1997, and Böge, F., "Back to the Places of the Future? The Transformation of Places and Local Identities in the 'New' South Africa. A Case Study of the Land Restitution Process in Simon's Town", Masters thesis, Freie Universität Berlin, 1999, and articles by Mesthrie, U., "Land Restitution in Cape Town: Public Displays and Private Meanings", *Kronos: Journal of Cape History*, Vol. 25, pp. 239–258, 1998/99; and Walker, C., "Relocating Restitution",

in land to those who were denied them for racially motivated reasons. So far, the programme has been mainly analysed in terms of its legal, administrative and organisational dimensions, with particular emphasis on the many problems that beset the restitution process in its early years.[4] This chapter focus on what might be called a "side effect" of the restitution programme, namely its stimulation of the production of memory. Examining a land claim in Kalk Bay, a small community in the Western Cape, it shows that the various stages of a land claim process involve the production and reshaping of representations of the past at a number of levels. It argues that because the restitution programme was not explicitly designed to produce new histories, the memories that emerged out of the land claim process escaped some of the constraints posed by more institutionalised attempts at shaping history in present day South Africa. More specifically, the land claim process was subjected to less of the pressure associated with nation-building, namely the requirement of reconciliation, forgiveness, and "leaving the past behind".

A case of forgetting

Before exploring how engagement with the restitution process shaped stories of dispossession and displacement in Kalk Bay, a few words need to be said about the context of this particular land claim.[5] I arrived in Kalk Bay, a small fishing community and seaside resort on the Cape Peninsula, in 1997 to conduct research on memories of the 1967 proclamation of the village as a white Group Area under the Group Areas Act (GAA).[6] Through archival research, I had established that the proclamation was a widely discussed – and, in the

Transformation, Vol. 44, pp. 1–16, 2000. The piece by Mesthrie is particularly useful for an overview of the actors and personalities "behind the scenes" in the TRC and the CRLR, as well as of technical and legislative differences between them.

4. See for example Brown, M., J. Erasmus, R. Kingwill, C. Murray and M. Roodt, *Land Restitution in South Africa: A Long Way Home*, Cape Town, Idasa, 1998; du Toit, A., "The End of Restitution: Getting Real about Land Claims," in *At the Crossroads: Land and Agrarian Reform in South Africa into the 21st Century*, edited by B. Cousins, Cape Town and Braamfontein, PLAAS and NLC, 2000.

5. This chapter is based on a study made possible by grants from the Centre for Public Sector Research (CEFOS) and the Swedish International Development Cooperation Agency (Sida).

6. The principal aim of the Group Areas Act of 1950, one of the central pillars of apartheid legislation, was to regulate the presence of coloured and Asian populations in urban areas.

liberal press, condemned – event, which greatly disrupted the community and sparked intense protests both locally and regionally. The proclamation made it illegal for non-whites to live in Kalk Bay, and forced some twenty coloured and Indian families (around a hundred and twenty individuals), mostly fishermen, to move. They resettled in designated Group Areas on the Cape Flats, some fifteen kilometres away from their boats and livelihood. Due to intense protests, however, the proclamation exempted a portion of land to allow a majority of the fishers to stay. Finally, sustained pressure led to the rescinding of the proclamation fifteen years later.

To my surprise, at the time of fieldwork, a majority of residents in Kalk Bay had forgotten, denied or were unaware that the village had ever been a white Group Area, and very few remembered that anyone had to move because of it.[7] In contrast, those who had moved from Kalk Bay and today live in various parts of the Cape Flats remembered the proclamation and its effects only too well. Partly because of my interviews, some of the former residents of Kalk Bay decided to participate in the government's programme of land restitution and submit claims for the homes they left behind.[8] I participated in this process by assisting with information leaflets about land restitution, facilitating meetings and inviting relevant individuals who informed the group about the restitution procedure. As a result, sixteen households, representing some forty individuals, lodged restitution claims with the CRLR on 31 December 1998 (the cut-off date for applications).[9]

In March 2000, the Kalk Bay Historical Association invited me to address their annual general meeting on the topic of the GAA proclamation. The meeting took place in the community centre in Kalk Bay. Current resi-

---

7. For the fishing community, the fight against the GAA, which eventually resulted in the rescinding of the proclamation in 1982, has become a dominant frame of remembering. The 'de-proclamation', which was widely reported in the newspapers, was interpreted locally as a victory not just over the government, but also over the very notion of apartheid. See Bohlin, A., "In the Eyes of the Sea: Memories of Place and Displacement in a South African Fishing Town", PhD, University of Göteborg, 2001; Bohlin, A., "Places of Longing and Belonging: Memories of the Group Area Proclamation of a South African Fishing Village," in *Contested Landscapes: Movement, Exile and Place*, edited by B. Bender and M. Winer, London, Berg, 2001.

8. During my fieldwork it became clear that although most people were familiar with the general features of the restitution programme, few of them knew that they were entitled to apply. I therefore provided information about restitution to those who were interested, something that no doubt influenced their decision to lodge land claims.

9. The claims are currently being processed by the CRLR.

dents made up the bulk of the audience. Most of them were from the white middle class, but a few were prominent members of the fishing community. A small number of former residents, now living in various suburbs on the Cape Flats, also attended the meeting. In my talk, I presented the GAA legislation, showed slides of houses that were sold because of the proclamation, and described how it disrupted the community. Among the current residents in the audience, the prevailing reaction to my presentation was one of surprise and dismay. Many had never heard of the proclamation, and those who had were under the impression that it had not affected anyone. Yet, while most members of the audience welcomed the opportunity to learn about the GAA, some after a while began to question whether anyone had in fact been forced to move, and indeed, even if this had been the case, whether such a memory was worth emphasising. A few of the relocated former residents clearly disapproved of these comments. One exchange stands out in particular. After a resident fisherman announced that as far as he knew, not a single person had to move under the GAA, a visibly upset woman in her sixties interrupted to say "But Jonathan, haven't you been listening? We had to move!" She went on to detail how she and her sisters lost the house that their grandfather had built on the slopes of Kalk Bay.

I describe this meeting in some detail because it vividly illustrates that history does not write itself. Even with the presentation of clear evidence of the disruptive effects of the GAA – photographs of sold houses, eviction notices, a copy of the deed of transfer of a property to the Department of Community Development[10] – members of the audience, white and coloured, held on to versions of the past that presented Kalk Bay as unaffected. The resilience of this selective memory shows the ease with which even a relatively recent event is denied or forgotten.

Land restitution and the production of memory

When the democratic government took power in 1994, it immediately began the work of addressing the legacy of the past by establishing a number of commissions.[11] While most of these address the past as it is embodied in the present, in terms of historically rooted patterns and structures of inequality,

---

10. The Department of Community Development was responsible for ensuring that proclaimed Group Areas developed in accordance with the GAA.

11. Examples are the Commission on Gender Equality, the National Youth Commission, and the Human Rights Commission.

two of the commissions were set up to engage more directly with the past itself. These were the TRC and the CRLR, which were given the task of addressing instances of past suffering and injustice as they are carried in living memory by those who were personally affected (notably, however, within the parameters established by the constitutional negotiations).[12]

Established to investigate human rights abuse during apartheid, the TRC was explicitly set up to produce a shared national history. Supplemented by archival research, some 22,000 statements from victims were collected in order to shed light on the nature and extent of human rights abuse during apartheid.[13] Based on these, around two thousand victims as well as some three thousand perpetrators of human rights abuse were invited to testify in public hearings that were broadcast nationally during 1996 and 1997. An extensive report subsequently published the findings of the TRC and was widely debated and analysed in the media.

In contrast to the TRC, the role of memory was for the CRLR mainly instrumental. The explicit aim of the land restitution programme is to produce reconciliation and "healing" of the nation through the return of, or compensation for, lost land rights.[14] To this effect, the CRLR invited individuals or communities who lost rights in land due to racially discriminatory laws or practices to apply for various forms of compensation. Rather than establishing a record of the past, in and of itself, the CRLR collected information from victims to facilitate the processing of applications for restitution. For this reason, the histories recorded in land claim processes have, compared with those of the TRC, largely remained out of the public limelight.[15]

---

12. For an overview of these negotiations see Walker, C., "The Limits of Land Reform: Rethinking 'the Land Question'", in Beall, J. and S. Hassim (eds), *State and Society in South Africa: Faultlines of Crisis and Sites of Stabilisation* (forthcoming).

13. Posel, D. and G. Simpson (eds), *Commissioning the Past: Understanding South Africa's Truth and Reconciliation Commission*, Johannesburg, Witwatersrand University Press, 2002, p. 3.

14. "Right in land" is by the CRLR defined as ownership of land as well as formal or informal tenancy or other form of residence in the same place for a minimum of ten years prior to removal. Compensation options include restoration of original land, or if not possible, alternative land, monetary compensation or access to various development projects.

15. The relative invisibility of such histories prompted historian Martin Legassick and Alan Roberts, then Western Cape Land Commissioner, to plan a project to combine restitution with various forms of memorialisation, a plan that has so far not materialised due to lack of funding. See Legassick's chapter in this book.

Nevertheless, the restitution programme is in a number of ways a significant site of production of a new "collective memory," despite not being explicitly designed as such. Firstly, the nation-wide collection of land claim forms, numbering some 60,000, is a unique memory bank of cases of displacement and dispossession that constituted some of the most far-reaching and destructive facets of apartheid. Although each four-page form outlines only the "hard facts" of dispossession, along with a few sentences on the hardship it caused, they provide a significant complement to the histories recorded by the TRC. While the TRC was event-oriented, and often focused on "heroic" victims and "evil" perpetrators, the land claim documents highlight structural and comparably low-key injustices experienced by ordinary South Africans.[16] At present, the land claim documents are not accessible to the public, but eventually they will be handed over to the National Archives in Cape Town, where, like the TRC report, they will be available to future generations.

A second "site" of public memory that has emerged from land claims processes is the research reports that were compiled by professional researchers, employed by the CRLR. Intended to facilitate the assessment and settlement of claims, every report outlines the historical circumstances of dispossession for each locality being claimed. Many of these professionally researched histories, which often involve innovative and multi-layered methodologies, have found their way into the news media, academic theses, journals and museums.[17]

---

16. See Mamdani, M., "Reconciliation without Justice", *Southern Review,* Vol. 10, pp. 22–25, 1997, who criticises the TRC for its focus on perpetrators, rather than the much broader category of beneficiaries of apartheid, and for highlighting the experiences of a narrowly defined group of victims as opposed to one that includes the majority of South Africans.

17. See for example Bantom, R., "A Study in the History of Protea Village and the Impact of the Group Areas Act", Honours thesis, University of the Western Cape, 1995; Broadbridge, H., "Relevant, Important and Credible: Reflections on Applying Anthropology in the South African Land Restitution Process", Masters thesis, University of Cape Town, 1997; Legassick in *Mail & Guardian,* 14–20 November 1997; Mesthrie, U., "The Tramway Road Removals", 1959–61, *Kronos,* Vol. 21, pp. 61–78, 1994. The District Six Museum in Cape Town, and the Simon's Town Museum on the Cape Peninsula, have assisted claimants with information for their applications, as well as displayed histories that have emerged out of such claims (see Rassool, C., and S. Prosalendis (eds), *Recalling Community in Cape Town: Creating and Curating the District Six Museum,* Cape Town, District Six Museum, 2001). Similarly, the George Museum in the southern Cape is planning an exhibition on forced removals, organised by a former researcher for the CRLR.

Finally, there is a range of both formal and informal activities of memory production that accompany a claim. In order to fill in the land claim form, the claimant, whether a representative of a community or a single individual, needed to provide information that proves the loss of rights to land. Besides official documents such as copies of title deeds, wills or marriage certificates, the CRLR also encouraged the submission of evidence of a more informal kind. Recognising that written documents such as lease contracts may be lacking, not least because leases may only have existed in verbal form, the CRLR accepts various forms of proof of residence such as old receipts, envelopes showing the old address, electricity bills, photographs and the like. In many cases, oral testimonies from old neighbours, as well as visits and "walkabouts" in former neighbourhoods, are also considered by the CRLR to determine which land rights were lost, and what compensation is reasonable. Rather than merely a straightforward bureaucratic exercise, lodging a claim thus involves a range of different forms of "memory work" – a labour of actively and consciously giving order and meaning to the past.[18] Below I examine how the specific requirements of the restitution framework initiated and shaped such memory work in the case of Kalk Bay.

Personal memories and public narratives

Once the decision to participate in the restitution process was taken, the claimants from Kalk Bay began the operation of translating their own, private memories into official narratives. As mentioned above, a land claim form must be accompanied by various types of evidence of the rights in land that was lost, as well as descriptions of circumstances before, during and after the dispossession. In order to meet these requirements, the claimants from Kalk Bay searched for birth and marriage certificates, photographs of childhood homes, old bills, letters, postcards and faded newspaper cuttings.

In informal meetings in private homes, as well as a formal meeting in a church in Kalk Bay, the group discussed the details and contents of the history of dispossession.[19] Comparing memories of dates and events, they pieced together a picture of who was born where, who rented from whom

---

18. Irwin-Zarecka, I., *Frames of Remembrance: The Dynamics of Collective Memory*, London, Transaction, 1994, p. 145. See also Gillis, J. R., *Commemoration: The Politics of National Identity*, 1994, Princeton, Princeton University Press.

19. I observed the application process in meetings, interviews and conversations but unfortunately left the country a few weeks before the group handed in their application

and which house was built when.[20] Differences between people's recollections were sometimes fundamental, leading to heated debates concerning various parts of the collective history that was being produced. Yet, although a mnemonic consensus would have been of benefit to the claimants, they did not always prioritise the discussion of "factual" information. The few times I intervened in the debate to offer information that I had come across during fieldwork, such as specific prices of properties, or the dates of property sales, I was often ignored, or if my facts contradicted what others were saying, politely told that I was mistaken. Compared with their own locally and experientially grounded memories, official records seemingly lacked relevance for the emotional and social evocation of past events that participants engaged in. At stake in the meetings was not so much the task of reconstructing events in chronological order in order to create an instrumental version of the past – ostensibly the reason for the meeting – but rather, the establishing of a social space in which "expressions of the value and significance of a lost past" could be articulated.[21]

One of the most striking aspects of the process of preparing the claims was how it shaped understandings of the Group Area proclamation and its effects. When I first spoke to former residents living in the Cape Flats, they explained that they had moved because of the GAA and frequently described the hardship this caused them in a few phrases, such as "it was very heartsore" (from Afrikaans *hartseer*, meaning sad) or "I'll never forget the day we moved." When later asked to describe the experience of moving in greater depth, however, many struggled to provide a coherent and detailed narrative. Compared with the elaborate and vivid memories of other aspects of life in Kalk Bay, descriptions of the move were fragmented, hesitant and interspersed with silences. These silences may be partly an effect of the passage of time, but the fact that people readily recalled detailed episodes from their daily lives before the move argues against this explanation. It is more likely that these silences reflect the private, personal and painful nature of such memories.

At the time of fieldwork, therefore, the proclamation of Kalk Bay as a white Group Area, while constituting a fundamental aspect of the past that

---

forms so was unable to see the final documents. What I describe here is therefore based on observations from various contexts related to the application process.

20. Some had been tenants while others had been owners of their properties.

21. Oliver-Smith, quoted in Brown, B.B. and D. Perkins, "Disruptions in Place Attachment," in *Place Attachment*, edited by I. Altman and S.M. Low, New York, Plenum, 1992, p. 294.

people assumed others were familiar with, was differently interpreted and conceptualised among different people. Each person had his or her own idiosyncratic perception of what occurred, and assumed others to have the same set of memories.[22] Many described seeing their former neighbours living in Kalk Bay as a confusing and at times painful experience that exacerbated feelings of failure and self-blame. A lack of knowledge of the precise workings of the Group Area legislation often reinforced perceptions of inadequacy. Not understanding why certain families managed to stay, despite the proclamation, people resorted to explanations that involved a range of possible alternatives.[23] At the same time, they looked for reasons for their own "bad luck". For example, two sisters believed that they had been forced to leave because their father was known to the City Council as a troublemaker. Others regarded the visits and threats from GAA officials as a test from God.

During the work required for the restitution claims, however, awareness of the legal and political aspects of the Group Area proclamation increased as people compared experiences, read through documents and listened to a presentation by a field researcher from the CRLR. Rather than interpret the move from Kalk Bay as to some extent a result of personal or religious conduct, they located the responsibility for the removals more squarely with the former regime, and particularly, with the "Group Areas". Increasingly, they came to identify themselves with the nationally recognised category of "victims of forced removals". Private and personal memories, previously associated by many with failure and stigma, were thus recast as moments in a national history of injustice that was shared with thousands of other citizens.

Yet, the extent to which claimants explicitly connected the land claim process to the project of nation-building, and more specifically, the extent to which they contrasted the injustice of the previous political system with the justice of the current one, differed. Some, as will be shown below, linked the restitution process to the TRC, and explicitly embraced the opportunity to insert their experiences into the official records after years of being excluded and marginalised on the basis of their racial identity. They regarded the proc-

---

22. Some believed for example that only non-fishing residents were evicted, while others thought only those who did not own boats had to leave Kalk Bay.

23. One man believed for example that those living next to the mosque were allowed to stay because of their connection with this consecrated property. The real reason certain families managed to stay outside the exempted area, however, was that these families lived in properties in which the registered owner was alive. Had any of these owners passed away while Kalk Bay was a proclaimed area, the remaining family members would have been forced to sell their houses.

ess as an opportunity to denounce the race-based politics of the former regime and to celebrate the non-racialism of the present government. Others rejected the discourse of non-racialism as superficial, and insisted on reading their present situation as one shaped by the experience of belonging to a historically emerged identity, that of being coloured. Contesting the idea of the present government as a guarantor of justice and equality, they nevertheless used the restitution process as an opportunity to express their anger and hurt towards the previous regime.[24]

Interpreting the restitution framework

Several commentators have noted that the restitution programme implicitly invites simplistic narratives of belonging, "rootedness" and "return" that obscure or ignore historical complexities, notably the developments that have taken place in the years since displacement.[25] To some extent, this was the case in the Kalk Bay land claim process. Yet, not everyone framed their experiences in terms of a static sense of belonging to Kalk Bay. The elderly claimants, especially, had no wish to return. Some mentioned that the steep hills and steps in Kalk Bay would be difficult to manage at their age, and in any case they felt that in the nearly thirty years since they left, they had established a sense of home and community on the Cape Flats. They contested any simple notions of "displacement" or "uprootedness" implicit in the restitution framework, and emphasised their sense of belonging to their current places of living. For them, the injustice of the GAA is firmly located in the past, and cannot be undone or even adequately compensated in the present. The primary value of lodging a claim, and of receiving compensation, is thus on a symbolic level: it is an official recognition of the unfairness of their experiences.

---

24. Not surprisingly, such differences largely coincided with political party affiliation. While the former category tended to sympathise with the ruling party, the African National Congress, the latter tended to support other parties such as the New National Party as well as parties on the political left.

25. See Böge, F., "Back to the Places of the Future? The Transformation of Places and Local Identities in the 'New' South Africa. A Case Study of the Land Restitution Process in Simon's Town", Masters thesis, Freie Universität Berlin, 1999, p. 55; James, D., "'After Years in the Wilderness': The Discourse of Land Claims in the New South Africa", *The Journal of Peasant Studies*, Vol. 27, pp. 142–161, 2000; Robins, S., "Land Struggles and the Politics and Ethics of Representing 'Bushman' History and Identity", *Kronos*, Vol. 26, pp. 56–75, 2000; Walker, C., "Relocating Restitution", *Transformation*, Vol. 44, pp. 1–16, 2000.

Some claimants explicitly pointed out similarities between the restitution meetings and the work by the TRC, which at the time had broadcast hearings on national television in which victims and perpetrators of human rights abuse under apartheid gave testimony. Like the victims in the TRC hearings, they said, they too had kept their stories to themselves for many years, and like them, they would now speak, "so that others can know what apartheid was like." Treating the land restitution meetings as a form of mini-TRCs, spaces where silence would give way to officially sanctioned, public disclosure of past suffering, people took the opportunity to vent experiences of various injustices. Not only did they describe hardship caused by the Group Area proclamation, but also related stories of how they had endured various other forms of racial discrimination, such as lower salaries than white colleagues, or the indignity of having to use segregated public transport. The meetings thus became fora for articulating and acknowledging a wide range of everyday injustices under apartheid.

Although the land claim meetings showed some similarity with the TRC hearings, they were also fundamentally different. Firstly, the land claim meetings were much less institutionalised. Because of the lack of capacity and resources within the CRLR, claimants have often had to invent their own ways of engaging with and organising the claim process.[26] It is also the objective of the CRLR that restitution should be a claimant-driven process. While the TRC hearings were strictly ordered affairs, designed and controlled by the TRC, and to some extent the media, the land claim meetings in the Kalk Bay case were largely informal and arranged by the claimants themselves, who set the agenda and decided what they wanted to discuss. This absence of outside, "top-down" control of the meetings had significant implications for the kinds of memories that emerged from them.

During the TRC hearings, Commissioners frequently intervened and reframed victims' testimonies, typically by recasting experiences of violence or death not only as meaningful moments in a wider liberation struggle, but also as sacrifices for the nation, the dead being declared "heroes".[27] In the land claim meetings, no such appropriation of people's memories occurred. The

---

26. Mesthrie, U., "The Truth and Reconciliation Commission and the Commission on Restitution of Land Rights: Some Comparative Thoughts", Unpublished paper, Conference on the Truth and Reconciliation Commission, University of Witwatersrand, 1999, p. 24.

27. Robins, S., "Silence in My Father's House," in *Negotiating the Past*, edited by S. Nuttal and C. Coetzee, Cape Town, Oxford University Press, 1998.

TRC hearings, which were grounded in a Christian tradition of confession, repentance and forgiveness, were structured in such a way that any expression of anger or bitterness would seem out of place, "an ugly intrusion on a peaceful, healing process." [28] In contrast, the moments of articulating the past in the restitution meetings were relatively unmediated, and expressions of frustration, anger or sadness were not smoothed over or silenced in attempts to achieve "healing," whether personal or national.

As a governmental institution, the CRLR would probably have preferred land restitution meetings to be marked by the same concern for peaceful healing as that of the TRC hearings. In fact, a field researcher from the CRLR who participated in one meeting, held in Kalk Bay, afterwards commented that he was concerned by the level of "upset feelings" among the claimants. Yet, his attempts to steer the meeting towards a serene mood of celebration, both of the restitution programme and of the fact that people had reunited in the place they were once evicted from, were unsuccessful as people treated the opportunity primarily as one in which to vent their frustration and sadness.[29] Significantly, however, such expressions of anger or loss were not accompanied by any calls for revenge or retaliation. On the contrary, people repeatedly emphasised that they wished nobody to go through what they had experienced.[30]

On a symbolic level, the restitution programme plays a crucial role in terms of how it defines the significance of the past in present day South Africa. Rather than sustaining the impression that transformation is already achieved, and that the divisions and tensions of the past disappeared with the emergence of the new dispensation, the restitution programme encourages local communities to face injustices in the present and to actively trace and address their roots in the past. One could question, however, whether the contractual nature of the restitution process does not contribute to the impression that such injustices can be redressed by a one-off deal, and indeed, whether compensation "cancels" them out. There is a risk that land restitution, rather

---

28. Wilson, R.A., *The Politics of Truth and Reconciliation in South Africa: Legitimizing the Post-Apartheid State*, Cambridge, Cambridge University Press, 2001, p. 120.

29. Once the meeting was over, however, the atmosphere did become more festive and celebratory, as former neighbours drank tea and socialised, some reconnecting for the first time in years.

30. In fact, such concerns initially caused some women to hesitate to lodge a claim, since they believed that this might cause the displacement of those currently living in their former homes. In terms of the Restitution of Land Rights Act, however, the state will expropriate property only under extreme circumstances.

than achieving a form of closure that insists on the continued significance of the past in the present, becomes another way of closing off the past. The extent to which this happens will depend largely on the support given by the government to people once the land claims are resolved, particularly in cases where communities resettle in their former living areas. To date, the lack of post-settlement support, in terms of infrastructure and resources, to relocated communities constitutes one of the biggest challenges to the integrity of the restitution programme as a whole.[31] Besides the suffering and squandered resources that such lack of support causes, the symbolic message is that people's memories matter only insofar as they can be used to write off the very past they concern.[32]

It should also be noted that the lack of resources of the CRLR, and its concomitant administrative openness, have had very different consequences for different communities. The Kalk Bay group, like many other urban or semi-urban claimants, had various social and educational resources to draw on when engaging in the process. They were able to capitalise precisely on the openness of the programme, filling the restitution framework with their own interpretations and understandings. In contrast, under-resourced rural communities were often either excluded altogether from participating in the programme, due to a lack of awareness of it, or able to do so only through active intervention by NGOs. The involvement by such organisations would have had particular consequences for how memories were mobilised and mediated in the land claims.[33]

Conclusion

Cherryl Walker, a former staff member of the CRLR, has identified a "master narrative" informing restitution, which has become a founding myth of the

---

31. See Lund, F., *Lessons from Riemvasmaak – Vol 2: Background Study,* London and Cape Town, Farm Africa and PLAAS, 1998, and Hall, R., *Rural Restitution,* Cape Town, PLAAS, 2003.

32. The legacy of the TRC is shaped by a similar dilemma, not least since government so far has failed to follow the recommendations of the TRC to compensate victims materially.

33. James, D., "'After Years in the Wilderness': The Discourse of Land Claims in the New South Africa", *The Journal of Peasant Studies,* Vol. 27, pp. 142–161, 2000. James argues for example that the communalist and inclusivist rhetoric adopted by some land NGOs obscures sharply differentiated historical experiences within communities.

new democracy, and which is too simple.[34] It contains a number of problematic assumptions such as the notion of homogeneous "communities" of claimants, void of internal divisions or conflicts, or the idea that history can somehow be reversed, disregarding the developments that have taken place in the years since removal.[35] The simplicity of this narrative is characteristic of expressions of "official culture", which represent reality in ideal, abstract terms in order to minimise social contradictions and divisions while seeking legitimacy for official, nationalistic projects.[36]

Yet, as John Bodnar argues, public memory, as a system of beliefs and views, emerges from the intersection of such official, nationalistic projects and vernacular expressions of reality based on lived experience in small-scale communities.[37] Although the land claim forms submitted to the CRLR may mirror the official script, with short catchphrases designed to convey to bureaucrats the essence of the history of dispossession, these are merely one facet of claimants' engagement with restitution. We saw how in the course of preparing the Kalk Bay claim, people engaged in broad, multifaceted memory work that allowed for a variety of responses to the master narrative. For some, claiming restitution was foremost a political project, inspired by the TRC, and they organised their memories according to public narratives of nation-building that linked suffering, victimhood and the idea of "return" with the legitimacy of the new nation. Others rejected implicit assumptions in the restitution framework, such as primordialist notions of belonging, or the idea that they were "displaced". Still others used the restitution opportunity to denounce specific actions and policies of the former government

---

34. Walker, C., "Relocating Restitution", *Transformation*, Vol. 44, 2000, p. 2.

35. For a discussion of the problematic notion of 'community' in land reform, see for example James, D., "'After Years in the Wilderness': The Discourse of Land Claims in the New South Africa", *The Journal of Peasant Studies*, Vol. 27, pp. 142–161, 2000; Kepe, T., *The Problem of Defining 'Community:' Challenges for the Land Reform Programme in South Africa*, PLAAS, 1998; Mokgope, K., "Community and Diversity: The Complexity of Interests in Land Reform – A Case Study of Gallawater: A Farm in the Eastern Cape," in *At the Cross Roads: Land and Agrarian Reform in South Africa into the 21st Century*, edited by B. Cousins, Cape Town and Braamfontein, PLAAS and NLC, 2000.

36. Bodnar, J., "Public Memory in an American City: Commemoration in Cleveland," in *Commemorations: The Politics of National Identity*, edited by J. R. Gillis, Princeton, Princeton University Press, 1994, p. 75.

37. Ibid.

without embracing the non-racial "oneness" of the new nation as promoted by the current government.

Seen from a wider perspective of collective memory making in South Africa, land restitution certainly has an important role to play. The 60.000 land claim forms collected nation-wide, half of which have been settled to date, represent beneficiaries that number hundreds of thousands. Whether restitution takes the form of relocation or monetary compensation, which so far has been the option privileged by government, the present challenge is to combine such redress with ways of remembering that involve, utilise and reflect diverse and historically specific experiences of dispossession. By their very nature, the histories recorded in land claims are grounded in local, lived experience, and, by their nature, refer to events that mostly took place in what today are white spaces. This spatial and "embodied" dimension of land claim histories should not be lost, since it carries great potential for bringing into public consciousness the way apartheid affected, and continues to affect, everyday life for vast numbers of South Africans.

CHAPTER 6

Reflections on practising applied history in South Africa, 1994–2002:

From skeletons to schools

Martin Legassick

Since about 1997, I have been dragged into what might be called "applied history" in South Africa. This has involved working for the Commission of Restitution of Land Rights (1999–2001), and on projects sponsored by the Department of Education's South African History Project (2001-). It has involved doing work as an 'expert witness' in a case brought by before the Land Court (1999-). It has involved a National Research Foundation financed project to study the post-apartheid transformation of the McGregor Museum in Kimberley, which subsequently informed decision-making of the Department of Arts and Culture (1998–1999). It has involved participation in a project, conducted by the South African Democracy Education Trust, to research the struggle for democracy between 1960 and 1994 (2001-).

All these developments started essentially by accident. In late 1992, I started researching the history of Upington on the Orange River in the northern Cape and paid my first field trip there in July 1993. The town I had first heard of in exile as the home of the Upington 26, people sentenced to death for "common purpose" in being part of a crowd involved in killing a black policeman in the local township, Paballello in 1985. When I was back in Cape Town, I met in Khayelitsha a person from Upington and first visited it in taking him home. I became fascinated with this town in fertile irrigated land surrounded by semi-desert and later discovered how its origins as a Baster settlement tied in with my earlier interest in the Griqua. However, my decision to investigate the local history of the area represented a conscious decision to move away from the contentious historiography of the main centres of our country, Johannesburg and Cape Town. I had been out of academia for ten years and felt that historiography had moved on from the debates of the 1970s and 1980s and wanted to reorient myself. Little did I know then what this would involve me in…

I began studying the history of Upington as an observer (though I was politically involved, there was little connection). But, from that, I was led to the use of history in resolving land claims, and became connected to those with such claims. "Applied history" for me, involves some direct connection with society outside the university, whether through claimants, public attenders of museums, recording oral history of political activists, educators and learners in schools, etc.

The September family

The second piece I wrote on the history of Upington concerned one Abraham September, a Baster who in the 1880s was the first to lead water out of the Orange River and undertake irrigation in Upington. After his death, the land he owned was taken from him by whites, illegitimately in the eyes of his descendants.[1] I had been concerned with land alienation from Basters to whites round the turn of the twentieth century. I was working with the Rev Aubrey Beukes of the DRC mission church in Gordonia and we accidentally ran into Gert September, a descendant of Abraham, while looking for someone else! We interviewed him and that evening I suddenly connected him with a document I had read in the archives concerning Abraham. Thus, the article came about.

As a result of this article, by the way, the history of Upington has been revised, and Abraham September is now figured in brochures on the area. Moreover, on 27 April 1997, Freedom Day, President Mandela spoke in Upington and dedicated a plaque reading:

> In commemoration of Abraham September, an ex-slave, who in 1882 was granted a farm along the Orange River and was the first person to discover the advantage of irrigating this land with water from the river. This led to the economic development of Gordonia but resulted in the eventual dispossession of the land belonging to him and his community by the colonial authorities.[2]

---

1. Published as "The will of Abraham and Elizabeth September: The struggle for land in Gordonia, 1898–1996", *Journal of African History*, Vol. 37, 1996, pp. 371–418. The first paper I wrote was a transcript of a taped interview, with introduction and notes, with Alfred Gubula, president of the UDF in the Northern Cape in the late 1980s and related to several of the Upington 26.

2. When I first presented this paper, at Basel in Switzerland, Professor Andre du Toit of UCT was in the audience, a descendant of J. Lutz, who engineered the expansion of the irrigation of the Orange River from the 1880s until at least the 1920s, and was

The September family was in fact only one of a number of families who regarded their land as having been taken illegitimately from them by whites. Several of these imagined that my research was then concerned with land restitution, but I insisted then that it was purely academic recovery of the past. My paper, however, overlapped with investigation of the September family's case by lawyers in Namibia. With the establishment of the Land Commission, the September family made their claim to it. It became the subject of a decision by the Land Claims Court, who denied their claim, although an appeal is being lodged against this.[3] The Land Commission initially supported the September family. However, with the merger of the Land Commission into the Land Affairs Department, it was instructed to withdraw its support from the family's claim. Ironically, the lawyer in this case for the (ANC government's) Land Affairs Department is a former NP member! (The position of the Land Affairs Department may not be unconnected with the fact that the value of the farm Uap – now some 14 well-irrigated river farms – may run into tens of millions of rand – and restitution to the September family would have to be paid by government.) Since 1999, I have been consulted by lawyers in the case, and in the appeal, I am supposed to appear as an "expert witness".

The Keidebees and Blikkies

Many of the Upington families who claimed illegitimate dispossession in the late nineteenth and early twentieth century had also later been evicted by the apartheid government from Keidebees in the 1960s. Keidebees was a classic coloured-African "location" whose origins went back to the late nineteenth century. Its coloured inhabitants were evicted to the existing location of Blikkies and its African inhabitants to the new township of Paballello. In September 1998, with Mike Abrahams of the UWC history department, I went to Upington to start to investigate the Keidebees removals. The area that once was Keidebees, like District Six, had been bulldozed but not rebuilt. We interviewed one person who took us to show us the ruins of his former

---

honoured for it. Du Toit asked about the historiographical relationship between Lutz and September.

3. David Daniel Jacobs and the Department of Land Affairs, re the Farm Uap28A and Erf 38 Upington, today known as part of erf13790, Upington: decisions of 28 February 2002 in the Land Claims Court of South Africa [Cases No LCC 3/98 and LCC 120/99].

house. It was a very moving experience, particularly for the Rev Aubrey Beukes, who we had been staying with, and who had lived for nearly twenty years in Upington without knowing that that piece of land was Keidebees. A committee existed of claimants from Keidebees and from Blikkies (from which Africans had been evicted to Paballello). The committee approached the Land Commission and asked for me to be the person to investigate and verify their claims. So once again, it was almost accidental that I started work for the Land Commission.

That investigation I undertook with enthusiasm. I personally went through the records of the Upington municipality from its inception in 1889 up to the 1960s. I went through the archives in Pretoria. I emerged with a fairly thorough picture of the racial shaping of the town of Upington over a century. What was interesting to me about this was (a) that the proposals for racial reshaping took place not under the post-1948 NP government but under the 1940s UP government (b) that under the NP government the main instrument was the 1945 Urban Areas Act, in particular the provisions – going back to 1923 but now more easily enforceable – that residence outside a declared location was forbidden (c) the way that action under this instrument intersected, but problematically, with the declaration of Group Areas.

There were 484 claimants from Keidebees (of whom 88 could not be traced) and 101 from Blikkies. They were all tenants of the municipality, not landowners. The Commission had very little experience with such claims. Indeed when I started there it was not settled that tenants were entitled to claim under the Restitution Act. Mike Abrahams was the principal research assistant and interviewed the claimants in Upington. I had managed to get from the archives lists of the occupants of Keidebees compiled at certain dates, 1946, and partial lists for the 1950s and 1962. We got aerial photographs of Keidebees from the mapping office in Mowbray. We had people in the Geography Department at UWC translate the photograph into a map of the site, with each dwelling marked with a dot. We had claimants try to identify the shack they lived in from the drawing as well as that of their neighbours. In this way, by a sort of triangulation method, we were able to piece together a picture of the community, of house numbers, who lived in them, and where they were situated. It was not perfect by any means. But because very few people had any documentary evidence of their stay in Keidebees, it was a means of verification of who had lived in Keidebees. It was also possible to work out from archival material when the removals began and when they ended, and to check this against the dates of individual files. A fully researched verification was possible, in which I felt confident.[4]

As a result of the success of this verification work, I was asked by Alan Roberts, Western Cape Land Commissioner, to undertake similar research on District Six in 2000. I was reluctant, but agreed in the end.

My regret about the Keidebees work – and, even more, the two Land Commission projects, which followed it – was an inability to link the history contained in the interviews with the history obtained from the archives. To have achieved such a linkage would really have been to write a transformed urban history.

The McGregor Museum

During 1997 I was approached by Vida Allen of the McGregor Museum asking me, as someone who had written on the Griqua,[5] to comment on a new exhibition on "Frontiers" that they were planning for the museum. Since UWC history department had developed in the 1990s a specialisation in public history I responded to this by not merely sending comments, but by initiating an investigation of the post-apartheid transformation of the museum together with other department members (and with the co-curator of the new exhibition, David Morris of the McGregor Museum) to investigate the post-apartheid transformation of the museum. Again, then, an "accident" led me into this project.

While concerned that the transformation should be of content – from white history plus static black "culture" to a dynamic history of all in the society – we were also concerned with form: with how museums should represent history. We raised the question of open-ended presentations, presentation of different senses of time and of causation, of non-expert conceptions of the past etc.

Through workshops, visits to the museum, and the work of researchers (again Mike Abrahams was centrally involved in this) we produced a number

---

4. M. Legassick and M. Abraham, "Keidebees/Blikkies locations: Research on community claim", Parts I, II and III, UWC, 2000.

5. See M. Legassick, "The Griqua, the Sotho-Tswana and the missionaries, 1780-1840: The politics of a frontier zone", PhD, UCLA, 1969; "The northern frontier to c. 1840: The rise and decline of the Griqua people", in *The Shaping of South African Society*, 1652–1840, (eds) R. Elphick and H. Giliomee, Longman, Cape Town, 1988.

of papers.[6] These centred on a critique of the overall content of the museum (including some of its outposts, such as the South African War battlefield of Magersfontein). My own paper dealt with the origins of the museum in diamond-dominated colonial Kimberley. Mike Abrahams' paper concentrated on issues to do with the staffing of the museum. He highlighted the domination of personnel and attitudes from the "old order", the failure to empower or promote long-time black staff, the fear of staff to express their opinions, and the stress under which many seemed to be working. Undoubtedly, his work at the museum had effects, because the subsequent period saw the resignation of the director and the appointment of a new director, and the promotion of several black staff members. The result has been a polarisation of staff over the research project, with some welcoming it and others hating it.[7]

Again, through essentially an accident, Ciraj Rassool and I stumbled on the most significant aspect of the museum research – the involvement of the first director, Maria Willman, in an embryonic trade in the dug-up skeletons of recently-buried San persons. This took place around the turn of the twentieth century, and the skeletons were collected by museums for the purposes of racial research. In going through the correspondence of Louis Peringuey, director of the South African Museum where Willman had worked previously, I came across letters in which someone named Pöch was mentioned. Ciraj knew him as an Austrian physical anthropologist and proto-Nazi racial researcher. I followed up his name on the computerised catalogue at the South African archives and we thus unearthed the material for our book *Skeletons in the Cupboard: South African museums and the trade in human remains,*

---

6. M. Legassick, "The social and intellectual milieu at the founding of the McGregor Museum in 1907", Unpublished, 1999; C. Rassool, L. Witz and G. Minkley, "The Castle, the Gallery, and the sanitorium: Curating a South African nation in the museum", Unpublished, 1999; C. Rassool, L. Witz and G. Minkley, "Who speaks for South African pasts?", SAHS conference, 11–14 July 1999; L. Witz, C. Rassool and G. Minkley, "No end of a history lesson: Preparations for the Anglo-Boer War centenary commemoration", *South African Historical Journal*, Vol. 41, 1999, South African war 1899–1902: Centennial perspectives, pp. 370–387; L. Witz, C. Rassool, and G. Minkley, "The Boer War, Museums, and Ratanga Junction, the Wildest Place in South Africa in the 1990s", Basler Afrika Bibliographen, Working Paper, No. 2, 2000, presented in Basel 10 February 2000; M.J. Abrahams, "Another Frontier? – impressions of post-apartheid transformations of historical representation at the McGregor Museum, Kimberley", Unpublished, 1999.

7. One of these has subsequently been trained at UWC and in the US under the auspices of UWC.

1907–1917.[8] We have argued for the mass reburial of the human remains violated in this way.

When we gave our paper at the South African Historical Society conference in July 1999, it attracted quite a lot of press attention.[9] Subsequently, to their credit, when we approached them, the SA Museum (now Iziko) and McGregor Museum agreed to publish our findings in a book, together with comments by archaeologists, physical anthropologists, and someone from Australia involved in restitution, and a reply from ourselves. In addition, the McGregor Museum organized a launch of our book together with a two-day workshop on the question of display of human remains in museums, 10–12 September 2001. At this workshop a resolution was taken, supported in particular by representatives of the National Khoisan Consultative Conference who were present, supporting the idea of repatriation of human remains. The issue attracted attention once again when the remains of Sarah Baartman were returned from France to South Africa. This included an editorial in the Sunday Times supporting repatriation: "It is not acceptable that, eight years into our democracy, our museums still hoard the remains of human beings."[10] I spoke at a public meeting on the subject in the South African Museum on 18 May 2002. The South African Museum had dragged its feet in responding practically to the findings of our book. However, at this meeting the director promised to hold a workshop within three months with representatives of Khoisan people to implement action. The director has now left the museum but it is to be hoped that the director who replaces him will pursue the matter.

8. Martin Legassick and Ciraj Rasool, 2000, *Skeletons in the Cupboard: South African Museums and the Trade in Human Remains, 1907-1917*, South African Museum and McGregor Museum: Cape Town

9. Ciraj Rassool was interviewed on SATV News on 14/7/1999 and Martin Legassick did several radio interviews on the subject of human remains. See also Yazeed Kameldien, "Skeletons in their cupboards: Museum morality questioned", *Cape Times*, 15/7/1999; Trevor Oosterwyk, "Body-snatchers leave museums with appalling legacy", *Sunday Independent*, 18/7/1999; Sven Ousman "Museums seeking ways to deal with their demons", *Sunday Independent*, 1/8/1999; M. Legassick and C. Rassool, "Gobbledygook obscures reality of grave-robbing", *Sunday Independent*, 8/8/1999; Leon Jacobson, "Dignity of the dead takes precedence over science", *Sunday Independent*, 15/8/1999.

10. "Royal city welcome for Saartjie", *Cape Argus*, 4/5/2002; "Khoi bodies litter SA's museums", *Sunday Times*, 5/5/2002; "More skeletons in our closets", *Sunday Times*, 5/5/2002.

District Six

In November 2000, a moving ceremony took place just near the Moravian Church that housed the District Six museum for a while. It was the formal handing back of the land in District Six to its occupants, forcibly removed by the apartheid regime mainly in the 1970s. President Thabo Mbeki, spoke, as did the ebullient then Minister of Land, Thoko Didiza, Wallace Mgoqi, Chief Commissioner of the Commission on Restitution of Land Rights, and Anwar Nagia – whose persistence in leading the struggle of District Six residents made him, more than anyone else, responsible for the event. It was attended by hundreds of former residents and their families. (This meeting was held shortly before local elections in Cape Town.) The restitution process for District Six had been stalled for some time. It was in fact research conducted by a team at UWC, directed by myself, which broke the logjam and enabled the ceremony to take place.

When I was asked to undertake this research, several people for whom I have a high regard argued that I should not take on the job because of the politics involved, which had already held up the restitution process. However, I agreed to do it, after the agreement of the Trust headed by Anwar Nagia had been obtained. I took on twelve researchers, and two people to supervise them. There then existed a District Six Claims Unit, under the auspices of the Land Commission. It had been initiated by Rhoda Kadalie but she had resigned. At the time, I took on the work the Unit had, I think, verified something like 40 owners' claims in a period of some two years. I was asked to research the claims of the tenants who numbered in the thousands – and was originally asked to complete the work in 3 months! I asked for six months, and eventually took eight. We conducted some 1,427 interviews, being unable to locate 224 claimants, and verified 672 claims. Most of the rest were outstanding because they did not submit the documents that they needed to.[11]

In the case of Keidebees and Blikkies, the claimants had lived basically in two areas, the coloured area of Upington, and Paballello. In the case of District Six, they were scattered all over the Cape Flats. The biggest concentration was in Lentegeur in Mitchells Plain, 200 of them. There were another 200 in the rest of Mitchells Plain, some 350 in the wider Athlone area (including Bonteheuwel and Langa), some 200 in Gugulethu, some 200 in

---

11. My first surprise, before the research even started, was to find that the list of claimants was held by the District Six Land Claims Unit in a data base that could not be electronically transferred to any other computer!

the Woodstock-Cape Town area, some 200 in Hanover Park, 100 in Grassy Park.

We organised centres for interviews, and hand-delivered letters to the claimants asking them to come for interview (this was arduous work).[12] After the interviews, we had to visit claimants again, usually more than once, to attempt to get relevant documentation from them.

I tried in relevant archives to get lists of tenant occupants of District Six properties before the evictions, and succeeded in getting only one, covering some streets. I typed this into my computer, and attempted to get correlations with the claimants. There was very little correlation. Claimants were also asked for their neighbours. But because of the political pressures to complete the work for a settlement, a similar exercise to what had been done in Upington was never performed. The claims were verified in eight months and in the majority of cases, claimants were able to provide some documentary evidence of the residence of the dispossessed in District Six.[13]

Although this research was completed in August 2000, and despite the "handing over" ceremony in November that year, as of mid-2003 not a single tenant had moved back to District Six, nor had any houses been built though they were reported to be "in the pipeline".

Western Cape African tenants

Shortly after the District Six research was completed, Alan Roberts again asked me to undertake research on African tenants who had been dispossessed in the Western Cape. Once again I was extremely reluctant. "Applied history" of this kind was beginning to get me down. On the District Six research, I had spent a considerable part of the year driving around the Cape Flats rather than really doing research.

My worries were initially confirmed when, despite repeated requests, no list of claimants could be provided to me before the research began. In the

---

12. This we decided to do after a preliminary attempt to rely on the Land Commission's postal service. We left letters for delivery on the relevant person's desk more than a week beforehand, and returned on the day on which we were to be at the interview site to discover the letters still on the person's desk. The person had gone on leave. We were to discover that persons at the Land Commission spent a considerable period of time on leave or at workshops.

13. M. Legassick, "District Six tenants' claims verification research", UWC, August 2000.

District Six case having the list had enabled planning of the way the interviews would take place. An initial interim list was provided only on 20th January – with 1097 names on it though the Commission had earlier told me that there were up to 3000 claimants.

When the project was first discussed with me it was portrayed as wholly concerned with removals in the Cape metropolitan area, and I was told that most of the claimants lived in Gugulethu. When I studied the initial list, however, I found, to my utter surprise, hundreds of names in Worcester as well as in Grabouw, Robertson, Ceres, Montagu, etc. The consequences were (a) the need to organise travel which had not been budgeted for (b) six times more archival research than had been planned for and (c) time and money potentially taken up in returning to distant areas to clarify or correct information provided by claimants.

I read and summarised an extensive academic literature on the removals from the 1940s squatter camps around Cape Town into Gugulethu and Nyanga – though I was wrongly told by the Land Commission's lawyer that this work was quite unnecessary! I also began archival work on the municipalities of Worcester etc, in none of which to my knowledge has the implementation of NP policy towards blacks been researched before.

In the end, the Land Commission was incapable of producing a final list of claimants. The list was finalised on the basis of data supplied by the Commission up to more than six months after the research began – and the bulk of the work on this was done by our own project manager. In the end, we had a list of 1928 claimants. In addition, each claimant should have had a file in the archives of the Commission. We found that 45% of the files of claimants interviewed could not be found. That is, since these people had made claims, for which the latest date was 31 December 1998, the Commission had mislaid nearly half of their files.

This made planning the research very difficult. We had to return to the same venues more than once, as new names were added to the list. This was not efficient. The fact that at the start of the research some claimants were on the list and other potential claimants, who knew where the venue was, were not on the list also caused immense problems for the researchers and for the project manager as those not on the list pestered to be interviewed. Secondly, compiling the list preoccupied the project manager until August, leaving her no time whatever to think ahead about problems like organising the capturing of the results of the interviews on the computer, collecting outstanding documents, etc.

Some five months into this research, I was summoned to a meeting with the Commission at which it was mentioned that there were problems with the work I had done on District Six! This was seven months after the District Six handing over ceremony! My report had been submitted at the end of August 2000, but the Commission did not request the files on individuals until January 2001! I do not believe that they studied the detailed tables in my report even then, and I believe that they muddled up piles of verified with piles of unverified files. Eventually I got hold of a critical report on the District Six work, which contained many false allegations. For example, we were told we had submitted a two-page report when it was 13 pages with 12 detailed tables totalling hundreds of pages! We were criticised for not undertaking Deeds Office research when we had been told at the start of the research that this was irrelevant for tenants! Other equally muddled claims were made which indicated that our report had not been read and understood.

The African tenants project was immeasurably more complicated than the Upington or District Six research. Instead of one, or two, areas from which people had been forcibly removed there were multiple areas. The main ones were: Windermere, Retreat, Athlone, Northern suburbs, Elsies River, Cooks Bush, Modderdam, Unibel, Werkgenoot, and the city centre in Cape Town. There were also Grabouw, Worcester, Ceres, Robertson, Montagu and a number of smaller areas. Moreover, as was the case with Upington, on the whole claimants were unable to provide documentary evidence of the residence of the dispossessed in an area. In many of these areas, in fact, there were no street addresses. Some claimants were able to say little more than that the dispossessed had lived "in the bushes". For proof of residence, one was therefore reduced to the provision of affidavits by two co-residents of the area (not relatives of the claimant). These were usually certified by police, who were often not at all familiar with what is involved. Thus whether the affidavits were reliable evidence was questionable. Ideally I would have wanted to have built up a Keidebees-like picture of each area – on the basis of aerial photographs and the questions asked regarding neighbours. In the absence of official documentation, the fall-back for verification I had used in Upington was collective methodology. But this was precluded by the demand of the Commission to have delivered to them individual files prior to the completion of the research process. Handing in individual files as "verified" on a month by month basis would preclude the "triangulated" cross-checking of each file against others and against the written documentation at the end of the research.

Let me give an example of lack of full research, which was implicit in the Commission's demand for immediate delivery of verified individual files. There was one person who had submitted five separate claims. For only one of these were all the documents available in the middle of the research. This claim could have been handed to the Commission as "verified". I did not want to do this without looking at all the claims together once the documents were in for them. Yet by the Commission's method, the person might already be paid on one claim without checking it against the other claims.[14]

The dispute over this led to delays in the Commission paying the project, which in my view constituted a breach of contract. Eventually the UWC lawyers had to be called in, and in the end, I terminated the project four months before its planned conclusion.[15]

Progressively from the Upington, through the District Six, to the African Tenants Project I had become sucked into the administrative as opposed to the academic side of the research. My mind felt drained of energy. I referred to production of sausages as in a sausage factory. My efforts to repeat Keidebees, to get some stimulation, were constantly rebuffed.

Memorialisation of forced removals

Before this falling out with the Land Commission, Alan Roberts and I had had discussions about the memorialisation of forced removals. He had undertaken to try and raise money for a project of this kind, which I drew up a proposal for. I argued that together with individual compensation (restitution) there needed to be some form of preservation of the memory of forced removals, to remind this and future generations of the oppressive experience, and to make sure that such actions never happened again. Such memorialisa-

---

14. M. Legassick and B. Bennett, "Western Cape African tenants' land restitution claims verification report" Parts I, II, III, UWC, December 2001.

15. There were additional problems. Discontinuity in management – the person in the Commission responsible for the project – meant that the criteria laid down to the project varied all the time, without real opportunity for discussion of these problems. In addition there was other obstruction of the work of the project, creating a situation and an atmosphere in which doing the research became an unwelcome chore rather than a pleasant task. Adversarial relations were created where previously there had been cooperation. I believe that it reflected disputes within the Land Commission Cape Town office over whether or not it was desirable to out-source work to academic institutions. So the 'accident' that I started to work for the Land Commission ended not too happily.

tion would assist in the retention of memory locally, and spread the experience to a wider national and international audience. Properly marketed, it could also be a stimulus to tourism.

The District Six Museum has pioneered a form of ongoing memorialisation with continued community input and participation. One of the ideas I had had regarding museums in the Northern Cape was the establishment at sites of interest – such as the still-surviving house of Abraham September on the farm Uap – of community-run mini-museums, which would also be centres for the collection of oral tradition. I had discussed this with the Minister of Education and Culture in the Northern Cape, Tina Jumat, an ex-UWC student – but she subsequently became confined to Education and dropped Culture. These plans were not pursued. Now they emerged in another form.

In District Six there had been a proposal, initiated from among the ex-residents, for the establishment of a park as a form of memorialisation. But District Six was only one of countless sites in the Western and Northern Cape and nationwide where forced removals took place. What needed investigation and discussion with the relevant communities was an appropriate and accountable form of memorialisation in each case of forced removals, uniquely appropriate to the particular place. It could take at least three forms (a) some form of spatial memorialisation (b) production of accessible written material for schools and for the wider public (c) production of audiovisual material such as tapes and films.

Spatial memorialisation would require teams of persons with heritage experience and knowledge of the removals in a particular area to visit areas of forced removal and restitution to discuss with the communities the appropriate forms. The teams would then produce plans and possibly, together with the community concerned, work out how to raise funds to implement the chosen project. Audiovisual material could include tapes of interviews with formerly dispossessed people about their experiences prior to dispossession, the act of dispossession, their experiences after dispossession and their experience of restitution.[16]

While doing the African tenants project I became particularly interested in Grabouw. Following 1963 people were forcibly removed here, some to Pineview in another part of Grabouw, and others to resettlement camps in the Eastern Cape such as Dimbaza. Most of these had been born in the Western Cape and though "black" and Xhosa-speaking they were regarded

16. M. Legassick, "Memorialising forced removals in the Western and Northern Cape: A proposal", 2001.

as foreigners in the Eastern Cape. Conditions in Dimbaza were terrible: at one time, 10–15 children were dying a day of malnutrition. The people were removed from areas including Newtown (a shack settlement) and Klipkop (a private location with stone houses). One such person removed to Dimbaza was Elizabeth Mentile. She returned to the Western Cape in 1983/4, initially living in Somerset West, and getting a job in Grabouw in 1987. In 1989, she led the re-establishment of a shack settlement in Grabouw. She is at present a councillor. Many of her friends in Grabouw were also removed to Dimbaza and have now returned. She was keen that the film Last Grave at Dimbaza should be screened in Grabouw, since very few residents had seen it. I also suggested to her the erection of some sort of monument in Grabouw to people removed from it who died in Dimbaza. A small museum display would serve a similar purpose. I also proposed the making of a documentary whose centrepoint would be the screening in Grabouw of Last Grave at Dimbaza and the reactions to this of residents, both those who lived in Dimbaza and those who did not.[17]

Neither of these projects – though they have a more academic content than the verification work – has come to fruition.

Curriculum 2005 and the teaching and writing of history

Many historians were unhappy with the way that the new curriculum proposals introduced under Bengu's tenure as Minister of Education affected the teaching of history. In particular, we were concerned that history was collapsed together with geography and civics up to Grade 10 (the previous standard 8). In addition, no attention was being paid to the revision of its content, as outcomes based education – the new idea – was concerned much more with method than with content.

When Arnold Temu became President of the South African Historical Society in 1997, he asked me to convene a panel to examine the teaching of history under Curriculum 2005. I did so, with people on it as diverse as Eddie Moloka (then of UCT) and Peter Kapp (an old NP stalwart at the University of Stellenbosch). In addition to them there were Uma Mesthrie and Peter Kallaway of UWC. We produced a statement, which in the end everyone except

---

17. M. Legassick, "Notes on a video documentary on forced removals from Grabouw", July 2000.

Peter Kapp agreed with. It was for some reason never published in the SAHJ but appeared in Kleio.[18]

South African Democracy Education Trust

At the University of California in Los Angeles in 1964, Ben Magubane was a fellow graduate student and we worked on anti-apartheid activity together. Ben became a professor at the University of Connecticut and retired back to South Africa in the mid-1990s. He was asked to direct the South African Democracy Education Trust, a presidential project to research the struggle for democracy between 1960 and 1994 and when he took up the offer asked me to be involved. Another "accident."

There are various consortia involved in SADET, in Pretoria, at Wits, in Natal, at Fort Hare, etc. I am coordinating the project in the Western Cape with a committee, which has at various times included Chris Saunders, Jeremy Seekings, Sipho Maseko (before his untimely and tragic death), Sean Field, Mohammed Adhikari, Uma Mesthrie, Harriet Deacon, Noel Solani, Barry Feinberg and Lungisile Ntsebeza. Currently there are a project manager/researcher and two other researchers.

In 2001, we concentrated mainly on the twenty-fifth anniversary of the "Soweto" uprising, and did research on what happened in the schools in the Western Cape. A number of interviews were done with activists and journalists of the time. This resulted in the production of an exhibition of some 11 panels, which was launched at a public meeting in Gugulethu on 11 August, the anniversary of the date of student marches in Langa and Gugulethu.

In 2002, we concentrated on research on the 1960s, doing dozens of interviews with activists of the time, together with research on trial records, etc. This was for a book on the 1960s produced nationally by SADET. It will be followed by books on the 1970s and 1980s, and volumes of interviews. There is a certain tension as to the extent to which the books will represent "history from above", of leaders, or "history from below" with the stories of ordinary activists.

The supervising board of SADET consists of representatives of the donors, MTN and Nedbank, together with the Minister for National Intelligence, Lindiwe Sisulu, the Minister in the President's Office, Essop Pahad, and military generals. It is rather a curious board to be supervising an aca-

---

18. "Statement by the South African Historical Society on the implications of Curriculum 2005 for history teaching in schools."

demic project. In particular Essop Pahad, while he has a doctorate in history from the University of Sussex, also spent many years in Prague on the staff of the Stalinist World Marxist Review. As yet however there have been no prescriptions from the board on the content of our productions.

A big problem has been our access to archives – in particular the security (military, police, intelligence) archives of the apartheid regime. The Truth and Reconciliation Commission had severe limits placed on its access to these archives and despite appeals to the board of SADET, we are at present faced with the same problem. Ben Magubane has however recently been appointed to head a committee to establish criteria for declassification of state documents.

A particular project that we in the Western Cape have been involved in since late last year is with Khumbula ("memory"), a community project in Worcester. Here we are involved in collecting material towards a local history of resistance in Worcester – a very well organized town with a mass of ANC followers even in the 1930s, and strong trade unions in the 1950s. Together with this we are developing the skills of local people in collecting oral history, and in general leadership.

South African History Project

The South African History Project arose out of the report of a panel on history and archaeology teaching in schools commissioned by the Minister of Education at that time, Kadar Asmal, in September 2000. The panel was chaired by Njubalo Ndebele, Vice-Chancellor of UCT, and consisted predominantly of university historians, though it also included M.P. Pallo Jordan. June Bam, a prominent history education theorist and a critic of the existing situation, and I were invited to give evidence to the panel.[19] Again, my "accidental" involvement in the SAHS panel earlier led to this. We subsequently did an initial draft of the panel's report, which appeared finally in November.[20]

The report started by identifying the values and value of historical learning, and also identified serious problems in teaching history in the schools. Innovative practices were less prevalent than rote learning. History was discredited and no longer seen as a core learning subject. There were serious

19. We had both recently attended a conference in Denmark on history teaching in the schools.

20. Report of the History Archaeology Panel to the Minister of Education, 14 December 2000.

problems with the curriculum. Teacher training presented a real problem, with seriously incapacitated teachers. The report recommended strengthening the substance and scope of the curriculum, strengthening teacher training, and producing new materials. It also recommended the establishment of a National History Commission to monitor the process of transformation.

The Minister's initiative showed his responsiveness to the criticism of Curriculum 2005 for not paying adequate attention to history. His response to the report has been to establish a Ministerial Committee composed largely of university historians, and to establish the South African History Project with June Bam as CEO.

Initially for SADET we decided in the Western Cape in November 2001 to hold a workshop on the practice of oral history, conducted by Sean Field of the Centre for Popular Memory at UCT. It was attended both by teachers and people from Khumbula. The SAHP jointly sponsored it, and has since sponsored three follow-up workshops during 2002. In the course of these more than 100 teachers and community activists have been given initial, and some more advanced, training in conducting interviews. The enthusiasm and commitment of the teachers – attending these workshops for a full Saturday – is very encouraging. Indeed, I have found it one of the most rewarding teaching experiences of my life. The main content of the workshops is practice sessions with interviewer and interviewee, with feedback from both and from the audience. This invariably produces creative and entertaining outcomes.

In the late 1980s, the UWC History Department was involved in a "mass" People's History Project, in a period when the first-year enrolment in history was some 2000. This attempt at capturing oral history had its strengths but also its weaknesses, and the lessons from it have informed the direction taken by many researchers at UWC. Some staff became quite disillusioned then with schoolteachers I think. Now the wheel has turned full circle, and once again UWC is involved with work in the schools.

What the history and archaeology panel described as the value and values of history is fairly much what I also think: its encouragement of civic responsibility and critical thinking, its training in the ability to contextualise and discriminate in judgement, its importance in the construction of identity, its interrogation of truth, relativity, and memory, its ability to present formerly subjugated and marginalized voices, its exploration of pathways of economic growth, its promotion of democratic values, its utility in the task of desegregating society.[21] In addition, it noted, the study of history is a sound vocational preparation for a wide range of jobs and careers.

Conclusion

What broader reflections do I have on these experiences? All of them have taken me out of the "ivory tower" of academia into the real world of people. Sometimes it has been into communities of "claimants", people with a specific and instrumental interest in history. At other times, it has been with history educators in schools, battling to interest and enthuse their learners (and indeed themselves) with the subject of history. At other times it has been with heritage workers in museums (McGregor, in Kimberley), or with aspirant heritage workers in the community (Khumbula in Worcester). At other times, it has been with political activists. I have become a private advocate (the September case) or a public advocate (human remains in museums).

In the Northern Cape, a schoolteacher called Jesse Strauss did research on a battle during the Anglo-Boer war, in which a force of the Northern Border Scouts, Baster men commanded by British officers, ambushed and inflicted serious casualties on a Boer commando. He told me how when he interviewed people, they all wept in telling the story, it was such a "geheim" (secret).[22] Most of the projects I have been engaged on have also involved collecting oral history. This is an emotional experience, as we have also discovered in SADET, or in interviewing for the Land Commission. Many people are still incapable of revealing what they did as underground activists, with the "need to know" syndrome still firmly with them. Others experienced the trauma of forced removals or of detention and torture. In "applied history" one cannot escape the emotions that people attach to their experiences of the past.

Many of these applied history projects that I have undertaken have involved a search for a (legal) "truth". Whether someone, or someone's ancestor, was dispossessed. Post-modernism has made this kind of quest unfashionable, yet "truth" is central to the conception of history in the public and popular mind. Practitioners of oral history know that memory is an unreliable source

---

21. See M. Legassick and G Minkley, "Current trends in the production of South African history", *Alternation: International Journal for the Study of Southern African Literature and Languages*, Vol. 5, No. 1, 1998.

22. See Jesse Strauss "Naroegas" and M. Legassick, "The battle of Naroegas: Context, significance, sources and historiography", *Kronos*, 21, November 1994.

of "truth" in this literal sense, but that through oral history, deeper truths are revealed.[23] There is therefore a constant tension in the practice of oral applied history between discovery of truth and discovery of representation.

In one way or another, applied history has seemed to involve relations with government. It is subject to all the usual tensions that apply in the relations between governments and academics. Governments want results (and sometimes results of their choosing). I pulled out of the Land Commission when the historical quest had finally been reduced to the mere findings of questionnaires. Academics tend to be more concerned with the journey of discovery itself.

---

23. See for example Alessandro Portelli, "The death of Luigi Trastuli: Memory and the event", in *The death of Luigi Trastuli and other stories: Form and meaning in oral history*, Albany, State University of New York, 1991.

CHAPTER 7

From apartheid to democracy in South Africa:
A reading of dominant discourses of democratic transition

Thiven Reddy

Discourses of democratic transition and consolidation orient how we interpret, talk about, consider thinkable, and debate the "miracle" of change in South Africa. These discourses – academic, state, and popular – variously interact to produce and reinforce a dominant narrative of democratic change. This chapter provides a reading of this dominant discourse. It shifts our attention away from the, "what happened in South Africa", or the equally familiar question, "what constitutes the best explanation of change" to provide yet another answer, towards the representation of change in discourses of democratic transition.

Three elements compose this dominant discourse structuring the way we view the change in South Africa. These are transitology or Third Wave perspectives, state crisis explanations, and configurative, event-history perspectives.

The first strand organises the conceptual framework of dominant discourse by providing the key categories of regime breakdown, transition, and consolidation. The second focuses specifically on those factors explaining the crisis of the Apartheid regime corresponding to the "regime breakdown" stage of transitology. The third involves the stringing together of "historic" moments into a coherent narrative corresponding to the "transition stage" in the transitology framework.

South Africa and discourses of democratic change

Discourses on democratic transition (transitology) attach a certain importance to the South African case. The South African transition resembles closely the

preferred model of change in transitology – transition by transplacement.[1]
This model values the relatively peaceful overthrow of the authoritarian regime, the leading role of regime and democratic opposition moderates in the
transition process, and the resulting political order where the constitution
protects individual civil rights in a capitalist social formation. Post-Apartheid
South Africa, defined by Tutu in 1999 as the "rainbow nation" society, holds
out the hope that it might succeed in creating a multicultural society. Lastly,
South Africa occupies a somewhat "special" place in dominant discourses
because it is often viewed as different to the rest of the continent.[2] In mainstream representations, the category "Africa" has often functioned as the signifier of a complex of negatives: underdeveloped, corrupt, violent, child-like,
traditional, place where primordial attachments reign etc. South Africa, by
contrast, is presented as a country that might deviate from continental patterns of post-colonial political development.

It is difficult to classify the voluminous studies relevant to democratic
regime change in South Africa. Mainstream approaches do however share a
positivist-empirical approach, valuing objectivist social science. These generally ignore the relationship of power and knowledge, and how discourses
constitute their objects of analysis.[3]

To make intelligible for our purposes this vast body of work, we could
distinguish three broadly defined perspectives: the literature examining the
global Third Wave of democratic transition,[4] an older body of work which
focuses on the comparative study of regime change and revolution,[5] and the

1. Giliomee, H., "Democratization in South Africa", *Political Science Quarterly*, Vol. 110,
   pp. 83–104, 1995; Guelke, A., *South Africa in Transition: The Misunderstood Miracle*,
   London, IB Taurus, 1999; Huntington, S., *The Third Wave: Democratization in the
   Late 20th Century*, London, University of Oklahoma Press, 1991.

2. Mamdani, M., *Citizen and Subject – Contemporary Africa and the Legacy of Late Colonialism*, London, James Curry, 1996; Southall, R., "The State of Democracy in South
   Africa", *Commonwealth and Comparative Politics*, Vol. 38, pp. 147–170, 2000.

3. Howarth, D. and Norval, A., *South Africa in Transition*, London, Macmillan Press, 1998.

4. Huntington, op. cit., 1991; Linz, J. and Stepan, A., *The Breakdown of Democratic Regimes*,
   Baltimore, Johns Hopkins University Press, 1978; O'Donnell, G. and Schmitter,
   P., *Transitions from Authoritarian Rule: Tentative Conclusions about Uncertain
   Democracies*, Baltimore, Johns Hopkins University Press, 1986.

5. Davies, J., *When men revolt and Why: A reader in political violence and revolution*, New
   York, Free Press, 1971; Gurr, T., *Why Men Rebel*, Princeton University Press, 1970;
   Johnson, C., *Revolutionary Change*, Boston, Little Brown, 1966; Moore, B., *Social
   Origins of Dictatorship and Democracy: Lord and Peasant in the Making of the Modern*

many South Africa-specific studies, configurative in approach, detailing the processes and events that make up the story of the South African transition.[6]

The Third Wave literature, constituting most of the transitology work, seeks to explain the democratic transitions that began in the mid-1970's in Southern Europe, and by the 1990's, spread to Latin America, Eastern Europe, Africa and Asia.[7] The first two waves, between 1828 and 1926, and 1943 and 1962, were followed by reverse waves of authoritarianism. It is not yet clear whether the Third Wave will follow the reverse pattern of the previous waves.[8] In this literature, the South African case is studied as part of the global Third Wave phenomenon.

The study of regime change and revolution, our second classification, occupies a special place in the field of comparative politics. Skocpol identified four conceptual approaches in this vast literature and each has been applied to South Africa: Marxist, social-psychological, structural-functionalist and historical-structural approaches.[9] The crisis of the authoritarian state is as key theme common to all these approaches.

Following Eckstein, I shall call the third type configurative, event-history studies because no explicit theoretical claims are made. Instead, these studies offer masses of detailed description of the key events, debates, and processes, organised into a recognisable narrative.[10] Typically, such works start with the un-banning of Black Nationalist organisations and the release of Mandela in 1990 and end somewhere between the first democratic elections in April 1994

World, Harmondsworth, Penguin, 1969; Skocpol, T., *States and Social Revolutions: A comparative analysis of France, Russia and China*, Cambridge, Cambridge University Press, 1979.

6. Friedman, S. and Atkinson, D., *The Small Miracle: South Africa's Negotiated Settlement*, Johannesburg, Ravan Press, 1994; Lodge, T., *Consolidating Democracy: South Africa's Second Popular Election*, Johannesburg, Electoral Institute of South Africa and the Witwatersrand University Press, 1999; Sparks, A., *Tomorrow Is Another Country: The Inside Story of South Africa's Negotiated Revolution*, Sandton, Struik, 1994; Waldmier, P., *Anatomy of a Miracle: The End of Apartheid and the Birth of the New South Africa*, London, Viking, 1997.

7. Huntington, op. cit., 1991.

8. Huntington, op. cit., 1991.

9. Skocpol, op. cit., 1979.

10. Eckstein, H., "A Perspective on Comparative Politics Past and Present", in H. Eckstein and D. Apter (eds), *Comparative Politics: A Reader*, New York, Free Press of Glencoe, 1963.

and the adoption in 1996 of the new constitution. Sometimes journalistic in character, these works describe in as much detail as possible "the key" political processes. Over time, certain events come to define the South African transition, contributing an important element to the production of the dominant narrative.

Framing of our understanding of change: transitology and the South African transition

The key areas of the transitology framework that determine how we approach democratic change in South Africa relate to the narrow definition of democracy, the metaphor of stages used to describe transition processes, and an understanding of democratic consolidation that emphasises democratic institutions and procedures. According to Diane Ethier, over the years, a developing consensus has been reached.[11] The research areas of transitology scholarship include the erosion of authoritarian rule, the conditions for democratic transition, the process of democratic regime change, and the consequences of such changes for the future democratic state.[12]

Huntington first establishes the notion of the "Third Wave" as a viable empirical category and then offers an explanation for its development.[13] He begins by defending a narrow definition of democracy along procedural and minimalist lines, identifies different paths and types of transition, and relates types of transition to different forms of authoritarian regimes. The elites, divided into standpatters and reformers, are the main historical actors. Simplistically, the conflict is represented as between regime supporters and the opposition. The entire process is divided into three neatly bounded stages: regime breakdown, transition and consolidation.

Huntington's work is typical of the general framing at work in transitology. In a progressive, linear movement, democratic institutions replace authoritarian institutions, and the subjects of this historical movement are the moderate elites. More precisely, we could criticise the following characteristics of this framework: it operates with a narrow, restricted conception of politics

---

11. Ethier, D., *Democratic Transition and Consolidation in Southern Europe, Latin America and Southeast Asia*, London, Macmillan, 1990, p. 3.

12. Share, D., "Transitions to Democracy and Transitions through Transaction", *Comparative Political Studies*, Vol. 19, pp. 525–548, 1987.

13. Huntington, op. cit., 1991.

and a minimalist, procedural notion of democracy; it assumes that the process of democratisation can be analytically divided into separable stages; it privileges the role of moderate elites; it emphasises the importance of institutions without dissecting the content of practices associated with key institutions, and it reduces democratic society to the mere existence of democratic political institutions. Despite these limitations, words such as "democratisation", "authoritarian", "transition", and "consolidation" are commonplace terms. Increasingly, there is little contestation over the basic framework of this discourse as it is applied to South Africa.

The contested concept of democracy

Transitology discourse leaves unexplored the relationship between chosen definitions and the kind of narratives that follow from them. All definitions exclude certain features of the world, and it is often the excluded features that constitute the source of conflict about the meanings of such terms. All definitions are, in some sense, tactical choices legitimating some rather than other stories about the world. Arblaster, provocatively, argues that the term "democracy" has gained popularity only in recent times because it does not pose a threat to the propertied classes. In the history of the concept, it is associated more with the rule of "the masses" rather than the elites.[14] Transitology discourses reduce democracy to narrowly defined political processes; those features of the political system defined in systems or structural-functionalist approaches.[15] Previously, work on democratic regime change had a broader conception of politics, where changes in state form were approached in relation to larger social processes such as "modernisation", global capitalism, or class conflict. Of the available understandings of democracy developed in the last two thousand years, the definitions by Dahl and Schumpeter, which emphasise the democratic method, elite decision-making, individual rights, and elections, are the ones preferred.[16] Dahl's concept of polyarchy consists of

14. Arblaster, A., "Democratic Society and Its Enemies", *Democratization*, Vol. 9, pp. 33–49, 1999.

15. Linz and Stepan, op. cit., 1978, p. 14.

16. Dahl, R., *Polyarchy: Participation and Opposition*, New Haven, Connecticut, Yale University Press, 1971; Schumpeter, J., *Capitalism, Socialism and Democracy*, New York, Harper, 1942; Share, D., "Transitions to Democracy and Transitions through Transaction", *Comparative Political Studies*, Vol. 19, pp. 525–548, 1987; Allison, L., "On the Gap between Theories of Democracy and Theories of Democratisation",

three characteristics: the existence of multiple socio-economic groups whose conflicts of interests are mediated through consultation (pluralism); the existence of multiple political parties drawing support from various classes, and where over time, all parties compete for the centre (multi-partyism); and lastly, the existence of constitutionally guaranteed individual and collective rights (constitutional rights).[17]

The commonly used definition in transitology discourse does not stray too far from the specific characteristics of democracy highlighted by Dahl and Schumpeter. For Schmitter and Karl, ruler accountability rather than citizen participation becomes the defining characteristic of value.[18] Diamond, Linz and Lipset identify competition, participation, and individual civil and political rights as the key features of democracy.[19] Huntington accuses those who adhere to a more substantive notion of democracy as simply "utopian" and "idealistic."[20]

This privileged conception of democracy excludes alternative meanings. Arblaster emphasises the contestability of the term. The reduced meaning of democracy – an emphasis on procedures, decision-making, individuals and elections – is an ideological and political project. The less threatening to the rich, the more acceptable the term has become.[21]

Besides closely resembling the polities of the advanced capitalist countries, the narrow definition of transitology ignores the everyday contestations over the meanings of democracy.[22] Finally, the narrow conception makes possible a stages metaphor, through which to organise our understanding of democratisation; the process is viewed in neatly bounded stages, without recognising its "messiness" where much of what really happens falls uneasily outside the established categories. And what Huntington views as the advantage of the narrow definition, making empirical verification possible, promotes a per-

Democratization, Vol. 1, pp. 8–26, 1994.

17. Ethier, op. cit., 1990.

18. Schmitter, P. and Karl, T.L., "What Democracy Is...And Is Not", *Journal of Democracy*, Vol. 2, pp. 75–88, 1991.

19. Diamond, L., Linz, J. and Lipset, S.M., *Politics in Developing Countries: Comparing Experiences with Democracy*, Boulder, Lynn Rienner Press, 1990; Linz and Stepan, op. cit., 1996.

20. Huntington, op. cit., 1991, p. 6.

21. Arblaster, op. cit., 1999.

22. Arblaster, op. cit., 1999.

spective that views the long term development of democracy exclusively in institutional rather than in broader participatory terms.[23]

The reliance on the metaphor of stages

Transitology frameworks rely on a metaphor of stages to organise our understanding of the process of democratisation – regime breakdown, transition and consolidation. This notion functions as the basis upon which to organise various research areas and debate. Some of the areas of debate concern the factors causing the collapse of the old regimes, relations between stages, factors causing each stage, defining characteristics of each stage, relations between regime types and the contents of each stage, relations between regime type and the kind of transition stage, different paths and their consequences for consolidation, and the relationship between structures and agency in each stage. The notion of democratisation as a process of stages requires a "starting point" and an "end-point." The starting point is the authoritarian regime in crisis. The end-point is a consolidated democratic regime. The conception of the authoritarian regime – that large undifferentiated category, which lumps together different state forms – is quite superficial; it is everything the democratic regime is not.

The relationship between process and stages is not absolutely clear. We are left unsure whether democratisation involves separate stages in a single process or whether each stage is a process in itself. Pridham, an astute analyst of the transition literature, adopts a less rigid differentiation between stages. He refers to "democratisation" as a "loose expression" covering the overall process of breakdown of the old regime and the consolidation of a new regime. [24]

Initially, transition studies assumed that each stage (breakdown, transition and consolidation) moved in a linear fashion, in the same direction from breakdown to consolidation. More recently, a pessimistic outlook is evident. Linz points out:

---

23. Huber, E., Ruishchemeyer, D. and Stephens, J., "The Paradoxes of Contemporary Democracies: Formal, Participatory, and Social Dimensions", *Comparative Politics*, Vol. 29, pp. 323–343, 1997.

24. Pridham, G., *Transitions to Democracy: Comparative Perspectives from Southern Europe, Latin America and Eastern Europe*, Aldershot, Dartmouth, 1995.

... the collapse of an authoritarian regime may or may not create the conditions for the successful establishment of political democracy.[25]

Burnell warns there is no guarantee the process moves unproblematically and inevitably from one stage to the next.[26]

The build-up of demands (from the internal and external environment) produces a crisis of legitimacy. For Schmitter, who steers a careful path between the influence of Johnson's structural-functionalism and Skocpol's statist perspective, the authoritarian regime in crisis is a unique feature of the Third Wave.[27] The inability to respond effectively to overwhelming demands places the authoritarian regime in a crisis. Why authoritarian regimes suddenly face a crisis and what constitutes the crisis of the state is a matter of dispute. Di Palma shifts the focus from factors outside the regime, such as opposition pressure, to pressures within it.[28] He argues that state crisis is generated within, a sign of "internal exhaustion" caused by growing inefficiency, increased expectations, disputes among organised interests and a crisis of confidence.

There is a consensus that the Apartheid regime was in crisis and was forced to initiate democratic reforms. Whereas Price identifies international, regional, and domestic factors as producing a crisis of social control of the Apartheid regime, Giliomee, identifying more closely with Di Parma, emphasises the source of reforms as elite driven and not directly related to opposition pressures. Nevertheless, both agree that the Apartheid state was experiencing a crisis of domination; they disagree on the source of the state crisis.[29]

Huntington identifies general causes for the Third Wave and only some have a bearing on explaining the South African transition.[30] His five inter-

25. Linz, op. cit., 1990, p. 108.

26. Burnell, P. and Calvert, P., "The Resilience of Democracy: An Introduction", *Democratization,* Vol. 2, pp. 1–32, 1999, p. 7.

27. Schmitter, P., "Speculations about the Prospective Demise of Authoritarian Regimes and Its Possible Consequences (I)", *Revista De Ciencia Politica,* Vol. 10, pp. 83–103, 1985.

28. Di Palma, G., "Government Performance: An Issue and Three Cases in Search of Theory", *West European Politics,* Vol. 7, pp. 172–187, 1984.

29. Price, R., *The Apartheid State in Crisis,* Berkeley, University of California Press 1990; Giliomee, H., "Democratization in South Africa", *Political Science Quarterly,* Vol. 110, pp. 83–104, 1995.

30. Huntington, op. cit., 1991, p. 47.

national causes are legitimacy problems, global economic growth and an ex-panded middle class, changes in the doctrine of the Catholic Church, the policies of powerful external actors at the end of the Cold War, especially the US, and the phenomenon of snowballing. The type of regime plays a mediat-ing role indicating how far regime elites are able to democratise without losing their strategic influence in the political and/or social hierarchy. He identifies the following regime types: absolutist, fascist, one-party, military, personalis-tic and racial-oligarchical. According to him, because the Apartheid regime (racial oligarchy) allowed for extensive competition (among white parties) be-fore it embarked upon greater citizen participation (reforms), good prospects for a successful democratic transition exist.[31]

There is a remarkable consensus in transitology on the different types of transitions and the role of the key actors. The crisis situation divides the regime elites into hardliners and moderates, and a similar process takes place among the opposition groups. Agreements are forged between the moderates on both sides producing the basis of the new democratic order. To overcome the crisis, according to Di Palma, a successful transition requires three crucial compromises, all present in the South African case: to continue with a state policy reproducing capitalist relations, to preserve the bureaucracy, and to obtain the consent of the Left.[32] Classifying types of transition depend on the behaviour of the moderate elites. Share classifies transitions according to whether the leaders of the authoritarian regime consent to the transition and the duration, gradual or rapid, of the transition.[33] He identifies the following four types: incremental transitions, transition through transaction, transition through protracted revolutionary struggle and transition through rupture.

Similarly, Huntington's main criterion is whether the regime elites or those from the opposition take the initiative and hold sway in determin-ing the main features of the post-authoritarian regime.[34] He distinguishes three types of transition – transformation, replacement, and transplacement. Transformation and replacement are opposite categories. In transitions by transformation, the regime elites take the lead to establish the new regime on its own terms. In transitions by replacement, the opposition groups dictate the terms of the new regime. The transplacement category describes a com-

---

31. Huntington, op. cit., 1991, p. 112.

32. Di Palma, op. cit., 1984.

33. Share, op. cit., 1987.

34. Huntington, op. cit., 1991.

promise situation where the moderates negotiate and compromise, excluding and/or marginalising the extremists in the process. These "centrist groups" are the democratic reformers in the regime and democratic moderates of the opposition forces. Linz makes a similar classification by distinguishing between the moderate reforma and the radical ruptura.[35] Share and Mainwaring agree with Huntington's classificatory scheme but use different classificatory labels – transaction, collapse and extrication transition types.[36]

Consolidation and the privileging of institutions

If the literature on types of transition emphasises the role of the elites in the process, the work on democratic consolidation emphasises the importance of institutions. There are many aspects of democratic society yet it is striking that political scientists tend to focus exclusively on the reproduction of its minimal conditions. The content of critical citizenship is hardly ever explored in international or comparative politics; it is heavily debated in political theory.[37] For Linz and Stepan, a consolidated democracy is one where democracy (the narrow definition) is "the only game in town." [38] It has behavioural, attitudinal and constitutional dimensions. The behavioural dimension refers to a situation where no "significant" group desires to remain outside the political system or regularly disobey the basic rules. The attitudes of the majority are significant. In a consolidated democracy faced with a political or economic crisis the majority will continue to adhere to the basic rules of the political system. There would be awareness that breaking these constitutional rules will incur severe penalties. The consolidation of democracy involves the significant "internalisation" of all three dimensions.

While Linz and Stepan focus on the positive features of a consolidated democracy, Schedler views a democratic society as consolidated when any threatening signs of reversal are absent.[39] Burnell and Calvert consider five conditions as necessary for democratic consolidation: civil society; political

35. Linz, J., "Transitions to Democracy", *The Washington Quarterly*, Vol. 13, pp. 143–164, 1990.

36. Huntington, op. cit., 1991, p. 114.

37. Allison op. cit., 1994.

38. Linz and Stepan, op. cit., 1996.

39. Schedler, A., "How Should We Study Democratic Consolidation", *Democratization*, Vol. 5, pp. 1–19, 1998; Schedler, A., "What Is Democratic Consolidation?", *Journal of Democracy*, Vol. 9, pp. 91–107, 1998.

society; constitutional basis or rule of law state; usable bureaucracy; and an economic society that is neither command nor pure market based.[40] Przeworkski places the occurrence of two consecutive elections and the uncertainty of outcomes that elections generally entail, as the key indicator of consolidation.[41] He argues that a democracy is consolidated when the ruling party loses after two elections and accepts the results. The change of ruling party indicates the degree of respect given to a key democratic value – democratic competition and respecting the outcomes of elections. As is evident the focus in transitology is on institutions and not the everyday quality of citizenship in democratic societies.

Crisis of state and event history perspectives

I suggest above that three elements make up the dominant discourse on democratic transition in South Africa – Third Wave perspectives, the notion of Apartheid state crisis, and key defining moments of the transition process organised into narrative form. Having discussed the Third Wave component and underscored that it functions as "the context", the organising framework, against which the South African transition is studied, I now turn to the other two elements. The second component is what I have called the "crisis of state" perspective. This notion of the crisis of the Apartheid state comfortably fits within the structure of transitology and its division of the process into stages; the regime breakdown stage is here the focus of attention. I will discuss the text of Robert Price, *The Crisis of the Apartheid State*, because it provides an excellent review of the main factors normally considered when explaining the collapse of the Apartheid state.[42]

Price explains the collapse of the Apartheid regime by drawing on the "bringing the state back" work of Theda Skocpol whose explanation of revolution relies on international and domestic structural factors that reduce the capacity of the state to maintain social control.[43] He systematically classifies the relevant factors into international, regional and domestic categories. At the international level, the disinvestment campaigns increased pressure

40. Burnell and Calvert, op. cit., 1999.

41. Przeworkski, A., *Sustainable Democracy*, Cambridge, Cambridge University Press, 1995.

42. Price, op. cit., 1990.

43. Skocpol, op. cit., 1979.

on Western allies to withdraw capital from South Africa. In an economy dependent on foreign capital, such as Apartheid South Africa, the disinvestments campaign severely affected capitalist growth. At the symbolic and psychological level, the equally successful cultural and sports boycotts adopted by the United Nations and Commonwealth Association made white South Africans aware of their pariah status as beneficiaries of Apartheid policies. The changing regional political situation applied further pressure on the Apartheid state. Here Black Nationalist movements sympathetic to the ANC and PAC seized power in neighbouring countries. Previously South Africa was surrounded and protected by white minority ruled regimes in Mozambique, Zimbabwe, Angola and Namibia. In response, the Apartheid state invested massively in military equipment and extended itself widely on different military fronts. It embarked on regular military campaigns to weaken the governments of neighbouring countries.

The domestic front involves various pressures, some structural and related to the economy, others political, and related to the waves of internal popular resistance. The relationship between Apartheid and the capitalist economy dominated South African studies in the 1970's. The Marxist position argued that Apartheid policies were compatible with the capitalist production mode; the Liberal position emphasised the contradictions, arguing that migrant labour policies undermined capitalist growth. Price pragmatically straddles both camps. Structural processes contributed to the intensification of resistance by urban blacks. The militant political consciousness of young blacks negated the efforts of political reform from above initiated by the Apartheid regime. It stimulated further protests. At the time of the unbanning of the ANC, PAC and Communist Party, the Apartheid regime was in crisis. A crisis of social control prevailed. The economy was in deep recession and, unless the regime embarked upon a different, more far-reaching political path, white property and security would be irreversibly endangered. The negotiated settlement opened the possibility of addressing some, if not all, of the factors that produced the state crisis.

The third scheme making up this system of thought and practice I have called the dominant discourse on the South African transition, is event history. It usually starts where Price ends and covers the key "moments" in the transition process. This would include: De Klerk's February 1990 speech to parliament announcing the unbanning of the ANC and other anti-Apartheid organisations; the release of Nelson Mandela from Pollsmore prison making world headlines; the Groote Schuur Minute marking the first public meeting between representatives of the government and the ANC; Mandela's tour of the townships, particularly his visit to Soweto; the opening session of Codesa one and the public clash between De Klerk and Mandela; the signing of the National Peace Accord; the presentation of the Nobel Peace prize to both Mandela and De Klerk; the assassination of Chris Hani, and lastly the first national elections and Mandela casting his vote.[44] These key events are entrenched in the dominant discourse defining the democratic transition.

To summarise the dominant discourse organises the story of the South African transition in a particular way relying on a familiar narrative structure: the phenomenon of Third Wave democratisation serves as the background context, to frame the narrative; the content of the crisis of the Apartheid regime explains regime breakdown, and the stringing together of key moments describes the details of the actual process of negotiations starting with the unbanning of black organisations and the release of key black political leaders. The dramatic aspect in the story comes, first with the breakdown, and then, the eventual resumption of negotiations. The story ends with the various agreements, the first democratic election, and the birth of a new South Africa.

Privileging, silencing and positioning of key concepts in the dominant discourse

We already know that in the move to foreground some themes function to exclude others or place them at the margins. I want to briefly highlight those themes found on the receiving end, those themes denied, ignored, and/or marginalised. We ought to recognise and appreciate the "messiness" of the transition. In privileging negotiations, the model of transition by transplacement makes negotiations and the settlement arrived at the defining feature of the process, and consequently, the elites become the primary subjects of historical change. I want to focus on just two aspects implied, yet absent, in this move of making elites the subjects of the transition. The first examines the significance and the different uses of the notion "the masses" for both regime and Black Nationalist elites that remain obscured in available representations. The second brings into sharper focus the presence of violence and the intermittent relationship between negotiations and violence, making if difficult, besides unconvincing, to naively disentangle them. The idea

---

44. Friedman and Atkinson, op. cit., 1994; Sparks, op. cit., 1994; Waldmier, op. cit., 1997.

of "the masses" permeates the entire transition process, being an "absence/presence", and where negotiation functions as a signifier for non-violence, violence and the brutality of the process are airbrushed out of the picture of regime change.

In academic "knowledge" and popular media production – the two main sites for the expression of the dominant narrative – the leaderships of the National Party and the ANC are the subjects of historical change, and more specifically, the figures of De Klerk-Mandela and Meyer-Ramaphosa; each leadership dyad conveys different meanings. The awarding of the Nobel Peace prize to both leaders contributes to and demonstrates the personalisation of the conflict. We associate a series of different signifiers to each of them: De Klerk, the moderate, reform-minded Afrikaner, professional yet cunning politician, the one leader who was brave enough to see a South Africa beyond Apartheid. Mandela, the moral symbol of struggles against injustice, the long-term prisoner, dignified in victory, disciplined party member, representing strong humanist-enlightenment values. The Mandela/De Klerk relationship has a primarily symbolic dimension, with them symbolising black and white South Africa respectively. The Meyer/Ramaphosa dyad does not stand for opposites, but the things they have in common (like their interest in fly-fishing!). Their relationship has a practical bearing, signifying the "behind the scenes" negotiations and "getting the job done". Little is said about the ideological, geographic, gender, and ethnic differences in the ANC and National Party. The salient difference is that between hawks (hardliners) and doves (moderates). A key issue is whether Mandela and De Klerk are able to control the hardliners in their respective camps. The "hardliner" category is a catchall container for anyone outside the party mainstream and supportive of the leader.

The construction of elites as central undermines the presence of ordinary people – "the masses" in the historical process. The presence of "the masses" signifies different things for the negotiating elites. On the regime side, "the masses" and the possibility of their increased participation in the political system represent everything that is reprehensible. The main strategic issue is how to keep "them" out and maintain an elite driven discourse of change. This translates into holding the ANC and its allies responsible for controlling "the masses", entailing an important discursive move. The notion of controlling "your people" and placing this ability to exert control as a test of leadership maturity assumes prominence. Besides viewing "the masses" as a threat, they are simultaneously viewed as a potential instrument against the ANC, and as easy canon fodder open to manipulation, which could be used to embarrass, and perhaps, even weaken the ANC.

In discourses of the ANC, the category, "the masses", performs quite different signifying functions. The category has a long tradition and privileged place in struggle discourses. The party leadership historically did not consider itself apart from its mass constituency. In a situation where leaders and led are considered as one undifferentiated unit, or as the "true and authentic representatives of the people", the ANC leadership resisted the label "elites" applied to itself and refused to grant it any legitimacy. Despite this notion of a close connection with "the masses", the mere use of the term suggests a differentiation between leaders and led, or vanguard (a word frequently used in ANC documents and speeches) and those open to mobilisation. Like the regime, the notion of "the masses" has important instrumentalist connotations for the ANC. It could be used as a weapon in the negotiating terrain. The threats and campaigns of "rolling mass action" made and embarked upon by the ANC at crucial moments in the negotiations demonstrates this view. At the same time, this instrumentalist relationship between party and "the masses" is a double-edged sword capable of moving the negotiations in a direction favourable to the ANC, but also opening the party to unintended consequences where it is unable to exert social control.

An unconvincing binary is set up between negotiations and violence in dominant narratives. These phenomena went hand in hand; the violence surrounding the negotiations was an essential part of the negotiating process. The phenomenon of violence produced a complex system of discourse – knowledge production, conferences, newspaper articles, special negotiations, monitoring groups.[45] The causes of violence are the focus of much debate where a few explanations compete: Third Force, primordial, party conflict, class conflict and scarce resource explanations. Three aspects of the violence stand out: first, the regime's representation of the violence as "black on black". In this move, the Apartheid state repositions itself as "neutral-arbiter", confronted by primordial-based groups killing each other. Second, the brutality of the violence, where the body of "enemies" is targeted often mutilating children and babies, introduced a new dimension to the conflict. It suggests a phase where an all-embracing conception of the targets of violence comes to the fore. Last, the ethnic/political dimension of Zulu migrants fighting trade

45. Pfister, R., "Violence during South Africa's political transition 1990–1994", Biennial Conference of the South African Historical Society, Pretoria, 1997.

union organised workers represents an interesting puzzle of the relationship between class, ethnic and rural-urban identities.

The assassination and figure of Chris Hani take on a marginalised position in transition narratives. Hani was an ambiguous figure. As leader of the SACP, he was located precariously between the traditional elites of the ANC and the more authentic representatives of "the masses." His death marks a significant turning point. It is the point of crisis in the negotiations where the situation could escalate into increased violence breaking down the entire process. Moderate leaders would be unable to control their supporters. The knowledge of this is presented as the "abyss" facing the elites, compelling them to renew their desire for a speedy democratic solution. The Hani assassination, discursively, makes the renewal of negotiations possible, and brings to the fore the fear of an uncontrollable mass in dominant discourses of transition.

The received discourse on democratic transition renders subordinate other discourses about democratic change, which compete against it and one another. If these are not marginalised by the dominant discourse, they are drawn into it; making them functional to the dominance of that discourse. From the many possible contenders, I shall identify three discourses classified by what they desire, bearing in mind that other criteria could also be used to identify alternative discourses about democratic change: "reform from above/ conservative"; revolutionary, and revenge discourses. Conservative discourses aim to maintain or make relevant as much of the old order and its everyday expressions as possible, to resist political change, and to organise the value system of the present around a blissful and non-conflictual past. The range of marginal, radical discourses would include those desiring revolutionary outcomes, seizing control of the state, and instrumentally using it to reverse as rapidly as possible generations of established social relations. Revenge discourses desire far-reaching reversal in the positions of whites and blacks and rich and poor; reversal associated with "getting back" at the previous holders of power. Partially related to these are those group rights discourses that have deep historical roots in South African politics, advocating cultural reassertiveness of various kinds. These and many others make for an extremely complicated picture. Some have reorganised themselves since 1994, others continue in slightly different forms, while some simply no longer exist.

In conclusion, the dominant narrative of democratic transition in South Africa produces a version of events that domesticates the messiness of the process of change. The focus on discourses of change in South Africa, taking those mentioned above into account, all interacting in various configurations, admits to a far "messier" process than that presented in transitology, state crisis and event history streams of dominant discourse. It will help to appreciate the continuities and ruptures between past and present politics, making for a richer, more complex, understanding of democratic regime change in South Africa.

PART II

THE HANDLING OF HERITAGE
AND THE
POPULARISING OF MEMORY

CHAPTER 8

The politics of public history in post-apartheid South Africa

Gary Baines

The question of whose version of history gets disseminated and institutionalized is a political one.[1] History, and more especially public history, is contested terrain. It is primarily in the domain of public history that battles over the meaning of the past are being and will continue to be waged in contemporary society. If those with the power to control the construction of the past have the means to shape memory, it is essential to understand how they do so. This entails examining the function of the state in reproducing history, especially in the sphere of education. Politicians, the media and cultural brokers also tend to become involved in cultural wars and so their interventions should be noted. And it goes without saying that those involved in the production of public history such as museum curators and heritage practitioners are key actors. It is also apposite to ask what role (if any) academic historians should play in the domain of public history. And the public, the consumers of this history, should not be ignored either. This chapter will seek to understand the politics of public history in post-apartheid South Africa.

Memory and the politics of public history

A desire to understand how public history functions in society is evident in the growing interest in the study of memory in scholarly discourse.[2] Memory, like history, is a reconstruction of the past from which meaning is derived. Obviously, however, history and memory are not synonymous. Pierre Nora

---

1. David Glassberg, "Public History and the Study of Memory", *The Public Historian*, Vol. 18, No. 2, 1996, p. 11.
2. Gadi Algazi, "Editorial: The Past in the Present", *History & Memory*, Vol. 13, No. 1, Spring/Summer 2001, p. 1.

holds that memory is in a permanent state of flux, open to the dialectic of remembering and forgetting, vulnerable to manipulation and appropriation, whereas history is a representation of the past, a critical discourse which is suspicious of memory.[3] In other words, history and memory are in a fundamental state of tension. In Marita Sturken's view, history and memory are "entangled rather than [necessarily] oppositional".[4] History and memory are often in contestation but they need not be. Indeed, there can be intersection or elision between history and memory for they are mutually constitutive. So the juxtaposition of history and memory is something of a false dichotomy to start with. What we are actually interested in is memory *in* history, the role of the past in history or, for that matter, in contemporary politics, and what Jurgen Habermas once called "the public uses of history".[5]

The emphasis in much of the literature, then, has been on the social construction of memory, particularly on efforts by the state and powerful political groups to invent traditions that could serve their interests.[6] But invention and manipulation do not go far enough in explaining how certain symbols assume dominance in public memory.[7] As all knowledge is political, and memory is a form of knowledge about the past, memory can usefully be conceptualised as a kind of "symbolic power" that can be marshalled in much the same way as material power.[8] Public memory reflects the structure of power in society because that power is always contested in a world of ideological differences and because cultural understanding is always grounded in the material structure of society itself. Public memory is a body of beliefs and ideas about the past that help a public or society understand both its past, present, and by implication, its future. It is fashioned in the public sphere in which various parts of the social structure exchange views. The major focus

---

3. Pierre Nora, "Between Memory and History: *Les Lieux de memoire*", *Representations*, Vol. 26, 1989, pp. 8–9.

4. Marita Sturken, *Tangled Memories: The Vietnam War, the AIDS Epidemic, and the Politics of Remembering*, Berkeley, University of California Press, 1997, p. 5.

5. Jan-Werner Müller, "Introduction: The power of memory, the memory of power and the power over memory" in Jan-Werner Müller (ed.), *Memory & Power in Post-War Europe*, Cambridge University Press, 2002, pp. 24–25.

6. This was pioneered by Eric Hobsbawm and Terence Ranger (eds), *The Invention of Tradition*, Cambridge, Cambridge University Press, 1983.

7. John Bodnar, *Remaking America: Public Memory, Commemoration and Patriotism in Twentieth Century America*, Princeton, Princeton University Press, 1992.

8. Müller, "Introduction", p. 25.

of this communicative and cognitive process is not the past, however, but serious matters in the present such as the nature of power and the question of loyalty to both dominant and subordinate cultures. Accordingly, historical memories are constantly refashioned to suit present purposes.[9]

The dominant memory emerges after a struggle between conflicting interpretations of historical events. The past becomes an explanation for the present, justifying the social or political order on the grounds that it was ordained by history. The dominant memory serves to validate a certain social order ordained by the past, to legitimate the status quo. Consequently, it prescribes what should be remembered (as well as how it should be remembered) and what should be forgotten. However, counter-memories can exist amongst individuals or groups in civil society who refuse to forget or remember what it prescribes. Such counter-memories exist in private spaces and individual minds and provide a potentially threatening undercurrent to the social order. Their ability to survive depends on what claims to political resources and state power the individual or group is able to muster.[10] For memory is capable of being appropriated, repressed or de-politicized by a variety of groups in civil society.

Obviously all state-sanctioned public acts of remembrance, commemoration or monumentalization tend to valorize the dominant or official memory. And yet it is not always possible to reach a consensus on the interpretation of a historical event to which people attach considerable significance. Particular versions of the past are selectively invoked to add credence and authenticity to truth claims,[11] as well as to assert a claim to a particular heritage and identity. Thus, historical representations such as a museum exhibit, war memorial, or commemorative ceremony are often deliberately ambiguous to satisfy competing factions.[12] Those working in museums, heritage sites, and community history projects confront the problem of historical representation on a regular basis and encounter perspectives on the past that their colleagues in universities and colleges are unlikely to engage. In presenting history to the public, they discover that they are engaged in a conversation. A desire to understand this exchange between historians and their audiences (or consum-

---

9. Daniel F. Bouchard (ed.), *Language, Counter-Memory, Practice: Select Essays and Interviews with Michel Foucault,* Ithaca, NY, Cornell University Press, p. 144.

10. Müller, "Introduction", p. 32.

11. Bodnar, *Remaking America,* p. 19, 15.

12. Glassberg, "Public History and the Study of Memory", pp. 13–14.

ers) has caused some academic historians to rethink their relationship with society and how to engage with public history.[13] The next section will discuss how academic historians in South Africa have responded to the exponential growth of public history, especially in the field of heritage.

Professional and public history in South Africa

The burgeoning of the heritage sector in South Africa has occasioned mixed reactions from professional historians. Some have welcomed it as a lifeline for history departments experiencing declining enrolments. They have embraced heritage and even taken to teaching courses in the field of public history and training students to work in the sector. Others are wary, sceptical or even suspicious. The UNISA environmental historian, Jane Carruthers, posted a briefing paper entitled "Heritage and History" on the H-Africa discussion network in 1998.[14] Following the lead of David Lowenthal, who regards heritage as antithetical to history,[15] she viewed the latter as a "higher" level of activity that included systematic research, evaluation of evidence and interpretation subject to the weight of previous research and the conventions of peer review. In this view, there exists a hierarchical schema of historical production in which the sub-genre of heritage produced by non-academics is innately subordinate to academic history. Heritage is deemed to be on a par with the antiquarian or "home-made" history produced by amateurs. A corollary of Carruthers' position would seem to be that the function of academics is to critique the heritage enterprise from the vantage point of their superior place in the sociology of knowledge. In other words, the scholarly discipline of history derives its authority from the expertise of its practitioners, which entitles them to function as custodians of the past. But is this the case? Or is the notion of "custodians of the past" problematical? Does the past belong to any one (group) in particular? Or does it belong to everyone and no-one?

---

13. Michael H. Frisch, "The Memory of History", in S.P. Benson, S. Brier & R. Rosenzweig (eds), *Presenting the Past: Essays on History and the Public*, Temple University Press, 1986, pp. 5–17.

14. Jane Carruthers, "Heritage and History", H-AFRICA Forum #2, H-NET, http://h-net.msu.edu/cgi-bin/logbrowse.pl?trx=vx&list=hafrica&month=9810&week=c&msg=sv82DZpkATFzGc7zqbkFKA&user=&pw=

15. David Lowenthal, *The Past Is a Foreign Country,* Cambridge, Cambridge University Press, 1985; *The Heritage Crusade and the Spoils of History,* Cambridge, Cambridge University Press, 1998; "Fabricating Heritage", *History and Memory*, Vol. 10, No. 1, 1998, pp. 5–24.

Such questions, which were ignored in the discussion thread prompted by Carruthers' paper, need to be more closely interrogated.[16]

Another – albeit more tangential – intervention in the debate about the relationship between history and heritage was made in an article by the foremost historian of Zulu history, Jeff Guy. It is clear from his piece entitled "Battling with Banality", that Guy is exasperated by the way in which the British invasion of Zululand of 1879 has been represented in military history texts aimed at the popular end of the market, as well as by how the story is recounted to tourists visiting battle sites. Guy asserts that "the heritage industry invokes a sentimentalized past which makes bearable a sordid and painful present".[17] I share his concerns insofar as heritage projects seek to promote nation-building in our fledgling and fragile democracy by sanitizing our past. The idea of a past that all South Africans can share is chimerical. Guy's article shows that there are a number of narratives of the Anglo-Zulu War competing for primacy in the marketplace of ideas. He decries the fact that academics have failed to counter the dominant imperial narrative of the invasion of Zululand purveyed by local historians and the heritage industry. He bemoans the

> ... failure of historians in the academy to fulfil one of their essential social roles
> – as guardians and propagators of informed, critical, disinterested history.[18]

This statement begs a number of questions: If we concede that historians do indeed have a social role, to whom are they responsible? To their own peers in the profession, the government of the day, those with vested interests, or the general public? Guy's use of the term "guardians" would seem to imply that historians should play the role of watchdogs over the production of partisan history for public consumption. He seems to believe that the heritage sector, unlike academia, is subject to the twin pressures of political expediency and the dictates of the market. He may be right, but is this reason enough for academics to summarily dismiss heritage? After all, it seems to me that "disinterested history" is something that even academics cannot attain.

---

16. A start has been made by Leslie Witz, Gary Minkley and Ciraj Rassool, "Who Speaks for South African Pasts?", paper presented to the Biennial Conference of the South African Historical Society, UWC, 11–14 July 1999.

17. Jeff Guy, "Battling with Banality", *Journal of Natal and Zulu History*, Vol. 18, 1998, p. 157.

18. Guy, "Battling with Banality", p. 168.

Many academics in South Africa have been slow to come to terms with what Ciraj Rassool has called "the fundamental reconstitution of the discipline of history".[19] Most practitioners still operate with the positivist assumptions that, provided reliable sources are available, past "reality" can more or less unproblematically be represented in stories written about or told about it in the present. The post-modernist notion that reality is socially constructed has undermined the premises of positivism. The constructivists hold that historical knowledge consisted of discourses about the past produced in a particular context, and that notions of "fact" and "truth" were anything but absolutes, relative also to particular times and places. Jacques Derrida's (in)famous statement that "there is nothing outside the text" has been often, perhaps wilfully, misunderstood by historians as meaning that what happened in the past cannot be known with any degree of certainty, as all versions of history are equally valid. Some historians reject the cognitive and epistemological paradigm shift of post-modernism as "relativism". They hold fast to empiricism and continue with business as usual. Others, like myself, have adopted a "soft" constructivist approach whereby we believe that there is an independent reality. This position allows for core facts about which there should be no disagreement. What is constructed is the meaning of events and the way they are construed in individual and collective memory. The predicament has occasioned considerable self-reflection within the historical profession causing uncertainty in some quarters and opening up new possibilities for others.[20] However, the public for whom such issues are too esoteric, has not lost its faith in history as the reproduction of "the facts".[21]

Amongst South African historians, Rassool is one of the few to recommend that academics engage constructively with heritage practitioners. He is also one of the few to have taken cognisance of the implications of the epistemological crisis for the history-heritage debate. He holds that it does not follow that academic history is superior to heritage by virtue of its rigorous methodology and peer review system. He reckons that heritage

---

19. Ciraj Rassool, "The Rise of Heritage and the Reconstitution of History in South Africa", *Kronos: Journal of Cape History*, Vol. 26, August 2000, p. 5.

20. T. Nuttall & J. Wright, "Probing the Predicaments of Academic History in Contemporary South Africa", *South African Historical Journal*, Vol. 42, 2000, pp. 26–48.

21. Joyce Appleby, "The Power of History" *American Historical Review*, February 1998, p. 2 citing Alasdair MacIntyre, "Epistemological Crises, Dramatic Narration, and the Philosophy of Science" in Gary Gatting (ed.), *Paradigms and Resolutions*, Notre Dame, Indiana University Press, 1974.

… can be seen as an assemblage of arenas and activities of history-making that is as disputatious as the claims made about the character of academic history.[22]

In other words, heritage is a form of public history produced by those outside the professional historical fraternity. Like academic history, it has its own set of codes and conventions and is equally contested. Academic historians do not have a monopoly on the production of historical knowledge. Public history is a particular kind of history making with its own rules. Promoters of cultural tourism might commodify the past for consumers who want souvenirs and pre-packaged memories. But there can be little doubt that history produced in the realm of public culture rather than the academy largely determines how the past is remembered by society at large. How should professional historians respond? Retreat into our ivory towers or get "down and dirty" by joining the battle in the terrain of public history? Turn a crisis into a challenge?

Obviously neither public history generally nor heritage specifically is above criticism. As well intentioned as many projects might be, they often construct simplistic versions of the past that amount to mythicization. We should interrogate projects that seek to validate or confer legitimacy on politically correct versions of the past. And we should critique official versions of the past and deconstruct the narratives that reify this sort of history. But I also believe that academics can and should make a constructive contribution with respect to how the past is represented in the public sphere. We should acknowledge that public history has a place in shaping the cultural and political landscape of post-apartheid South Africa.

Nation-building and identity politics in post-apartheid South Africa

According to Benedict Anderson, a shared history is the crucial element in the construction of an "imagined community". This facilitates identity formation that enables disparate individuals and groups to envision themselves as members of a collective with a common past, present and future.[23] Whoever wields power has the wherewithal to decide who is included and who is excluded from the "imagined" community. History has served as a "school of

---

22. Rassool, "The Rise of Heritage", p. 5.

23. Benedict Anderson, *Imagined Communities: Reflections on the Origins and Spread of Nationalism*, New York, Verso, rev. (ed.) 1991, p. 15.

patriotism" for it has been used to construct the master narrative of the "imagined community" of the nation. The congruence between the development of history and European nationalisms from the early nineteenth to the late twentieth century is well documented. South Africa's apartheid regime also put history to equally utilitarian uses in order to construct an exclusive Afrikaner and then, later, a more inclusive white nationalism. Collective memory might be the key to reinforcing a sense of national identity,[24] but in societies in transition national identity can be contested and collective memory fluid. In post-apartheid South Africa, history has played a rather more ambivalent role in framing a master narrative, which seeks to realign collective memory with a new national identity thereby re-defining what "being South African" means.

The failure to construct a new national master narrative in post-apartheid South Africa can partly be attributed to the emergence of identity politics. Joyce Appleby contends that:

> [I]t may once have been important to construe the nation as the holder of the collective experience for our "imagined" community, but the trope carries too much baggage to persist. The identity politics of our day have emerged precisely in reaction to the claims of the nation to represent a homogenized people.[25]

Appleby may have had the Western nation state in mind but identity politics has come to play a crucial role in many multicultural societies, especially those like South Africa in a state of transition. Stakeholders and cultural brokers from a variety of political persuasions and communities have become engaged in attempts to renegotiate the meaning of the country's past and their own place within it. Old versions of the past have come to be regarded as either redundant or unacceptable, and previously dominant ideologies have been challenged. With the assertion of sub-national identities in the context of the fissiparous forces caused by globalization, new (hi)stories are being constructed to replace extant ones. This growing interest in ethnic, local and even family history seems to suggest that we have entered a post-nationalist era with a proliferation of particularist histories and memories.[26] Representa-

---

24. Müller, "The power of memory", p. 21.

25. Appleby, "The Power of History", p. 11.

26. John Gillis, "Introduction" in *Commemorations: The Politics of National Identity*, Princeton University Press, 1994, pp. 3–24; Charles Maier, "A Surfeit of Memory: Reflections on History, Melancholy and Denial", *History and Memory*, Vol. 5, 1993, pp. 136–52.

tives of cultural, ethnic, linguistic, religious, regional and other particularist identities are seeking their own "sites of memory". For instance, the erection of the Sarah Baartman memorial can be regarded as a manifestation of Khoisan revivalism. The mobilisation of ethnic "minorities" occurs in a situation where race still serves as a significant social category and marker of difference. Groups such as white Afrikaners have invoked their own versions of the past in order to justify their claims to a discrete cultural identity, as well as being a constituent part of the nation. When certain historians apparently questioned the wisdom of including Boer War leaders in the pantheon of heroes of the liberation struggle to be honoured in Freedom Park, the journalist Max du Preez responded:

> ... we [Afrikaners?] should rescue our history from the clammy claws of our nation's historians ... we should never allow anyone to manipulate it to serve any kind of political or other purpose...We should claim our common history as South Africans, otherwise we will remain the victims of the past.[27]

Du Preez's call for a consensual history shows that he favoured the promotion of reconciliation and nation-building so long as provision was made for his reading of the past. Indeed, national identity and collective memory survive only to the degree that they accommodate individuals' demands for a usable past.[28] But in a multicultural society like South Africa, it is difficult to juggle all competing claims for an equitable share of the past.

In this climate where there is a lack of consensus as to how the nation should be defined, two discourses appear to be competing for primacy. These discourses are constructed through historical memory and the interplay of different social forces. They are not necessarily mutually exclusive, but do exist in a state of tension. The first might be termed "rainbowism" and is in keeping with the ANC's tradition of non-racialism.[29] Its proponents emphasize that South Africa has a common, shared history. The Truth and Reconciliation Committee (TRC) has been the most public attempt to refashion a collective, national memory for the sake of reconciliation and laying to rest the

---

27. Max du Preez, "Rescue our rich national history from academics", *The Cape Argus*, 20 December 2003.

28. John R. Gillis, "Review Essay: Remembering Memory: A Challenge for Public Historians in a Post-National Era", *The Public Historian*, Vol. 14, No. 4, 1992, p. 98.

29. Gary Baines, "The rainbow nation? Identity and nation-building in post-apartheid South Africa", *Mots Pluriels*, No. 7, 1998, http://www.arts.uwa.edu.au/MotsPluriels/MP798gb.html.

beast of the past.[30] This vision stresses the need to forge a co-operative future from the cauldron of our conflict-ridden past. The second discourse might be termed "Africanism" or Afrocentrism for it proclaims African leadership of the national liberation struggle and of government. At its most benign, it allows for non-Africans to cross cultural borders either way and identify with the African majority.[31] In its more strident form, it posits a version of the past that is exclusive and foregrounds a triumphalist narrative of resistance. This is epitomized by President Mbeki's "People's History" project, which seeks to construct an official history, which would make the liberation struggle the master narrative of our national history. "Africanism" endorses nation-building albeit of a different form to "rainbowism".

Since 1994, the ANC's nation-building project has been fraught with contradictions. Initially, the state downgraded history in the school syllabus, especially in Curriculum 2005, which was subsequently scrapped. Subsequently, the curriculum has been revised so as to accord history a more central place as a discrete subject. A new series of school history textbooks called *Turning Points* initiated by the Institute for Justice and Reconciliation, was commissioned. It was launched in April 2004 by (former) Minister of Education, Kader Asmal with these words:

> … we are starting to build a truly South African [education] system that enables us to teach the truth about our history. For so long, the facts were deviously manipulated and we need to look at the kind of memory we are building for our children. We need to build an inclusive memory where the heroes and heroines of the past belong not only to certain sectors, but to us all.[32]

Similar sentiments might have been expressed by Asmal's predecessors, but little was done to promote an "official" national history by the Department of Education. In fact, it was the heritage sector under the direction of the Department of Arts, Culture, Science and Technology (DACST) that carried much of the responsibility for developing a nation-building paradigm in

---

30. Colin Bundy, "The Beast of the Past: History and the TRC" in W. James & L. van de Vijver (eds), *After the TRC: Reflections on truth and reconciliation in South Africa*, Cape Town, David Philip, 2000, pp. 9–30.

31. Kwesi Kwaa Prah, "Africanism and the South African Transition", *Social Dynamics*, Vol. 23, No. 2, 1997, p. 14.

32. http://www.dailynews.co.za/general/print_article.php?fArticleId=391377&fSection 2004/04/12.

the Mandela era.[33] It established new "sites of memory" – memorials, monuments, public holidays, national symbols, commemorative events and civic rituals – so as to foster both reconciliation and a new national identity in South Africa. But the emphasis has begun to change under Mbeki as the ANC as government and organisation falls into line with his vision of the African Renaissance and begins to reclaim its radical heritage and African past. For instance, it has underwritten a project to produce a new ANC-centred history with the launch in 2001 of *The Road to Democracy* series to be published by the South African Democracy Education Trust (SADET). These tensions between the common past articulated by the rhetoric of "rainbowism" and a conflictual one associated with "Africanist" discourse will become more apparent when we examine the narratives constructed by museum curators in the next section.

Curating the past in and on behalf of the new South Africa

Since 1994, numerous new sites of memory have been commissioned to remember aspects of South Africa's reconfigured past. These include national, local and community-based public history projects. Certain of these, especially battle sites, memorials and monuments, have sought to promote nation-building by emphasizing a shared rather than a conflictual past. Others have celebrated ethnic-nationalist history. Still others have focused on telling the stories of local communities but have inserted these within the master narrative of national history. In some instances, the initiative for the establishment of these sites came from civil society or the private sector. Funding has come solely from central, regional or local government in some cases, whilst in others one or more of these tiers of government has formed a partnership with the private sector. I will focus on museums in the discussion that follows.

As state-funded institutions, South African museums give material form to authorized versions of the past, which in time become institutionalized as public memory. In this way, museums invariably – although not always – anchor official memory.[34] During the apartheid era, museologists insisted on

---

33. Nuttall & Wright, "Predicaments of Academic History", p. 34.

34. Patricia Davison, "Museums and the reshaping of memory" in Sarah Nuttall and Carli Coetzee (eds), *Negotiating the past: The making of memory in South Africa*, Cape Town, Oxford University Press, 1998, p. 145. There have been cases, such as the Smithsonian's proposed Enola Gay exhibit in 1995, where museum curators have challenged the meaning of an event in public memory. In this instance, the commemorative voice

the objective nature of their exhibits and the knowledge conveyed by them. Since then it has been widely acknowledged that:

> ... the conceptual frameworks that order collections and underpin exhibitions also mirror dominant forms of knowledge.[35]

For museums are not simply repositories of artefacts but active producers of knowledge. They employ a discourse which, in Foucauldian terms, is a historically specific material practice that produces knowledge and establishes power relations between subjects who occupy specific positions – in this case, curators and the public. In other words, museums tend to reproduce the unequal political relationships of a society. And the ability of ethnic groups and local communities to have their version of history accepted as the public history rests on their access to power and resources. In recognizing that they are part of civil society and should provide spaces where members of society can explore and make sense of their past, certain museums have in recent years sought to involve communities in their projects so as to give them a sense of ownership of their heritage.[36] But this has not always been the case for a variety of reasons. I wish to examine two instances – one a municipality-initiated and the other a foreign-funded project – that bear this out.

Danish museum curator Maria Rytter, in conjunction with Faaborg Prison Museum, produced an exhibit in 1999 simply called "Nelson Mandela". Sponsored primarily by Danish funders, it was handed over to the Robben Island Museum in 2001. Following its display in one of South Africa's premier cultural tourism attractions, it has become a travelling exhibit under the name "Long Walk to Freedom".[37] It derives its title from Mandela's autobiography (co-authored by Richard Stengel) and tells, in part, the life story of Mandela and how this intersected with the resistance struggle against apartheid. It consists of 34 display boards with captioned photographs and texts, as well as artefacts such as a South African Police uniform, a replica of Mandela's Robben Island prison cell, and items associated with the hard physical labour performed by political prisoners in the limestone quarry on Robben Island.

---

prevailed over the historical one and the exhibit in its original form was cancelled.

35. Patricia Davison, deputy director of the South African Museum, Cape Town, cited by Praeg, "Transformation and the politics of memory", *Grocotts Mail*, 2000.

36. Sandra Klopper, "Whose Heritage? The Politics of Cultural Ownership in Contemporary South Africa", *NKA Journal of Contemporary Art*, Vol. 5, 1996, pp. 34–37.

37. I viewed it at the Albany Museum, Grahamstown.

The structure of the display would seem to suggest an attempt to marry a "slice of life" thematic focus on the prison experience of Mandela with the broader (and chronological) history of his role as a political leader. In fact, much of the exhibit concerns the experiences of the Rivonia Trialists and other political prisoners on Robben Island. Mandela is depicted as a dignified leader of men despite the dehumanizing circumstances of his incarceration. The display also deals with Mandela's subsequent transfer to Pollsmoor and Victor Verster prisons from whence he entered into negotiations with the De Klerk government that resulted in the release of all political prisoners and the dismantling of apartheid.

The exhibit was constructed during the "honeymoon period" of the Mandela era when national reconciliation was high on the agenda, and when the rhetoric of "rainbowism" was ubiquitous. It is clear that the curator was influenced by the expressions of goodwill by former political enemies who were prepared to sink their differences in order to find a way out of the protracted conflict and the spiralling levels of violence. There is reference to the "miracle of the negotiated revolution". The main text reflects admiration for Mandela and his selfless efforts to secure a peaceful political transition. The teleological narrative leads the reader/viewer along the path of reconciliation. The final display board has the heading *The Power of Reconciliation* and shows photographs of a reunion between former political prisoners and warders. The sub-text would seem to be that even functionaries of the apartheid regime had sufficient humanity to recognize that all that separated them from the erstwhile inmates had been the politico-judicial system that they were obliged to enforce. The exhibit undoubtedly extols the magnanimity of Mandela and his associates in being willing to forgive their former oppressors but suggests that their jailers, too, were honourable men. Sources cited include James Gregory's *Goodbye Bafana: Nelson Mandela, My Prisoner, My Friend* (1995) and stories relayed by another prison warder named Christo Brand. These acknowledgments would seem to imply that Mandela's former jailers were quite prepared to tell their stories once Mandela had emerged as an icon. In this way, their own stories were refashioned to coincide with the history of reconciliation in the new South Africa. And the exhibit serves to validate the nation-building process.

History is not only reworked to reflect changing political circumstances but it may be appropriated by civic and political leaders. This can be illustrated with reference to the sequence of events and circumstances surrounding the proposed development of a museum in the century-old township of New

Brighton. Port Elizabeth's local authority – previously the City Council and now the Nelson Mandela Metropole – has a long-standing commitment to upgrade the Red Location, which is the oldest part of the township. It was envisaged that the first phase of the project would entail the erection of a Freedom Struggle Museum and the restoration of corrugated iron houses from which the Red Location derives its name. The project was launched in June 1998 with an architectural competition designed to solicit a suitable design for a cultural complex, which was to include an art gallery, a creative art centre, a market, a library, a hall, conference centre and visitors' accommodation.[38] On 1 April 2003, the Metropole's Executive Mayor Nceba Faku performed the sod turning at a ceremony to mark the commencement of what was now to be called the Red Location Cultural Museum. The Metropole's communications manager, Roland Williams, said that the project "formed part of the council's strategy of upgrading previously disadvantaged communities". He added that the Red Location had "major political significance".[39] The project has been inextricably connected to a political vision of why New Brighton's past should be remembered; a version of New Brighton's history which invokes the history of the struggle against apartheid and commemorates it as a "site of resistance". This vision that New Brighton be remembered in this way was first articulated by certain (former) Councillors.[40]

Since being mooted, the Red Location Cultural Museum project has been owned and promoted by the Mandela Metropole and the heritage tourism industry in Port Elizabeth. The project has taken some five years to get off the ground even though the central government promised to match the funding budgeted by the Metropole. While the authorities claimed to have consulted with Red Location residents to ascertain how the money should be spent, they ignored their express wishes when they insisted that priority be accorded to the development of infrastructure and the provision of essential services rather than the cultural/historical precinct. Nonetheless, the Metro has proceeded with the project. Irrespective of the motives of its initiators and planners, the project represents a real danger that outsiders might impose

---

38. *The Municipality of Port Elizabeth, Competition for the Transformation of Red Location,* Port Elizabeth, 1998, p. 8. This publication was compiled by Albrecht Herold.

39. *Eastern Province Herald,* 2 April 2003, "Mayor kicks off Red Location museum project".

40. It appears to represent the vision of former Cllrs Rory Riordan and Jennifer Bowler. See *Weekend Post,* 24 June 2000, p. 6, "Vision of township apartheid museum becoming a reality".

their vision of what New Brighton's past should mean for those who have lived there. It is not my wish to denigrate struggle heroes, but the struggle for liberation was not the only defining experience of New Brighton's residents. Richard Werbner holds that the "right of recountability" entitles citizens to have their memories made known and acknowledged in the public sphere.[41] Insofar as they have been heard – as with the TRC hearings – the voices of New Brighton residents have been framed by the master narrative constructed by public memory and/or official history. If ordinary voices do not fit the dominant narrative, they are silenced and exit the space of public memory. Although this need not necessarily mean that they are forgotten, they most certainly are marginalised. For when memory is repressed or de-politicised by groups in civil society, it is deprived of its claims on political resources and state power.[42]

Whereas personal memory based on the individual's lived experience fades with the passage of time, the authority of public memory increases for it becomes the more widely accepted version of the past.[43] The public memory of New Brighton's past privileges the experiences of political activists over those of ordinary people. The stories of their everyday lives have been subsumed by the triumphalism of struggle history. As the liberation struggle becomes the dominant narrative of our national history, the stories of smaller communities are subordinated to this master narrative. So New Brighton is remembered as a "site of resistance" and a "stronghold of the ANC". This is typified in reminiscences published in books, journals, web sites and local newspapers that lionize both living and deceased "heroes of the struggle" who happened to have lived in the township. And this will, no doubt, provide the template for the fashioning of New Brighton's public history when it comes to be written and displayed in the Red Location Cultural Museum.

41. Richard Werbner, "Beyond Oblivion: Confronting Memory Crisis", in R. Werbner (ed.), *Memory and the Postcolony: African Anthropology and the Critique of Power*, London, Zed Books, 1998.

42. Müller, "The power of memory", p. 32.

43. Barbie Zelizer, *Remembering to Forget: Holocaust Memory through the Camera's Eye*, Chicago, University of Chicago Press, 1998, p. 3.

Conclusion

I believe that the quality of the country's transformation to democracy can be improved through dealing openly with the past. Conversely, forced silence and forgetting might derail the process. We should avoid repeating the mistakes of the past when the poor and oppressed were generally excluded from or confined to the margins of the apartheid master narrative that legitimated white supremacy. The disempowered had to construct their identities in counter-memories that existed outside the authority of official history. Their stories have, belatedly and to some extent, been recovered through cultural heritage projects, oral history, memoirs and some social history. The recovery and recognition of the memories of poor and oppressed groups will provide a corrective to the reification of the official version of South Africa's past; perhaps even constitute a true people's history. However, it cannot be taken for granted that counter-memory is automatically liberating, or that such counter-memory should have legitimacy per se. Counter-memory might contribute towards preserving another version of the past, but it does not necessarily follow that it is the truth.

So, instead of manipulating public memory and subverting the past in pursuit of a political agenda, we should accept and even welcome conflicting and competing memories as an inevitable part of the transition to democracy.[44] If public memory is to be more than a dominant mythology, new ways of evoking multiple memories and a plurality of historical voices will have to be found.[45] This means providing for open-ended or non-prescriptive readings of the past so that audiences may negotiate the diverse meanings that any site/display/exhibit/artefact holds for them. In post-apartheid South Africa, this is the responsibility of professional and public historians alike.

---

44. Müller, "The power of memory", pp. 32–34.
45. Nuttall and Coetzee, "Introduction" to *Negotiating the past*, p. 14.

CHAPTER 9

The transformation of heritage in the new South Africa

Christopher Saunders

To define heritage as "what is left behind after the historic event has taken place"[1] is surely inadequate. "Heritage" includes what is created in the present to remember the past by, such as names given to places and monuments. Heritage is often a recreation of the past, an act of remembrance, through the giving of a name, the erection of a monument or the way objects are displayed in a museum. This is clearly different from the critical study of the past, the primary concern of historians. While history, as a critical discipline, has had a rough ride in South Africa since 1994, as the chapter in this volume by Colin Bundy shows, the heritage industry has boomed, as efforts have been made to correct the inherited legacies of the past. Some historians have become "heritage specialists", writing critically about aspects of heritage and training those entering the heritage industry, for while posts in History Departments at universities have been hard to come by, numerous posts have opened up in recent years in heritage.[2]

Along with the growing inter-relationships between "history" and "heritage", however, have come new tensions. Some historians have criticised heritage practices, and stressed the differences between the study of the past, on the one hand, and the concern with preserving aspects of the past on the other. For their part, some heritage practitioners have been critical of historians for not engaging with heritage, and have accused them of failing to see its significance. At a conference held at the Rand Afrikaans University, Johan-

---

1. J. Deacon, "Heritage and African History", paper given at conference on history, memory and human progress, Rondebosch, October 2002, p. 1.

2. From the late 1990s a joint post-graduate Diploma in Museum and Heritage Studies was offered by the University of Cape Town, the University of the Western Cape and the Robben Island Training Programme.

nesburg, in June 2002 under the title Heritage Creation and Research: The Restructuring of Historical Studies in Southern Africa,[3] the then Director of the Robben Island Museum, in a keynote address, launched an attack on historians (and he chose to emphasise the fact that the great majority of them are white and male) for not recognising the value and importance of heritage. He interpreted what certain historians had written on the differences between "history" and "heritage" as constituting an attack on heritage itself, and sought not only to come to its defence, but to suggest that heritage was becoming the new paradigm in historical studies.[4] This followed a trend in international scholarship to praise transformations in heritage and be critical of the failure of historians to keep pace.[5]

This chapter is mainly concerned with exploring, through a very selective range of case studies, some of the achievements and inadequacies, the pitfalls and the promises, of the new heritage industry in South Africa. It considers how much transformation there has been since 1994, in the naming of South Africa's public places, in its monuments and its museums, and asks why there has not been more. And in conclusion, it offers a few reflections on the role that historians should play in relation to the heritage sector.[6]

3. Some of the papers from this conference are included in *Historia,* Vol. 47, No. 2, 2002.

4. A. Odendaal, "'Heritage' and the Arrival of Post-Colonial History in South Africa", unpublished paper, 2002. Odendaal wrote from a privileged position, being a white male himself, his only connection with a university (Western Cape) was as Honorary Professor of History and Heritage Studies. He was insufficiently critical of the many failings of the heritage industry, in which he had been a leading player. There had for example been no effective response to the numerous criticisms of false statements made by the guides on Robben Island to visitors over the years.

5. E.g. D. Chakrabarty, "Museums in Late Democracies", *Humanities Research*, Vol. IX, No. I, 2002, p. II: "...memory and experience...will play as important roles in the politics of democracies as the disembodied knowledge academic disciplines aspire to. Museums, more than archives and history departments have travelled the distance needed to keep up with changes that mark late democracies."

6. A first version of this chapter was prepared as a lecture delivered in Denmark in 2000 on a "History and Democracy" exchange. I have updated the contents to reflect the situation as of early 2003. I wish to thank June Bam, who later came to work with the South African History Project, and our Danish hosts for making my first visit to Denmark so enjoyable.

The process of restructuring

The names given to public places, and the nature and content of museums and monuments, reflect power relations in any society. In South Africa, they were products of a colonial past, when a settler elite ruled. The ethnology exhibitions of museums were notorious for perpetuating a set of racial stereotypes. As late as the 1980s, when South Africa moved to a new tricameral constitution, bringing Coloureds and Indians into central government, museums were classified into either own affairs (White, Coloured or Indian) or "general affairs". Into the 1990s, most museums tended to preserve white heritage, and to the extent that black history was portrayed at all, it was to be found in museums of anthropology, natural history and physical science. This was most obvious in Cape Town, South Africa's cultural capital, where the South African Cultural History Museum presented artefacts relevant to the Western tradition back to Graeco-Roman times and then relating to the history of whites in South Africa, while a separate Bo-Kaap museum was established for Moslem or Malay culture, and plaster-casts of San or Bushmen – the "first nation" – remained in the South African Museum, which was devoted mainly to natural history and science.[7]

From the time of the transfer of political power in 1994, the ANC-dominated government's Department of Arts and Culture has been trying to redress imbalances in heritage, and promote a more egalitarian culture, as part of the general process of transformation. Now for the first time the explicit goal of the Department was that the heritage sector should serve all South Africans. Previously marginalised communities should now have their cultural heritages recognised. A set of well-funded "legacy projects" were formulated at national level to give content to this goal. The stated aim was to reflect the diversity among the people of the country, while at the same time to help build shared values, to aid the nation-building project.

But there was no massive, over-night transformation in the heritage sector. Arts and Culture has not been a high priority in the government's plans. The ministry is a lesser one, which has been headed by a non-ANC member of the de facto coalition government, Dr Ben Ngubane of the Inkatha Freedom Party. In the ministry's 1999/2000 budget, which had to fund science and technology as well as arts and culture, R38.4 million was allocated to 27 museums, but the Robben Island Museum alone received R21.9 million, or

---

7. In 1964, objects relating to European culture were removed from the SAM to the newly established South African Cultural History Museum.

57 per cent .[8] Inertia and bureaucratic delays impeded progress, and there was deliberate blockage by those who did not want change. Much time was taken up with restructuring, with the National Monuments Council becoming part of the South African Heritage Resources Agency (SAHRA), and museums being linked in various groupings, Northern, Southern (named Iziko, meaning "the hearth" in Xhosa), and Eastern.[9] The national Department has sought to offload decisions for change to provincial and local authorities, and there are particular reasons for lack of action at those levels. In neither Kwa-Zulu Natal nor the Western Cape did the ANC hold power at the provincial level; only within the last year (2002–3) did the ANC win control of the Cape Town unicity and then the province. In a democratic order, the process of change had to involve discussion and consultation, and it was often not clear who the relevant stakeholders were. More generally, the fact that South Africa had experienced, not a victory of one side over the other but a negotiated settlement meant that the emphasis fell, especially during the presidency of Nelson Mandela (1994–1999), on cautious change and reconciliation. Abrupt change was thought politically unwise. On the other hand, changing names, monuments and museums was one of the easiest and least costly ways to bring about transformation. What, then, has happened since 1994? Let us consider first the naming of public places, especially those named after historic events or people.

Historical naming

In South Africa, fewer indigenous place-names survive than in, say, the United States. This reflects both the destructive nature of the conquest of the country and the extent of racism involved, for because blacks were regarded as inferior, the names they themselves used for places tended to be ignored by the conquerors. Since 1994, there has been some attempt at redress. The redrawing of the provinces in the 1993 constitution, increasing them in number from four to nine, enabled some black African names to be introduced soon after the transfer of power (Mpumalanga, Gauteng). The changing of pro-

---

8. *Sunday Independent*, 7 March, 1999, p. 11. The 1998/99 budget had been R39.4 million. In 2000 the Robben Island budget was reduced to R21.2 million, *Cape Argus*, 1 March 2000. By contrast, R2 million that year went to six colonial and apartheid-era monuments.

9. The creation of a central flagship museum complex was complicated by the fact that it would cross provincial boundaries.

vincial names is ongoing, with the Northern Province deciding in 2002 to change its name to Limpopo. At the same time, a number of leading towns in the Limpopo Province lost the names given them for their Voortrekker founders and received African names; Pietersburg became Polokwane, for example. With the introduction of new metropolitan areas, the opportunity arose to find African names that could be used in place of colonial names for the major cities: Pretoria became part of the larger Tshwane metropole, Port Elizabeth now falls in the Nelson Mandela metropole, Durban in the eThekwini metropole. But across the country, the overwhelming majority of the old names remain, even in most African townships.

In 2001, a new mayor of Cape Town, Peter Marais, proposed that two main streets in Cape Town, Wale and Adderley Streets, be renamed after F.W. de Klerk and Nelson Mandela. This aroused much opposition, and a judicial commission found that the process involved in proposing new names had been flawed and dishonest. So the names remain unchanged. The City Council did decide that in future, any renaming should be undertaken in close consultation with the relevant community, but there was more talk than action. Though it was announced that the names in the Cape Town township of Gugulethu, which were mere numbers following NY, standing for "Native Yard", would be changed, there was no agreement on what names were to take their place.[10] The range of mountains beyond the Cape Flats, named by the Dutch in the seventeenth century the Hottentots' Holland, retained its name, despite the fact that "Hottentot" had long had a derogatory connotation. When students at a University of Cape Town residence were polled to find a new name for their apartment block, called Forest Hill, they could not come up with any agreed alternative, so that name too was retained. One issue that often arose was whether it was appropriate to use the name of a living person. While in the Namibian capital of Windhoek, numerous names now reflect the names of distinguished living visitors, in South Africa there was resistance to using the names of living people, in part because of the poor record set in this regard by the previous National Party government, which had allowed the names of its politicians to be given to new ventures. A major road in Pretoria was named for Nelson Mandela, but the use of the names of living people was relatively rare. Instead, in most cases when names were changed the new names were neutral and non-historical/political. Verwoerd-

---

10. "Gugulethu folk won't live in racist NY any more", *Cape Argus*, 1 May 2002. At the same time, the nearby township of Khayelitsha was given new names, mostly of struggle heroes: "Heroes Names for Khayelitsha", *Cape Argus*, 5 May 2000.

burg, originally named after the architect of apartheid, now became Centurion, and when the first Minister of Water Affairs after 1994 insisted that the apartheid-era names for major dams be dropped, they were not re-named after people: the Verwoerd became the Gariep Dam, the Khoi name for the Orange River, for example. Cape Town's D.F. Malan airport, named after the first apartheid-era prime minister, became simply Cape Town International Airport, and Jan Smuts airport, named after the last pre-apartheid era prime minister, Johannesburg International. On the other hand, the Department of Education's main office building in Pretoria is now named after Sol Plaatje,[11] the greatest black South African intellectual of the early 20th century, and the Chelmsford Dam, named after the British general who led the imperial troops into Natal in 1879, has become the Ntshingwayo Dam, after the senior general in Cetchwayo's Zulu army.[12] Such changes, easy to make, could have great symbolic importance as reflecting a new vision of the past.[13]

Public monuments

Since the transfer of power, few existing public monuments have been removed. The removal of the statue of Verwoerd from public display in Bloemfontein in 1994 was a rare example, similar to the swift removal of the statute of Cecil Rhodes in Harare, Zimbabwe, when that country became independent in 1980.[14] In Cape Town, there was a brief attempt to "redo" some of

---

11. *Sunday Independent*, editorial, 4 June 2000. This editorial pointed out that the homes of Robert Sobukwe in Masizakhe, adjoining Graaff Reinet, and of Steve Biko in Ginsberg are not functioning national monuments.

12. R. Kasrils, "Zulu victory over British inspires the renaming of KwaZulu-Natal's Chelmsford Dam", *Sunday Independent*, 6 August 2000. Other names that were changed were those of ships and submarines in the South African Navy: the SAS Magnus Malan became the SAS Makhanda, the SAS P.W. Botha became SAS Shaka.

13. Soon after coming to power, the new government changed the names of a number of the public holidays, and in the interests of reconciliation the new names were "neutral": Sharpeville Day became "Human Rights Day", Soweto Uprising Day "Youth Day" and the September holiday merely "Heritage Day". 16 December, the anniversary of the battle of Blood River/Ncome, formerly commemorated as "Dingane's Day", "Day of the Vow" and "Day of the Covenant" now became "Day of Reconciliation". Umkhonto we Sizwe chose that day to launch its armed struggle in 1961.

14. There are plans to put the toppled Verwoerd statute up again, this time in the Afrikaner enclave of Orania, on the Orange River, where there is a much smaller Verwoerd statute.

the statutes; the statue of General Louis Botha, the first prime minister of a united South Africa, which stands outside Parliament. It was draped in a blanket and the face transformed, so that Botha became a Xhosa initiate. But the statue was soon restored to as it had been, and officials often said that it was wrong to tamper with, or destroy, existing monuments, for that would be to destroy history. So Queen Victoria remains in her place outside the Parliament buildings in Cape Town, and Cecil Rhodes still stands in the Cape Town Gardens close by, and is memorialised also on the slopes below Devil's Peak. A suggestion made by a Member of Parliament that epitaphs should be added to statutes of people like Louis Botha, pointing out that they were architects of racial domination, has so far elicited no positive reaction.[15] Instead, new monuments have been created, to tell the "other side of the story", to commemorate the previously marginalized. At the site of the battle of Blood River or Ncome in KwaZulu Natal (December 1838), descendants of the original Voortrekker victors and other Afrikaners had erected a laager of ox-wagons as a memorial in 1971. A new monument, to the Zulu who died, was now built with government funds and unveiled on the 160th anniversary of the battle.[16]

In *When Smuts Goes*, a prediction of what would happen in South Africa after an Afrikaner nationalist government came to power, Arthur Keppel-Jones outlined a racial conflict that ended with the blowing up of the Voortrekker Monument, with the last apartheid ruler cowering in its basement as it was reduced to rubble. But today the Voortrekker Monument, opened with great fanfare in 1949 and symbol of Afrikaner nationalism, continues to loom over Pretoria. Umkhonto we Sizwe, the armed wing of the ANC, decided not to target the Monument in the 1980s because it knew how much its destruction would anger Afrikaners.[17] After 1994, the new government chose not to interfere with the Monument, except to cut funds to it, so that now it derives most of its funds from entrance fees. Instead, the new government decided to set up another substantial museum alongside it, on Salvokop, an adjacent hill overlooking Pretoria. In 2002 President Mbeki unveiled a plaque to mark the launch of this new Freedom Park project, and professional architects from anywhere in the world were invited to submit proposals for the site, in a com-

---

15. M. Ramgobin, "SA Whites should review past ideas", *Cape Times*, 15 September 2000.

16. *Cape Times*, 17 December 1998. This was a Legacy Project.

17. Information from Indres Naidoo, Cape Town, March 2003.

petition with substantial monetary prizes.[18] Namibia has recently aped Zimbabwe in erecting a "Stalinist Heroes" Acre, identical to that in Harare, on a hillside overlooking Windhoek. The aim of the Freedom Park project was to create something unique and special, which will not only commemorate the recent liberation struggle, but offer a view of "the entire South African story".[19] How successful this will be remains to be seen.

Other new monuments include that for the Mozambican President Samora Machel, at the place where he was killed when his plane crashed under mysterious circumstances just inside South African territory; the women's memorial, unveiled on Women's Day 2000 at the Union Buildings in Pretoria to commemorate the women's anti-pass gathering in 1956,[20] and monuments to Mahatma Gandhi in Pietermaritzburg and to Enoch Sontonga in Johannesburg, the composer of the larger part of the present national anthem, which combines the old and the new in a gesture of reconciliation.[21] A statue unveiled to Steve Biko, martyr of Black Consciousness, in East London was, ironically, made by a white artist, and the funds for it were donated mainly by white admirers, mostly foreigners.[22] More recently, new monuments have been unveiled to commemorate the pass-protesters who were shot at Sharpeville on 21 March 1960,[23] those who died in the violence during the

---

18. See for example, the full-page advertisement for the project in *Sunday Times*, 1 December 2002. R140 million has been voted for the project in the 2003 budget.

19. Freedom Park, conceptual document, Pretoria, 2003. In opening Parliament on 14 Feb. 2003, President Mbeki said: "as a contribution to building the self-image that attaches to a proud nation, we shall continue this year with the project to build the first phase of the Freedom Park Monument… We are confident that the best of our architects, designers and other creative workers, together with others from the rest of Africa and other parts of the world will avail their talent for the construction of a Freedom Park that we hope will stand out as an important tribute to the dignity of Africans and all human beings."

20. It takes the form of a grinding basin, in which a stone is set, for the slogan of the time was: "You have struck a woman, you have struck a rock."

21. The Enoch Sontonga memorial at his grave in the Braamfontein cemetery was unveiled on Heritage Day 1996. The present national anthem remains a mixture of what he composed and part of "Die Stem" / "The Voice", the pre-1994 anthem.

22. C. Rassool, L. Witz and G. Minkley, "Burying and Memorialising the Body of the Truth: The TRC and National Heritage", paper presented at conference on Public History: Forgotten History, University of Namibia, August 2000. Those who donated money included Richard Branson, Richard Attenborough and Kevin Kline, leading actor in the movie *Cry Freedom*.

23. *Sunday Independent*, 17 March 2002.

early 1990s in Thokoza on the East Rand, and the victims of apartheid-era atrocities in Cape Town. The latter were much criticised by the families of the victims for having been erected without prior consultation with them.[24] The Truth and Reconciliation Commission, in its 1998 Report, proposed the idea that a form of reparation to victims could take the form of memorials to be erected to those who had suffered and died in the recent liberation struggle, perhaps similar to the wall of remembrance for the Vietnam War in Washington D.C. Some have even suggested that places of death and torture – most notoriously, the farm of Vlakplaas, outside Pretoria, the "heart of the whore"[25] – should also become national monuments.

Museums under transformation

Turning to museums, we find here too that the scorecard is mixed. Though existing monuments can usually not be altered, museums can be, and some have begun to take up the challenge of moving into the post-apartheid era. This has meant, in some existing museums, adding to what already exists; new displays on the history of blacks were added on to the existing pantheon of settler and white pioneering achievements. Of the new museums created, one of the best known is the Mandela Museum, opened in February 2000 at three sites in the Transkei: at Mveso, his birthplace, at Qunu where he grew up and in the town of Umtata, where the main museum is housed.[26] Other new museums include the Hector Peterson Museum in Soweto, at the place where he was shot on 16 June 1976, sparking off the Soweto Uprising,[27] and the privately funded and built Apartheid Museum outside Johannesburg, at the site of the Gold Reef City casino. Though the University of the Witwatersrand historian Phil Bonner was a key adviser on the content of

---

24. The memorial unveiled on 21 March 2000 to the Guguletu Seven, gunned down by the police in 1986 in cold blood, was described by one of the mothers involved as "an insult": *Sunday Times*, 29 October 2000. A similar reaction had been evoked to a sculpture unveiled in Athlone, a Cape Town suburb, to commemorate the so-called "Trojan Horse" incident in 1985, in which three children were shot and killed by police hidden in the back of a railway truck.

25. J. Pauw, *In the Heart of the Whore. The Story of Apartheid's Death Squads*, Halfway House, 1991.

26. See L. Callinicos, *The World that Made Mandela*, Cape Town, 1999.

27. *Sunday Independent*, 16 June 2002; *Sunday Times*, 2 December 2001; www.apartheid-museum.org; Cf. A. Levin, "The Substance of Style", *Sawubona*, August 2002.

the Apartheid Museum, the selective nature of the displays has come in for considerable critical comment.[28]

Elsewhere, change was less dramatic. Though President Mandela spoke out against natural history museums containing exhibits of indigenous people, the South African Museum (SAM) in Cape Town was able to resist government pressure for some time. The lifelike plaster casts of the thirteen San men and women who lived near Prieska in 1912 have now been boarded up and whether they will ever be displayed again depends on "consultation with the community".[29] But the SAM still exhibits the art of indigenous people, such as the Lydenburg heads and the Zimbabwe birds (one of which was returned to Great Zimbabwe in Zimbabwe, from which Cecil Rhodes had taken it), and most of the displays at the South African Cultural History Museum remain Eurocentric; despite now being called the Slave Lodge, only one or two exhibits concern slavery as such.[30]

A number of the new museums established – such as Museum Africa in Johannesburg, the African Window, a satellite of the National Cultural History Museum in Pretoria, and the KwaMuhle Museum in Durban – represent the lives of ordinary black people. Their collections fill obvious gaps, but they are special museums relating to black life, and so continue an unfortunate separatist tradition.[31] Perhaps the best-known new museum to be criticised along such lines was the District Six Museum in Cape Town, which commemorated the proclamation of District Six as a white area in 1966, the forced removal of its people and the destruction of the area.[32] In 1989 a group

---

28. E.g. on the absence of Helen Suzman, icon of above-ground anti-apartheid resistance of the 1960s and 1970s.

29. M. Gosling, "Museum's Bushmen Exhibit to Close Today", *Cape Times*, 3 April 2001. Before the display was boarded up, some attempt was made to show how the exhibit had developed, and a box asked for opinions on the exhibit. Cf. P. Davison, "Museums and the Reshaping of Memory", in S. Nuttall and C. Coetzee, *Negotiating the Past: The Making of Memory in South Africa*, Cape Town, 1998.

30. These were, in mid-2001, a pipe, a piece of lace, a birth certificate and a slave ownership paper: "Museum to Dust Itself Off", *Sunday Times*, 3 June 2001. Very imaginative ideas for transforming the museum were made, over many years, by Robert Shell, now of the University of the Western Cape, but these came to nothing.

31. One new museum that escaped such strictures was the Lyandle Migrant Labour Museum in Lwandle township at Somerset West: L. Oliver, "Tough Lives of SA's Migrant Labourers Set in Memory", *Saturday Argus*, 22 April 2000.

32. C. Rassool and S. Prosalendis (eds), *Recalling Community in Cape Town: Creating and curating the District Six Museum*, Cape Town, 2001.

of ex-residents – then involved in a "Hands Off District 6" campaign – came up with the idea of founding a museum as a way to bring the former residents together again. This became linked, after 1994, to the land claim that the District Six people lodged with the Commission for Land Restitution. From the start, there was much community involvement in the new museum, and since it opened in 1994, its central exhibit has remained a map of the former District covered by a plastic sheet; visitors who remember special sites – such as the house in which they used to live – mark the place on the plastic, and there are other sheets on which names can be recorded. The original street signs, fortuitously found, are also exhibited. The idea is to reclaim the history of the District.[33] Early critics claimed that the displays suggested a story of a Golden Age in which people lived together in harmony and peace; there was romanticisation and much nostalgia for a lost community. In reality, said the critics, the District was often far from being a place of harmony and racial integration; just because it was under threat, it was neglected and much of it became a slum; for decades it was an area in which gangsters operated openly, even if they were not a major threat to the community and were not involved in violent crime. Other critics did not like the museum being located in a building that had been a Methodist Church, when many other faiths had been represented in the District. And the museum focused, it was said, on the history of the District as a place where Coloured people lived, and relatively little on the history of the Africans who, especially at an earlier date, had lived there in considerable numbers.[34] District Six was only the most notorious of many Group Areas removals in the Cape Peninsula, and its history needed to be seen in the context of Group Areas removals in the area as a whole.

Fortunately, professional historians have always been closely associated with the management of the District Six Museum, and most of the criticisms have now been addressed in new displays recently opened at the museum. These give due attention to the Africans who were expelled from the District, and to other communities in the Cape Peninsula affected by Group Areas. This close interaction between historians and heritage professionals has been less successful in relation to the new addition to the Robben Island Museum, now a world heritage site, which, as we have seen, has attracted a dispropor-

---

33. See esp. I. de Kok, "Cracked Heirlooms", in Nuttall and Coetzee, *Negotiating the Past*, pp. 63ff.

34. Some were not removed until the early 1960s: see esp. Nomvuyo Ngcelwane, *Sala Kahle District Six*, Cape Town, 1998, a wonderful evocation of District Six by an African woman.

tionate amount of funding from the state.[35] The way the Island has been marketed, as both a symbol of hope and of tragedy, has come under critical scrutiny from within the Museum.[36] For long the house on the Island lived in by the leader of the Pan-Africanist Congress, Robert Sobukwe, lay neglected and off the tourist-route, while a R40 million new Nelson Mandela Gateway to Robben Island, opened by Mandela himself on 1 December 2001, incorporated a poorly-displayed collection of artefacts relating to the museum.[37] Some critics argued that such a large sum should rather have been spent on a new museum of resistance and slavery.[38]

History and heritage

History and heritage should not be confused. Historians provide an interpretation of what happened in the past. Those involved with heritage are concerned with specific aspects of that past. It is the duty of historians to judge heritage critically, and to point to its inadequacies and failings. Such criticisms should not be misconstrued as an attack on heritage as such.[39] Ideally, the two should work in constructive harmony and tension.[40] Herit-

---

35. H. Deacon, "Remembering Tragedy, Constructing Modernity: Robben Island as a national monument", in Nuttall and Coetzee, *Negotiating the Past*, ch. 11.

36. Ibid.

37. Cf. M. Morris, "Gateway to our Past and our Future", *Cape Argus*, 1 November 2001, and "A Forlorn Symbol of Exclusion", *Cape Argus*, 8 November 2001.

38. Robert Shell, author of a seminal work on Cape slavery, has taken the lead in arguing for new slave exhibits at the Cape, and tried to access UNESCO Slave-Route funds for this.

39. In the United States, academics regularly criticise museum exhibits and ideas for new museums, but in South Africa there is no tradition of this. Cf. e.g. E. Foner, *Who Owns the Past?*, New York, 2002.

40. In opening up discussion of the relationship between "history" and "heritage", in an H-Net Africa Forum, October 1998, Jane Carruthers quoted the overstated view of David Lowenthal in "Fabricating Heritage", *History and Memory*, 10, 1, 1998: "History seeks to convince by truth ... Heritage exaggerates and omits, candidly invents and frankly forgets, and thrives on ignorance and error. Time and hindsight alter history, too. But historians' revisions must conform to accepted tenets of evidence. Heritage is more flexibly emended. Historians ignore at professional peril the whole corpus of past knowledge that heritage can airily transgress ... History tells all who will listen what has happened and how things came to be as they are...Heritage everywhere not only tolerates but thrives on historical error."

age professionals should respect the knowledge on which historians can base their comments, and the wider context they can introduce into discussion of heritage sites. Professional historians should be given more opportunities for engaging in heritage projects, and should seize such opportunities to make constructive contributions.

Many wish now to put the past to rest and move on. It may be, then, that the first decade after 1994 will be seen in the future as a golden age for transformation in the South African heritage sector, for all the shortcomings mentioned above. In this process of transformation, historians have played a relatively minor role. It is to be hoped that in the future they will work together with heritage practitioners, not in opposition to them, with each being aware of their own special roles and responsibilities.

CHAPTER 10

Reframing remembrance:

The politics of the centenary commemoration of the South African War of 1899–1902

Albert Grundlingh

The passage from the 20th to the 21st century was an occasion to recall one of South Africa's most devastating wars. The British scorched earth policy during the latter part of the conflict reduced the republics of the Transvaal and the Orange Free State almost to a wasteland. Boer women and children who died by the thousands in the hastily constructed British concentration camps to house those being swept from the veld, far outnumbered republican battlefield casualties and constituted about ten percent of the total Boer population. Moreover, the war involved all groups in South Africa and had a significant social and political impact on black people. It was indeed a war that had the potential to be remembered, even a hundred years later.

What has been called the "cult of centenary", has become increasingly important in "perpetuating, revising or creating public perceptions of past events and people."[1]

The main aim of this chapter is to analyse the dynamics of commemoration, bearing in mind that the contours of remembrance have been substantially revised through major political changes in South Africa.[2]

The state and commemoration of the war

The advent of the centenary of the war was marked by considerable ambiguity in African National Congress (ANC) circles. The public representation of the war, as a seminal event in Afrikaner history, had a long association with

---

1. R. Quinault, "The cult of the centenary, c. 1784–1914", *Historical Research,* Vol. LXXI, No. 176, 1998, p. 303.

2. A revised and longer version of this chapter is to be published by the Journal of Southern African Studies.

sectarian nationalist politics. Moreover, it was not a war, which was made to loom large in the memory of black oppositional groupings under apartheid; they had more than sufficient other armoury in their ideological arsenal to draw upon for historical legitimization.[3] The question then arises why a new government should wish to help commemorate a war that had been a white public reserve for the greater part of the century.

For the predominantly white National Party, whose support base included many Afrikaners who could claim a direct historical interest in the war, there was no doubt that the event should be commemorated.[4]

The initial indecision of the state on the matter led to some strange prohibitions. At Bloemfontein during a show in March 1998 to promote tourism in the Free State, a planned war exhibition was vetoed by the local legislature on the grounds that it was too "sensitive."[5]

It was only towards the end of 1998 that the state decided through a cabinet decision to support the centenary. For the Department of Arts, Culture, Science and Technology (DACST) an alternative was to play down or officially ignore the event. The risk, however, it was argued, was that the commemorations might have developed their own dynamics, not unlike the 1938 Voortrekker centenary celebrations, which saw a massive mobilization of Afrikaners across class and other divides. Although such a possibility, given the dramatically different circumstances between 1938 and 1999, was rather remote, the spectre of spirited right wing Afrikaner resistance kept preying on the minds of those in power. The other option was that the decision should be left to the individual provinces, but a strong counter argument was that the provinces lacked the necessary capacity to undertake a project of this kind. The possibility of embarrassingly contradictory interpretations emerging from the provinces as to what the centenary was supposed to mean in a new dispensation, was considered a further risk. The decision then was to adopt the commemorations as a national legacy project, alongside other

---

3. B. Nasson, "Commemorating the Anglo-Boer War in post-apartheid South Africa", *Radical History Review*, Issue 78, 2000, p. 150. See also T. Lodge, "Charters from the past: The African National Congress and its historiographical traditions", *Radical History Review*, Issue 46/7, 1990/91, p. 161.

4. *Die Burger,* 12 May 1998, "Wes-Kaap sal oorlog herdenk (translation.) See also *Beeld,* 10 September, "NP wil regering betrokke hê by oorlog"; *Rapport,* 3 May 1998, "Staat erken nog nie eeufees."

5. *Die Volksblad,* 11 March 1998", Anglo-Boereoorlog is te sensitief vir Bloemfontein"; *Die Volksblad,* 2 March 1998, "Kenner verstom oor verbod op uitstalling".

initiatives such as the Nelson Mandela museum, the Constitutional Court in Johannesburg and Freedom Park in Pretoria.[6]

Besides these considerations, it also has to be borne in mind that the centenary was the first major heritage event to be marked under an ANC government. Moreover, it promised to attract international attention, particularly as the advent of commemorations was to overlap with the Commonwealth conference to be held in South Africa at much the same time. Many Commonwealth countries, of course, participated in the war and this provided further impetus for the ANC to highlight the passing of a colonial world and to put the spotlight on the new incumbents of power.

Over the years the memory of the war has congealed into a particularly solid body of cultural and historical understanding and the government might well have wished for more pliable material to work with. The timing of the centenary could obviously not be changed, but the state could still try and leave its imprint on the commemorative proceedings. Ministers and directors of arts and culture in the various provinces were advised to take a particular interest in the event so as "to broaden its representation."[7] Government also made its influence felt by renaming the war as the Anglo-Boer South African War;[8] a clumsy composite of names that had little chance of being generally accepted. The Anglo-Boer War, a more traditional name for the war, proved difficult to dislodge in the public mind. Most scholars, though, preferred the term "South African War" to indicate that all groupings in the country were affected.

The National Party in pressurizing the ANC in 1998 to take a stand on the centenary had hoped that the state would be involved as a facilitator in supporting the event, but that it would refrain from exerting control.[9] The arrangement was not to be that simple. Although civil society was to be allowed a certain latitude, once the state had decided to participate, it could not afford to be outflanked and had to give a particular emphasis to proceedings.

---

6. G. Dominy and L. Callinicos, "Is there anything to celebrate? Paradoxes of policy: An examination of the state's approach to commemorating South Africa's most ambitious struggle", *South African Historical Journal*, p. 41, November 1999, pp. 389–391. See also *Rapport*, 18 June 1998, "Regering en oorlogsherdenking".

7. Dominy and Callinicos, "Paradoxes", p. 396.

8. DACST notes on government programme for the commemoration of the centenary of the Anglo-Boer War, October 1999. (In private possession.)

9. *Die Burger*, 12 September 1998, "Regering moet nou alles insit om ABO herdenking te laat slaag".

This much became clear when the War Museum of the Boer republics in Bloemfontein, which since 1994 had played a leading role in planning the commemorations, suddenly found itself under siege. Advisors close to DACST had some appreciation of the fact that the institution was aware of the need for a re-interpretation of the war and that it had also sponsored research into black participation in the war, but ultimately:

> ... given the previous ethos and uncertain institutional positioning of the museum, it is perhaps not the most effective institution to drive the process.[10]

With little regard for the museum work that had been patiently and assiduously performed since 1931, much of it voluntarily, the state moved in under the banner of restructuring and transformation. As the museum received a subsidy from the state, it was financially vulnerable. But the state did not use an economic weapon; it targeted the museum council. The existing council was not opposed to adjusting their composition after consultation, but that was not enough. With the stroke of a pen, the entire composition was swiftly and drastically changed. Predominantly Zulu speakers, with no or little knowledge of the war, were imported from Kwa-Zulu Natal to fill six of the nine positions on the council. The original council was decimated; only three members from the Free State who had a direct and longstanding interest in the work of the museum were allowed to remain.[11] Not surprisingly, this development gave rise to considerable dissatisfaction on the part of the museum establishment. The impression was created, it was argued, that the state "wished to deny Afrikaners even their own memories and sentiments related to key events in their history."[12]

The museum hierarchy decided to retaliate. Having their representation on the council slashed to an absolute minority and having members without the necessary expertise unilaterally foisted upon them on the eve of the commemorations, were considered ill advised if not perverse. They prepared a court interdict against the relevant minister, Ben Ngubane, in which he was accused of not applying his mind to the matter and being unduly in-

---

10. Dominy and Callinicos, "Paradoxes", p. 396.

11. *Beeld*, 22 April 1999, "Nuwe herrie oor museum"; *Beeld*, 29 April 1999, "Minister, oorlogsmuseum skik oor raad."

12. *Beeld*, 19 April 1999, "Twyfel heers oor maghebbers se siening van Afrikaners." (Translation.)

fluenced by officials with "irrelevant, ideological and prejudiced motives."[13] Wiser counsels then prevailed and the matter was settled out of court with a new board consisting of seven members appointed by the minister and seven by the museum.

The official launch of the centenary commemorations was planned to take place in the Free State. Initially a large sports stadium in Bloemfontein was considered as a venue. However, the plan was rejected and the reasons for not following it through reflected the state's anxiety about publicly moving into uncharted cultural waters. DACST advisors made these reservations clear:

> There is a strong possibility that a public event will not turn out the way the organizers designed it. The ABSAW is not yet seen by the majority of black South Africans as a significant event in their history and there is a strong possibility that the crowd in the stadium will be very small, despite the presence of the president. Another possibility is (particularly if there is little black participation) that the event may be used as a rallying focus for right wing minorities.

In the light of this, a "more appropriate form for the launch" was considered to be a "small elite event with a high media presence."[14] The masses, so it seems, could not always be relied upon.

Eventually it was decided to have a launch just outside Brandfort, a small town north of Bloemfontein. It was ostensibly a suitable place as there were war graves of Boer and British combatants, as well, it was claimed, of a black concentration camp victim. Brandfort is also the town where Winnie Mandela, the former wife of Nelson Mandela, was held under house arrest by the apartheid government, but whether this also fed into the choice of venue is conjectural.[15]

The launch indeed turned out to be a grand affair as seven luxury air-conditioned busses left Bloemfontein on Saturday 9 October, followed by a cooling truck with refreshments, cool drinks and mineral water for the hordes of ambassadors, politicians, invited guests and hangers-on.[16] Clearly, the launch was not meant to be a re-enactment of what happened a century earlier when

---

13. Court Papers, Supreme Court of South Africa, Case 99/1457, 9 April 1999, War Museum vs Minister of Arts, Culture, Science and Technology. (Translation.)

14. Undated DACST notes on government programme for the commemoration on the centenary of the Anglo-Boer War. (In private possession.)

15. http//woza oct 1999/ 25.htlm, "Whose remembering the war?"

16. *Die Volksblad*, 11 October 1999, "Party bly weg omdat regering herdenking kaap".

a solitary Boer fighter might have left his family and homestead on his trusty steed with provisions for thirty days to join his comrades on commando.

The crowd which gathered at Brandfort was predominantly black, comprising many schoolchildren. They gathered some distance from the dignitaries congregated at the fenced off podiums. Conspicuous by their absence were the whites who traditionally attended public ceremonies of this kind in the halcyon days of Afrikaner nationalism. As one journalist observed:

> Nary to be seen were the bearded, solid pipe-smoking Afrikaners of yore in velskoens, slouch hats and colourful "kappies" and Voortrekker dresses. Nowhere in sight was a Vierkleur or even a venerable ox-wagon. Instead, virtually the only white men in view were the substantial numbers of uniformed police and military personnel who lined the perimeters of the various ceremonial sites – and, of course, a smattering of gorgeously attired members of the diplomatic community.[17]

The appearance of President Thabo Mbeki was met with shouts of "Amandla Baba" and shrill ululation. Not everything proceeded as planned. There were shouts of glee when a burly white sergeant-major slipped and fell as he clambered to a vantage look-out point on a rocky outcrop. But this was followed by a respectful silence as "Baba" himself raised an admonishing hand.[18] It is somewhat doubtful how many of the crowd had a fair grasp as to what they were supposed to commemorate. Many had just come to see Mbeki and others with placards thought it was the opportune time to make known some more pressing concerns: "We beg our second black president to alleviate the poverty in Brandfort."[19]

A distinct African flavour was added to the occasion in an unmistakable attempt of symbolic inversion by having young black girls dressed up in white bonnets and Voortrekker dresses to represent Boer women, and black boys were put on display in red coats and bobby helmets to represent British soldiers. "While one must presume that the intention was not to be comic," a bemused historian commented, "this outlandish spectacle certainly took some planning imagination."[20]

---

17. *The Citizen*, 11 October 1999, "SA War remembered in different style".

18. *The Citizen*, 11 October 1999, " SA War remembered in different style."

19. *Die Volksblad*, 11 October 1999, "Party bly weg omdat regering herdenking kaap."(Translation.)

20. Nasson, "Commemorating", pp. 155–157.

Mbeki's oratory was to be the high point of proceedings. In a speech finely crafted for the occasion he hit all the right notes; paying homage to all those who fell, emphasizing the importance of black participation and dwelling on the need to use the past in a positive way for nation-building purposes. Complete with a couple of Afrikaans sentences added in praise of the "dapper boerevegters" (brave Boer fighters), his pleas for reconciliation in the aftermath of strife were well received by the Afrikaans press.[21] Equally well received was the Duke of Kent's speech, on behalf of the British government. It came as close as British reserve would allow to presenting South Africans with a public apology for the loss of women and children in the camps.[22]

The potential impact of these speeches, however, was somewhat blunted through planning oversights, deliberate or otherwise, which contrasted badly with the nation-building rhetoric of Mbeki. The organisers neglected to invite an Afrikaner representative to the podium, ostensibly because the Boer republics no longer existed and therefore a suitable representative could not be found. This questionable defence only rankled Afrikaners further; it was like having a wedding without a bride they retorted. When wreaths had to be laid on Boer graves, the director of the War Museum had to be hastily summoned.[23] It is for this reason, it was claimed, that the white inhabitants of Brandfort stayed well clear of proceedings. A spokesman said:

> The government hijacked the commemoration of the war between Boer and Brit. The Duke of Kent passed by, giving us a royal wave, and was afforded the opportunity to speak. A descendant of the Boers, however, was not allowed to pay tribute to the Boers. The descendants of the Boers feel that their faces have been pushed in the mud. Some of them even regarded it as the final victory for the British.[24]

The launch was not only less inclusive and representative than history would have dictated, but also more carefully stage-managed than it appeared. It transpired that the grave of what was supposed to be the black concentra-

---

21. *Business Day*, 11 October 1999, "Mbeki praises Boer fighters"; *Beeld*, 12 October 1999, "Versoening"; *Die Burger*, 12 October 1999, "Oorlog en versoening".

22. http//www. afrika.nl/news/09.10.99.htlm. Text of speech.

23. *Die Volksblad*, 9 Oktober 1999, "Onmin in herdenking"; *Die Afrikaner*, 15 October 1999, "Net Swartes by herdenkingsfees"; *Die Volksblad*, 11 October 1999, "Party bly weg omdat regering herdenking kaap."

24. *Die Volksblad*, 11 October 1999, "Party bly weg omdat regering herdenking kaap." (Translation.)

tion camp inmate, which Mbeki paid tribute to, was actually that of a farm worker buried at the time of the war. Authentic black concentration camp graves were two kilometres away. The director general of DACST virtually admitted that they were aware of this, but "that it would have spoiled the ideal of a single commemorative event in one place."[25]

Despite omissions and inaccuracies, the state had succeeded in staking its official claim in the moulding of the war heritage. This was to be carried over into the public arena.

Public discourses on black participation in the war

As far as general awareness of the nature of participation in the war was concerned, the issue of black involvement made a long overdue entry onto the public stage. It was somewhat misguided though to claim, as one journalist did, that historians had "torn out the page" on black vicissitudes during the war.[26] On the contrary, progressive historians working on the war had all but exhausted the topic during the previous 30 years.[27] That the issue only surfaced in the public arena after such a lapse of time, had everything to do with an altered climate of public opinion and little with the alleged neglect of professional historians.

Once in the public sphere, the question of black fatalities became a matter of considerable interest. A salient feature in the discourse of the commemoration of the war was the discovery of an increasing number of black war graves, especially concentration camp victims. Both the Afrikaans and the English language press announced these findings in banner headlines.[28] The keenness to report on this, prompted one reporter to take a rather jaundiced view:

---

25. *Cape Argus*, 15 October 1999, "Row over black Boer War monument"; *Die Volksblad*, 2 February 2000, "Regte begraafplaas van ABO slagoffers opgespoor"; *Die Volksblad*, 9 February 2000, " Besluit oor begraafplaas geregverdig"; *Beeld*, 2 February, "Monument se ligging is beslis verkeerd."

26. *Saturday Star*, 14 September 1996 "How Boer war historians tore out the page on blacks".

27. Nasson, "Commemorating" p 162; A. Porter, "The South African War and the historians," *African Affairs*, Vol. 99, No. 397, 2000, pp. 640–641; C. Saunders, "Blacks in historical writing on the Anglo-Boer South African War", *New Contree*, 47, 2000, pp. 127 –136.

28. For example *The Star*, 14 September 1999 "Search for site of black camp"; *Cape Argus*, 11 October 1999 "How blacks died"; *City Press*, 18 April 1999 "South Africa's forgotten POW's"; *Cape Argus*, 26 September 2000 "Graves rewrite history of blacks in Boer War";

Some ... newspaper coverage seems to have been reduced to only one aspect of the war: the participation of black compatriots, and some journalists have without a hint of irony turned into serial gravediggers. So caught up are they in this new assignment that they can't see the war for the graves.[29]

The rate at which black graves were claimed to be discovered, caused a measure of concern for certain Afrikaner groupings. They saw in this a deliberate intention to inflate black casualties so that, for political reasons, these could surpass the number of whites who had perished in the camps. With this accomplished, ran the argument, the Afrikaner history of suffering could be proportionally reduced and presented as of lesser importance than before.[30] This, however, was somewhat of a minority view.

Less suspicious and more pervasive was a pragmatic attempt on the part of Afrikaner cultural brokers to welcome the new development and to project, under the rubric of nation-building, a common bond of suffering between Afrikaners and black people. The British could now be put in the dock and on the basis of a conveniently constructed "common" anti-imperialist past, the old white elite could try and speak to the new black elite.[31]

Such an interpretation, which failed to take into account the subsequent apartheid interlude, was just too ingenuous to make much headway. It also underestimated the extent to which the new black elite sought to manoeuvre itself onto the moral high ground and preferred to conduct exchanges on nation-building on their own terms. Ben Ngubane, opening an exhibition at the War Museum in Bloemfontein on 8 October 1999, started his speech off cautiously enough by genuflecting to the notion of mutual suffering, but could not restrain himself for too long before he had to claim "that notwithstanding the general suffering across the colour divide blacks suffered even more"

Sunday Independent, 16 May 1999, "Deaths of thousands of Africans come to light"; *Die Volksblad*, 26 May 1999 "Nog swart grafte ontdek; *Beeld*, 17 April 1999 "Speurtog na Anglo-Boereoorlog se swart konsentrasiekampe"; *Die Burger*, 11 November 1999 "Nog swart grafte"; *Die Volksblad*, 9 February 2000 "Nog ABO begraafplase kan later ontdek word".

29. http//woza.za.forum2/Oct 99.Boer war25.html.

30. *Die Afrikaner*, 17 January 1999 "Segsman vir die swartes"; *Rapport*, 17 October 1999, "Moenie Boere uit die oorlog skryf nie".

31. *Rapport*, 17 October 1999, "Erken Swartes se rol in die oorlog"; *Die Burger*, 9 October 1999, "Oorlog skep band Afrikaners en Swartes; *Financial Mail*, 2 October 1999, "A congress of anti-colonial victims". See also G. Cuthbertson and A. Jeeves, "A many-sided struggle for Southern Africa", *South African Historical Journal*, 41, 1999, p. 7.

during the war.[32] The tragedy of a hundred years earlier was now recast as an almost tawdry spectacle of the Olympics of suffering. Afrikaner nationalists, of course, were past masters of invoking the concentration camp catastrophe for political purposes particularly in the thirties and forties.[33] Sixty years later, a "new set of skeletal people were to rise up from those terrible days" of the war to participate in the séance of a new round of politicians.[34]

Although there can be no doubt as to the tribulations of black people in the war, it is an oversimplification to emphasise this to the exclusion of much else. Black people were not only victims. Some tried to be masters of their own fate as far as circumstances allowed; there were those who decided to join the fighting forces on specific terms if possible, while others profited from increased agricultural markets brought about by the need to feed British troops. There was also an awareness in certain areas of the Transvaal that as a result of the war, the props of colonial society were being loosened and that this offered new opportunities to try and reclaim land that had been lost before.[35]

These specific and more varied dimensions of black involvement failed to enter into the public arena during the centenary. A partial explanation for this may simply be that the full extent and nuances of black participation were not that widely known at the time of the centenary. However, a more convincing argument is probably that even if such information had been more readily available, the "suffering" dimension would still have surfaced as the prime commemorative aspect. While the other angles were not completely without the potential to be codified into useful ideological constructs to be used in the present, there is little to compete against "suffering." Having already laid claim to the high moral ground as a result of the iniquities of apartheid, the additional revelation of black vicissitudes a century ago was a bonus to be timeously deployed, if so required, in the public sphere. The discourse of victimhood is a powerful one; particularly when there is a convenient and rich fund to draw upon.[36]

---

32. Address of Ben Ngubane, 8 October 1999. (In private posession.)

33. A. Grundlingh, "The War in Twentieth-Century Afrikaner Consciousness", in D. Omissi and A. Thompson, *The Impact of the South African War,* London, 2002, pp. 24–28.

34. Nasson, "Commemorations", p. 163.

35. Nasson, "Commemorations", p. 163. The standard work on the topic is still that of P. Warwick, *Black people and the South African War of 1899–1902,* Cambridge, 1983.

36. For a discussion on victimhood see *New York Review of Books,* 8 April 1999 "The joys

The enthusiastic endorsement of "suffering", however, was not welcomed across the board. In certain unreconstructed Africanist circles, it was argued:

> … that the obsessions of black politicians to claim the Anglo-Boer War reflects, if anything, the extent of psychological damage suffered by black people as a result of colonialism.[37]

In this view, the war was viewed merely as a squabble between colonial overlords, and black people "… couldn't even sit down comfortably and watch the fight, because they no longer owned any land to sit on." Since neither side asked black people to enter the conflict on equal terms, "there is nothing in this centenary for their descendants to celebrate."[38] Any association with the war was accordingly inappropriate and showed an "unhealthy identification with the master" and "to emulate him is a pathology that afflicts the oppressed all over the world."[39]

Both discourses had their own internal political logic, but in terms of the impact and cultural purchase, it is probably safe to claim that despite the media prominence given to black participation and the jockeying for moral positions, the centenary failed to stir the imagination of black people to a significant degree. "The vast majority of ordinary black South Africans have little knowledge as far as the Anglo-Boer War is concerned", one black commentator noted.[40] It was after all a war that had taken place well outside living memory and even if some oral recollections survived, as they certainly did,[41] it was too much to expect, given the tumultuous twentieth century and the predominant effect of apartheid, that one distant event amongst many other more recent ones would be etched in collective memory. Neither was it necessary, beyond the ritual incantation of a superior moral position, for

---

and perils of victimhood".

37. *Sunday World,* 17 October 1999, "Victims of the white man's war"; *Mail and Guardian,* 15 October 1999, "It was a white man's war"; *Sunday Times,* 17 October 1999, "Boer War had nothing to do with blacks."

38. *Mail and Guardian,* 15 October, "It was a white man's war".

39. *Sunday World,* 17 October, "Victims of the white man's war".

40. A. Sekete, "The black people and the Anglo-Boer War: How did they see it?" *Knapsak,* May 2002, 41.

41. See for example *Die Volksblad,* 28 March 1999 "Oorlog te sensitief"; *Die Volksblad,* 19 January 1997, "Dinamiese wêreld gaan oop toe navorsing oor oorlog begin." These articles contain evidence of black recollections of the war.

those in power to invoke a particular legacy of the war to bolster their political legitimacy. With an overwhelming majority in the 1999 election, the ANC hardly needed an unlikely platform such as a war between whites a hundred years previously, to cement its position.

Afrikanerdom and the commemoration of the war

While the war was deeply woven into the fabric of Afrikaner national consciousness during the first half of the century, it did not present itself as an occasion to celebrate. The Boers after all had lost the war and one does not celebrate defeats. This was in contrast to the Great Trek centenary commemorations in 1938, which had much more of a celebratory ring, linked to the successful 19th century Boer settlement in the interior of South Africa. The fiftieth anniversary of the outbreak of war in 1949, a year after the narrow National Party victory at the polls, allowed some respite from the historical legacy of loss, which had permeated so much of Afrikaner thinking after the war. Afrikaners could now start to put the war behind them; in 1948, they had regained what they had lost in 1902.[42] The future seemed bright and so inviting that the historian, D.W. Kruger, could confidently proclaim on the anniversary of the war in 1949 that "the sun has risen for the Afrikaner and now it is Africa for the Afrikaners."[43]

In 1999 with a black government in power, this vision had all but evaporated. Nor was it possible to rekindle the embers of the memory of a war that helped to stoke the Afrikaner nationalist fires of the thirties and forties. Whereas impoverished whites had formed a substantial section of Afrikanerdom at the time and political hostility was mainly directed at imperialistic English speakers, sixty years later Afrikaners had become predominantly middle-class and no longer felt inferior to English speakers.[44] Symbolically there were parallels between an emasculated Afrikanerdom of 1999 and the defeated Boer republics of a hundred years earlier. However, in terms of realpolitik in 1999 only the foolhardy would have thought of invoking a receding memory as a viable political rallying point.

---

42. A.Grundlingh, "The War in Twentieth Century Afrikaner Consciousness."

43. D.W. Kruger, "Die Tweede Vryheidsoorlog in ons nasionale ontwikkeling 'soos die son uit die môrewolke'," *Koers*, Vol. xvii, No. 2, p. 67.

44. H. Giliomee, "Streef na onafhanklikheid van gees", *Afrikaans Vandag*, Oktober 1999, p. 2.

Nevertheless, it was in the arena of cultural politics that the war could still speak to Afrikaners in a meaningful way. Much of this had to do with the re-negotiation of identity. The commemoration of the war coincided with a period of considerable drift in Afrikaner society; besides the loss of political power, old cultural sureties had disappeared or were under threat while the future looked increasingly uncertain.

One Afrikaner commentator summed this up:

> ... after the election of 1994 there was a notable escapist tendency among Afrikaners. Some escaped into the other-worldly idea of nation-building, others fled overseas, whilst a larger number sought their salvation in individualism ... economic prosperity and personal enrichment.[45]

To this can be added that the commemoration allowed some Afrikaners another escape hatch – that of the past. In the run-up to the centenary, Afrikaners as a group had to come face to face with disturbing presentations of their immediate apartheid past. Unsettling revelations from the Truth and Reconciliation Committee, reflecting Afrikaner excesses during apartheid, added to a sense of unease and disillusionment. Under these circumstances, the coming centenary of the war was viewed in some circles as an opportunity to showcase a heroic period in Afrikaner history for which they did not have to apologise.[46] More generally, the commemoration provided an opportunity to withdraw from a present where tensions between black and white seem to persist, and to find relative solace in what now may appear as an almost brotherly conflict between white and white that had already fully exhausted itself and no longer presented a threat of any kind.[47]

In the Afrikaans press, a noted author, Etienne van Heerden, aptly noted that circumstances were ripe for nostalgic indulgence and that the centenary offered a mythological space where ethnic nesting could take place.[48]

---

45. D. Goosen, *Voorlopige aantekeninge oor Politiek,* Orania, 2001, p. 63. (Translation.)

46. A. Grundlingh, "The War in Twentieth Century Afrikaner Consciousness", p. 24; *Southern Cross,* 6 October 1999, "A century on."

47. P. Louw, "Gee swaarkry van die oorlog nuwe sin", *Afrikaans Vandag,* October 1999, p. 15.

48. *Die Burger,* 1 October 1999, "Oppas vir goedkoop nostalgie". Also F. Davis, *Yearning for yesterday: A sociology of nostalgia,* London, 1979.

Recalling the war and extrapolating from that in such a way allows for the juxtaposition of a somewhat idealised, yet troubled past, with a foreboding present.[49]

Centenaries present themselves as crafted occasions for the merging of past and present, and nostalgia is one binding element in this process. Yet, it was not unthinking, uncritical, non-reflective immersion in nostalgia that marked the way in which Afrikaners remembered the war. There was a strong awareness that the apartheid past had failed and that Afrikaners now had to adapt to a new order. In line with this realisation, for the most part, a deliberate attempt was made to acknowledge the role of black people and view the conflict not only in local but also in international terms.[50]

There were, however, select groupings clustered together as the "Volkskomitee vir die herdenking van die Tweede Vryheidsoorlog" which harked back to distant memories of a time when the war explicitly provided an ideological arsenal to promote Afrikaner ethnic politics of the day.[51] The basic message stayed the same, even if it was dressed up in a more modern idiom than 50 years earlier.[52]

Such exceptions apart, overall there was a tendency to downplay the potential political ramifications of the war and to steer away from active public promotions of such agendas. The trend, in fact, was towards personalising and privatising the memory of the war – a notion that involved safeguarding a realm of experience from being appropriated and moulded by agencies with overt political aims.[53] The war was not expected to perform a specific wider function. The politics of the personal took a cultural form; for example, the re-recording, recollecting and preserving of material related to the war. Many of these narratives were of a purely anecdotal nature and were devoid of explicit messages that could be construed to have a meaning in the present.[54]

---

49. *Beeld*, 21 August 1998, "Wat ongedaan gemaak is, weer opgebou?". (Letter from Dr WF te Water, Standerton, Translation).

50. F. Jacobs, "Die herdenking van die Anglo-Boereoorlog in oënskou", *Knapsak*, Vol. 14, No. 1, May 2002, pp. 3–10.

51. S. Agten, "Een veranderende oorlog: de Geschiedschryving van de Anglo-Boereoorlog, 1899–1902", Licentiaat verhandeling, Catholic University, Leuven, 2002, pp. 92–93.

52. *Rapport*, 2 Junie 2002, "Heft burgers! Hoor Brandfort".

53. Compare J. Bailey, "Some meanings of the 'private' in sociological thought", *Sociology*, Vol. 34, Vol. 3, p. 384.

54. *Die Volksblad* in the Free State and *Die Burger* in the Western Cape published such material on a regular basis throughout the commemorative period. Some of those

Of course, the very act of collecting can in itself be seen as ideological, as it is often, at times quite unwittingly, spurred on by wider pressures in society.

Essentially though, the intention was not to make a grand political statement, but to accomplish memory work in a space specifically carved out for the retention and reworking of remembrances. "When memory is no longer everywhere, it will not be anywhere unless one takes the responsibility to recapture it through individual means," the French historian, Pierre Nora, has aptly noted.[55]

What also prompted the cautionary salvaging mode of memory, was the implosion of much of the earlier Afrikaner ethnic constructs of history. Cultural entrepreneurs now had to dig carefully among the debris to recover and reconstruct those building blocks considered worthy of being retained and that could be re-used in the overall construction of a new identity.

In form and content, the commemorations often bore a local character. Families visited gravesites of relatives or battlefields where ancestors fought, while many small towns used the opportunity to recall specific events that took place in the vicinity. The format of the commemorations varied: mock battles, community barbecues and dances, torch processions, marathon running, exhibitions and lectures or a combination of these activities.[56] Unlike the 1938 Great Trek centenary celebrations when the symbolism of the Trek was clearly defined and spelt out in a very deliberate manner in every town,[57] in 1999 the commemorative proceedings of the war were not marked by an all encompassing single cohesive message of memorialisation.

Each town gave its own imprint to proceedings. Nor were all these gatherings sombre and solemn occasions. At Machadodorp, during the war a temporary capital for the Transvaal republic after the fall of Pretoria in June 1900, the high point of the proceedings was supposed to be the symbolic arrival of

---

in the Free State were collected in two volumes: N. Nieman (ed.), *Ons lesers vertel,* Bloemfontein, 2001 and 2002.

55. Cited in J. Gillis, "Memory and identity: The history of a relationship", in J.R. Gillis (ed.), *Commemorations: The politics of national identity,* New Jersey, 1994, p. 14.

56. For example *Die Volksblad,* 23 November 2001, "Louw familie hou saamtrek"; *Die Volksblad,* 9 October 1999, "Fakkels in Bethlehem"; *Die Volksblad,* 19 January 2000, "Colesberg wedloop"; *Die Volksblad,* 12 October 1999, "Herinneringe aan die oorlog word 'n werklikheid"; *Rapport,* 6 June 1999, "Feesprogram in 2001 en 2002".

57. For the Great Trek centenary see A. Grundlingh and H. Sapire, "From feverish festival to repetitive ritual? The changing fortunes of Great Trek mythology in an industrialising South Africa, 1938–1988", *South African Historical Journal,* Vol. 21, 1989, pp. 19–27.

Paul Kruger. Once "Oom Paul" was duly received, the attention shifted to the tent where liquor was served. It was not too long before the townspeople turned the occasion into a festive one. The foot-stomping rhythms of American country and western music blared across the town square as Machadodorp made merry. Traditional Afrikaans music, once standard fare at such occasions, seemed to have been forgotten. A reporter noted wryly: "Not the 'Hartseerwals'. Not 'Ou Ryperd'. No, it was 'Hand me down that bottle of Tequila, Sheila!'"[58]

What was particularly remarkable during the commemorations, was the considerable growth in Afrikaans literature on the war. At least a hundred titles, some of them reprints, appeared and sold well in a market not known for huge sales.[59] The literary explosion not only mirrored a revitalised interest in the conflict, but also a probing and questioning attitude. One bestseller was a novel dealing with the darker side of Boer treachery and war crimes.[60] Besides literary works, several plays were produced of which some focused on the ethnic and racial tensions spawned by the war.[61] In addition, the South African produced television documentary, "Verskroeide Aarde" (Scorched Earth), which covered a variety of angles drew much praise as well as a considerable number of viewers.[62] Certain art works also sought to rework traditional themes. In an exhibition in Pretoria, a bronze statue depicted a young Boer woman on horseback, wearing only a Voortrekker bonnet and what was described as a:

> ... very sado-erotic corset covered in sharp pins reminiscent of something between a punk and a porcupine.[63]

---

58. *Rapport*, 11 June 2000, "Paul Kruger ruk-en-rol op Machadodorp volksfees". (Translation.)

59. *Die Burger*, 27 September 1901 "ABO steeds gewilde tema"; *Rapport*, 17 October 1999, "Oorlogsboeke verkoop soos soetkoek."

60. *The Sunday Independent*, 2 August 1998, "Anglo Boer War spawns milestone in new fiction"; http//www.mweb.co/litnet/leeskring/mentz/ Chris van der Merwe, "Die verstommende verskietende ster ooit"; *Beeld*, 11 May 98, "Kragtige debuutroman"; L. Renders, "Tot in die hart van boosheid: twee resente Afrikaanse romans oor die Anglo-Boereoorlog", *Literator*, 20, 3, November 1999, pp. 117–121. The book was that of C. Coetzee, *Op soek na Generaal Mannetjies Mentz*, Cape Town, 1998.

61. *Die Burger*, 1 April, "KKNK herdenk ABO met die opvoerings".

62. Interview with H. Binge, producer, at Stellenbosch, 2 March 2002.

63. *Pretoria News*, October 1999, "A different angle on history".

This statue was seen as a way of crossing old boundaries and merging fashion, historical memories and eroticism into a new form. Overall, these developments reflected intensive memory work in a designated cultural space and a creative engagement with identity through the reframing of remembrance.

Under the twin impact of the disintegration of apartheid and the declining power of the National Party, a gradual erosion of traditionally constructed Afrikaner culture had long been in evidence before the centenary.[64] This assisted in opening the way for a more varied approach. The commemorations then, provided Afrikaners with an opportunity to re-evaluate a particularly dramatic period in their history and to rework it, relatively free from previous political agendas and restraints, into a more kaleidoscopic whole without necessarily translating this into a fixed leitmotif for the future. Of course, some renditions of the war preferred to be rooted in an earlier period, but perhaps the outstanding feature of the commemorations was the cultural dynamism released to find new answers to abiding questions in a non-prescriptive way.

Tourism and the commemoration of the war

Particularly in Kwa-Zulu Natal, the politics of the commemorations played itself out mainly in the arena of tourism. There were high hopes, not always based on realistic assessments that the centenary would bring in thousands of tourists.[65] The area had a number of battlefields such as Talana, Colenso, the dramatic setting of Spioenkop, Vaalkrans, Tugela Heights and of course also the siege of Ladysmith, Mainly tourists from Britain, and to a lesser extent the Netherlands were targeted.

The logic of tourism dictated that the commemorations had to be cast in promotional language that offered an enticing package. One tour was advertised as a recreational blend of "Battle Fields and Outdoor Adventure"; tourists could "experience the echo of fierce clashes of gunfire" or visit "the lonely memorials of brave soldiers", while "the towns along the route have their own unique charm and attractions, scenic hiking trails, farm resorts, arts and crafts, game viewing and many more outdoor attractions."[66] Moreover,

---

64. D. O'Meara, *Forty lost years: The apartheid state and the politics of the National Party, 1948–1994,* Johannesburg, 1996, pp. 368–372.

65. *The Natal Witness,* 5 March 1998, "Will the Anglo-Boer War centenary see a tourist invasion?"

66. Cited in P. Maylam, "Not the South African War: Commemorating, commercialis-

besides South African War battlesites, the area could also boast with very marketable sites from the Anglo-Zulu War of 1879. "Where else could you get two wars for the price of one and some magnificent scenery to boot?" it was asked.[67]

There was no shortage of tour operators, some styled as "Anglo-Boer War Tour Brokers". Thus Brigadier Jim Parker CBE assured potential tourists from Britain that he was "...an acknowledged expert on inbound specialist military tours."[68] Not to be outdone was Major Jamie Bruce, a man who professed that "he just loves playing with toy soldiers." He promised to meet tourists in full military regalia; brown hob-nailed boots, turn-of-the-century British army regulation khaki and a pith helmet.[69]

At the Talana battlefield, close to Dundee, the local museum recruited a cast of 75 "British soldiers", 35 "Boers", eight Indian stretcher-bearers and several black scouts to stage a mock battle. Locally manufactured uniforms were exact copies of the originals and period experts were called in to choreograph proceedings. Visitors were also able to stroll through the Boer and British camps, sampling bully beef or *moerkoffie en beskuit* (traditionally brewed coffee and rusks).[70]

Underlying the tourist representation of the war were two related impulses. One was a strand of white male military culture with a long tradition, which in part revolved around regiments like the Natal Carbineers amongst others.[71] Palpable interest in military matters of this kind was reflected in the opening of the Natal Carbineers museum just prior to the start of the war commemorations, and a flourishing military history society, which made much of the battlefields of the province.[72] It was military enthusiasts from

ing and obfuscating the war", Unpublished paper, August 2000, p. 2.

67. J. Hattingh, "The centenary commemorations of the outbreak of the war as a tourist attraction", *Knapsak*, 14, 1, May 2002, pp. 32–33; also *The Natal Witness*, 23 November 1998, "Watch your back on the battlefields."

68. *Official Guide to the Commemorative Programme in Kwa-Zulu Natal*, p. 3; *Business Day*, 6 November 1998 "Lord of the manor faces a battle."

69. *Business Day*, 6 November 1998 "Lord of the manor faces a battle".

70. *South African Country Life*, October 1999, "Window on the world of Khaki and Boer".

71. See R. Morrell, *From boys to gentlemen: Settler masculinity in Natal*, 1880–1920, Pretoria, 2001, 139–175.

72. *The Daily News*, 16 February 1998, "A museum at long last"; "Kwa-Zulu Natal", *Military History Journal*, 12, 2, December 2001, p. 74.

these ranks who had a strong guiding hand in commemorative proceedings and the packaging of battlefield tours.[73]

The other current has a bearing on the ideological ramifications of battlefield tourism. It is misleading to regard such tourism as value free, as its narrow focus tends to shut out a fuller understanding of the social and political impact of war and allows stereotypes to go unchecked. The "here we are lads" experience of a battlefield does not encourage searching questions as to what such a presence might have meant a century ago and even less what its significance is in the present. As the historian, Jeff Guy, writing on the representation of the Anglo-Zulu War battlefields, has noted:

> ... explanations why thousands of armed men from Britain were marched into foreign territory, looted cattle, burnt homesteads and killed their occupants, are unnecessary. The fact that an independent African kingdom was destroyed ... can be ignored. That this was done with deceit and racist brutality can be brushed aside.[74]

Much the same point in much the same language can be made as regards the British invasion of the Boer republics.

The fact that Kwa-Zulu Natal had a ready and convenient supply of battlefields available for tourist consumption, made it easy to slip into a mode where unquestioning representation could prevail. Whereas both blacks and Afrikaners had in varying degrees to renegotiate their understanding of the war, for white English speakers in the province this was not really necessary as they had their answer in tourism.

Besides the peculiar regional dynamics at work, the "tourist gaze" in itself also contributed to the way in which the war was represented. Not broadly interpretative history, nor the diverse considerations of local people, essentially governed the commemorations. Although battlefield tourists are probably more knowledgeable than most, they are also more demanding in what they want to see and this in turn determined the format of what marketing specialists glibly called "the battlefield product."[75]

Associated with the "product" is the perception that the killing-fields of yesteryear are the potential moneyspinners of today. Whilst it would be churl-

---

73. Compare *The Daily News*, 7 September 1998, "Tours of the KZN battlefields"; G. Torlage, "World travel market and the South African war centenary commemorations", *Innovation*, 14, June 1997, p. 19.

74. J. Guy, "Battling with banality", *Journal of Natal and Zulu History*, 18, 1998, 164–165.

75. Compare Hattingh "Tourist attraction", p. 34.

ish to suggest that a heritage industry that creates employment opportunities and brings in foreign currency should fashion itself along purist academic lines, commemorations and the commercialization of the past often trouble historians as they mask the deeper import and significance of history.[76] The centenary of the war was no different, nor given the imperatives of commemorations, could it really have been otherwise.

Conclusion

Commemorations by their very nature, give their own shape and form to public understanding of the past. Debates over commemorations, are not primarily to pit one version of the past against another or to assert the authority of academic scholarship, but are geared to invite inquiry to try and explain the way in which commemorations as such are constructed to derive maximum benefit from the past in the present.[77] In this respect Ian Buruma has made the salutary point that "memory is not the same as history and memorializing is different from writing history."[78]

In reviewing the construction of the commemoration, the apogee of the state's involvement was probably the official launch at Brandfort. For the rest of the almost three years the state only sporadically genuflected in the direction of the centenary. It would appear that once it had exhausted whatever political mileage it could get out of the occasion, it left civil society to its own devices. In public, a significant discourse was about black participation in the war and this was conducted along lines designed to establish the high moral ground. For Afrikanerdom, the commemoration of the war involved much memory work as earlier received memories of the war had ceased to have the same purchase for a new generation in a changed environment. In Kwa-Zulu Natal, the logic of war tourism ensured that existing perceptions remained largely outside the realm of critical interrogation. The nuances and differences that emerged during the commemorations served to underline the

---

76. For example P. Maylam, "Not the South African War", p. 11; L. Witz, G. Minkley and C. Rassool, "No end of a history lesson: Preparations for the Anglo-Boer War Centenary Commemoration", *South African Historical Journal*, Vol. 41, November 1999, pp. 370–371.

77. Compare P. Carrier, "Historical traces of the present: The uses of commemoration", *Historical Reflections*, Vol. 22, No. 2, 1996, p. 445.

78. *New York Review of Books*, 8 April 1999, "The joys and perils of victimhood."

general assertion that historical memory is "always contextual, partial and subject to self-interested manipulation and obfuscation".[79]

---

79. M. Kenny, "A place for memory: The interface between individual and collective history", *Society for Comparative Study of Society and History*, Vol. 41, 1999, p. 425.

CHAPTER 11

Structure of memory:
Apartheid in the museum

Georgi Verbeeck

A museum in Johannesburg

When one drives through the gloomy southern suburbs of Johannesburg, one would not directly expect a prestigious memorial that is devoted to the history of apartheid in South Africa. The Apartheid Museum's surroundings are somewhat absurd. The Museum is located in Gold Reef City, a Wild West scene in the African savannah. This complex, named after the empty gold-mine of Johannesburg, accommodates an enormous casino and a real "theme park". An environment, which resembles that of Las Vegas or Disney World, seems to contradict the political message of a monument that is devoted to South Africa's controversial history. Despite the serious political message, this museum is also a symbol of the ironic character of the post-apartheid era. After all, the history of South Africa has taken revenge. Under the puritan administration of the National Party, casinos in white South Africa were forbidden. They were tolerated in the black "homelands", where the whites could live it up in a type of decadent entertainment that the rulers of these "Bantustans" generously provided. For visitors from overseas the few amuse-ment parks that existed in the old South Africa could hardly serve as sources of thrilling entertainment. After the 1994 democratic elections, these restric-tive regulations on all sorts of decadent entertainment finally disappeared. And for its part, apartheid was placed in the museum. Or at least that was the intention.

Finding the entrance of the museum is a peculiar experience. It is in the middle of an enormous car park with an old-fashioned roller coaster in the

Paper delivered at the Centenary History Conference at the University of Stellenbosch, April 2004. The author wishes to thank Jeanne d'Arc Elhage for her assistance with the translation of this chapter.

background. The contrast cannot be greater; on one side a row of cars parked in the shade of palm trees and on the other a building surrounded by an indigenous African landscape.[1] After 2001 when the museum opened its doors, the government gave permission to build a casino provided an additional "social responsibility project" plan was added. The investors wanted a museum, which resembled the Holocaust Museum in Washington D.C. However, one can question the validity of the museum as a kind of moral spin-off of "big business". Furthermore, and above all, "Big Business" invests in entertainment. With a lot of money at stake, the legendary business duo from Johannesburg, Solly and Abe Krok are behind this R100 million enterprise.[2]

Museum director Christopher Till, who was the former executive producer of the Johannesburg Biennale, supports the museum's location. According to Till, Johannesburg is the most suitable city to accommodate the museum. Around the turn of the last century, a dramatic population growth and convergence of people took place. Different ethnic groups clashed with each other in the new industrial metropolis of the country. Blacks had been expelled from their land through colonial wars and poll taxes on their agricultural activities. White farmers had fled the countryside and had come to the cities as a result of the Anglo-Boer War. Complex networks of both economic interaction and ethnic segregation emerged. As a consequence of these events, the social laboratory of apartheid originated.

Dealing with the past

South Africa is putting its past behind it in a way that is not comparable to Germany or the former Eastern block.[3] In 1994, a proper process of *tabula rasa* was not pursued. This had a lot to do with both the nature of the regimes themselves and the transitional period that followed after their collapse. The apartheid regime had never reached the perfection of a monolithic dictatorship. As a form of "domestic colonialism" its repressive nature should be more

---

1. "The Aesthetics of Disappearance. In Conversation with Jeremy Rose", unpublished interview, acknowledgements and thanks go to Sean O'Toole.

2. Davie, Lucille, "The powerful Apartheid Museum", April 9, *City of Johannesburg, Official Website.*

3. Verbeeck, Georgi, "Een nieuw verleden voor een nieuwe natie. Een Duits model voor Zuid-Afrika?", in Jo Tollebeek, Georgi Verbeeck and Tom Verschaffel (eds), *De lectuur van het verleden. Opstellen over de geschiedenis van geschiedschrijving aangeboden aan Reginald der Schryver*, Louvain, 1998, pp. 535–564.

precisely described in terms of social and economic discrimination than in terms of political dictatorship. It constituted an exceptional form of ethnic oligarchy. That means that within the boundaries of the white community basic norms of a democratic constitutional state were largely maintained. The transformation process cannot be compared to that of Eastern Europe. South Africa underwent a political transformation process just after the dismantling of the apartheid state. Social and economic transformation has been considerably slower since then. South African macro-economic development is still characterized by basic "North-South contradictions", which usually manifest themselves on a global level, but are apparent "in one country" here. Due to long term traditions of internal colonialism it will still remain a place were the First and Third World meet in one country. The system of apartheid had established a hypocritical façade, which obscured this reality. Now that this façade has disappeared, these basic contradictions and the accordingly unequal development have become manifest. The education system, the economy and public administration are still very burdened with the past.

The framework of the political legislation of racial segregation has disappeared, however, the social and economic contrasts, which stem from this, are still largely maintained. The beneficiaries of the old regime, mainly the white communities, have not disappeared and instead continue an existence as an ethnic minority within a culturally plural society. Politically condemned to powerless and fragmented opposition but socially and economically virtually unaffected, they mostly maintain their position of the well-to-do middle class.[4] The post-apartheid transformation process naturally eroded some social structures and patterns of interactions between black and white. There is an increase in poverty in the lower white classes and a growth in the black bourgeoisie. However, there is almost no question of a major turn around. Therefore, the museum in Johannesburg does not play the same role as for instance the (ultimately controversial) "House of Terror" in Budapest[5] or the still to be established "Museum of Communism" in Warsaw.[6] The museum does not, and cannot, really close a painful chapter of the nation's history in the sense that it puts the past in a museum. The museum is part of a re-education policy. It calls for a new sense of public responsibility: a sense of aware-

---

4. Terreblanche , Sampie, *A History of Inequality in South Africa 1652–2002*, Pietermaritzburg, 2002.

5. Brochure: *Terror Haza Andrassy ut 60 , House of Terror*, Budapest, 2002.

6. *SocLand Muzeum komunizmu. Museum of Communism (under construction)*, Warsaw, 2003.

ness about shameful injustice from the past has to lead to better relations between the citizens of the Rainbow Nation.

Visiting a museum

Thus, the Apartheid Museum presents itself as a mirror for the new nation. The reactions at the opening were very positive. In *Beeld*, Elise Tempelhoff recounts a cyclic story in the museum that suggests a catharsis; the oppressed and the oppressors were only really liberated in 1994.[7] The visitor to the museum will inevitably think of the procedure that is also used in the Holocaust Museum in Washington. Whether one chooses a "white" or "non-white" pass determines the life path one will follow during the journey through the labyrinth of the apartheid-state. The museum's message is linear; the simple principal of racial segregation itself undoubtedly leads to chaos, misery and destruction. The outside of the building (straight lines mostly under an aqua blue African sky) recalls images of terror and repression. Claustrophobic feelings overwhelm the visitor.[8] Curious one wanders through a wall of mirrors in which one cannot be sure who is watching whom. But it is only when one is inside that the labyrinth really begins. Photographs, fragments of motion pictures and texts, text panels, billboards and all kinds of objects are shown. There is an exemplar of the feared "casspirs", the armoured motor vehicles that the police used in oppressing political revolts. Execution poles symbolize the number of political prisoners that were condemned to death by the apartheid regime. Television fragments show Mandela on the eve of his trial or prime minister H. Verwoerd defending his policies. Of course, there are the well known signs with: "slegs vir blankes" or "non-Europeans only". The visitor gets to know almost all the aspects of life under the apartheid regime: the banal and bizarre sides of an existence in which racial obsession played the main role, the ideology and its execution, oppression and resistance. This has to result in an overall picture. Therefore, the museum describes its objectives as "a non-prejudicde and historically accurate reconstruction of the twentieth century South-Africa."[9]

---

7. *Beeld*, November 28, 2001.

8. "New Apartheid Museum Opens", *The Universal Zulu Nation*, 17 December 2001.

9. Brochure: *Apartheid Museum*, Johannesburg 2002. See also: www.apartheidmuseum. org.

The museum without any doubt strongly impresses the visitor. In general the press is positive about the project, which is described as "shocking and brilliant".[10] Especially the symbiosis of content, architecture and natural environment are highly appreciated.[11] The fact that the museum is embedded in the landscape can create a strange effect, but for many it is very invigorating. The museum is the work of a multidisciplinary team of architects, curators, historians and museum designers. Witwatersrand professor Phillip Bonner acts as a history consultant. As a social historian, he makes sure that the past of apartheid is not reduced to a few dramatic moments and highlights and that the forgotten layers of the population and the anonymous masses will also be represented. Stephen Hobbs and Kathryn Smith serve as artistic advisors. All forms of multimedia are prominently present. For all of these reasons, the museum could become a major tourist attraction in the growing network of museums and monuments devoted to South Africa's recent history. This includes, for instance, the "Soweto tour" in Johannesburg, where foreigners and locals can visit locations that remind them of the daily life and the struggle against apartheid like the Hector Pieterson Museum that is connected to the revolt of 1976.

Elsewhere in the country, there is Robben Island or the District Six Museum in Cape Town. The classic memorials of the apartheid regime have undergone a gradual transformation, such as the "Voortrekkersmonument" in Pretoria or the museum of the Anglo-Boer War and the "Women's Monument" in Bloemfontein.[12] Thus, a new historical culture has emerged.[13] The discussion about the memorial at Blood River proves that this cannot happen without a struggle. Blood River has been a white nationalist sanctuary but was recently completed with a Zulu monument as a political historical adjustment. To quote Stellenbosch professor Albert Grundlingh, "it's always about the same thing: the tension between the former symbolical power and the actual political power."[14]

10. *Mail & Guardian*, December 5, 2001; *Beeld*, November 5, 2001.

11. O'Toole, Sean, "The Structure of Memory. Johannesburg's Apartheid Museum", *Arththrob. Contemporary Art in South Africa*, March 2002.

12. Grundlingh, Albert, "A Cultural Conundrum? Old Monuments and New Regimes. The Voortrekker Monument as Symbol of AfrikanerPower in a Postapartheid South Africa", *Radical History Review*, Issue 81, 2001, pp. 95–112.

13. Refer to: Verbeeck Georgi, "Verzoening door herinnering? Afrika Historische cultuur in Zuid-Afrika", *Nieuwste Tijd*, 3 November 2001, pp. 62–76.

14. "Voortrekker Monument changes in the new SA", *Mail & Guardian*, 7 May 2003.

Criticism and comparison

Criticisms about the museum, coming from those who feel that they are disadvantaged in some way, cannot be avoided. It is found that the museum emphasizes too much the importance of the ANC in the struggle against apartheid. The role of other resistance groups such as the PAC, the SACP, or of other distinguished individuals, is far less expressed. For example, there have been criticisms towards the fact that the progressive white resistance, represented by Helen Suzman, is almost neglected.[15] The question is raised now who will receive more or less attention in the museum. It therefore nourishes the thoughts and the fear that a new kind of historical dogmatism is arising, whereby the current political majority is pushing their historical vision forward. In general, one can notice that the museum emphasizes the large forms of resistance (Sharpeville, Soweto, the armed struggle) and pays far less attention to how the apartheid machinery functioned within various layers of society. This resentment at the "insiderism" is not surprising. It reminds us of the cultural debates in Germany reflecting the comparable sense of resentment towards any effort to focus on the motives and deeds of those who are responsible for crime and oppression. A nation not only consists of victims and heroes, but of bystanders and perpetrators as well.

"Racial discrimination is now where it belongs, in the museum", reads the political message of the Apartheid Museum.[16] This naive optimism can instigate objections and irritation from different directions. A museum that sets the past in concrete, silences the debate and concludes history. Justice is no longer done to the "living past". When history is connected to injustice, the museum actually gives a moral license to the modern day visitor. It is this very *Schlußstrich*-strategy that has kicked up a lot of dust in Germany, at the construction of national historical museums in Bonn and Berlin. "History in the museum" can lead to closure of the personal and collective confrontation with the past. As for the Nazi past in Germany a museum of national history contradicts the moral demands of *Vergangenheitsbewältigung*, the typical German expression to refer to the process of coming to terms with the past. Simultaneously, although in a different way, this matter also arose in Johannesburg. Putting apartheid in a museum can result in a self-absorbed, yet lying ideological self-depiction of the "New South Africa". John Matshikiza is

---

15. Britt Youens, "Apartheid Museum does Helen Suzman a great disservice", *Focus: A publication of the Helen Suzman Foundation*.

16. Brochure *Apartheid Museum*, Johannesburg, 2002.

tied to the Wits Institute for Social and Economic Research and a columnist for the *Mail & Guardian*.[17] He does not hide his sarcasm. Apartheid is in no way over, referring to the painful poverty and contrasts that still mostly originate in racial segregation. The apartheid museum is a "white" initiative, financed with "white" ("Jewish" as Matshikiza puts it) money and it can make many whites think the soothing thought that apartheid is "finally finished and klaar". Speaking of irony in history, the Kroks' fortune was built in the apartheid era through selling some sort of skin cream that was supposed to make the faces of black women lighter. Therefore, what gives them the right to appoint themselves as the curators of the past? When obtaining a permit for the casino, the smart businessmen wanted to repay a moral debt and in the form of the museum "to give something back to the community". What specifically goes for the Krok duo may apply to the white community in total. "Apartheid? What a horrible thing, thank God it's over!" Could this be the first thought of every embarrassed white person that leaves the museum?

Similar objections have been expressed by Nadine Gordimer when she compared the Apartheid Museum to the Holocaust Museum in Washington DC and the brand new *Jüdisches Museum* in Berlin.[18] Her resentments towards the financial machinations that lie at the core of the museum are very outspoken, because she experiences it as a hurtful insult that damages the dignity of the anti-apartheid struggle.[19] According to her, putting history in a museum represents double danger. It closes history unjustly, as Matshikiza also states. If it contains a universal message – as a repudiation of racism or ethnic cleansing and genocide – a museum also provides a roof to everyone who actually does not want to learn for the future. Confrontation with a violent past, in accordance with to the social-pedagogical function, calls for a *Nie wieder* (never again). At the same time, the murdering continues all over the world. And the visitors in Washington, Berlin or Johannesburg – they may well just be visiting a museum.

Some would call the entire project a form of "political prostitution". It is the kind of criticism that is typical of the sceptical attitude that many white

---

17. "History in the making" *Mail & Guardian*, 30 November 2001; "A State of permanent transition", *Mail & Guardian*, 3 February 2003.

18. "Washington, Berlin und Johannesburg. Dreierlei Gedenken", in *Die Tageszeitung*, 15 August 2003. (The German edition of *Le Monde Diplomatique*, Nr. 7131.)

19. At the moment, Solly and Abe Krok are entangled in a strange juridical dispute about their brand name *Apartheid Museum*, which is being challenged in court by business rivals. Refer to: *Sunday Times*, 22 June 2003.

South Africans have taken and of the growing fear that the ideological line of the ANC will take on threatening forms. They see the Apartheid Museum as a political project that is intended to burden the white minority with feelings of guilt. A new corrupt elite is using fashionable and politically correct recipes to defend its newly achieved wealth and to confirm its growing cultural dominance. Following the precedent of J.M. Coetzee, the big silence has begun with disillusioned old liberals. A few of them are sick of the tensions in the country, turned their backs on politics or are planning to emigrate haunted by horror stories about crime, "degrading values" and AIDS.

Nation-building?

Is the Apartheid Museum just another example of the eternal quest for "nation-building" in the new South Africa, through closing its painful and controversial past? And what can the European perspective learn from these proclaimed ambitions?[20] In the early days of the old East Germany the building of a national image of history played a crucial role in the regime's ideological legitimacy, and therefore in the right of existence of a separate state. The class struggle model from the fifties and sixties that had given rise to a "partial" and, especially, to a very one-sided image of history, was replaced by a harmony model in the seventies and eighties. Historiography explicitly set itself the task of securing the claims to as broad a historical heritage as possible. Thus the GDR was supported by a noteworthy paradox. By claiming to be the lawful heir of the entire German history, they wanted to perpetuate a continued existence as a *separate* state.[21] This construction was a boast, as became evident when the two German states rapidly reunited. The restoration of national unity was preceded by the restoration of a common past.

Similar dynamics are also at work in South Africa. The new South Africa is trying to project the political model of consensus on the past. The harmony being pursued must be reflected in a common past. Common memory be-

---

20. Verbeeck Georgi, "A New Past for a New Nation? Historiography and Politics in South Africa. A Comparative Approach", *Historia*, Vol. 45, No. 2, 2000, pp. 387–410.

21. Some conclude (to my mind, unjustifiably so) that the building of a "national image of history" in the GDR made the factual reunification in 1989/90 possible. See: Brinks, J.H., *Die DDR-Geschichtswissenschaft auf dem Weg zur deutschen Einheit. Luther, Friedrich II und Bismarck als Paradigmen politischen Wandels,* Frankfurt a.M. /New York, 1992, pp. 309–313.

comes the matrix for a new South African national culture. Rehabilitation for previous injustice still remains *historical* rehabilitation. For the damages they suffered, people are also demanding a rightful place in history.

The German example shows that unity-thought and the projection of national consensus on the past are *un*desirable. In Germany as well as in South Africa or any other country, it is recommended to remain wary of the temptations of a certain kind of consensus thought. It is desirable to take into account the fact that the danger of such an institution is that of a new dogmatism and a new intolerance.[22]

Despite factual historical differences there is, however, one noteworthy point of similarity between dealing with the past in Germany and in South Africa. In both cases, historical thought fits into a framework of "assimilation of the past". This means that dealing with the past is not an isolated matter, but is linked to the establishment of a democratic political culture.[23] Despite factual differences, the situations in Germany and in South Africa show a striking resemblance here. In both countries people have an idealistic view of history, according to which knowledge of history has a purifying function. It is most entrenched in the old GDR-slogan: *Aus der Geschichte lernen, heisst siegen lernen!* But a more or less comparable historical and philosophical optimism is characteristic of historical culture in the Federal Republic. Here, a dominating elite still swears by a permanent commemoration of "Auschwitz" as a condition for democratic stability (Jürgen Habermas). National ideology in the new South Africa starts from the same axiom: *Reconciliation through Truth.*

Is the Apartheid Museum a successful tourist attraction or a source of contention? One of the biggest objections that can be expressed is directed at the self-cleansing character of the whole project. It would be correct to pose the question whether a private initiative can or should aim for public goals. On the other hand, one could challenge that fact by saying that the direct government interferences may pose an even greater danger. The criticism would have been even tougher if the Apartheid Museum had, in fact, become an icon for the ANC ideology. There are already enough elements present that are thought-provoking. Like the naïve optimism that lies in the dichotomy of the "Leitmotiv" of the museum: *Tragedy and heroism. Tyranny*

---

22. Adam Heribert, van Zyl Slabbert Frederik and Moodley Kogila , *Comrades in Business. Post-Liberation Politics in South Africa,* Cape Town, 1997, pp. 102–103.

23. Grünenberg Antonia (ed.), *Welche Geschichte wählen wir?* Hamburg, 1992, especially pp. 7–22.

and freedom. Chaos and peace.[24] Modern society certainly does not expect this kind of historical dogmatism and dualistic conception of history. Reflecting on its message, the museum should hold up a mirror to the contemporary public. It should reflect on the past, without closing the past. Inevitably, this will cause an unpleasant feeling for many. One can only wonder whether the legacy of apartheid is ready yet to be locked up in a museum.

24. Brochure: *Apartheid Museum*, Johannesburg, 2002.

CHAPTER 12

Building the "new South Africa":

Urban space, architectural design, and the disruption of historical memory

Martin J. Murray

It is quite unfashionable these days to use apartheid as a reference point when trying to find the roots of South Africa's economic and political problems. In the name of reconciliation, a blanket amnesia is being imposed on South Africans: what you forget you forgive, and what you forgive you reconcile yourself to. The only problem with this rather generous approach to history is that there are lessons to be learned from the past. This somewhat utilitarian fact aside, there is something distinctly sad about losing one's past, however bitter one might feel about some of it.[1]

The steady growth of such arcadian pleasure-palaces as festival marketplaces, showcase shopping arcades, upscale malls, and themed tourist destinations in the "new South Africa" is one of the most visible expressions of an underlying structural logic, or a set of aesthetic conventions, governing the invention of new spatial landscapes after apartheid.[2] The driving force behind a great deal of the restructuring of urban spaces comes from the narrow, profit-seeking perspective of corporate builders and financiers, real estate developers, architectural and design professionals, and municipal authorities who, in a largely depoliticized fashion, are concerned about the advantageous placement of the "new South Africa" in the highly competitive global economy. They thus myopically focus their attention on improving the marketability of South Africa's aspirant "world-class" cities by strengthening their positive image, their

---

1. Achmat Dangor, "Apartheid and the Death of South African Cities", in Hilton Judin and Ivan Vladislavic (eds), *Architecture, Apartheid and After*, Rotterdam, NAi Publishers, 1999, p. 359.

2. I would like to thank Catherine Burns and Merle Lipton for helpful comments on an earlier version of this chapter presented at the Collective Memory and Present-Day Politics in South Africa and the Nordic Countries Conference, Centre of African Studies, Copenhagen University, 22–23 August 2002.

qualities of life, and their cultural accoutrements. In the triumphant world-culture of consumption, packaged built environments like cultural heritage sites, luxurious convention centres, and glitzy "shoppertainment" extravaganzas have become vital instruments promoting the distinction, desirability, and prestige of a place.[3] This kind of self-conscious "place-making" is an essential component of postmodern urbanism. For local business associations, downtown merchants, property managers, and urban planners, the creation of themed entertainment destinations offers the possibility of a new sense of urban vibrancy and vitality in the face of the widespread perception of cities after apartheid as disorderly, dangerous, and chaotic. Festival marketplaces, heritage theme parks, and waterfront revitalization schemes appeal to the consuming tastes of the affluent middle-classes, overseas tourists, and itinerant spectators alike. When juxtaposed against the pervasive and disturbing image of the post-apartheid city as a frightful place of disruption and decay, the detached, effete, and gaudy appearance of these ornamental architectural compositions – expressed by both spatial and symbolical distance – becomes even more exaggerated and attenuated.[4]

    This spatial configuration epitomises what Christine Boyer has termed the "city of illusions" – an evolving urban landscape which eagerly transforms sites into showcase "promotional spaces," while simultaneously ignoring the accumulated realities of homelessness, unemployment, and social injustice.

---

3. The literature is extensive. See Judith Kenny, "Making Milwaukee Famous: Cultural Capital, Urban Image, and the Politics of Place", *Urban Geography*, Vol. 16, No. 5, 1995, pp. 440–458; M. Christine Boyer, *The City of Collective Memory: Its Historical Imagery and Architectural Entertainments*, Cambridge, Massachusetts, The MIT Press, 1994, pp. 1–8; Ada Louise Huxtable, *The Unreal America: Architecture and Illusion*, New York, The New Press, 1997; David Crouch (ed.), *Leisure/Tourism Geographies: Practices and Geographical Knowledge*, New York and London, Routledge, 1999; M.V. Levine, "Downtown Redevelopment as an Urban Growth Strategy: A Critical Appraisal of the Baltimore Renaissance", *Journal of Urban Affairs*, Vol. 9, No. 2, 1987, pp. 103–124; Nan Ellin, *Postmodern Urbanism [Revised Edition]*, New York, Princeton Architectural Press, 1999, pp. 267–296; Dennis Judd, "Constructing the Tourist Bubble", in Dennis Judd and Susan Fainstein (eds), *The Tourist City*, New Haven and London, Yale University Press, 1999, pp. 35–53; Jon Goss, "Disquiet on the Waterfront: Reflections on Nostalgia and Utopia in the Urban Archetypes of Festival Marketplaces", *Urban Geography*, 17, 3, 1996, pp. 221–247; and Charles Rutheiser, *Imagineering Atlanta: The Politics of Place in the City of Dreams*, London and New York, Verso, 1997.

4. See David Harvey, "Between Space and Time: Reflections on the Geographical Imagination", *Annals of the Association of American Geographers*, Vol. 80, 1990, pp. 418–434; and Boyer, *The City of Collective Memory*, pp. 1–2, 3–5.

In South Africa's cities after apartheid where the plight of the poor invades everyone's daily routine and there is virtually no escape from the tangled skein of poverty and wealth, of crime and greed, and of hard-scrabble existence and luxurious living, the affluent and well-to-do classes have retreated en masse into fortified enclaves of luxury, partitioning themselves off from the disagreeable parts of the city. Although seldom connected physically with each other, these "well-designed spaces of visual identity" are linked imaginatively to each other, to other cities, and to a shared discourse of "historicized" cultural interpretations. The steady expansion of these privatized spaces catering to the urban middle-classes has only reinforced the already existing fragmentation, division, and separation that characterized cities under apartheid rule.[5]

Such themed entertainment destinations as enclosed luxury malls, revitalised waterfronts, wildlife and nature preserves, and "heritage" theme parks are sites of cultural expression that are regulated by entrepreneurial values and guided by corporate marketing strategies. Image-conscious corporations in the "new South Africa" have played an increasingly visible role in sponsoring museum exhibitions, theatrical performances, sporting events, cultural festivals, and national celebrations. New technologies of cultural production and consumption have come to dominate crucial nodal points of urban space, turning these sites into new marketplaces constructed from inward-looking architectural designs and catering to fashionable life-styles. The wealthy and well-to-do propertied classes thrive within the make-believe fantasy realm of these "hyper-real" image spectaculars, safely cocooned behind material fortifications and the symbolic denial of the persistent poverty of the truly disadvantaged. These stylized pleasure-domes do not allow for critical perspectives grounded in values and moral economies located outside the marketplace, beyond the mesmerizing allure of spellbinding images, and in opposition to the fetishized commodification of everyday life. The attractiveness of entertaining spectacle in the "new South Africa" has spawned a kind of selective

5. M. Christine Boyer, "The City of Illusion: New York's Public Places", in Paul Knox (ed.), *The Restless Urban Landscape*, Engelwood Cliffs, New Jersey, Prentice Hall, 1993, pp. 111–126, especially pp. 111, 116, 119–120; M. Christine Boyer, "Cities for Sale: Merchandizing History as South Street Seaport", in Michael Sorkin (ed.), *Variations on a Theme Park: The New American City and the End of Public Space*, New York, Hill and Wang, 1992, pp. 181–204; and M. Christine Boyer, "The Great Frame-Up: Fantastic Appearances in Contemporary Spatial Politics", in Helen Liggett and David Perry (eds), *Spatial Practices: Critical Explorations in Social/Spatial Theory*, Thousand Oaks, California, Sage, 1995, pp. 81–109.

amnesia, a collective "letting go" if not outright forgetting of the sordid past. These luxurious pleasure-palaces, festival marketplaces, and showcase entertainment venues of the "new South Africa" promote a false reconciliation across the racial and class divide that treats the apartheid past as a "dead" historical relic that has been left behind, overcome, and superseded.[6]

The future – unforeseeable in its detail, but predictable in its broad macrohistorical contours – inhabits the present moment as the contingent outcome of a multitude of causal mechanisms. In their understanding and use of the historical past, in their inclusionary and exclusionary spatial practices, and in the values they espouse, festival marketplaces and other themed entertainment destinations bring together in microcosm their own peculiar vision of the "new South Africa", that is, its actual conditions of everyday life, its relations of power, and its modes of existence. These places contain within themselves important clues to the possible futures which are as yet unrealized.[7]

The enchantment and spectacle of place: The Victoria and Alfred Waterfront

> Here, at the tip of Africa, lost in legend, wrapped in history, absorbed in harbour activity, teeming with life and energy, is Cape Town's own Waterfront.[8]

> The Victoria and Alfred Company can give Cape Town the equivalent of three or four gold mines, handled on strictly business lines, using the Disneyland syndrome of thinking and acting big.[9]

The creation of the Victoria & Alfred Waterfront (V&AW) Company in 1988 heralded the beginning of a state-inspired initiative to attract capital back to the underdeveloped and largely redundant industrial dockland precincts of Cape Town. The area is located on the Atlantic seaboard, close to the city

---

6. For the source of some of these ideas, see Boyer, *The City of Collective Memory*, pp. 64–65; Margaret Crawford, "The World in a Shopping Mall", in *Variations on a Theme Park*, pp. 3–30; and John Hannigan, *Fantasy City: Pleasure and Profit in the Postmodern Metropolis*, London and New York, Routledge, 1998.

7. See Howard Caygill, *The Colour of Experience*, London, Routledge, 1998, pp. 57–59, 93–97.

8. Victoria and Alfred Waterfront publicity brochure, 1991/1992.

9. Errol Friedman, "Dockland: Foreign Interest Growing", *Cape Times*, 11 February 1988.

centre and with easy freeway access to the affluent southern suburbs, yet ironically its historical development has been functionally and physically separate
from the city and its residents. In relinquishing control over the 83.2 hectares
of unused port, warehousing, and storage facilities in the historic harbour
area, state and municipal agencies gave the V&AW Company a mandate to
revitalise the site as a tourist and commercial venue that would respect the
ongoing operations of a working harbour.[10] By restoring old buildings and
remaking them as "cultural heritage" sites, and by removing the dilapidated
"eye-sores" that were beyond repair, the V&AW Company transformed the
derelict built environment into what Harvey in another context has referred
to as a "centrepiece of urban spectacle and display."[11]

The masterplan follows the blueprint established by successful international precedents.[12] The insertion of tourist-related infrastructure (vast parking lots, easy entry and exit, children-friendly amenities, and up-to-date
security systems) and renovated retail, hotel, and office facilities has been
coupled with an enthusiastic adoption of the style-and-form template which
makes the "waterfront experience" almost identical across the world. Components common to old port sites – warehouses, sheds, drying docks, quays,
cranes, windlasses and bollards, and the like – bind together docklands redevelopment schemes everywhere all around the globe. Yet what distinguishes
the Victoria and Alfred Waterfront project from other revitalization models
is that shopping, entertainment, and tourist amenities sit alongside the traditional working harbour. The maritime ambience is set by the sights, sounds,
and smells of an actual working harbour, which is also home to a deep-sea
fishing fleet, a glitzy marina for pleasure boats, and the point of departure for
cultural-heritage excursions to the historic prison site at Robben Island.[13]

10. See D. Kilian and B.J. Dodson, "The Capital See-Saw: Understanding the Rationale
for the Victoria and Alfred Redevelopment", *The South African Geographical Journal*,
Vol. 77, No. 1, 1995, pp. 12–20; and P. De Tolly, "Cape Town's Central Waterfront",
Architecture SA, Vol. 3, 1992, pp. 23–26.

11. David Harvey, *The Condition of Postmodernity: An Enquiry into the Origins of Cultural
Change*, New York and London, Basil Blackwell, 1989, p. 271.

12. The real estate developer James Rouse has been perhaps the most influential and
well-known figure in helping to shape thinking about the historic "re-use" of under-
utilized, central city retail districts. Rouse is credited with creating the new typology
of "festival marketplaces". See Ellin, *Postmodern Urbanism*, pp. 84–85.

13. See Christine Muwanga, *South Africa: A Guide to Recent Architecture*, London, Ellipsis,
1998, pp. 40, 42.

In seeking to enhance the success of the Victoria and Alfred portside development, the private-public partnership of real estate developers, financiers, urban planners, and municipal authorities set out to duplicate successful strategies of postmodern waterfront revitalisation elsewhere. In the visual "sameness" of architectural styles, mixed-use services, and varied entertainments, the Victoria and Alfred Waterfront resembles similar docklands revitalisation projects undertaken in Boston, Hong Kong, Sydney, San Francisco, Toronto, New York, Baltimore, and elsewhere. The incremental process of dockland redevelopment included the restoration of historic buildings, the construction of an exhibition centre and museum, a fish market, fashionable restaurants and other eateries, entertainment venues, souvenir shops, office space and berths for harbour tours, plus a leisure boat marina, hotel accommodation, vast parking lots, and exclusive residential condominiums located within the New Basin Precinct.[14]

One distinguishing feature of the feverish post-modernizing of contemporary cityscapes has been the discovery of the visual possibilities of previously discarded landscapes and their reclamation as urban amenities.[15] In forging a fragile alliance of commerce and conservation, the V&AW Company set out to carefully recreate a historical ethos of romance and spectacle. In co-opting existing symbolic, aesthetic, and cultural attributes of the once vibrant site, the Company actively recycled and marketed old buildings of historic significance. The historic preservation of these aging buildings laid particular stress on the maritime theme. The Victorian style of many of the early structures was repeated in several entirely new buildings, notably the right-angle extension of the historic Harbour Cafe Building (1903). Over the course of inte-

---

14. P. De Tolly, "Cape Town's Central Waterfront", *Architecture SA*, Vol. 3, 1992, pp. 23–26. Real estate developers have constructed a mini-island with 60 apartments surrounded by water as part of a R600-million residential marina. It is anticipated that this marina, on the site of the old tank farm, will eventually contain about 500 homes. Designed by architects Revel Fox and Company, the waterfront apartment buildings include such distinctive features as pergolas, lattice screens, shaded verandas, and French doors behind Marseilles-type balconies ("R600m Marina to be Built", *Sunday Times,* Cape Town, 21 February 1999).

15. See Edward Relph, *The Modern Urban Landscape*, Baltimore, The Johns Hopkins University Press, 1987, pp. 258–259; B.S. Hoyle, D.A. Pinder and M.S. Husain (eds), *Revitalising the Waterfront: International Dimensions of Dockland Redevelopment*, London and New York: Belhaven Press, 1988; and Adrian Mellor, "Enterprise and Heritage in the Dock", in John Corner and Sylvia Harvey (eds), *Enterprise and Heritage: Crosscurrents of National Culture*, London and New York, Routledge, 1991, pp. 93–115.

grating new elements with existing docklands structures, traditional designs informed and highlighted the overall planning that went into establishing a sympathetic architectural unity and stylistic coherence.[16]

The V&AW Company incorporated three existing buildings into a major shopping and entertainment complex integrated around a central arched galleria with its pitched roofs, clerestory top-lighting and elaborate exposed ironwork. Designed by Louis Karol Architects to resemble a 19th-century Victorian transportation terminal, the Victoria Wharf shopping centre offers an additional zone of retail and entertainment space that consists of more than 230 separate establishments. These and other refurbished landmarks of a bygone Victorian age have become reassuring reference points in what is often an entirely new milieu.[17]

The V&A Waterfront treats the old port facilities of Cape Town as a work of art, painstakingly refurbished and carefully designed for ostentatious display as well as for commercial use.[18] The large promenade, with its multi-purpose amphitheatre situated in front of the Victoria Wharf shopping centre, creates a large, open space that enables visitors to enjoy, and, if they wish, to become part of the surrounding public spectacle and outdoor festivities.[19] Part of the visceral appeal of festival marketplaces like the V&A Waterfront can be found in the visual aesthetics created by the meeting of horizontal and vertical spaces, the complex and nuanced textures, the rhythmic motions of water and boats, the loquacious presence of maritime animals, and the subtle changes of colour and mood with the time of day, the weather, and the season. But more important to the commercial function of festival marketplaces is the pervasive theme of transportation, both literally as departure to new and exciting destinations, and metaphorically as a welcome escape from the mundane routines of everyday life.[20]

16. Neil Veitch, "The Waterfront: A New Vision", *Waterfront and Harbour: Cape Town's link with the Sea*, Cape Town, Human & Rousseau, 1995, pp. 101–107, esp. 104–105.

17. See Veitch, "The Waterfront: A New Vision", in *Waterfront and Harbour*, pp. 104–105; and L. Karol, "Getting the Very Best", *The Waterfront Review*, Vol. 2, 1992, pp. 23–26.

18. See Boyer, "The Great Frame-Up", pp. 98–99.

19. See D. Kilian and B.J. Dodson, "Forging a Postmodern Waterfront: Urban Form and Spectacle at the Victoria and Alfred Docklands", *South African Geographical Journal*, Vol. 78, No. 1, 1996, pp. 29–40, esp. 36–37.

20. See Goss, "Disquiet on the Waterfront", p. 237.

This assemblage of hybrid, plural spaces resembles what the "contextualist" architect Colin Rowe has called "collage city," where diverse elements of an imaginary urban landscape are woven together into a cohesive whole.[21] At the V&A Waterfront, architectural openness is a metaphor for social inclusiveness, and the articulation of the walkways, shops, cafes, and restaurants suggests the freedom of the street and unity of social life. Festival marketplaces provide a carefully cocooned arena in which sightseers can wander aimlessly, seek enjoyment, shop, dine, and socialise freely, separated from the discomforts, dangers, and social pathologies associated in the popular imagination with the disorderly public spaces of the city. They offer welcome respite from the threatening realities of racialised poverty, homelessness, and over-crowding in the teeming streets of the dangerous city.[22]

As recycled remnants of the invented past, festival marketplaces make use of "cultural heritage" and the revival of discarded historical styles as vehicles to enhance the art of consumption. The historical tableaux of festival marketplaces consciously present a "symbolic public life", that is, a set a shared meanings that develop out of the common experience of particular settings and rituals in public space that ideally kindle social bonds between impromptu communities of strangers.[23] Narratives accompanying festival marketplaces reduce a class-stratified, heterogeneous urban population to a class-flattened, multi-ethnic "imagined community" that "joins the capital of the wealthy, the ideas of the intellectuals, and the labour of the working classes in a unitary history of urban progress" that implies an unbroken continuity with the past.[24] The V&A Waterfront is a sanitized Disneyesque world of entertainment, leisure, and recreation, whose acknowledgement of its unique cultural landscape is largely limited to fragmented images of the history of Cape Town. At this revitalized harbourplace, tourists, shoppers, and sightseers can experience a "squeaky clean, romanitised reconstruction of the past."[25]

21. See Colin Rowe, "Collage City", *Architectural Review*, August 1975, pp. 65–91; and Colin Rowe and Fred Koetter, *Collage City*, Cambridge, Massachusetts, MIT Press, 1978.

22. See Huxtable, *The Unreal America*, pp. 75–76; and Goss, "Disquiet on the Waterfront", pp. 229–230.

23. See Boyer, *City of Collective Memory*, pp. 47, 416–420.

24. See Goss, "Disquiet on the Waterfront", p. 228.

25. Simon Goudie, Darryll Kilian, and Delinda Dodson, "Postmodern F(r)ictions: History, Text and Identity at the Victoria and Alfred Waterfront", *Architecture SA*, May-

From its origins in the seventeenth century as a replenishment station at the southern tip of the African continent to its present-day metamorphosis as an aspirant "world-class" tourist city, Cape Town has undergone successive waves of restructuring that have not only altered its physical landscape but also imprinted one idealized spatial vision after another on the malleable urban fabric.[26] With the construction of the V&A Waterfront, Cape Town has donned yet another mask: the return to a regime of normalcy. In the spirit of Cape Town's earlier incarnations, the V&A Waterfront is an allegory of its own time. As the most far-reaching addition to the outward appearance of the cityscape after the end of apartheid, this harbourfront revitalisation scheme is a mediation on the perplexity of the organization and use of urban space in the "new South Africa". If the deliberate destruction of District Six remains a lasting symbol of the cruelty and absurdity of the "apartheid city", then the V&A Waterfront epitomizes the roseate post-apartheid vision of "a future alive with possibility and promise."[27]

The revival of the Waterfront as a surrealistic entertainment site reflects the scripted normalcy of the post-apartheid social order. In this narcissistic vision of the "new South Africa", the uplifting story of the rebirth of derelict and unused docklands holds a powerfully inspiring message for the uncertain times after apartheid. Conceived at a time when white minority rule was at its end and the transition to non-racial parliamentary democracy was just beginning, the V&A Waterfront has come to symbolise the idealized corporate vision of the "new South Africa": a vast playground-by-the-sea, open and inviting to all citizens across the racial divide who can afford to partake of its earthly pleasures. Despite its utopian rhetoric of inclusiveness, the V&A Waterfront consists of little more than a contained and rational concentration of entertainment venues and spectacular displays – a surreal oasis of order carved out of the redundant docklands, and separated from the vast wasteland of the Cape Flats.

In an era of triumphant global capitalism, festival marketplaces like the V&A Waterfront have come to constitute the reigning prototype for the or-

---

June 1995, pp. 26–27, 29–30; and Muwanga, "Central Cape Town", pp. 40–41.

26. See John Western, *Outcast Cape Town*, Berkeley and Los Angeles, University of California Press, 1996; and Jennifer Robinson, "Power, Space, and the City: Historical Reflections on Apartheid and Post-Apartheid Urban Orders", in David Smith (ed.), *The Apartheid City and Beyond: Urbanization and Social Change in South Africa*, London and New York, Routledge, 1992, pp. 292–302.

27. Veitch, *Waterfront and Harbour*, p. 7.

ganization and use of the symbolic "public spaces" of the future. Like enclosed shopping malls and other themed specialty retail centres, they are profoundly ambivalent and even contradictory places that articulate both sides of the schizophrenic tension between a genuine desire for vibrant urban life and rational strategies of social control. On the one hand, they offer a comfort zone where visitors can sample a veritable smorgasbord of visual delights, bodily pleasures, and diversionary entertainments.[28] On the other hand, festival marketplaces mobilise and exploit utopian impulses in the service of crass commercialism. They are surreal dream-houses of contemporary consumer capitalism, largely dependent upon ideological manipulations, formulaic aesthetics, and exclusionary practices.[29] Like other themed entertainment destinations, festival marketplaces contrive to be everything that they are not: that is, "carefully orchestrated corporate spectacles" masquerading as genuine public spaces. The illusion of an open, freely-shared space and civil public realm is possible only through private ownership and social regulation. The prospect and the promise of spontaneous festivity and theatricality are made in a context of organised entertainment and rigorously maintained public order. Opportunities for liminal encounters with "the Other" largely depend upon the deliberate exclusion of social difference.[30] Instead of contributing to the enlargement of the public life of the city, they merely reproduce an illusionary spectacle of spontaneous sociality and meaningful social interaction.[31]

The genealogy of festival marketplaces like the V&A Waterfront can be traced to urban renewal and revitalization schemes that emerged in the 1960s as a welcome panacea to rapid deteriorization of North American city centres, with their blighted core business districts, declining inner-city property tax base, and "white flight" from urban neighbourhoods to the sprawling suburbs. The dozen or so "world-class" waterfront revitalization projects (typical-

---

28. See Dennis Judd, "The Rise of the New Walled Cities", in *Spatial Practices*, pp. 144–146; and Jon Goss, "The Magic of the Mall: Form and Function in the Built Environment", *Annals of the Association of American Geographers*, Vol. 83, 1993, pp. 18–47.

29. See Goss, "Disquiet on the Waterfront", pp. 221–247; Loretta Lees, "Agoraphobia, Heterotopia, and Vancouver's New Public Library", *Environment and Planning D*, 15, 3, 1997, pp. 321–348; and David Sibley, *Geographies of Exclusion: Society and Difference in the West*, London and New York, Routledge, 1995, esp. pp. 72–89.

30. See Sharon Zukin, *Loft Living: Culture and Capital in Urban Change*, Baltimore, The Johns Hopkins University Press, 1982, p. 190; and Goss, "Disquiet on the Waterfront", p. 240.

31. See Boyer, "The City of Illusion", p. 119.

ly situated near port facilities, rivers, lakes, or even canals) around the world descend from early urban redevelopment plans like the former chocolate factory premises in San Francisco renamed Ghirardelli Square in 1964, and Faneuil Hall Market Place and the adjacent Quincy Market in Boston.[32] The patriarchal figure of the stylized "festival marketplace" motif, the developer James Rouse, set in motion a trendy preservationist movement toward what Margaret Crawford has called the "successful packaging of 'authenticity'."[33] This retrofitting of obsolete built environments, refurbished with up-to-date conveniences and insinuated into the existing urban fabric by their absorption into a commercial setting, offered a viable and attractive alternative to their gradual decay and eventual demolition.[34] The steady expansion of these cloned and packaged indoor shopping malls, or what real estate developer Jon Jerde has enthusiastically endorsed as the "third millennium city", has gone hand-in-hand with the cordoning off and subsequent devaluation of genuine public spaces, like streets, parks, plazas, and other sites of outdoor assembly and entertainment.[35]

The ostentatious conceits of fabricated "heritage"

Generally speaking, cultural heritage sites entail the restoration of existing places that have fallen into disrepair or the creation of entirely new locations, retrofitted to give the look and feel of something significant and meaningful retrieved from the past. The act of preservation itself necessarily involves a whole series of interventions and innovations. The consolidation of what otherwise threatens to disintegrate can easily metamorphosize into a process of embellishment or even invention. What may begin as a rescue operation, designed to preserve the relics of the past, passes incrementally into a work of restoration in which a new environment has to be created in order to turn fragments into a meaningful whole.[36] The motive behind such "invented tra-

32. See Diane Ghirardo, *Architecture after Modernism*, New York, Thames & Hudson, 1996.

33. Margaret Crawford, "The World in a Shopping Mall," in Sorkin, *Variations on a Theme Park*, pp. 3–30.

34. See Huxtable, *The Unreal America*, pp. 96–97; and Ellin, *Postmodern Urbanism*, pp. 84–85.

35. See Mike Davis, "Urban Renaissance and the Spirit of Postmodernism", *New Left Review*, Issue 151, 1985, pp. 111–112.

36. Raphael Samuel, *Theatres of Memory. Part I: Past and Present in Contemporary Cul-*

ditions" is often the hackneyed packaging of a sanitised version of the past as a commodity for present consumption with profit-making as the driving force. Under these circumstances, historical tradition is at best refitted as a soi-disant museum culture, where stress is typically laid upon a sanitized and popularized version of "local history" and how things once-upon-a-time were made and consumed, exchanged and sold, and seamlessly integrated into a long-lost and often romantized daily life, where virtually all traces of oppressive social relations are expunged.[37] With the increased emphasis on image-making in urban design, it is not surprising that real estate developers and corporate planners have looked to the entertainment industries – the masters of "imagineering" – for ideas about how to build heritage theme parks, leisure resorts, and other sites of fanciful enjoyment.[38]

Sites of memory like the District Six museum, the Mayibuye Centre, and the Robben Island tour and exhibition genuinely struggle with perplexing questions of historical accuracy, political relevance, and national identity. In contrast, there is no such pretence in ersatz "heritage" theme parks like Gold Reef City, a sprawling leisure and entertainment complex located on the southern fringe of the Johannesburg CBD at the former site of the long-abandoned Crown Mines facilities.[39] In constructing a built environment intended to simulate a frontier gold mining town in the grasp of Rostowian "take-off" at the turn of the last century, the corporate owners of this entertainment extravaganza have created an imaginative encounter with a fantasy-filled past. Gold Reef City invites its patrons to sample the exhilarating, bawdy excitement of early Johannesburg, circa 1890–1920. Promotional brochures boast that this fun-filled place is "Africa's greatest theme park", an

ture, New York and London, Verso, 1994, pp. 172, 178, 303–304.

37. See Harvey, _The Condition of Postmodernity_, p. 303.

38. See Charles Rutheiser, "Making Place in the Nonplace Urban Realm: Notes on the Revitalization of Downtown Atlanta", in Setha Low (ed.), _Theorizing the City: The New Urban Anthropology Reader_, New Brunswick, New Jersey, Rutgers University Press, 1999, pp. 317–341.

39. Many of the ideas expressed here are taken from Cynthia Kros, "Experiencing a Century in a Day?: Making More of Gold Reef City", _South African Historical Journal_, Vol. 29, 1993, pp. 28–43; and Cynthia Kros, "Visiting History on the Week-End: From Colonial Williamsburg to Gold Reef City: An Exercise in Scrutinising Public History", _Africa Perspective_, Vol. 2, No. 1, 1993, pp. 104–111.

entertainment destination that "brings back to life that exciting era" when Johannesburg was a "roistering, rollicking Mining Town."[40]

By situating itself at a location that was once dedicated to the arduous task of deep-level mining, Gold Reef City at least obliquely shares the preservationist fondness for industrial archaeology: the resurrectionist urge to salvage the long-abandoned machinery and equipment of a glorious "industrial age" slowly but surely slipping into the oblivion of historical forgetfulness. The centrepiece of Gold Reef City is Crown Mines No. 14 shaft: a representative sample of eye-catching mining headgear left behind when the Crown Mines facilities were demolished. Arching upward and silhouetted against the sky, this conspicuous landmark is one of the last remaining totems of authenticity, a physical reminder of something truly original about the site itself. As with similar ersatz retrieval projects, exquisite relics of the past function as a point of access for refurbishing the site to serve contemporary pecuniary interests.[41]

Whatever else it represents, Gold Reef City is the most extravagant, ostentatious, and tacky commemoration of a physical site whose primary touchstone is literally a special kind of rock: gold-bearing ore, first discovered in surface outcroppings on the Witwatersrand main reef. The geological exhibit located nearby retells the story of the initial discovery of gold and the subsequent efforts to extract and process the ever-elusive gold-bearing ore deposited in thin ribbons deep underground. Taken as a whole, the social site itself – the stylized replicas of old buildings, souvenir shops, thematized eateries, live performances, museological artifacts, scattered detritus of redundant mining technologies – commemorates the national founding (or originating) myth of South Africa as a largely unsettled but highly contested frontier zone where "modernizing" European settlers encountered "traditional" Africans.[42]

As exercises in commercial entertainment, heritage theme parks attract visitors through a variety of representational strategies: exclusion and error, deliberate vagueness and ambiguity, conflation of past and present, and mod-

---

40. This quotation and the following ones are taken from promotional materials distributed at Gold Reef City.

41. Some of the ideas expressed here and in subsequent paragraphs are borrowed from Barbara Kirstenblatt-Gimblett, "Plimoth Plantation", in *Destination Culture: Tourism, Museums, and Heritage*, Berkeley and Los Angeles, University of California Press, 1998, pp. 189–200.

42. See Leslie Witz, "Beyond Van Riebeeck", in Sarah Nuttall and Cheryl-Ann Michael (eds), *Senses of Culture: South African Culture Studies*, Cape Town, Oxford University Press, 2000, pp. 318–343.

ification to accommodate the whims of taste and fashion, or the pressures of the marketplace.[43] The governing logic that informs the design of such heritage-inspired attractions as Gold Reef City corresponds to what MacCannell has called "staged authenticity".[44] The promoters of this theme-o-ramic, theatrical stage-set have made only the slightest effort to re-create a historically accurate and chronologically-situated setting, preferring instead to work with a strategy of historicized bricolage where period and place are promiscuously blended into a hodge-podge of make-believe. Heritage theme parks like Gold Reef City place a premium on "hands-on" experience – visceral, kinaesthetic, thrilling, intimate – that is more akin to carnivalesque masquerade than having a pedagogical commitment to learning something new about what happened in the past and why. What is lost in historical comprehension of site itself is gained in immediacy and exhilaration. The "experience" itself represents an exemplary exercise in mock historical re-enactment, an invitation to take an imaginary journey back in time. Its brazen, commercial theatricality invites us to indulge in a kind of momentary fantasy-play, to suspend historical judgement under the guise of "having a good time".[45]

Heritage theme parks like Gold Reef City are a genre of cultural performance, a mezmerizing spectacle of visual enjoyments constructed in such a way as to give the appearance of realism and spontaneity, and to instil an aura of authenticity. If there is a unifying thread to these mock exercises in historical reconstruction, it is the quest for immediacy, the search for a past, which is palpably and visibly present.[46] As a way of seeing and using the past, this kind of "heritage" has more in common with invention, fantasy, and myth-making than with historical accuracy and truth. In the name of broadening its popular appeal and satisfying discordant tastes, the makers of "heritage" create simulacra of a sanitised past that never actually existed.[47] Two thematic orientations – the mimetic re-creation of a frontier mining town combined with theatrical performances celebrating African "tradition" – converge at Gold Reef City to produce an "effect of the real" that is modelled on a kind of

---

43. See Nuala Johnson, "Review of David Lowenthal, The Heritage Crusade and the Spoils of History", *Journal of Historical Geography*, Vol. 24, No. 4, 1998, p. 507.

44. Dean MacCannell, *The Tourist: A New Theory of the Leisure Class*, New York, Schocken, 1976.

45. See Kirstenblatt-Gimblett, "Plimoth Plantation", pp. 194–195.

46. See Samuel, *Theatres of Memory*, p. 175–176; and Kirshenblatt-Gimblett, "Objects of Ethnography", in *Destination Culture*, pp. 57–65.

47. See Samuel, *Theatres of Memory*, p. 242.

Geertzian "experience-near" of simulated time-travel and the visual engagement with the life-worlds of others.[48]

Amnesiacs delight: Xanadu and the Lost City

In their most egregious manifestations, counterfeit heritage sites travesty the historical past by substituting amusing ersatz and tacky kitsch for genuine artefacts and memorabilia, and offer a bogus simulation that does not even bother to pretend to faithfully imitate anything that actually happened or really existed.[49]

The exemplar of this "fantasy-island" approach to a make-believe past is Sol Kerzner's Lost City, a glitzy, $300 million themed resort and entertainment complex carved out of eighty arid acres of what used to be the Independent Homeland of Bophuthatswana. Located around 100 miles northwest of Johannesburg, the Lost City rises incongruously out of the featureless bushveld like a gigantic, overscaled movie set. Kerzner, an out-spoken and flamboyant South African real estate developer, created Sun International, which developed and owns the gambling resort Sun City in Bophuthatswana, of which the Lost City is the crown jewel. On the eve of South Africa's first non-racial general elections in 1994, Sun City boasted 1.5 million visitors a year, mainly white South Africans seeking ribald adventure outside the boundaries of the strict moral codes that had banned gambling, nudity, and other sorts of lascivious behaviour in their own country. With the addition of the Lost City, the number of visitors a year to the resort and gambling complex has more than doubled.[50]

From start to finish, the experience of Lost City entails a kind of wilful self-deception about the nature of social reality, about history and one's place in it. It is a surreal place that combines visual deceptions with fictional narratives about a mythical past that makes no pretence to mimicking an

---

48. See Kirshenblatt-Gimblett, "Objects of Ethnography", in *Destination Culture*, pp. 3, 4–5.

49. Robert Hewison, *The Heritage Industry: Britain in a Climate of Decline*, London, Metheun, 1987, pp. 132–133; Huxtable, *The Unreal America*, pp. 72–89; and David Lowenthal, "Identity, Heritage, and History", in John Gillis (ed.), *Commemorations: The Politics of National Identity*, Princeton, New Jersey, Princeton University Press, 1994, pp. 41–60.

50. The ideas for this and the following paragraphs are taken from Richard Stengel, "South Africa's Theme Park: Dinosaurland", *The New Republic*, 208, 4 January 1993, pp. 11–12.

actual place or time. Lost City is the quintessential simulacrum, the identical copy of which no original ever existed. In order to give the Lost City a semblance of identity, the corporate developers invented a "fictional history" out of whole cloth. In this purely fanciful "myth of origins", the Lost City is a pretend-place that was built many centuries ago by a prescient tribe of environmentally correct and spiritually pure aesthetes. Buried by a volcano sometime during the Dark Ages, the city had only recently been discovered and painstakingly excavated. Like Kublai Khan's Xanadu, Kerner created an imaginary world that abounds with sacred rivers, royal temples, and monumental totems. Like Xanadu, it is a pure figment of a fertile imagination, a fictionalized place where nothing in it is real.[51]

The Lost City is totally absorbed in architectural discourse. First, there is the discovery of an "other" place, one whose whereabouts were unknown and one, which was suspended in time, preserved in a time warp. Second, this place is then identified, mapped, or marked in some way to distinguish it as unique, unusual, or special. This "rediscovery" has the effect of calling attention to its otherness, and then bringing this otherness under control. Gradually, any trace of otherness is reduced or made to disappear by making it similar to what is already known. Lastly, in order to compensate for the assimilation and inevitable disappearance of the otherness of the site, there is an attempt to reproduce or establish an artificial otherness with reified images as a kind of textual, visual, or spatial "gaming" which masks its actual reality.[52] At Lost City, architecture is left to reveal its own often fantastical personality. The building designs offer a bizarre mix of pretentiousness and airy whimsy. The corporate builders of the Lost City have abandoned the modernist impulse toward universalism, purism, and functionality in architectural design in favour of pluralism, contextualism, and hybridity. The spatial layout of the sprawling premises resembles a postmodernist decorative pastiche, a celebratory moment of ephemeral surface appearances lacking in any genuine intrinsic depth. Its eclectic geometrical design, architectural motifs, and decorative ornamentation are fashioned more in the spirit of fiction than of function.[53] Its elaborately overscaled and theatrical pseudo-architecture – with its clever

---

51. Kerzner also owns thirty other hotels, most of which are casino-resorts that were located in the so-called "independent Homelands".

52. See Sarah Chaplin, "Heterotopia Deserta: Las Vagas and Other Spaces", in Iain Borden and Jane Rendell (eds), *Intersections: Architectural Histories and Critical Theories*, New York and London: Routledge, 2000, pp. 207–208.

53. This phrase is borrowed from Harvey, *The Condition of Postmodernity*, p. 292.

stress on facile eclectic illusion, on image over substance, and on artifice over art – receives all the attention, and is generally accepted as the real thing. The main building, the 338-room Palace Hotel, consists of a dizzying and disconnected melange of architectural styles: elaborate Romanesque arches, bulky Moorish towers, and colourful Byzantine mosaics. With its free play of styles and historicist allusions, the elaborate ornamentation of the Lost City conforms to what might be called the "magical realism" school of postmodernist architecture. Lyrical displays of animals step outside of real-life wildlife settings to create imaginary worlds of myth and mystery. Giant sculpted antelope heads form flying buttresses for the hotel's twin towers, which are topped by cupolas that are shamelessly faked to resemble something carved out of giant elephant tusks. Repetitive and serialized images, modified to fit the context, symbolize the flamboyant hyperbole of this make-believe place. Sweeping, phallic elephant tusks are ubiquitous features in the Lost City: from the crossed tusks in the elevators to elephant tusk pencils in the elegant rooms. With friezes of ancient animals on a faux rock wall, the main casino resembles the Caves of Lascaux except for its flashy gambling tables. The Bridge of Time, the elongated skywalk linking the gambling casino to the hotel, is crisscrossed with phony hairline cracks. The fake rocks, like the elephant tusks, are fashioned from welded steel and wire mesh, sprayed with cement, and covered with an "authentic-looking" fiberglass patina.[54]

The corporate developers of the Lost City have created a fake fantasy world of pure imagination, where the false is more beautiful, tantalizing, and entertaining than the real.[55] A grand fan-shaped pool with timed six-foot-high waves – a surfers' delight – that break onto a white sandy beachfront which spreads out from the rear of the hotel. An "endless River" flows into the "Royal Baths" and feeds five different water slides, including the daunting "Temple of Courage", the centrepiece water extravaganza with a frightening 250-foot drop. An expansive, sixty-acre faux jungle, which features an artificial rain forest, a desert, and a swamp, almost completely surrounds the hotel. To create this stylized designer jungle, Kerzner imported 1.6 million plants and shrubs, including a forty-eight-ton Baobab tree from the eastern Transvaal near the Kruger National Park. According to the Guinness Book of World Records, this Baobab is the largest transplanted tree in the world – a true "factoid" of insignificant significance. At the Lost City, even the absence

54. Stengel, "South Africa's Theme Park: Dinosaurland", pp. 11–12.
55. See Harvey, *The Condition of Postmodernity*, pp. 95, 97–98.

of the sea can be overcome: Big Surf, an indoor environment featuring a machine that creates a giant, and perfectly predictable, wave every 90 seconds, all for the pleasure of desert surfers.[56]

Despite the Sisyphean efforts to create an "other-worldliness" at the Lost City, the actual realities of the "new South Africa" manage to intrude. The patterns of employment at the Lost City replicate existing racial divisions in the country. The virtually-all-white managerial staff dress in black tie, whereas every black worker occupying the lower rungs of the employment hierarchy seems to wear some sort of costumed attire. The black doormen are outfitted in flowing robes and jewelled turbans; the black cleaning ladies are clad in brightly-coloured dashikis with matching sashes. The black waiters at the Tusk Bar are dressed in leopard-print vests. Black gardeners wear safari-like outfits.[57]

What the Lost City and other similar Disneyesque fantasy-making environments have in common is their suspension of disbelief, the skillful expertise of their creative illusion, their crafty, shrewd showmanship and advertizing genius, and the de novo construction of a cleverly edited, engineered, and marketed version of a chosen place or theme. Fantasy make-believe and the selective re-creation of a surrogate "reality" have become an undifferentiated whole, two sides of the same coin, in which the shift of function to mesmerizing entertainment cancels out the meaning and value of history and form. Without a genuine attachment to actual existence, what is borrowed, appropriated, or copied acquires validity over the source. The rejection of the historical past, or at least the unwillingness to come to grips with it in favour of something easier and more pleasant, is not a new South African phenomenon. There is a long history of invention and fabrication of the past to serve vested interests. So much of what has masqueraded as South African history has been created out of wishful thinking or fashioned out of whole cloth. So much has been invented by those who had an interest in sanitizing or erasing the past, or had a remarkable instinct for the exploitation and alteration of the historical past to serve some new and unrelated purpose or context.[58]

---

56. William Kowinski, *The Malling of America: An Inside Look at the Great Consumer Paradise*, New York, Morrow, 1985, pp. 232.

57. See Stengel, "South Africa's Theme Park: Dinosaurland", pp. 11–12.

58. For the source of these ideas, see Huxtable, *The Unreal America*, pp. 41–42.

In the Lost City, the real implodes and disappears, replaced by the "hyper-reality" of the image.[59] For some, this taste for a shrewdly programmed artificial experience with its phantasmagorical collage of images represents "a chic superrealism with a cutting-edge cachet, a perversely trendy avant-guarde." Unlike cultural heritage sites that at least gesture toward the veracity of images, places like the Lost City have no such problem of degenerative authenticity. The Lost City is an enchanting place that has lost touch with (relinquished its connection) with its referents in the real world. Nothing contained within its spatial boundaries is admired for its ability to replicate reality, only for the remarkable simulation that its skillful "masters of illusion" have been able to achieve. The selective manipulation of its sources is a deliberate, expressive distortion that can be its own art form. Simulation, as distinct from resemblance, has no origin or referent, for the model replaces the real.[60]

The remarkable ménage-à-trois of entrepreneurial self-interest, state-of-the-art technologies of simulation, and masterful marketing all come together at the Lost City. The privileging of image-spectacles like the Lost City is not an innocent undertaking, devoid of ethical considerations and political value judgements. The sheer grandeur and majesty of the Lost City generates what Leach calls an "aesthetics of intoxication".[61]

It is a surreal non-place where meaningfulness is so shallow, depthless, and without substance that it dissolves into a vacuum of kitsch imitations of genuine compassion, empathy, and emotional attachment.[62] What the Lost World offers is a bathetic parody of the truly creative powers of imagination, a callow, child-like world of make-believe fairy-tales that infantilizes the intellect and stifles critical thinking. It is a self-absorbed, cocoon-like place catering to the vanity, hypocrisy, and self-indulgence of the privileged classes.[63]

59. See Eco, *Travels in Hyperreality*, pp. 30–31, 40–44.

60. Quotations are from Huxtable, *The Unreal America*, pp. 10, 87.

61. See Neil Leach, *The Anaesthetics of Architecture*, Cambridge, Massachusetts, MIT Press, 1999, pp. 2–3, 18–19.

62. For the source of these ideas, see Stjepan Gabriel Mestrovic, *The Coming Fin de Siecle: An Application of Durkheim's Sociology to Modernity and Postmodernity*, New York, Routledge, 1991, p. 15.

63. Jean Braudrillard, *Simulations*, [Paul Foss, Paul Patton, and Philip Beitchman, trans.], New York, Semiotext(e), 1983, pp. 23–24.

The corporate art of "placemaking" and the erasure of collective memory

Entertaining places like the V&A Waterfront, Gold Reef City, and the Lost City have insinuated themselves into the popular mind as the embodiments of what the "new South Africa" has to offer its citizens. By strictly regimenting the organization and use of space, corporate planners have created places that can accommodate diversity and complexity in the post-apartheid era. By recycling familiar images and implanting them in local settings, corporate planners have fashioned symbolic landscapes in which a fragmented social order after apartheid can participate in the reassuring myth of a shared "rainbow" culture. In the idealized world of the corporate imagination, themed entertainment destinations have largely dispensed with racial animus because they offer pluralized sites where consuming citizens across the racial divide can freely choose amongst a veritable medley of earthly pleasures without fear of confronting the annoyances of city-life. Despite their up-beat promotional rhetoric, these pleasure-sites deliberately sidestep the unresolved tension between the ideals of communitas and civitas and the practical politics of exclusivity. In the corporate vision, socioeconomic betterment can be accomplished without undue sacrifice because, just as the rising tide lifts all boats, the powerful forces of entrepreneurial initiative and market competition will trickle down to benefit the poor.

In festival marketplaces and other themed entertainment destinations, nostalgia for a lost time is exploited to commercial effect. In the view of Eric Hobsbawm, "invented traditions" are those practices that seek to establish continuity with a suitable past through the creation of rituals and rules, through the use of historically-loaded symbols, or simply through repetition as a way of implying a connection with what came before. In short, the "invention of tradition" is the process of creating shared understandings that promote a collective sense of continuity with a largely fictitious, or fictionalized past.[64] Those cultural heritage sites and other themed entertainment destinations which foster a sense of historical continuity with a "suitable past" are prime examples of what Dorst calls "traditionalization", or the production of historical "authenticity" as a consumable image. The historical past – whether real or imagined – becomes a spectacle: it is selectively arranged

---

64. Eric Hobsbawm, "Introduction", in Eric Hobsbawm and Terence Ranger (eds), *The Invention of Tradition*, Cambridge, Cambridge University Press, 1983, pp. 1–14, esp. pp. 2–4.

by corporate planners to validate what appears to be an accurate and truthful portrayal of what once existed some time ago.[65] Carried to the extreme, the "invention of tradition" produces a kind of "hyper-reality", a surreal condition that, as Umberto Eco points out, must be absolutely fake in order to be better than anything real.[66] It is here where the pretence of historicism or preservation, which depend upon reference to a certain original, is superseded by the effort to produce an encompassing environment that effectively transcends its source of inspiration.[67]

65. John Dorst, *The Written Suburb: An American Site, an Ethnographic Dilemma*, Philadelphia, Pennsylvania, University of Pennsylvania Press, 1989, pp. 16–17.

66. Eco, *Travels in Hyperreality*, pp. 7, 8, 30.

67. See Nan Ellin, *Postmodern Urbanism*, pp. 162–163.

PART III

INTERPRETATIONS OF
SOUTH AFRICAN HISTORY

— CHAPTER 13 —

Whose memory – whose history?
The illusion of liberal and radical historical debates

Bernhard Makhosezwe Magubane

The colonization of South Africa and its designation as a "white man's country" is a grim and sordid affair.[1] It is a tale of brutal aggression, broken pledges, and treachery. Even when we celebrate the "new South Africa", we should not forget the deep wounds that it left in the hearts and minds of its victims. Any history of South Africa worth its salt must take into account those deep wounds, especially now that we have a government, which is committed to healing and national reconciliation, and to building a better South Africa for all its peoples.

I am going to be bold and probably provocative and state that the nature of white domination and exploitation of indigenous peoples remains elusive and enveloped in clouds of mystifications. From 1969, following the publication of the first volume of the *History of South Africa* edited by Monica Wilson and Leonard Thompson, a stream of books, collection of essays, reviews and dissertations have appeared in which liberal interpretations of South African history were challenged and debunked by radical or Neo-Marxist interpretations. These debates, at least to a non-historian, like myself, never confronted what it meant for black folks to be treated as non-persons in the country of

---

1. South Africa is littered with statues of generals who conquered the country. The cities and towns, hospitals, bridges and city squares are also named after conquerors. The Africans on the other hand are treated simply as part of the landscape. In 1955, during his whirlwind tour of the country, Mandela (*Long Walk to Freedom*, 1994, p. 155) found himself offended by the fact that colonial towns were named after brutal colonizers. As he put it: "From Durban I drove south along the coast past Port Shepstone and Port St. Johns, small and lovely towns that dotted the shimmering beaches fronting the Indian Ocean. While mesmerized by the beauty of the area, I was constantly rebuked by the buildings and streets that bear the names of white imperialists who suppressed the very people whose names belong there."

their birth. Or indeed, what it meant to be white and to be proclaimed a member of the superior race!

To be an African, in particular in South Africa, meant and still means to suffer privation, on a daily basis. But among South African historians, it seems not to have been a very important issue. French scholars, on the other hand confronted white settler colonialism in Algeria head on. Frantz Fanon in his various writings, especially in the *Wretched of the Earth*; Albert Memmi in 1965 in *The Colonizer and the Colonized* or Jean-Paul Sartre in his various writings confronted the Algerian situation in a way that none of those who engaged in the South African debate ever did.

It is probably unkind to ask: "whose history" and "whose memory" has been written and argued about in South Africa? Can one have History when one is invisible *to* History? To state that a colonial and white supremacist society breeds and needs a racist historiography is a cliché. Where the fact of colonization was accompanied by acts of genocide against the indigenous peoples, racism became blatant and naked in its rationalization of the acts of brutality. And where the indigenous peoples were spared death and were factored in as instruments of production and servants of the colonizing society, the veil of racism became almost impenetrable. Theal's racist *oeuvre* in South Africa served this purpose well, as I will show below.

Forces that emerged victorious in the struggles between the colonizer and the colonized created South African history, as written by recognized historians. If one looks at the history of higher education in South Africa, there is no question that the forces that endowed its institutions were the major beneficiaries of African helotry. Major buildings in all South African universities tell the story more eloquently than I can[2]. They celebrate the "generosity" of those who endowed some of these institutions, from what Rhodes said were funds derived, as he put it from "starving Kafirs".[3] No doubt, these endowments were not altruistic, but were to buy *silence* on certain of their activities. In short, can one really understand South African history without understanding the role of those who were the beneficiaries of African exploitation and dehumanization in the mines and farms, and the sugarcane agro-industry of Natal?

---

2. The statue of Cecil John Rhodes on a horse and pointing north in front of the University of Cape Town is one such obscenity.

3. See my "Round Table Movement and its influence on the historiography of Imperialism", in Magubane, *African Sociology – Towards a Radical Perspective*, Trenton, New Jersey, Africa World Press, 2000.

Let us acknowledge, indeed, that the subjects we choose to study, the questions we ask, the concepts and theories we use, are not neutral, or motivated by purely academic concerns. What we study has a lot to do with relations of power. This at least to me is no better exemplified than in the so-called disputes between liberal historians and academic Marxists. When I read and reflected on these debates, I was always nagged by the question: Where is the black story of suffering? Why were certain questions never raised, or when raised, tended to be dealt with in a perfunctory manner? Indeed, why are African voices silenced in South African historiography?[4]

What is striking about the historiography of South Africa is that each generation seems to think that history began only yesterday and what happened a day before yesterday is "ancient history" that has no relevance for today's problems. I agree with Lonsdale who says that historical processes are to be understood, over the longest possible spans of time.[5] The African, since the advent of the Age of Europe and capitalism has constituted "the wretched of the earth", to use Fanon's apt phrase or, in fact, because of his enslavement Christian theology and racial science made him the outcast of evolution. South Africa's colonial experience cannot be separated from that gruesome reality of genocide and mayhem. During the 19th century when minerals were discovered in South Africa and when the country was being constituted as a White Dominion in the British Empire, the African was constituted to play the same role that Africans as slaves had played in the Americas.

The rape of Africa involved much international intrigue and considerable sanctimonious bilge. Britain conspired with Italy against France to gain the Sudan and protect Cecil Rhodes' dream of an unbroken Cape-to-Cairo British Empire; Germany played France against Italy and Britain allowed Germany to take over Togoland and the Cameroons. Many secret treaties were signed with a cynical eye on the inevitability of future open conflict, as was exposed after the First World War. To salve their conscience and greed, European powers proclaimed their actions to be humanitarian, honourable, and a "civilizing mission". What has this to do with South African history?

---

4. Take for instance, *South African Capitalism and Black Political Opposition*, edited by Martin Murray, Cambridge, Massachusetts, 1982. It contains only three contributions by black scholars. There is not a single article devoted to the ANC or the PAC. Even worse Ruth First's rejoinder to Mafeje's article was not included. To me the title of the book is misleading, to say the least.

5. Lonsdale, John, "From Colony to Industrial State: South African Historiography as seen from England", *Social Dynamics*, Vol. 9, No. 1, 1983, p. 67.

One of my interests in this history is that it enables me to establish patterns. Are there parallels, for instance, between the disenfranchisement of African-Americans in the United States and the denial of the franchise to black people in South Africa?

The legacy of colonialism

Following the abolition of slavery, to control and direct African labour to where it was needed most, several institutional mechanisms were devised to define, confine, and reduce the African worker to pure labour. Of these the pass system and its application only to Africans is unique. Originally devised for indentured white immigrants, free Coloured workers and emancipated slaves, the pass system anchored the master and servant relations and lasted until 1990. The economic development that accompanied the mining industry and even the industrialization, instead of ameliorating the enforcement of the pass laws, in fact entrenched them even more. The pass laws survived South Africa's capitalist growth and precipitated the Sharpeville massacre. Temporarily suspended, they were re-introduced and enforced with even more rigour. To argue that economic development would ameliorate racial oppression is a terrifying parody of serious academic investigation that is either wilful or due to blind ignorance of the nature of capitalism. It suggests sterile theorizing at its worst.[6]

The enslavement, conquest, land dispossession, exploitation, and oppression constitute a historical totality of horror, whose structures are bound together in such a way that any one of them considered separately is an abstraction. It is not an aggregate sum of the African experience.

This chapter is a synoptic review of the debates that divide liberal and Neo-Marxist paradigms. But before that, I want to interrogate briefly nineteenth century and early twentieth century writers to see what issues they considered important, and what light they can throw on our understanding of the present debates. To study the concerns of nineteenth and early twentieth century historians is to understand how historians as they study bygone times, are actually immersed in the problems of their day.

In South Africa, Theal's history writing and that of his successor Cory is a classic demonstration of history as politics. The theory of white racial

---

6. From the point of view that in the social sciences, it is important to distinguish between what David Harvey in 1973 called "status quo", "revolutionary", and "counter-revolutionary" theories. David Harvey, *Social justice and the city*, London, 1973.

supremacy dominated the political practice of white settler colonization. And Theal's racist historiography justified the earlier practice of genocide against the San and the Khoi whom Theal's historiography had reduced to the status of sub-humans. In his 1893 synthetic volume: *South Africa*, the so-called "Bushman" and "Hottentot" are described as follows:

> The aborigines of South Africa were savages of very low type. They were pygmies in size, yellowish in colour, hollow-backed, and with skins so loose that in times of famine their bodies were covered with wrinkles and flaps. On their heads were rows of little tufts of wiry hair hardly larger than peppercorns, and leaving the greater portion of the surface bald . . . To the European no people in any part of the world were more unattractive.[7]

If the San and the Khoi are not human, but "savages of very low type" it follows that only the Europeans are real human beings entitled to inherit their earth. Indeed, Theal, bases the Dutch and British title and settlement in South Africa on the grounds of the sub-humanity of the original owners:

> The settlement of the Europeans in the country was disastrous to the aborigines. Bushmen were still numerous along the interior mountain range, but in other parts of the colony there were hardly any left. One may feel pity for the savages such as these, destroyed in their native wilds, though there is little for regretting their disappearance. They were of no benefit to any other section of the human family, they were incapable of improvement, and it was impossible for civilized men to live on the same soil with them, it was for the world's good that they should make room for a higher race.[8]

This was the intellectual atmosphere in which Great Britain and the Boers carried out their late wars of conquest and their dispossession of indigenous chiefdoms and kingdoms. It was also Theal who, using what he called "classical sources", first peddled the spurious theory that the so-called Bantu were intruders in South Africa. In their movement south, he said they had pillaged and massacred whoever was on their way.[9]

History entered the public domain as the revelation of the inherent pattern of cultural and political development.[10]

7. Theal, George M., *South Africa,* London, Fisher Unwin, 1894, p. 1.

8. Theal, George M., *History of South Africa since September 1795*, London, George Allen & Co., 1887–1919, Vol. 4, p. 382.

9. Theal, George M., op. cit., Vol. 1, p. 432.

10. Schreuder D.M., "The Imperial Historian as a Colonial Nationalist: George McCall

In the decade leading to the Anglo-Boer War and after the creation of the Union, two writers compared developments in the United States and South Africa. In 1897, Lord Bryce's book, *Impressions of South Africa* was published. It was a sequel of the book he had written on *The American Commonwealth* in 1888. Within the British Empire, he said South Africa was an anomaly, fitting neither the model of self-governing white settlement colonies in the temperate zones nor that of dependent crown colonies in the tropics. In Australia, New Zealand and Canada the aborigines had been dying out, but in South Africa the Natives were increasing. This, he said created "the general difficulty of adjusting the relations of a higher and lower race", that was "serious under any kind of government", but in South Africa presented:

> ... itself in the special form of the construction of a political system which, while democratic as regards one of the races, cannot safely be made democratic as regards the other.[11]

Maurice S. Evans wrote that the Union of South Africa:

> ... was ruled by the white electorate, they are responsible for the government of a people five times as numerous as they are.

> The majority of the governing group do not understand the question in all its bearing. Their chief concern is with the economic development of the country, the part they are to play in it, and the reward they are to get for these activities. The native is of interest to them only so far as he assists to this end...[12]

After the establishment of South Africa as a white Dominion in the British Empire, where African labour power had been factored in as a permanent source of capitalist accumulation, Theal's raw racism was not *kosher* any more. In the post-World War I era, liberal history and anthropology emerged; but now purged of the concerns of Lord Bryce and Evans about the denial of the franchise. Macmillan's history by frequently ignoring the issue of the franchise,[13]

Theal and the Making of South African History", in Studies in *British Imperial History*, Vol. 9, (ed.) Gordon Martel, New York, St. Martins Press, 1986, p. 98.

11. Lord Bryce, *Impressions of South Africa,* New York, Negro University, The American Commonwealth Press, 1969 (reprint of the 1897 edition, org. (ed.) 1888), p. 347.

12. Evans, Maurice S., *Black and White in the Southern United States: A Study of the Race Problem in the United States from a South African Point of View,* New York, Longmans, 1915, p. 8, p. 50.

13. Macmillan was the first South African historian to be the recipient of a Rhodes schol-

and anthropology by rejecting the historical method in the study of "primitive" society, justified the status of Africans as a subject race. The leading personalities in this division of labour were W.M. Macmillan, a Scottish born historian at Wits University and Radcliffe-Brown, also British, first chairperson of Philosophy and Anthropology at the University of Cape Town.[14]

In his book *Africa Emergent: A Survey of Social, Political, and Economic Trends in British Africa*, Macmillan dealt with the denial of the franchise to Africans. He revealed the attitude of most white South Africans: that before the spread of education had produced any considerable body of Africans ready and eager to claim full citizenship: liberal doctrine fell out of fashion:

> Experience of the hard struggle to survive in Africa has bred in the white man on the spot a spirit very different from the sublime self-confidence of the nineteenth century. With them it is less than ever a question of bringing civilization to the African, but rather of protecting the white man against what is conceived to be dangerous competition from the black.[15]

Even if Macmillan did not like the growing Afrikaner influence and distanced himself from the worst cases of super-exploitation of Africans, he approved of what he saw as the overall civilising effects of classical British colonialism,[16] and he had no real understanding of radical African resistance:

> The position of Africans in wage employment is governed first by their own weakness. African helplessness everywhere allows European employers of small means, agriculturalists and others, to use political power to further their own interests...[17]

---

arship. But he was not the original choice. Toby Muller, father of the historian C.F.J. Muller so disapproved of Rhodes that he declined the fellowship. It was then given to Macmillan, who was the runner-up. He sailed to England in 1903. (Cf. Saunders 1988, pp. 48.)

14. For the circumstances that led to the appointment of Radcliffe-Brown to the Chair of Anthropology at the University of Cape Town, see *African Studies*, Vol. 49, No. 1, pp. 90. For a discussion of Radcliffe-Brown's methodology and its anti-history in the study of African society, see my *Making of a Racist State: British Imperialism and the Union of South Africa, 1875–1910*, Trenton, New Jersey, Africa World Press, 1996, especially Chapter xv.

15. Macmillan W.M., *Africa Emergent: A Survey of Social, Political, and Economic Trends in British Africa*, Faber & Faber, London, 1938, pp. 15.

16. Macmillan W.M., op. cit., p. 14.

17. Macmillan W.M., op. cit., p. 241.

What is striking in Macmillan's historiography is the degree of silence about the disenfranchisement by the South Africa Act of 1909 compared to his objections to late segregation measures such as the Hertzog Bills passed in 1936–37. To say that the "the position of Africans in wage employment is governed first of all by their own weakness" is one of the grossest injustices. The fact of the matter is that white labour policies, as Lord Bryce, and Evans, and the Simonses have pointed out, emerged from an election system approved by Britain.[18] What Hertzog called the "white labour policy" after his election in 1924, had already been anticipated by Lord Milner in his speech declaring that he did not want a white proletariat in South Africa. Even if Macmillan had critical opinions to the disenfranchisement and favoured Cape Liberalism and its qualified franchise, it is clear enough that he never saw South Africa from the point of view of the black majority and that he did not see the possibility of one-man-one-vote as a realistic alternative.

Olive Schriener described what she called, the financial and speculative attitude towards the native, by great syndicates, companies and chartered bodies, the individual members of which are seldom or never brought into any personal contact with natives whose lives they control:

> For them the native is not a person hated or beloved, but a commercial assert. To these persons the native question sums itself up in two words: cheap labour.[19]

In 1930, the year I was born, an interesting conference was held to look back on what the State of the Union was like as its 21st birthday approached. Hofmeyr, one of South Africa's greatest liberals, edited the volume: *Coming of Age: Studies in South African Citizenship and Politics.* He was not optimistic. According to Hofmeyr, the fear arose from two sources: first was that gold was a wasting asset, but even more threatening and troubling to men's minds:[20]

---

18. Simons H.J. & R.E. Simons, *Race and Class in South Africa:* 1850–1950, Penguin Books, 1969, p. 98.

19. Schriener, Olive, *Thoughts on South Africa*, New York, Frederick Unger, 1923, p. 310.

20. In the 1920s and 1930s, while liberal historians were agonizing about the "threat" of the Africans who were "refusing" to succumb to Darwin's laws, a New African Movement was questioning African historiography as it was then written and taught. In three articles entitled "The Evolution of the Bantu" that appeared in *Umteteli,* 14, 21, and 28, November 1931, H.I.E. Dhlomo complained about "the lack of chastening helpful power of criticism and controversy" that "was due to the fact that South African history is written by members of one race from their own particular point of view. Until we have history written by Natives from their point of view, Union

... was the presence of what European South Africa regards as the black cloud – the native with his numerical superiority of three to one ... A generation ago men gave little thought to the problems of the relations between white man and black. The military power of the Bantu had been broken, he had been forced into subjection, he was giving his labour with docility and submission – and so the Europeans could devote all their attention to disputes among themselves. But in our day the man in the street or on the farm has become alive to the existence of a native problem; an election has been fought on the issue of the "native menace", and the phrase has come to be part of the thinking ...The native – the savage, cruel, wily foe of the past, whom he, the white man, has crushed into submission – will he not do him some evil yet?[21]

For Hoernle on the other hand the problem was that:

The Natives are part of the 'population' of South Africa, but they are not part of the 'people.' The 'people' are the Whites, and they are willing to tax themselves for the education of White children, recognizing this to be essential for the main-tenance of White superiority over all non-Europeans, as well as for citizenship in a White self-governing state. They are not willing to tax themselves, or to spend the revenues of 'their' South African estate (e.g., millions paid annually into the State by Gold Mines), for the education of a racially-alien group, the members of which might become, by that education, competitors of Whites in the economic field and demand political rights.[22]

When the Union of South Africa was created as a white Dominion in the British Empire, there was wishful thinking that Boer and Briton would fuse into a single, prosperous, White South African nation that would be able to

---

history will remain incomplete and one sided." He pleaded for a "history which is guided by principles of humanism, rather than dictates and niceties of scholasticism." Also, Dhlomo regretted the fact that "Natives cannot get access into public librar-ies and into the archives department, and therefore cannot make use of historical records that lie unknown or partially understood by writers... ." We should remember also that Dhlomo and all Africans who had access to education received it in mis-sionary schools, themselves expressions of the triumph of European colonialism and imperialism. See also A.F. Hattersley in his book, *South Africa, 1652–1933*, Thornton Butterworth, London 1933.

21. Hofmeyr, J.H., *Coming of Age: Studies in South African Citizenship and Politics*, Cape Town, 1931, pp. 1–2.

22. Hoernle R.F.A., *The Problem of Race*, Johannesburg, The Society of Jews and Chris-tians, 1937, p. 19. In his autobiography, he returned to the black "problem" in South Africa. By now, he saw it as the ultimate problem. Hoernle R.F.A., *Studies in philoso-phy*, London, George Allen & Unwin, 1952, p. 200.

face the "black menace". John X. Merriman, the last prime minister of the Cape Colony, Louis Botha, the Transvaal prime minister and the first prime minister of the Union, and General J. C. Smuts, Botha's right hand man and later prime minister believed that since Boer and Briton "sprang from a common stock" and both were protestants, "there was nothing to prevent them from intermingling in every possible way." It was Botha's wish that all "White South Africans" should be welded into "one South African nation".

The generation of British who came to South Africa at the time had no doubt about South Africa being a British country. In 1916, in the midst of the war, General Smuts joined Prime Minister Lloyd George's cabinet.

Discussing what British policy towards the Boers should be, Buchan pleaded for understanding. The Boer, he said, "was the easiest creature in the world to govern." He was not easily made drunk with the ideals of ordinary democracy:

> If the Boer is once won to our side we shall have secured one of the greatest colonizing forces in the world. We can ask for no better dwellers upon the frontier. If the plateaux of our Central and East African possessions are to be permanently held by the white man, I believe it will be by this people who have never turned their back upon a country which seemed to promise good pasture…With all her colonizing activity, Britain can ill afford to lose from her flag a force so masterful, persistent, and sure.[23]

In other words, as he saw it, the numerically dominant Afrikaners could be factored into the new Union as Britain's instruments in its imperial ambitions and also they could play the role of "fall guys" to absolve the British of any blame concerning white supremacy.

This brief excursion into the debates surrounding the formation of the Union highlights a few truths feared by liberals of later years. That in a vital sense and regardless of anything else, the Africans and European settler interests in South Africa were sharply counterpoised by virtue of the contradictory position assigned to them by British imperialism. The wars fought between Africans and white settlers in the nineteenth century demonstrated not only the capacity for ruthlessness and savagery of Boer and British imperialisms, but created conditions whereby the Africans were reduced to "slaves" of white capital.

---

23. Buchan, John, *The African Colony: Studies in the Reconstruction,* Blackwood, 1903, p. 75.

How then did later liberal and Neo-Marxist history deal with the problems raised in the nineteenth century by Theal in his *oeuvre* and in the first half of the twentieth century by Hoernle, Hattersley and Hofmeyr?

The above provides the context in which liberal and Neo-Marxist debates must be understood. To continue the claim that South Africa was a "white man's country" in the face of post-World War II developments would have been foolhardy. Instead, historians, consciously or unconsciously, had to change the terms of the debate, in my opinion often as part of an effort to retain the substance of white hegemony in South Africa.

Liberal history

It is almost pathetic today to read liberal historians, who abstract South Africa's capitalism from the project of creating a white Dominion, and argue that racism is incompatible with its growth, and blame Afrikaner racism on the *frontier* or on the fact that they missed the Enlightenment and its liberal ideas. From this, they argued that capitalist development would ameliorate racism. The vested interest in capitalism by liberals bred what Gordon calls "a comfortable facticity of bad faith".[24]

In 1969 and 1971 Professor Monica Wilson, an anthropologist, and Leonard Thompson, the doyen of South Africa's liberal historians, combined their erudition to produce as editors, the *Oxford History of South Africa*.[25] When the work was published, it was supposed to be a milestone. It was billed as the "first post-colonial history of South Africa" and made a conscious effort to escape from the old imperial clichés. In light of the events that took place from 1990 to 1994, the *OH* could be regarded as the ultimate word of liberalism's irrelevant wisdom. And like everything written by liberal historians on South Africa it exemplifies wishful thinking and the limits of bourgeois thought. It was unable to go beyond the limits imposed by its interest in the *status quo*.

When the *OH* was published, it elicited an unprecedented number of responses. There was a veritable cottage industry of reviews and monographs critical of this or other aspect of these volumes. The *OH* embodied all the problems of partial histories. Social and political narratives set awkwardly next to chapters written by anthropologist, archaeologist, economist and so-

---

24. Gordon Lewis R., *Fanon and the Crisis of European Man: An Essay on Philosophy and the Human Sciences*, New York, Routledge, 1995, p. 39.

25. Wilson, Monica and Thompson, Leonard M. (eds), *The Oxford History of South Africa*, Oxford, Clarendon Press, 1969–71.

ciologist. In 1990, *A History of South Africa* by Thompson was published. This general synthesis was obviously an attempt to make up for the weaknesses of the *OH*.[26]

I am not sure if the editors of the *OH* were aware of the irony of the editorship of their endeavours by an anthropologist and a historian. In a colonial situation, Africans were studied and conceptualized by anthropologists because they belonged to what Eric Wolf later described as "People Without History".[27] That is, the study of Africans grew up as an applied discipline, conducted mainly by anthropologists for the purpose of managing them so that they could be controlled and exploited.

General Smuts praised Monica Hunter's *Reaction to Conquest, Effects of Contact with Europeans on the Pondo of South Africa*.[28] Smuts tells us that he had met Monica Wilson as a young student when she was on her way from South Africa to Cambridge:

> I then warned her against a common failing of South Africans to be unduly preoccupied with larger political aspects of our native problems, and urged her to get at the facts and cultivate a disinterested scientific outlook before forming large-scale conclusions. How well this advice has been followed is proved by this book.[29]

No wonder. At Oxford and Cambridge, where most anthropologists were trained, they were not trained for a life of pure science and scholarship but for entry into governmental service in the Empire. Perry Anderson reminds us that:

> British anthropology developed unabashedly in the wake of British imperialism. Colonial administration had an inherent need of cogent, objective information about peoples over which it ruled. The miniature scale of primitive societies... made them exceptionally propitious for microanalysis ... British anthropology was thus able ... to assist British imperialism.[30]

---

26. Thompson, Leonard M., *A history of South Africa*, New Haven, Yale University Press, 1990/2000.

27. Wolf, Eric R., *Europe and the People without History*, Berkeley, UCP, 1982.

28. Wilson, Monica (Monica Hunter), *Reaction to Conquest: Effects of Contact with Europeans on the Pondo of South Africa*, Oxford University Press, 1936.

29. Smuts, 1936, p. vii, vi.

30. Anderson, Perry, "Components of the National Culture", in *English Questions*, London, Verso, 1992, p. 93.

As I see it, the *Oxford History* was itself really an ideological acknowledgement of the emergence of radical African nationalism in the era of the collapse of European hegemony. Let me examine more closely the ideas and assumption of liberal historians against historical and contemporary developments. That seems to me the only test of the adequacy of any theoretical assumptions; their capacity to enable us to understand historical trends.

I see the *Oxford History of South Africa* as a case of using selective history to underpin post-World War II political concerns and in effect to freeze the status quo. For example, in volume I, we are told that: "the central theme of South Africa" involved the "interaction between peoples of diverse origins, languages, technologies, ideologies and social systems."[31] The authors also tell of the difficulty of writing the history of a society, which they say, has become "rigidly stratified", and they refer to recent histories to illustrate the point that "nearly every one of them embodied the point of view of only one community."[32]

The authors move on to discuss what they consider five misleading assumptions that they say shaped historical writing on South Africa. The first assumption is that South African history began with the discovery of South Africa by the Portuguese. To make up for this they include a chapter of recent archaeological evidence. The second fallacy, they say, is the assumption that traditional African societies were static; they did not undergo structural change. A third fallacy is that physical type, language and economy are *necessarily* correlated. The fourth and fifth fallacies are, they said, the assumption that each of the four physical types formed a "pure race" which had the exclusive occupation of a specific area and remained isolated from the others, and the assumption that it is absurd and it is improper for the historian to be concerned with social structures and improper for the anthropologist to study all races.[33]

The nine chapters of volume I tell their own story. The liberal master concept describing South Africa as a "plural society" was ideological.[34] It

31. Such emotive words as "conquest", "land dispossession", "racism", "racial oppression", have been expunged from the discourse of the OH.

32. Wilson, Monica & Leonard Thompson, *The Oxford History of South Africa*, London, Oxford University Press, 1969/71, Vol. I, pp. v-vii.

33. Wilson, Monica & Leonard Thompson, op. cit., pp. vii-ix.

34. I define the word "ideologies" here as world-views which do not care to study the real history of relations between victor and vanquished, or between exploiter and exploited. They have built their theories on arbitrary social constructs, such as the so-called plural

corresponds to what Harvey calls status quo theorizing. So too was the endeavour of Thompson and company to assert the "African factor". One is struck by the influence Theal still must have had on the assumptions of the two volumes. Except now, efforts are made to sanitize "the fact of conquest". For example, in Volume I Monica Wilson repeats Theal's justification for the wars of settler conquest:

> Such a history of dispossession on a frontier by settlers better armed and organized is not unique. A 'Trail of Tears' forms part of the history of many nations, and dispossession had, indeed, already occurred in South Africa as Bantu-speakers pressed on San.[35]

Elsewhere she tells us that:

> Conflict was also within individuals who pursued incompatible ends. The most obvious incompatibility was between maintaining separation of white and black and trading with Africans, employing them as labourers, and preaching the Gospel ... In its widest sense the conflict was between isolation and wide-scale interaction; between a tribal outlook and a universal one ... and the cleavage did not coincide exactly with differences in race or language.[36]

This is the essence of an ideological explanation. The resulting body of explanations is nothing but arbitrary constructions. The whole exercise cannot explain anything. The passages cited contain many "misconceptions" about what settler colonialism was about. Obviously, Wilson is trying hard to fit the Africans into the liberal framework. The intellectual inertia or indifference to historical reality exhibited by Wilson can be explained by Freudian theory as resulting from an individual's wish to hide what is shameful, fearful, and socially unacceptable. The dispossession of the Africans and its consequences are extremely unpleasant to contemplate and equally unpleasant to explain.

---

society. Consequently they prevent us from understanding the society in which we live and the possibility of changing it. They are world-views which correspond to standpoints of classes and social groups whose interests in the existing social order make it impossible for them to see it as a whole. The theory of plural society is part of bourgeois ideology, not because it expresses the immediate interests of the ruling class or is developed by it, but because it is limited in theory by the limits of bourgeois society in reality; because its development, including even its criticism of bourgeois society, is governed by the development of bourgeois society and unable to go beyond it.

35. Wilson, Monica & Leonard Thompson, op. cit., p. 253.

36. Wilson, Monica & Leonard Thompson, op. cit., p. 271.

In a chapter "The South African Dilemma" that Thompson contributed to a book edited by Louis Hart, *The Founding of New Societies,* he attributed Afrikaner racism simply to the fact that they were isolated from the European ideas of democracy:

> Although the Afrikaners have now mastered modern educational, industrial, and military techniques, the basic ideas of the majority, including their political leaders, remain those, which crystallized in the seventeenth and eighteenth century. Bred in isolation from the mainstream of Western thought; they have rejected three of the dynamic modern impulses – liberalism, socialism, and democracy. A fourth – nationalism – they accepted; but they perverted it because, unlike other nations, they do not form a majority.[37]

The second volume of the *Oxford History of South Africa,* covering the years 1870 to 1966, reveals everything that is obscene about liberalism. In the South African edition of the volume, there appears in the "acknowledgement" page, a note, warning the reader that:

> Legal opinion on the chapter by Leo Kuper entitled 'African Nationalism in South Africa 1910–64' was to the effect that it infringed South African law in many respects, mainly by references to books and articles dealing with African Nationalism, policy statements of the African National Congress, and statements by African leaders. In the circumstances, the publishers and editors decided that the better course was to exclude Professor Kuper's chapter from the South African edition. It is with great regret that the decision has been taken to exclude the scholarly contribution; but it is available, in precisely the form in which it was written, in this edition of the History.

There are two other contributors who expressed regret in their footnotes that they were unable to cite writings of three "banned" stalwarts of the liberation movement, Professor H.J. Simmons, Mr. Govan Mbeki, and Mrs. Helen Joseph. It is important to note that the decision to exclude Kuper's chapter, was a voluntary, self-imposed and anticipatory censorship. To their shame, Professors Wilson and Thompson did the dirty work of the apartheid regime. I know for a fact that Professor Kuper pleaded with Thompson that honour and intellectual integrity demanded that the censorship be done by the South African regime, but it was to no avail.

---

37. Thompson, "The South African Dilemma", in Hart, Louis, *The Founding of New Societies: Studies in the History of the United States, Latin America, South Africa, Canada and Australia,* Boston, 1964, p. 178–218.

I could not agree more with this scathing indictment by Professor Hyam:

> In light of this self-inflicted mutilation, the editors' and publishers' continuing claim that their project has been executed 'in the belief that the central theme in South African history is interaction between people of diverse origins, languages, technologies, ideologies, and social systems on the South African soil' begins to look like a piece of hollow hypocrisy … It was bitterly disillusioning to discover what is perhaps the most prestigious University Press in the world placing itself in the pathetic position of depriving Africans in the Republic of their history.[38]

It is important to understand what was at stake in South Africa in 1909, when the South Africa Act that denied Africans the franchise was passed by the British parliament. In my 1996 book, *The Making of a Racist State: British Imperialism and the Union of South Africa 1875–1910*, I have dealt with forces that were involved in shaping Britain's geo-politics in the nineteenth century. From the 1870s, the doctrine of social imperialism was a compelling force in Britain. The Social Imperialist movement proposed to meet the threats to Britain's strategic position and commercial supremacy by a consolidation of the political unity of its white dominions, which, given their resources, would make Britain self-sufficient. The dream of Greater Britain, of a federation of Anglo-Saxon settler states, organized as an economic and political bloc within the world economy and strong enough to maintain its independence and prosperity, is a dream that has faded. From 1875 to 1931 when the Statue of Westminster was passed, it was pursued with vigour as a major geopolitical alternative.

The unification of South African colonies as a white dominion had to do, first with the new policy of social imperialism aimed at expansion in an era in which Britain found itself challenged by new powers. On top of this the discovery of the richest gold mines in the world, which could however only be made super-profitable by the super-exploitation of black labour, made the disenfranchisement of blacks imperative.

The Anglo-Boer War (1899–1902) was long regarded as one of the greatest triumphs of the new social imperialism. Julian Amery has described it as a masterstroke of policy:

> Few victories in British history have done more to increase Britain's economic or military power. After the peace of Vereeniging British settlers and British capital

---

38. Hyam Ronald, "Are We Nearer an African History of South Africa?" *The Historical Journal*, Vol. xvi, No. 3, 1973, p. 617.

poured into the country. Today it has become Britain's second most important market in the world and the ground where well over £1000 million British capital are profitably invested.[39]

Modern racism in South Africa had more to do with this historical development than with the ancient frontier heritage that liberal historians have chosen to focus on.

Let me add a comment on another major liberal work, *South Africa: A Modern History*, by Davenport. Like Thompson, he does not convincingly confront the issues of colonialism, when he writes about what he calls the birth of a plural society:

> Oppressed in the early years by natural disasters and by periodic Xhosa cattle raids, the 1820 Settlers became acclimatized to their new surroundings as the frontier Boers had done before them, developing the physical and moral toughness and the harder race attitudes common to the inhabitants of turbulent frontier districts, yet helping to bridge the gap between Colonial and African society, which warfare had tended to widen.[40]

The language that Davenport uses acts almost like anaesthesia. It is smooth and soothes the pain. Before you know it, you are in a stupor.

The conservative and liberal historians from G.M. Theal to Thompson, consciously or unconsciously, were apologist for the brutal acts of British imperialism. Thus in searching for the origins of racial oppression, the liberals focused on the Boers who are pitied for having left Europe before liberal influences of democracy had taken root. In his *History of South Africa: Social & Economic,* De Kiewiet put the case for Afrikaner backwardness and racism in these dramatic terms:

> The Boers moved inland not to found a new society and to win new wealth. Their society was rebellious, but it was not revolutionary. Fundamental innovations in the use of land or in social practices were not easily made in their minds. They trekked in spite of the Industrial Revolution, moving away before it reached them. In one sense the Great Trek was the eighteenth century fleeing before its more material, more active, and better-organized successor.[41]

---

39. J. L. Garvin, Julian Amery, *The life of Joseph Chamberlain*, Vol. 5, 1901–1903: *Joseph Chamberlain and the Tariff Reform campaign*, 1969, p. 998.

40. Davenport T.R.H., *South Africa: A Modern History* London, third edition, 1987, p. 44.

41. De Kiewiet, C.W., *A History of South Africa: Social and Economic,* Oxford, Clarendon, 1941, p. 58.

But using the pre-liberal attitude of the Boers as a scapegoat does not explain for instance how the United States of America, a country, if ever there was one, which was a child of the Enlightenment and its ideas, entrenched racism. One of the great theoreticians of American liberal philosophy is none other than John Locke, who wrote the Fundamental Constitution of Carolina when it was colonized in 1669. He said, among other things, that: "... every freeman of Carolina shall have absolute power and authority over his negro slaves, of whatever opinion or religion."

The illustrative passages from more recent liberal historical writing raise the question if the events of 1994 make everything written by liberal historians nonsense?

Liberal history of South Africa rarely ventured beyond a timid empiricism. The fate of liberal history, and indeed, all South Africa's social science can make us pessimistic about the function of the social sciences. Liberal history was a victim of subjectivism, that is, the interest of white settlers was taken for granted. Everything else had to be accommodated to the maintenance of the *status quo*. This type of history engaged itself with a process that Foucault and others have termed "normalization" which led to a routinization of the injustices of conquest.

Professor Z.K. Matthews, the first graduate of Fort Hare Native College, not only felt the mental anguish of being subjected to the white version of South African history, but cried foul at racist assumptions that left Africans out of the story of South African history:

> As African students in a land dominated by Europeans, we were in a peculiarly uncomfortable position. Our history, as we had absorbed it from the tales and talk of our elders, bore no resemblance to South African history as it had been written by European scholars ... The European insisted that we accept his version of the past and what is more, if we wanted to get ahead educationally, even to pass examinations in the subject as he present it. It was one thing to accept willingly and even eagerly the white man's world of literature and science. It was quite another to accept his picture of how we all came to occupy the places in life now assigned to us.[42]

In colonial situations, the study of historical memory requires therefore the study of cultural struggles and of contested truths between victor and victim. Since the Dutch East India Company established the victualling sta-

---

42. Matthews, Z.K. (Wilson, Monica (ed.)), *Freedom for My People. The Autobiography of Z.K. Matthews: Southern Africa* 1901–1968, Cape Town, David Philip, 1981, p. 58.

tion at the Cape, labour power has loomed large in the discourse. The whole story revolves around that whether we think of the importation of slaves from Malaya, Indian indenture labour to work the sugar cane fields of Natal or indeed, the importation of Chinese labour to work in the mines after the Anglo-Boer War.

Both Monica Wilson's and Leonard Thompson's volumes and Davenport's history claiming to be devoted to interaction between blacks and whites are devoid of any reference to the voices of the oppressed, whose condition and demands were embodied in their national movements. These movements could not be wished away, they embodied the dreams of lost freedoms and sovereignty. African resistance and white conquest shaped South Africa's relations of domination, the crucible of its relations of production.[43]

It seems strange that the *Oxford History* did not deem it necessary to devote a specific chapter to the subject of race and racism. Maybe it was another of those subjects about which the less said the better for our interactions! The trouble with liberal historiography, according to Hughes, "is that it is not political enough":

> [I]t serves as an anaesthetic against the pain of too much reality. Bringing it all under a neat conceptual scheme, finding theoretical grounds for optimism about change, when there are grounds – these things help make life bearable...[44]

Radical or Neo-Marxist historiography

What is called the "Marxist", "Neo-Marxist", or "radical revisionist" school of history was developed in the 1970s by students and professors, who had lost their role as interlocutors between the powers that be and helpless Africans. Some of them, who had been members of the student organization, NUSAS, had felt the pain of rejection by the Black Consciousness Movement and its demand for black power. In Europe, Althusser and his student Poulantzas were in vogue and in England, the New Left was the fashion. Even though Marxist ideas had existed in South Africa from the turn of the century supported by communists and by trade unionists of Marxist or Trotskyite persuasion, the young revisionist scholars of the 1970s seem not to have been

---

43. Lonsdale John, "From Colony to Industrial State: South African Historiography as Seen from England", *Social Dynamics*, Vol. 9, No. 1, 1983, pp. 78–79.

44. Hughes K. R., "Challenges from the Past: Reflections on Liberalism and Radicalism in the Writing of Southern African History", *Social Dynamics*, Vol. 3, No. 1, 1977, p. 55.

very aware of these early traditions. To what extent they were frightened away from taking up these early debates by the 1950 Suppression of Communism Act, we will never know.

In 1969, the same year Volume I of the *Oxford History of South Africa* was published, Jack and Ray Simons' *Class and Colour in South Africa 1850–1950*, was also published, building on the older Marxist tradition. Whilst the former produced a veritable cottage industry, the latter was completely ignored by the Neo-Marxists.

In South Africa, Marxist and socialist ideas go back to the last quarter of the nineteenth century. However, they came with British emigrant workers. The workers who came to South Africa were recruited mostly from the adventurous sectors and they came to South Africa with the hope of making their own fortunes in the new colony. Most of them were already infected with the culture of white supremacy and racism.

Among the earliest leaders of the socialist movement in South Africa was Wilfrid Harrison, the evangelical socialist of the Social Democratic Federation (SDF), who later became a founding member of the Communist Party. For him, "the pigment in a man's skin, which was a medical mystery", was not an issue.[45] On the other hand, "capitalism, the cause of colour prejudice, and exploitation in general" was. According to Simons:

> Members of the SDF...tried to put their theory to the test. H. MacManus quoting in his Belfast twang from William Morris and the Bible; Hunter mixing socialism with temperance; H.B. Levinson relying on economic determinism; Arthur Noon propagating Christian socialism, and Harrison, armed revolt, took their messages to racially mixed audiences in District Six, in Salt River, and at the foot of Van Riebeeck's statue in Adderley Street.[46]

Archie Crawford, the founder and editor of the *Voice of Labour*, was in 1914 deported by Smuts. His paper advertised and published extracts from the works of Marx, Engels, Plechanov, De Leon, Eugene Debs, Blatchford, and Keir Hardie, and made the first systematic attempt to spread the doctrines of revolutionary socialism.

---

45. Quoted from Forman, Lionel (Forman, Sadie and Odendaal, Andre (eds), *A trumpet from the housetops: Selected writings,* (The Mayibuye Centre, University of Western Cape), London, Zed Books / Ohio University Press / David Philip, 1992, p. 42.

46. Simons H.J. & R.E. Simons, *Race and Class in South Africa: 1850–1950*, Penguin Books, 1969, p. 139.

The story of early socialism in South Africa is full of contradictions. As the Simonses put it, the contrast between the African militancy and the passivity of white workers did not escape the International Socialist Review. In 1910, Tom Mann visited South Africa from Australia and was struck by the situation he experienced in the Witwatersrand, the principal centre of gold mining. The wages of white workers were "received at the expense of the Native Kaffir, not of the profit receiver." In addition, he said:

> ... the natives are fed and lodged in compounds on the mines. The cost of feeding the Kaffir is only about four pounds a year.[47]

This, he said, explained the passivity of white workers.

Jones and Bunting, the International Socialist League's leading theoreticians gave two reasons for the white workers' passivity. First white workers had been corrupted by racialism: "Slaves to a higher oligarchy, the white workers of South Africa themselves in turn batten on a lower slave class." They compensated for their inferior class status by lording it over Africans. More intolerant than any other working class, the whites were more parasitical. Appeals to international unity could never evoke a sincere response from the rank-and-file so situated.[48]

Given the political status of the African, most white workers feared any association with their struggles. In the first general election of the Union of South Africa, the so-called Labour Party had come out with a platform of segregation for the "Kaffirs". Though some of their leaders attempted to base their thoughts on Marxist ideas, they made damaging theoretical errors by ignoring the national question.

This was the context in which the Communist Party of South Africa was formed. In South Africa, the Party had to learn that parliamentary elections were less important because three-fifths of the population were disenfranchised. Secondly, the Party had to ask itself this important question: Did the principle of unity apply to the national liberation movement? South Africa was "a unique case" of ruling and subject races jostling together. However, it was also the epitome of what was happening on a world scale.[49]

---

47. Mann, Tom, "Diamond Mining in South Africa", *The International Socialist Review*, Vol. XI, No. 1, 3, July 1910, p. 3.

48. Simons H.J. & R.E. Simons, op. cit., p. 189.

49. Simons H.J. & R.E. Simons, op. cit., p. 269.

Brief as it is, this review of early socialism in South Africa is important. It serves to put in perspective the problems of neo-Marxism. Jack and Ray Simons' book, according to Saunders, formed a bridge between the earlier, polemical and often politically engaged Marxism and the radical academic Marxism of the 1970s.[50] In 1964 Jack Simons, then Professor of Native Law and Administration, was barred from teaching at the University of Cape Town under the terms of the 1950 Suppression of Communism Act. Ray Alexander, his wife, who in 1954 had been elected to parliament by African voters, was prevented from taking her seat because she was "listed" as a communist. It seems ironic to me that the later radical historians could flaunt their Marxism without incurring any penalty.

The Simonses called their book, not a history, but "an exercise in political sociology on a time scale". Their purpose, they said, was not merely to recover the history of the left-wing political movement, they also wanted to move beyond description to an analysis of the dialectical relation between class interests and racial interests, between radical politics and the "national movement". That is, they wanted to study black resistance to the oppression of blacks. Their book was banned and its possession was a criminal offence.[51]

What lessons did the Neo-Marxists learn from the debates and dilemmas of early socialists in South Africa? The Neo-Marxist "movement" never grew beyond being an intellectual exercise. In the late 1970s and early 80s, it is true that some of their members gave invaluable help to the emerging African trade unions. But compared to the South African Communist Party, they never became a force of any consequence. Because the Neo-Marxists ignored the historical lessons of early socialists, they failed to realize, how distant their culture was from the reality of the very workers they counselled. In my opinion, they never understood the dialectical relationship between class and nationalism.

Just as the liberal historical revisionism of Wilson and Thompson had arisen to meet the challenges posed by Third World struggles, the Neo-Marxist current, when it criticized the liberal paradigm, was immersed in the problems of the age. That is, its interests, preoccupations, and concerns. In fact, it was the process of decolonisation taking place around the world and in Africa in particular that provided them with their most important key to the past.

---

50. Saunders Christopher, *The Making of the South African Past*, Cape Town, David Philip, 1988, p. 166.

51. Ibid.

The radical historians created an opening to the left, but their range of awareness was narrow. Hughes says that what seems to have touched the heart in the writings of most of these authors "is merely the abstract pain."[52] The radical historians have produced an enormous body of historical dissertations (many later published as books), articles, and reviews. Their flagship publication was the *Journal of South African Studies*, their main publishing house was the *Ravan Press*, and their most important institutional affiliations were the Institute of Commonwealth Studies at the University of London and Witwatersrand University. Some of the new historians were trained either at Sussex or at Oxford.

When one reads the contributions of the Neo-Marxist historians, the infrequency of discussions of the national liberation movement and its struggles strikes one very forcefully. The banning of the ANC and the PAC seems to have suggested that the national aspirations of the Africans were no longer realistic. This was in spite of the yeoman effort of Professors Thomas G. Karis and Gail M. Gerhart, who over many years were collecting and preserving *A Documentary History of African Politics in South Africa, 1882–1990*. In 1970, Peter Walshe poorly served the nationalist struggle in his book *The History of the African National Congress*, dealing with its so-called respectable years. As Lonsdale has noted, it was a study in failure.[53] As I view the matter, Neo-Marxist historiography most of all was a confused mixture of ideas borrowed from Nicos Poulantzas, Edward Thompson and the British and French New Left.

Let me briefly review what Neo-Marxist historians thought were the key issues they had to deal with in their endeavours. The important collection, *Labour, Townships and Protests – Studies in the Social History of the Witwatersrand* from 1969, edited by professor Belinda Bozzoli, is concerned with "local" social history. Because, Bozzoli argues:

> South Africa's colonial and post-colonial past has imposed particular class and structural patterns upon particular regions...[54]

52. Hughes K.R., "Challenges from the Past: Reflections on Liberalism and Radicalism in the Writing of Southern African History", *Social Dynamics*, Vol. 3, No. 1, 1977, p. 55.

53. Lonsdale, John, "From Colony to Industrial State: South African Historiography as Seen from England", *Social Dynamics*, Vol. 9, No. 1, 1983, p. 70.

54. Bozzoli B. (ed.), *Labour, Townships and Protests – Studies in the Social History of the Witwatersrand*, Johannesburg, Ravan Press, 1979, p. 2.

We are told of the "enormous and significant" differences between such areas as the Western Cape, the Eastern Cape, Natal, and the Rand. This means, obviously, that a complete understanding of South Africa needs many more local histories.

Like Wilson and Thompson, Bozzoli and her associates, wanted to decolonize South African history but by concentrating, in their case, on the contribution of the "common man" and "the people", while Wilson and Thompson did this by "including" not only the pre-European evidence of South African history but also the "contributions" of the various peoples of South Africa. For Bozzoli, the key theoretical concept that informs the book is "class", for Wilson and Thompson, as we have seen, it is what they call "interaction".

In an assessment of the contribution of Neo-Marxist scholars Belinda Bozzoli tells us that for a growing number of white students and intellectuals, Marxism, stripped of its Stalinist accretions and with its emphasis on class, offered a coherent alternative to liberalism on the one hand and black nationalism on the other. The strikes of the early 1970s, according to Bozzoli, provided what appeared to be a powerful confirmation for activists that Marxism and class analysis were now the appropriate tools for the South African society. Whites in Cape Town, Durban, and Johannesburg, she tells us, played an important and courageous role in the difficult birth of an independent trade union movement in the remainder of the 1970s.[55]

We need to ponder these assertions and conclusions. The events of the 1980s and the emergence of the ANC as the custodian of African nationalism and as a premier force, make all this read like yesterday's newspaper. I must confess that I find the argument and the main postulates of both liberal and Neo-Marxist studies to be exercises in irrelevance and they revealed a gross misunderstanding of the African reality and especially the nature of the Africans' struggles. For the previous two hundred years or so, the White masters of South Africa had denied Africans their nationhood. Z.K. Matthews writes that, as the world emerged from World War I:

> When President Wilson published his 14 Points, the phrase, 'self-determination for small nations' caught the ears of Africans. Did the 'nations' to which he referred include us? Did he mean us, the black peoples of Africa, too? At Fort Hare we talked of little else. The consensus was that the makers of the world did not count us as a nation or as part of any nation. We used to argue over the meaning of the word nation itself. We were of different chiefdoms and languages. We

---

55. Bozzoli, Belinda and Delius, Peter, "Radical History and South African Society", *Radical History Review*, Issue 46/7, p. 23, 1990.

lived in South Africa, but we were not regarded as part of the South African nation...[56]

To dismiss and deny the validity of African nationalism the way Bozzoli and Delius did is a gross disservice to the course of African liberation. Central to post-World War II South African history has been the struggle of the masses of the oppressed – Coloureds, Indians, and indeed, members of the Communist movement and some whites – under the banner of the Congress Alliance. No aspect of the history of South Africa, whether of the working class or women's liberation, can be understood without taking into account the history of struggle of the African National Congress. Whose interests were being served by the backhanded dismissal of African nationalism? To the degree that the national struggle is minimized – not to speak of being ignored – to that degree the historiography is false and could even be considered to be racist.

It is ironic that just as President Wilson's call for self-determination had raised hopes for African students like Matthews, the Afrikaners too had been similarly inspired, especially when the British government seemed to endorse Wilson's call. In 1919, they sent a delegation to Switzerland to demand the restitution of the republican status of the Transvaal and the Orange Free State as it was before the war of 1899 to 1902. Lloyd George, who received their petition refused, pointing out to the Afrikaner delegation the advantages of the dominion status, which South Africa enjoyed, and which gave whites in the Union full control of their own destiny, while allowing their representatives to take part in international affairs on a basis of complete equality with Britain and other nations.

Contrast this with the reception of the South African Native National Congress (as the ANC was called then); like the Afrikaner delegation the ANC delegation had gone to Switzerland to petition that the time had come to make further claims on behalf of the African population. The ANC delegation argued that Africans had remained loyal throughout the rebellion of 1914 and had made a not inconsiderable contribution to South Africa's war aims in a non-combat capacity. They now asked for a hearing. The Congress delegation pleaded for the removal of the colour bar. L.S. Amery, one time member of Milner's kindergarten, and now under-secretary for the colonies, dismissed their pleas. He informed them that the South Africa Act, which

---

56. Matthews, Z.K., (Wilson, Monica (ed.)): *Freedom for my People. The Autobiography of Z.K. Matthews: Southern Africa* 1901–1968, Cape Town, David Philip, 1981, p. 58.

had made Africans pariahs in their own country, could not be changed at the request of one section of the population.

On this backdrop, to dismiss African nationalism, as many liberals and Neo-Marxists did, was similarly a gross injustice to the African people. The African struggle in South Africa was not simply for inclusion in what was called a "plural society", but was a struggle in a society made up of oppressor and oppressed, and of exploiters and exploited. It was a struggle for power. South Africa was a society in which those who opposed the inhumanity of white minority rule were tortured and killed because the system could not be maintained in any other way. Given this reality, Africans suffered as blacks and as workers, and their struggle could not be reduced to either category. The African national struggle predated and anticipated the formation of the working class and its struggles. This seemingly obvious observation explains the important role played by the ANC today in South Africa, especially the alliances it formed with other entities in the Congress Alliance that included the Communist Party of South Africa.

In a review of what he called "a developing controversy over the nature of South African history" between "liberal and radical" historiographies of South Africa, Harrison Wright, made some interesting points. However, his efforts were marred by his partiality toward the liberal position and his outright hostility to the Neo-Marxist position.[57] The controversy, which was set off by the publication of the *Oxford History of South Africa*, centred on the problem of the relationship between South Africa's capitalist development and racial oppression.

To understand the liberal/radical controversy in South Africa, it is important to put it into historical context. It is important to remind ourselves how the denial of human rights to Africans first took place. The wars of conquest that lasted through the 19th century were a traumatic experience for the African chiefdoms and kingdoms. They were dispossessed of their lands and confined into reservations where they would be made available as cheap labour for what was now called "white South Africa."[58] Colonies were acquired by force and the colonized were governed by domination.[59]

---

57. Wright, Harrison M., *The Burden of the Present. Liberal-radical controversy over Southern African history*, Cape Town, David Philip, 1977.

58. Bernhard Magubane, *The Making of a Racist State: British Imperialism and the Union of South Africa 1875–1910*, Trenton, NJ, Africa World Press, 1996.

59. See for example Sartre in Albert Memmi's, *Colonizer and Colonized*, 1967, pp. xxiv-xxv, (also London, Souvenir Press, 1974).

The post-World War II decolonisation movement, had posed for the colonizer everywhere the question whether he and his children would have a place in the new nation. The liberal and radical paradigms were attempts by beneficiaries of colonial usurpation to transcend that legacy. Both the liberal and radical paradigms feed on memories of historical betrayal. Their transcendence does not really involve accepting the reality of a new nation in which Africans, by virtue of the demographic reality are the majority. The liberals have become part of the *status quo*. In the case of the radicals, white intellectuals have sought to liquidate the national aspirations of the Africans in favour of a leading role for themselves.

What theoretical paradigm then captures the relations between what in the late 19th century were called "subject races" and "ruling races"? Does the concept of "plural society" favoured by liberals capture the essence of black/white relations that are the consequence of conquest? Does the concept of class as used by radical or Neo-Marxists in the South capture what it means to be a member of the "subject race"? The controversy between liberals and Neo-Marxists has an air of unreality. As white minority rule reached its nemesis, one could not avoid looking at its terminal agony with the too-wise eyes of those who knew the end of the plot in advance, who knew that this debate was an illusion all along.

Only the ANC gave African national aspirations a voice, which would constitute them into a future nation and restore to the Africans that which the colonizer had usurped.

Conclusions and prospects

Coming to the end of this survey of South African history as it has been written by liberal historians and the challenges that were made in the 1970s by radical or Neo-Marxist historians; the question still remains, at least for me: What is the meaning of 1994?

When Nelson Mandela, our first president, proclaimed in front of multitudes of people gathered at the Union Buildings, which were designed by Sir Herbert Baker at the behest of Cecil Rhodes, I could not but be reminded of the fears and anxieties, expressed by Hofmeyr in 1930. He feared that: "some day little brown children will play among the ruins of the Union Buildings", and wondered at the same time what would happen to his offspring.

For almost eighty-two years, the Union Building had been the seat of white supremacy, and now it was the site, as Mandela put it "of a rainbow gathering of different colours and nations for the installation of South Africa's first democratic, non-racial government."[60] In July 1990, my wife and I returned to South Africa for the first time since December 1961, when I left the country, wondering if I would ever come back. In 1990 I was struck by how much poorer our people had become since I left. At the same time, the white population could not have been richer.

The history of our struggle, which brought about 1994, is still unfortunately a closed book to most of our people. Like someone who has long been struck with amnesia and begins to recover, a nation that does not know its past, or cares to understand the past history of men and women who sacrificed everything to bring us 1994, cannot understand the significance of 1994. Decades of falsification of our history have induced the collective amnesia that I have tried to expose in this article.

In 1961, to celebrate Freedom Day June 26, *Fighting Talk* devoted a volume to some chapters from South African history.[61] Ruth First, who edited the volume, wrote the introduction, entitled *In the Presence of History*. We need to remember what she said then, when dealing with historical memory in the new South Africa. Many of the events and incidents dealt with in that issue of *Fighting Talk* did not appear in any standard history text. Almost without exception, they were chapters within the range of living memory. Many readers, like many of those who wrote the articles, had taken part in that kind of event and had themselves been makers of history. They were men and women, who moved by the injustices, did what had to be done -- what their conscience and their passions drove them to do. They lived their lives as they chose, struggling forwards as best they could without thought or consciousness that they were thus making the history of this country. But looking back on the tale revealed in these chapters, who can doubt that here South African history was in the making?

There were few heroes of gigantic statue in these episodes, few dramatic moments in which the face of a country is suddenly transformed. Instead there is the record of a multitude of indecisive and inconclusive struggles, of strikes won and lost, of campaigns completed and uncompleted; there are multitudes of nameless faceless ordinary people, some few remembered but many forgotten. Can this be history?

60. Mandela, Nelson, *Long Walk to Freedom*, London, Little, Brown, 1994, p. 541.
61. *Fighting Talk*, Vol. 15, No. 5, 1961.

History has been defined as the study "of the growth of nations". By this definition, as I see it, the struggles of the damned of the earth are the essence of history. It is their struggles that embodied the spirit of the new South African nation that was born on May 10, 1994. We need to recover these struggles and the men and women, who individually and collectively made this non-racial nation a possibility. Most of what has been written until now from the above-mentioned perspectives about the African experience has not fully taken into account the African memory, and therefore cannot adequately explain what happened between 1652 and 1994. My central argument, therefore, is that any discourse on historical memory in South Africa which deals with the experience of the African people should of necessity focus on the African memory, something which is glaringly absent from past South African historiography.

— CHAPTER 14 —

Four decades of South African academic historical writing:

A personal perspective

Christopher Saunders

I assume we all agree on the importance of historiography. The way historians conceptualise the past helps shape a society's collective memory. Yet at the beginning of the new millennium, little is being written on the development of South African historical writing, despite post-modernist concerns with how historical knowledge is produced, and with self-reflection. The only two book-length surveys of South African historiography in English appeared in the same year, as long ago as 1988,[1] perhaps not entirely coincidentally when the apartheid era was moving to a close. Since then only perhaps half a dozen articles have appeared that deal directly with South African historiography.[2] There are many reasons for this. When history can be seen as little relevant to a fast-changing present, when one of the leading figures in the field, Shula Marks, can be told by a South African immigration official, in 1994, that "we don't need historians any more",[3] historiography can too easily be dismissed – especially now that Shula Marks herself is no longer writing about it[4] – as little more than the musings of ageing white men.

---

1. K. Smith, *The Changing Past*, Johannesburg, 1988; C. Saunders, *The Making of the South African Past*, Cape Town, 1988. In Afrikaans, the main account remains the even earlier F.A. Van Jaarsveld, *Omstrede Suid-Afrikaanse Verlede*, Johannesburg, 1984.

2. I refer to the most important of these in the footnotes that follow.

3. E. Foner, *Who Owns the Past?*, New York, 2002 and cf. E. Foner, "'We Must Forget the Past': History in the new South Africa", *South African Historical Journal*, Vol. 32, May 1995.

4. E.g. S. Marks, "Recent Developments in the Historiography of South Africa", in R. Samuel, (ed.), *People's History and Socialist Theory*, London, 1981; "The Historiography of South Africa: Recent Developments" in B. Jewsiewicki and D. Newbury (eds), *African Historiographies*, Beverly Hills, 1986; "Rewriting South African History", lecture, University of London, 1996. Her most recent, partially historiographical essay is in *Interventions*, Vol. 3, No. 1, 2001. Cf. also I. Smith, "The Revolution in South

Some of what I am about to say may indeed seem to be little more than such musings. My original idea was to make my paper entirely autobiographical, and to try to explain why I had written what I had written over more than three decades. It would, I think, be useful if more historians of South Africa did produce such reflective surveys. Too much about the making of our past goes unrecorded; few historians write about their own writing, and many leave no papers, meaning that their writing careers cannot be recreated in any depth.[5]

What I have decided to offer is more modest: some personal, and therefore very partial reflections on South African historiography, mainly from three vantage points, and emphasising work done in South Africa itself and in Cape Town in particular, as that was where I was based. Because I began to study South African history at the University of Cape Town (UCT) in the early 1960s, I am now able to look back over forty years of personal engagement—often peripheral, I am the first to admit – with South African historical writing. My first vantage point, then, is when I was a student. I do not consider the 1970s in any detail, but jump to the early 1980s, roughly the mid-point of the forty years since I first studied South African history at UCT, and thirdly I consider the present situation, and reflect on how things have changed. What follow, then, are mostly personal reflections, some of them autobiographical, some likely to be provocative, focused mainly on when I began my engagement, the mid-point in my involvement in South African historical writing, and today. I hope that other historians will follow my example and offer similar reflections, based on their own careers, and that, where they think it necessary, they will challenge my interpretations.

The 1960s and 1970s

First, then, let me consider the early 1960s. It was when I was a student at UCT that I first heard Leonard Thompson, who had become the Professor of History at UCT a few years before and was now leaving Cape Town to settle in the United States, call for the decolonisation of South African history. This was enormously exciting, as offering the possibility of what seemed an

African History", *History Today*, February 1988.

5. J.S. (Etienne) Marais, who taught at UCT until 1945 and then at Wits, and wrote three seminal books, is an example of a historian who left no significant collection of papers.

overturning of what had been written to that time. I have argued elsewhere, and see no reason now to change my view, that the Africanist breakthrough of the 1960s, led by Thompson and his UCT colleague Monica Wilson, the joint editors of the two volume *Oxford History of South Africa*, John Omer-Cooper, an ex-South African then teaching at Ibadan University in Nigeria, and, a little later, a former UCT student who completed her PhD at the University of London, Shula Marks,[6] did represent a fundamental shift in South African historiography. These historians were of course influenced by earlier work, especially that of the early liberal historians W.M. Macmillan and C.W. De Kiewiet, but it was only in the early 1960s, under new influences from tropical Africa in particular, that professional historians first fully accepted the fact that the majority of the population deserved equal attention, and began to study African societies and social movements in the same way as white ones. Yes, there were non-academic precursors, dismissed by the professional historians as amateurs, and authors of mere polemics. When I studied at UCT in the 1960s, I remained ignorant of the earlier Africanist work by the Unity Movement activist Hosea Jaffe and his colleague Dora Taylor, with its stress on conquest and dispossession, and argument that white liberals and missionaries had abetted these processes.[7] While this interpretation had no direct impact on later scholarship, the work of the early Africanists influenced a new generation of graduate students, who were to build on the foundations laid by the pioneers and carry scholarly Africanist work in new directions. We can see now that the contributions made by the early Africanist historians had many limitations – for one thing, they tended to overstress African agency – but the basic assumption, that South African history was about the study of all South Africans, was, once made, so obvious that while the process of decolonising South African history was an ongoing one, by the end of the 1960s – say with the publication of the second volume of the *Oxford History* in 1971 – the ground had been laid for the different, much

---

6. Though she began teaching an Africanist course on South Africa in 1964, it was some years before she published a significant Africanist work: *Reluctant Rebellion*, Oxford, 1970. Cf. A. Cobley, "Does Social History Have a Future? The Ending of Apartheid and Recent Trends in South African Historiography", *Journal of Southern African Studies*, Vol. 27, No. 3, September 2001, p. 613, n. 1.

7. Mnguni (H. Jaffe), *Three Hundred Years*, n.p., 1952; Majeke (D. Taylor), *The Role of the Missionaries in Conquest*, n.p., n.d., 1952.

more sophisticated Africanist phase of the 1970s, concerned primarily with socio-economic themes.[8]

As a student at UCT, I knew what Thompson and Wilson were doing – I was fortunate to work as research assistant for Wilson for the first volume of the *Oxford History of South Africa* for some months in 1965 – and their work appealed to me because it seemed almost revolutionary, in relation to the previous historiography, and because its anti-apartheid purpose was so clear. Unfortunately for historians in South Africa Thompson decided, for political and career reasons, to settle in America,[9] and at the University of Los Angeles he directed a number of graduate students to the African history of South Africa. I might have been one of them, for he arranged a scholarship for me to go to California for doctoral studies, but by then I had been seduced by Oxford, where I had first gone to take another undergraduate degree. When I came to choose a subject for a doctorate at St. Antony's College, I found no historian prepared to supervise a thesis on an Africanist topic, and so I wrote a thesis that was primarily about the reasons for and process of imperial expansion, and only peripherally about the impact of that expansion on the people of the Transkei.[10] When I eventually had my Oxford viva, after I had completed my thesis while now teaching at UCT, the imperial historians Ronald Robinson and Geoffrey le May were mainly interested in whether I had emphasised sufficiently the imperial concern with the sea-route around the Cape. I had seen no evidence that concern with the sea-route played any role in imperial expansion into the Transkei, nor evidence of any significant concern on the part of Cape or Natal politicians with labour, though I later realised that my reading of the evidence had been blinkered by my concern at the time with political and constitutional rather than economic issues. And so my own Africanist work was marginal, though I long remained interested in aspects of the history of the Eastern Cape,[11] while, after returning to UCT

---

8. This work was especially to be seen in J. Peires, (ed.), *Before and After Shaka*, Grahamstown, 1979.

9. C. Saunders, "Leonard Thompson's Historical Writing on South Africa", *South African Historical Journal*, Vol. 30, May 1994.

10. C. Saunders, "The Annexation of the Transkeian Territories", D.Phil thesis, University of Oxford, 1972. It was published under the same title in *Archives Yearbook for South African History*, 1976.

11. C. Saunders and R. Derricourt (eds), *Beyond the Cape Frontier,* Cape Town and London, 1974; B.A. le Cordeur and C. Saunders, (eds), *The Kitchingman Papers,* Johannesburg, 1976; C. Saunders, "The Hundred Years War: Some Reflections on African Resistance on the Cape -Xhosa frontier", in D. Chanaiwa (ed.), *Profiles in Self-Deter-*

in 1970, I became increasingly involved in researching the history of black Africans who had moved from the Eastern Cape to Cape Town.[12]

The 1980s

There is much more that I could recall relevant to the development of South African historiography in the 1960s and 1970s, but let me skip past the revival of African urban history from the time of the Soweto Uprising and come to the early 1980s. By then, thanks in part to the excitement generated by the work of the Neo-Marxists, students were clamouring to take history courses, and at UCT there were twice as many historians as a decade earlier. By the 1980s, history was widely seen as the leading discipline in the humanities, thanks largely to the radical historians, who had by the early 1980s for over a decade made the running in opening up new themes, whether the rise and fall of the peasantry or the class nature of the gold-mining industry. Though apartheid was still to go through its last and most brutal phase, there were signs that we were entering the end-game.

In history-writing interest had clearly shifted from the pre-colonial – a high-point was the conference held at Rhodes in 1979, which brought together Jeff Guy, J.B. Peires, Julian Cobbing, Phil Bonner, John Wright and others, and led to the publication of *Before and After Shaka* – to the mineral revolution and after.[13] The most fundamental development that had taken place by the early 1980s was the shift to social history. Nineteen eighty-two, the middle year in my four decades, happens to be the year in which one of the most brilliant works in the new social history appeared, Charles Van On-

---

mination, Northridge, Calif., 1976; C. Saunders, (ed.), C. Brownlee, *Reminiscences of Kaffir Life and History*, Pietermaritzburg, 1977; C. Saunders, (ed.), W. Dower, *The Early Annals of Kokstad and Griqualand East*, Pietermaritzburg, 1978; B. le Cordeur and C. Saunders, (eds), *The War of the Axe*, Johannesburg, 1981.

12. C. Saunders, "Not Newcomers: Africans in Cape Town", *South African Outlook*, February 1978; C. Saunders, "F.Z.S. Peregrino and the South African Spectator", *Quarterly Bulletin of the South African Library*, March 1978; C. Saunders, "Segregation in Cape Town: The Creation of Ndabeni", in Africa Seminar: Collected Papers, I, University of Cape Town, 1978; C. Saunders, "From Ndabeni to Langa, *Studies in the History of Cape Town*, Cape Town, 1979; C. Saunders "Africans in Cape Town in the Nineteenth Century: A Preliminary Outline", *Studies in the History of Cape Town*, Vol. 2 , 1980.

13. Peires, (ed.), *Before and After Shaka*. The title was odd, for its authors sought to get away from personalities and address socio-economic aspects of African societies.

selen's studies in the social and economic history of the Witwatersrand, *New Babylon, New Nineveh*. Grassroots history, concerned with ordinary people and – sometimes to an exaggerated extent – with the marginalised – the best of the new social history linked the micro with the macro and the social with the political and economic. Like most of the radical historians, Van Onselen was trained as a sociologist rather than a historian and he was not based in a History Department, but at an Institute of Social and Economic History at the University of the Witwatersrand.

With the Wits history workshop, which had first met in 1978, firmly established, social historians were as much as odds with the structural Marxists as with liberals. Though publication of *The Burden of the Present* by the American historian Harrison Wright in 1977 had stirred up strong exchanges,[14] by the early 1980s, as I remember it, the steam was beginning to go out of the so-called liberal-radical controversy because extreme views on either side had been marginalised and because the pluralists – as the liberal historians began to call themselves – agreed with much of what the radicals said. The radicals' initial over-emphasis on class, and denial of the salience of race and ethnicity, were being challenged, by Debbie Posel among others.[15] Though Merle Lipton's *Capitalism and Apartheid* had not yet been published, there was an increasing acceptance by all that the "historical" relationship between apartheid and capitalism had changed over time. Those radical scholars who continued to attack liberal history often attacked stereotypical views from a much earlier era, not what the pluralists of the 1970s and 1980s believed. We certainly did not believe that capitalism would on its own undermine apartheid, for example.

In an essay in a recently-published collection, Neville Alexander, a leading black intellectual, takes me to task for having suggested in *The Making of the South African Past* that by the mid-1980s a convergence between liberal pluralist and radical revisionist views was taking place. After quoting from my book he says that my words remind him "of a kind of historiographical truth and reconciliation commission", and that what I wrote:

---

14. H. Wright, *The Burden of the Present. Liberal-Radical Controversy over South African History*, Cape Town, 1977 and "The Burden of the Present and its Critics", *Social Dynamics*, Vol. 6, No. 1, 1980.

15. D. Posel, "Re-Thinking the "Race-Class" Debate in South African Historiography", *Social Dynamics*, 1983.

... amounts to a premature closure of a continuing debate, one which is being conducted at very different levels in quite different domains and disciplines under the general rubric of the implications and consequences of globalisation.[16]

But that is surely a quite different debate, and not one that continues among historians in South Africa, a point I shall return to below. I agree with the thrust of what Bill Freund said in 1994, if not all the precise words he used:

> The disputes between liberals and Marxists, the revisionism that emphasises the position of women, rural people or others left out, these are really quarrels within a master-narrative. For our master-narrative is not class or male superiority or even Marxism, it is simply the Struggle. The 'really revolutionary road' would be to start writing a South African history that did not revolve around the axis of the struggle against the construct of South Africa as a white world.[17]

Freund's highlighting of the importance of the master narrative of "the Struggle" leads me to jump to the present, to say something about historical writing now that more than ten years have passed since Nelson Mandela succeeded F.W. de Klerk as South African President.

The 1990s

The transfer of power that took place in 1994 was not matched by any significant new historiographical development. Some had expected that with the birth of the new South Africa would come a new kind of history-writing designed to aid the nation-building project, as had happened in tropical Africa with the coming of independence. One possible new direction was a black African nationalist one that would stress the African contribution to the exclusion of others, and see whites as merely intruders into an essentially African country. Another was the kind of reconciliation history alluded to by Neville Alexander, an attempt to bring people together, to match the rainbow-nation of Mandela and Desmond Tutu. Such attempts as there have been to write such history have produced eccentric results. Having in 1995

---

16. N. Alexander, *An Ordinary Country,* Pietermaritzburg, 2002, p. 23.

17. B. Freund, "The Art of Writing History", *Southern African Review of Books,* September/October, 1994. Freund continued: "the liberal-cum-radical school of South African historiography, has long since achieved total victory, real hegemony ... In my own work, I keep striving for a kind of marriage of history and political economy that asks questions left out when apartheid occupies centre stage."

wondered whether "a new Theal waits in the wings with a reconciliation history",[18] Norman Etherington, an Australian-based historian of South Africa, has in his recently-published *Great Treks*[19] set out deliberately to write "truth and reconciliation" history, suitable, he says, for the new democracy. This leads him to claim, absurdly in my view, that the early 19th century black treks he writes about are of equal significance to the Boer trek of the late 1830s.[20] If what historians writes aids reconciliation so much the better, but reconciliation should not be their goal.

To explain the absence of a new direction in historiography in the 1990s, Martin Legassick and Gary Minkley point to the nature of the negotiated revolution.[21] It is certainly true that the transfer of power in South Africa, unlike the decolonisations of tropical Africa thirty years before, was the result of a set of compromises between parties representing the ruling white minority and the majority, the one agreeing to give up political power, the other accepting a liberal democratic constitution and agreeing to work within the existing capitalist framework. But Legassick and Minkley, in my view, fail to acknowledge the importance of the fact that the historiographical equivalent to the dramatic political change of 1994 had taken place decades earlier: as I have suggested above, South African history was decolonised long before the political "decolonisation" – as some interpret it – of 1994.[22] A third reason for South African historical writing not having taken any new direction is that history has been in crisis for much of the past decade. Those of us who teach in South Africa can of course write at length about this. All I will do here is merely mention that few black historians have obtained and retained academic jobs. Some who got such posts have moved into government or the private sector.[23] Posts in history have disappeared with the fall-off in student

18. N. Etherington, "Reconsidering Conflicting Historical Narratives in the Context of Post-Apartheid South Africa", unpublished paper, 1995.

19. N. Etherington, *The Great Treks*, London, 2001.

20. C. Saunders, "Great Treks?" *South African Historical Journal*, Vol. 46, 2002.

21. M. Legassick and G. Minkley, "Current Trends in the Production of South African History", *Alternation*, Vol. 5, No. 1, 1998.

22. Cf. C. Saunders, "The Transitions from Apartheid to Democracy in Namibia and South Africa in the Context of Decolonization, *Journal of Colonialism and Colonial History*, Vol. 1, No. 1, 2000.

23. Dr Eddy Maloka, for example, gave up his lectureship at UCT to become adviser to the Premier of Gauteng, and then the Executive Director of the Africa Institute of South Africa. Other historians have taken jobs at the Human Sciences Research

interest in history.[24] Though this is to some extent a world-wide trend away from history, for which post-modernism must surely bear some blame, it has been accentuated in South Africa, where students take subjects either directly relevant for jobs at a time when the teaching of history in schools is declining, and therefore there is no demand for history teachers, or that seem more directly relevant than history for the world they are about to enter.

Today no major controversy divides the historical profession in South Africa. Certainly a whole range of new questions are being asked, about memory, public history, representation, gender, the social history of medicine, and many other topics, and all this indicates that South African history is far from dead. Much of the new work reflects global trends, and to some extent its very existence is a reflection of the normality that has come to the "new South Africa". But – and here I will be controversial – much of the new work is narrow and specialised and of limited general significance; much of it is faddish or related more to heritage than history as such. Writing in 1990, Colin Bundy could say that "fragmentation and over-specialisation is not yet a major problem".[25] He would find it difficult to say the same today. In the 2002 South African Historical Society newsletter, which lists publications of the past year by historians at South African universities, among the numerous publications listed it is difficult to find anything that is likely to be remembered in the future.[26] Yes, Jeff Guy of the University of Natal has given us another wonderfully detailed study of Harriette Colenso, but his *View across the River*, and my colleague Nigel Penn's lively book on eighteenth century characters in Cape Town, *Rogues, Rebels, Runaways*, are very readable micro studies; they only deal with major issues indirectly.[27] Paul Maylam's

---

Council rather than in the universities.

24. This was particularly the case at the historically black universities, such as North-West, but was also the case at, say, the Pietermaritzburg campus of the University of Natal.

25. C. Bundy, "An Image of Its Own Past? Towards a Comparison of American and South African Historiography", *Radical History Review*, Issue 46/7, 1990, p. 135.

26. The exceptions to this would include Paul Maylam's book, cited below, and, say, Jane Carruthers, *Wildlife & Warfare:The Life of James Stevenson-Hamilton,* Pietermaritz-burg, 2001. Though interesting new work is being done in relatively new sub-fields of medical history, gender history, public history and environmental history, most of this work is narrow in focus.

27. J. Guy, *The View across the River,* Cape Town, 2002; N. Penn, *Rogues, Rebels, Runaways: Eighteenth Century Cape Characters,* Cape Town, 1999.

recent book on race and racism does tackle such issues head-on, but his is for the most part a synthesis of previous work.[28]

Patrick Furlong, an ex-South African US-based historian, concludes his recent survey of South African historiography by saying that:

> ... finding appropriate themes now will be as hard for those steeped in opposi-tional traditions as for Afrikaner historians reduced to analysing the apparent failure of a communal past.[29]

But is this the case? We do not have any history of the Cape, let alone of many aspects of Cape history, and there is much that we do not know about such major themes as the impact of modernity on African societies or of glo-balisation, a topic mentioned recently, as we have seen, by Neville Alexander. In my view, it should not be difficult to select relevant topics for research. But instead, much time is taken up with the production of commemorative publications, or ones that merely add detail to what we knew already. For ex-ample, we knew twenty years ago that blacks had played a significant role in the South African War, and yet that is a theme recently much pursued, while five major collections, at last count, have been published on that war in the past three years.[30] Though historians should take advantage of centenaries, is so much attention to this war justified, when we still lack, say, any satisfac-tory history of, South Africa's much more recent war in Namibia/Angola?[31]

---

28. P. Maylam, *South Africa's Racial Past: The History and Historiography of Racism, Seg-regation, and Apartheid*, Aldershot, 2001.

29. P. Furlong, "South Africa" in K. Boyd (ed.), *Encyclopaedia of History and Historians*, London, 2000, II, p. 1118.

30. D. Lowry, (ed.), *The South African War Reappraised,* Manchester, 2000; I. Smith, (ed.), *The Siege of Mafeking*, Johannesburg, 2000; J. Gooch (ed.), *The Boer War: Direction, Experience and Image*, London, 2000; K. Wilson (ed.), *International Impact of the Boer War*, Chesham, 2001; D. Omissi and A. Thompson, *The Impact of the South African War*, Basingstoke, 2002; G. Cuthbertson, A.M. Grundlingh, and M-L. Suttie (eds), *Writing a Wider War: Rethinking Gender, Race, and Identity in the South African War*, 1899–1902, Athens, Ohio University Press / Cape Town, David Philip Publisher, 2002.

31. I myself contributed to two of these collections instead of writing up my history of South Africa in Namibia, though in one of the two papers I did attempt a comparison between the South African War and the recent liberation struggle. Cf. C. Saunders, "Reflections on the Significance of the South African War", *Kleio*, 2000. At the end of the centenary of the war, I planned to compare the compromise that ended the war with the compromise that ended the conflict in the early 1990s, but that paper re-mains, alas, unfinished. Nor have I worked up for publication the paper I was asked to give on my first visit to Copenhagen, two years ago, on "Why Apartheid Collapsed",

Though it is now almost three years since the five volume Truth and Reconciliation Report appeared, few historians have commented on them, let alone subjected them to any detailed critique.[32] Though access to sources *is* a problem for research on the last twenty years, this is not a sufficient excuse.[33] The South African Democracy Education Trust (SADET) "Road to Democracy" project, which is doing extensive interviews with veterans of the struggle, is of great potential importance. But much of the best work on South African history continues to be done outside the country, where pressures are less and resources greater. An example is the work of Diana Wylie, an American based at Boston University, who has recently published *Starving on a Full Stomach: Hunger and the Triumph of Cultural Racism in Modern South Africa*.[34] Alas, it remains the case that the majority of those who do serious research in our archives do not live in South Africa.

When one thinks back to the early 1980s, and to the early 1960s, one is struck by the clear and obvious political purpose that directed so much of the most significant historical work done at both those now distant times. Since 1994, South Africa has become "an ordinary country", to use the title of Alexander's recent book, and linked to the rest of Africa as never before, in an era when the production of new historical knowledge has virtually collapsed in much of the continent.[35] With the old anti-apartheid political purpose gone, South African history-writing is now much more diffuse and difficult to categorise, which is surely one of the reasons why there is no recent survey of it. Let me close with a question that is rhetorical rather than historical, for it concerns the unknown future. It puts in other words what Legassick predicts in an interview with the United States based labour historian Alex Lichtenstein in a recent issue of the *Radical History Review*,[36] a prediction that the

a theme, which remains, remarkably, almost untouched by South African historians.

32. But cf. D. Posel and G. Simpson (eds), *Commissioning the Past*, Johannesburg, 2002; C. Saunders, "Historians and the TRC", *Focus*, February 2003.

33. Cf. S. Ellis, "Writing Histories of Contemporary Africa", *Journal of African History*, Vol. 43, 2002.

34. D. Wylie, *Starving on a Full Stomach: Hunger and the Triumph of Cultural Racism in Modern South Africa*, Charlottesville, Virginia, 2001.

35. Whereas in the 1970s historians based in Nigeria and Kenya published important monographs and were frequent contributors to leading international journals, in the last decade there has been virtually nothing of significance coming out of the History Departments of the universities in those countries.

36. A. Lichtenstein, "The Past and Present of Marxist Historiography of South Africa",

close relationship that has existed in the past between our history-writing and our politics will be re-established. The question is this: For a new invigoration of our historiography, do we have to wait for a future populist challenge to the prevailing neo-liberal hegemony?

Radical History Review, Issue 82, 2001.

CHAPTER 15

The role of business under apartheid:
Revisiting the debate

Merle Lipton

This chapter reviews recent acrimonious debates about the role of business under apartheid.[1] It sketches out the contending positions in order to high-light a striking feature – the increasing similarities behind the conflicting rhetoric about what was actually happening in South Africa (SA). Some of the historical, philosophical and psychological issues underlying this paradox are then discussed.

The starting point is the conflicting testimony presented to the Truth and Reconciliation Commission (TRC) on the role of business under apartheid.[2] Some of those testifying argued that the course of events since 1990 – the willingness of the ruling white elite to negotiate a non-racial, democratic con-stitution for SA – confirmed the liberal argument that the interests of, and pressures from, business were contributing to the erosion of apartheid and conversion of the ruling elite to the view that a negotiated ending to apart-heid was desirable and possible. But others denied that the historical record gave support to this view and reiterated the argument of the Neo-Marxist re-visionists that business was the major supporter and beneficiary of apartheid, only switching its support at the last moment when the demise of apartheid became unstoppable.

This chapter uses the terms liberals and Marxists in which this debate has been cast, although these categories are often misleading and fail to reflect the

---

1. The UK's Economic and Social Research Council (ESRC) provided funding for this research project, based at Sussex University. Contact address: 15 Eaton Place, Kemp-town, Brighton, BN2 1EH (mlipton@onetel.com).

2. The TRC was set up in 1996 to establish the facts about the causes, nature and extent of gross violations of human rights under apartheid. Special hearings were held on the role of business, the media, and medical profession. The references here are to the Business Sector Hearing.

wide, fluid and overlapping spectrum of intellectual positions. In particular, the term "liberal" covers a wide range of views, evident in its different meanings in the USA and Europe. In pre-1990 SA, liberals were non-communists who opposed apartheid; they ranged from social democrats concerned with poverty and inequality, to libertarians mainly concerned with the rule of law, political freedom and civil rights.

This debate about the role of business was closely linked to questions of political strategy, such as whether the international community should impose economic sanctions on SA. Some liberals, such as Donald Woods, Colin and Margaret Legum and Peter Hain, favoured sanctions. But most liberals, while not against some pressures on SA, wanted the maintenance of external contacts and influence and opposed comprehensive economic sanctions aimed at damaging the economy, which they regarded as a major generator of domestic pressures for reform. It is hardly surprising that this close link to political strategy added to the intensity and polarisation of the debate before 1990. What is surprising is the continued acrimony over these issues in post-apartheid SA, and the persistence of the negative view of the role of business, and of the white liberals to whom business is perceived as linked.

I was struck by the persistence of this negative view of the business role because, since 1970, I have been researching the conduct of business in SA, and observed at first hand its mounting pressures against a widening range of apartheid policies. This pressure came both from individuals, such as Harry Oppenheimer, and from business organisations, such as the Federated Chambers of Industry (FCI) and Associated Chambers of Commerce (Assocom). From the 1970 election (when the ruling Afrikaner National Party defeated a challenge from its Herstigte right wing), these pressures contributed to the erosion and scrapping of many apartheid measures. Indeed, by 1990, when President de Klerk unbanned, and began negotiations with, the ANC, there was little left of what the ANC itself had defined as the core features of apartheid, such as job reservation, pass laws, legally segregated education, the restrictions on black access to training and apprenticeships, home ownership and business opportunities, and the legal restrictions on social mixing and inter-racial sex and marriage. By 1990, most of the legally entrenched apartheid measures had been abolished, with some notable exceptions, such as the Land Act and franchise laws.

There was, and remains, extreme racial inequality and a huge task of socio-economic transformation. But the legalised and institutionalised measures, which were the distinctive feature of apartheid, had been abolished.

And these had not gone easily, but only after fierce battles, in many of which business and liberals played an active and public role. It was this process, which led some of us to argue that SA was on a reformist course. Thus, it was not the case that everyone was surprised by the "miracle" that supposedly occurred during 1990–94. Rather, the transition to majority rule seemed to confirm this analysis and to contradict the Neo-Marxist argument that capitalism and apartheid were inextricably linked.

Two other features of the continuing disputes about the role of business merit comment. First, SA's post-apartheid settlement occurred at a time of narrowing ideological differences, with a significant shift by the ANC from the socialist policies of the Freedom Charter. These included "nationalisation of the banks, mines and monopoly industry" – a principle reiterated by Nelson Mandela on his release from prison in 1990, but thereafter soon abandoned. I am not here implying approval of the ANC's current policy, with priority for the empowerment of a smallish elite and, thus far, little redistribution to the poor. I am merely noting that the dramatic shift in ANC policy fits uneasily with the continuing anti-capitalist rhetoric evident at the TRC hearing. Second, the post-apartheid policy of reconciliation has been evident in the ANC's conciliatory attitude towards the former ruling Afrikaner National Party (NP) and other elements of the White Right, and also towards its rivals Inkatha and the PAC. But there is little sign of reconciliation in the ANC's acrimonious relations with white liberals. Instead, the ANC's relations with the English press, the opposition Democratic Alliance, and to a lesser extent, with white business, are often strained.

The resurfacing at the TRC hearings of the Neo-Marxist analysis, with its negative view of the role of business and hostility towards white liberals, and the continuing tensions between the ANC and white liberals, stimulated me to revisit the debates of the apartheid years. This review suggests that there is less disagreement about the facts – what business said and did and how the government reacted – than the polarised rhetoric suggests. The difference is mainly over the interpretation of these facts. And this, in turn, rests upon differences in the underlying (and largely implicit) assumptions, values and theories about human behaviour and social change of the contenders in this debate.[3]

First, a prior question – how relevant are these historical disputes to post-apartheid SA? The TRC hearings, and the exchanges between the ANC and

---

3. At the NAI/CAS Copenhagen conference, at which draft papers for this book were presented, Hans Erik Stolten challenged me to respond to accusations that the Neo-

white liberals, confirm the close links between perceptions of the historical issues and current political issues, such as whether business should pay reparations to the victims of apartheid and whether SA should adopt an affirmative action or black empowerment policy. The past is constantly invoked in relation to claims/entitlements on the one hand and responsibilities on the other hand. Thus, the history matters and is perceived by all parties as relevant.

This very sensitivity leads some to argue that it is unwise to dig up the past and expose the truth about our appalling past behaviour to one another. Partly for this reason, the establishment of the TRC was contested, and both Mandela and de Klerk initially opposed it. Some academics agree with this "bury the past" approach, but I do not believe it is desirable or feasible. Revelation of the truth might on occasion worsen relationships; but it might also improve them. I believe that SA is a case of this, and that a fuller understanding of the messy, complex truth about the role of business under apartheid holds out the hope of improved relationships in post-apartheid SA. Even if I did not believe this, I would regard it as the duty of academics to tell the truth about the past as straightforwardly as they can, regardless of any feelings of political solidarity or personal loyalty.

Contending analyses of the role of business

The liberal analysis was not that business led a long, heroic struggle to overthrow apartheid. It was as follows: the interests of business in relation to apartheid were never homogeneous, and business had a mixed record. This included support from white farmers and mineowners for apartheid measures such as the Land Acts and pass laws. It also included opposition from manufacturing and commerce to the restrictions on black education, training, and home ownership and to the job colour bar, which was opposed by all major business interests, including farmers and mineowners. The generally conservative mineowners were involved in virtual civil wars with white labour over the job bar in 1907, 1913 and 1922. Thus, both the pro- and anti-apartheid strands within business have a long history, predating the formation of the

---

Marxists have made about the work of liberals, especially myself. These accusations relate both to substantive historical and to historiographical questions – who said what, and when. To avoid the historiographical issues clouding the argument, they are dealt with in the Appendix at the end of the book.

Union of SA in 1910, and including phases of conflict thereafter, particularly during World War II and at the time of Sharpeville.[4]

Thus, the interests of business were not static but changed over time. From the 1960s (the period covered by the TRC hearings), business criticism of apartheid strengthened in response to the NP's attempt to shore up apartheid against the forces of industrialisation and urbanisation. My own analysis focused on the growing need for a more educated and skilled workforce as the economy mechanised, and on the need for a larger domestic market – requirements inhibited by apartheid. From the late 1960s, a growing convergence of business pressures against apartheid emerged. By the mid-1970s, the traditionally conservative Chamber of Mines and Afrikaans Business Association (though still not the SA Agricultural Union) were supporting the pressures of the FCI and Assocom for economic and social reforms.

These growing pressures from business coincided and interacted with other economic and political changes. Within the white elite, the pro-apartheid forces were weakened, both because of the declining economic need for apartheid on the part of white labour, the white bureaucracy and white farmers and also because of the declining political power of these conservative forces. There were also increasingly effective political pressures from blacks, whose numbers, education, income levels and bargaining power grew rapidly. Finally, there was the impact of external influences and pressures as SA became more integrated into the international economy and society. I am not here making judgments about which pressures were the most effective, but pointing to an increasing range of pressures, including from business. These business pressures were not limited to behind-the-scenes lobbying, but were

---

4. Liberal versions include: Michael O'Dowd's 1964 paper, "South Africa in the light of the stages of economic growth", reprinted in A. Leftwich (ed.), *South Africa: Economic growth and political change*, 1974, Allison & Busby, London; N. Bromberger, "Economic growth & political change in South Africa", in Leftwich, *Idem*; Bromberger & Hughes, "Capitalism & Underdevelopment in SA", in J. Butler et al. (eds), *Democratic liberalism in SA*. 1987; J.B. Knight, "Has capitalism underdeveloped the labour reserves of SA?" *Oxford Bulletin of Economics and Statistics*, Vol. 42, 1980; M. Lipton, "White farming: A casestudy of change in South Africa", *The Journal of Commonwealth and Comparative Politics,* March 1974; "South Africa: Authoritarian Reform?" *World Today,* June 1974; "British investment in SA: Is constructive engagement possible?" in *South African Labour Bulletin*, October 1976; "The debate about South Africa: neo-Marxists and neo-liberals", *African Affairs*, Vol. 78, 1979; Monograph on migrant labour, *Optima,* Vol. 29, No. 2–3 of 1980; and *Capitalism & Apartheid: 1910–84,* Gower, 1985, republished in 1986 with an Epilogue updating the book.

public and well-documented. Many observers commented on fact that business in SA was noticeably to the left of government.

If this is so well documented, why and how do the Neo-Marxists and others deny it? A close examination of their recent publications, and of some of the testimony before the TRC, shows that – despite their continuing hostile rhetoric about the role of business – they no longer deny it.[5] Their argument that capitalism and apartheid were not only compatible, but functionally and inextricably linked, has been replaced by at least some recognition of the well-documented facts about the growing opposition of business to apartheid and the growing conflicts between business and government. However, the Neo-Marxists continue to interpretate this process negatively, and they conclude that they did not contribute to the erosion of apartheid.

This view is reflected in Cosatu's lengthy testimony to the TRC, based on the Neo-Marxist analysis, in which business is bracketed together with the apartheid regime, as its ally and handmaiden. Cosatu tersely notes that business pressed for, and frequently secured, the reforms listed above. However, it then dismisses their significance for the following reasons:

i) that business pressures were driven by the self-interested motive of reducing the rising economic costs of apartheid;

ii) that the intention of business was not to abolish apartheid, but to secure limited adjustments, which would actually strengthen apartheid by making it more adaptable.

Whether or not one accepts this rationale for dismissing the significance of business pressure, it confirms that there were such pressures. Despite the continuing polarised rhetoric, there is thus a narrowing of differences about the facts – what business said and did, and how the government reacted – but a very different interpretation of these facts. These differences in interpretation raise questions about the underlying model or theory of why people behave as they do and how social change takes place, as well as about the possibility of establishing historical truth.

A few brief points follow about the different assumptions about behavioural and social theory that underlie these conflicting interpretations. Analyses and judgments of motives and intentions rest on theories about what drives

---

5. See Cosatu's testimony to the Business Sector Hearing of the TRC in November 1997 in which they cite Dan O'Meara, *Forty Wasted Years: The apartheid state & the politics of the National Party*, Ravan, 1996.

human behaviour and what is normal. Despite our limited understanding of this, even careful, scholarly social scientists make sweeping generalisations about the motives and intentions of people on the basis of vaguely formed assumptions, which are often implicit and not clearly stated. I suggest as a hypothesis that all humans are driven by an often ambiguous, contradictory mixture of motives, of which they are often unaware; that self-interest is a major component in the behaviour of most people – whether in business, trade unions, government or academic life; whether blacks or whites, liberals or Marxists; and that self-interest does not preclude enlightened or altruistic feelings.[6]

Relevant to intentions is the phenomenon of unintended consequences: well-intended actions sometimes have appalling consequences, while actions that are not consciously well-intentioned can have good effects. Surely, it is the effects of actions that matter most. Our limited capacity to understand or manage the effects of our actions should make us wary of attaching too much weight to imagined motives and intentions rather than to their more observable effects.

Also problematical are the implicit models and assumptions about the nature of social change made by those who distinguish between genuine reforms and pseudo "neo-apartheid" measures. I incline to the belief that history proceeds more on the basis of ad hoc measures and cock-ups than by deliberate social engineering. But there are governments with ideological blueprints, which they try to implement. This included apartheid theorists such as Prime Minister Verwoerd, who strove to make apartheid more workable and acceptable by adapting and modernising it, via his "separate development" policy. Fortunately, Verwoerd's ideological project of setting up "independent" Bantustans, where blacks were to exercise their political rights, was not supported by most businesspeople, particularly not by English and foreign capital, which dominated the SA economy outside agriculture. At one stage, Afrikaans business, closely tied to the government, and in receipt of many favours from it, supported this policy. But as its economic implications became clearer – the constraint on economic growth imposed by the exclusion of blacks from skilled work; the expensive and failed attempt to decentralise labour intensive industries to the Bantustans – even the Afrikaanse Handelsinstituut (Business Association) backed away from 'separate development' and shifted towards supporting the FCI and Assocom in lobbying

6. Matt Ridley, *The Origins of Virtue*, Viking, London, 1994; Gary Runciman, *The Social Animal*, HarperCollins, London, 1998.

against one aspect of apartheid after another – eventually moving towards acceptance of an integrated, common society.

Yet, by a tortuous process of reasoning, these reforms – which the ANC had long called for – came to be defined as neo-apartheid measures and dismissed as part of a Machiavellian master-plan to ensure the survival of apartheid. The rationale for this was that they aimed at the adaptation rather than the complete and rapid overthrow of apartheid. Hence reforms such as the scrapping of restrictions on black mobility, access to jobs, ownership of houses and businesses, the extension of trade union rights – measures which when carried out elsewhere in the world were hailed as major reforms – were dismissed as "neo-apartheid".

But what then is "real reform"? This reasoning implies that it means "changing the whole system" and "starting with a clean slate". But social change seldom happens this way, and attempts to stage such total revolutions invariably reveal that it is impossible to change everything at once, as was the case in Russia, Cambodia, Ethiopia, and elsewhere. Meanwhile, programmes of incremental change, whatever their motives, often have far-reaching, long-term consequences, whether or not these were intended by their advocates.

When the ANC came into power in 1994, soon after collapse of communism in eastern Europe and Africa, it had already modified its revolutionary aims and adopted a more gradual, reformist strategy. But even this modest programme is proving difficult to carry out. And this is hardly surprising. Societies are organic entities, with complex networks of relationships and institutions that tend to resist rapid change. Profound changes generally take place incrementally and gradually – for reasons that New Institutional Economics is helping us to understand. These reasons include the fact that people, poor as well as rich, are risk-averse and cautious and usually resist drastic, quick changes. And this too is a universal trait of human behaviour – for good or for ill.

I suggest as a definition of "genuine reform" in SA, changes that undermined the hierarchical, racial, principle, i.e. not changes for separate but equal education or housing, or the extension of business rights in separate areas, but changes that involved a shift towards a common, non-racial society – even if the pace was slower than many wished.

Another reason cited by the Neo-Marxists for dismissing the significance of business pressures is that, even if the reforms are accepted as significant, they were due to pressures, not from business, but from trade unions, NGOs, the armed struggle, and/or sanctions. It is odd that Marxists should argue thus, because it is surely central to a Marxist analysis that, in a capitalist system, it is the pressures from capital, which are decisive. One would expect that a coherent Marxist analysis would view business pressures as a crucial factor in both the establishment of apartheid and, later, in its erosion. Many great social transitions are facilitated by splits within the ruling elite, and it would be surprising if the long – drawn-out battle within the white oligarchy did not play a significant – which is not to say the sole or even leading – role in the erosion of apartheid.

There are also realpolitik reasons why the Neo-Marxists, and others, deny that white business contributed to the erosion of apartheid, including the fear that business might use such credit as an excuse for not contributing to reparations, for opposing redistribution, and for declining to take a back seat politically in post-apartheid SA. Also relevant is the rivalry and jockeying for power within the former anti-apartheid opposition, all of whom want to claim credit for ending apartheid and many of whom are competing for positions and influence with the ANC. Apart from the long-standing rivalry between the (predominantly white, coloured and Indian) Marxist and liberal activists and intelligentsia, there is a new actor on the scene – the emerging black elite, who previously played a subdued role in this debate. At the TRC hearings, the Black Management Forum adopted an analysis of the relationship between capitalism and apartheid similar to that of the Marxists, while advocating the nurturing of black capitalists, who will be the equals of, or perhaps supplant, whites. In this case, the anti-capitalist rhetoric needs to be scrutinised to see whether their argument is really about capitalism or whether it is about who its beneficiaries should be. Thus, this debate is relevant to political strategy, and to future race and class relations in SA.

Some fear that any credit given to white business will be used by them as an excuse to oppose social reform. However, the case for redistribution, in SA or elsewhere, rests on the coexistence of extreme wealth and poverty. Declining to take a simplistic view of SA's complex, messy history does not reduce the urgent need to address its acute problems of poverty and inequality. To recognise that business played a positive role is not to deny that there has been a history of systematic racial discrimination, nor is it to deny that rich whites – even though they may have wanted apartheid less than poorer whites – benefited from, and became the most visible symbols of, the inequality and privilege associated with apartheid. It would be wrong and foolish of white business not to recognise that there is an appalling inheritance that needs to be righted. But continually berating and demonising people, while denying the positive aspects of their historical contribution, is not necessarily the way to get the best out of them.

The complex, messy, unheroic, but not entirely discreditable, truth about the role of business under apartheid has the potential to provide a more realistic basis for building a common society than simplistic models of a society composed of demons and saints. Facing the truth about SA's past involves recognising how regrettably alike we all are and how ambiguous, volatile and confused are our motives and intentions. This chastening recognition brings us closer to the truth and provides the realistic long-term basis for living together.

APPENDIX: HISTORIOGRAPHICAL ISSUES

At the Copenhagen conference at which the papers for this book were presented, Hans Erik Stolten challenged me to reply to allegations about the work of liberal historians, including myself, that were made by the Neo-Marxist revisionists and some of their admirers. I welcome Stolten's action in placing on the agenda allegations that have circulated widely, but only occasionally appeared in print.[1]

These allegations relate to the work, and the professional ethics, of both past and contemporary liberal historians, and to their interpretation of SA history since the mid-17th century. I address these wider themes elsewhere; here I focus on the allegations made in relation to the debate about the role of business. Briefly, the charge against contemporary liberals is that – apart from the inadequacies of their analysis, and their role in providing a rationale not only for business interests, but also for apartheid – they have drawn heavily on, while failing to acknowledge and refer to, the work of the Neo-Marxist revisionists – work that has, they claimed "transformed and revolutionised" SA history.[2]

Some of these charges are concisely set out in Stanley Greenberg's influential review of *Capitalism and Apartheid* in which he claims that:

> Lipton's work ... is curiously out of touch with the scholarship on SA ... She manages not to engage the work of others ... [in particular] barely any of the Marxist scholarship of the last decade receives mention ... while Lipton seems to engage the Marxist critique of SA capitalism, she does so only through phantom authors and arguments ... vague positions attributed to nobody in particular.[3]

Greenberg claims that among the relevant works to which I did not refer are scholarly radical journals such as the *Journal of Southern African Studies* and *South African Labour Bulletin*, as well as his book, *Race and State in Capitalist Development*.

However, *Capitalism and Apartheid* contains references to Greenberg's work on pages 5, 190, 417, 437, 442, 443 and 445. These references are not confined to footnotes, but include discussion of his arguments within the text. Chapter 1 sets out the

---

1. See Stolten's conference paper "The discussion of the relationship between capitalism and apartheid: Elaborations over Lipton's position" on his website: http://www.jakobsgaard-stolten.dk/ and then go to | History Conference | Links to unpublished papers from the NAI/CAS conference on South African history. Stolten has dissociated himself from many of these allegations. I appreciate his editorial action in giving me the opportunity to place my response to them on the record here, uncomfortable though this has been for him. Apart from the issues of historiographical and professional ethics discussed in the Appendix, Stolten's paper raises major questions about the liberal historical interpretation, particularly the roles of mining capital and white labour, and about the moral duty of historians in situations of intense political conflict. I respond to these in my forthcoming book, *Liberals, Marxists and Nationalists: Competing interpretations of South African history*.

2. For example, C. Saunders, *The Making of the South African Past*, 1988, Barnes & Noble.

3. *Social Dynamics*, Vol. 13, No. 2, 1987.

Blumer/Greenberg thesis as one of the four main positions in the debate. Chapter 5 sets out my reasons for rejecting the Blumer/Greenberg thesis that capitalists readily adapted or "nestled" into the apartheid structures.

Greenberg also claims that I ignored the work of non-Marxist scholars such as Lodge, Giliomee, du Toit and Yudelman. However, there are references to these authors on pages 329, 411, 417, 418, 440, 449, 450, 452 and 456. I did not refer to Yudelman's book, which was published in 1983, the same year that my book went to the press.

A further damaging allegation by Greenberg is that, apart from the failure to cite major secondary works, *Capitalism and Apartheid* makes little use of primary sources, except for a heavy reliance on unattributed interviews. Greenberg writes:

> Lipton's analysis depends for its interpretation of recent events on interviews ... Yet nowhere does she indicate anything about these interviews: how many, with whom, or the structural positions [of the interviewees. The fact that] ... these interviews were off the record and therefore unattributable is no excuse for indifference to standards of evidence.

Capitalism and Apartheid contains over 1,000 citations of sources.[4] Thirty of these, less than 3%, are references to my interviews; and many of these interviewees are identified by their names or positions.[5] Most of these interviews were conducted during a time when free speech was restricted, books banned, and critical researchers and journalists were harassed so that many of them found it prudent to leave the country – soon to be followed (under the supposedly business-friendly Botha regime) by outspoken business critics such as Gordon Waddell, Chris Ball and Tony Bloom. People were scared of the Vorster/Botha securocrats and nervous of speaking frankly about sensitive policy issues that academics abroad could safely debate.

These constraints on revealing the identity of interviewees were later attested to by Greenberg himself who wrote, in his 1987 book, *Legitimating the Illegitimate*:

> To ensure the anonymity of those interviewed ... I have been purposely vague ... I have not given the dates of interviews ... to cover my tracks.

Quite so!

The footnotes also confirm that *Capitalism and Apartheid* was heavily based on primary sources, including official government papers; commission reports and sta-

---

4. Many of the 852 numbered footnotes refer to multiple sources. Additional references were cited in the statistical material used in the 14 Tables.

5. For example, the trade unionists Anna Scheepers and Arrie Paulus, cabinet minister Treurnicht and opposition MP, Schwarz; the Director of Assocom, Chief Economist of the SA Agricultural Union, and officials of the Bantu Affairs Administration Boards. Some interviewees insisted on confidentiality and were referred to as factory manager, senior NP politician, official in Department of Economic or Bantu Affairs, etc

tistics; parliamentary debates; the SA press; and (published and unpublished) reports and memoranda of organisations of employers, workers, and other NGOs.[6]

Secondary sources included a wide range of contemporary scholars (including the Marxist and non-Marxist scholars whom Greenberg incorrectly alleged were omitted) and journals, such as the Journal of Southern African Studies and SA Labour Bulletin, which Greenberg claimed, inexplicably, that I did not use.

Despite the readily refutable nature of the allegations by Greenberg et al., the mud has stuck. This is evident in the credibility given to these allegations by respected radical scholars, such as Hans Erik Stolten and Bill Freund, who grind no personal axes and, in their reviews, strive to rise above partisanship. Thus Stolten, in his original draft paper, recorded the widely repeated allegation that:

> ... among the work of Marxists whom Lipton strives to avoid is Dan O'Meara, of whose well known work Lipton was apparently not aware [although she] .... kept building on (his) well-founded research.

Capitalism and Apartheid also contains references to O'Meara on pages 268, 370, 438, 449 and 458. These too are not confined to footnotes. On p. 370, I wrote:

> O'Meara is one of the few Marxists who confronted the problem of Afrikaner nationalism, treating it, like white racism, as functional for the interests of capital.

Likewise, Freund (in his critical but constructively challenging review) is presumably influenced by these frequently reiterated allegations when he regrets that *Capitalism and Apartheid* does not refer to the work of Bozzoli (to whom there are, in fact, references on pages 161, 435, 438, and 449).[7] In similar mode, Freund chides me for failing to refer to books published in 1983, '84 and '85 and even to a book, which was "forthcoming", i.e. not yet published when Freund wrote his review in 1987! Freund also regrets that:

> It is peculiar that Lipton does not engage with more recent writers (and that she) ... fails to point out the significance within SA's intellectual history of the 1970s revisionist work ... which produced material on which Lipton and others can stand and move forward. 1970s revisionism need not be rejected but rather used critically.

It is often remarked that people are quick to suspect others of sins they are themselves inclined to. An examination of the work of both Greenberg and O'Meara suggests that the boot is indeed on the other foot, and that it is they who seem to be "striv-

---

6. Official reports cited included the seminal reports of the 1930s and 1940s commissions on "native" and economic policy; the du Plessis/Marais and Reynders reports of the late 1960s and early 70s; the Wiehahn and Riekert reports of the late 1970s. Also cited were unpublished reports of employer and worker organisations. My fieldwork included interviews with many of the members, including chairpersons, of the 1970s commissions, as well as with many of the experts giving evidence before them. Interviews were also held with officials and members of the major employer and worker organisations.

7. *Transformation*, Vol. 4, 1987.

ing to avoid" any references to my work. Greenberg's *Race and State* contains one reference to my work, and there are no references in his subsequent publications, despite the notable shift in his analysis towards my arguments and methodology.[8] There is no reference to my work in O'Meara's articles or his book, Volkskapitalisme, although his verbal denunciations of my work at seminars at Sussex University and elsewhere, suggested a keen awareness of its existence.[9]

As even a cursory examination of the work of liberals such as Bromberger, Bell, Hughes, and myself shows, we did respond and refer to the work of the revisionists. (Indeed Greenberg himself, inconsistently accuses me of giving excessive attention to the work of Johnstone and Legassick!) It was they who conducted the written debate as though we did not exist, while the shifts in their arguments in response to our research, and their verbal denunciations of us at seminars and conferences – revealed that they were well aware of our work. Often, it is unclear whether we are accused of not reading the work of the Neo-Marxists; for using their work without attribution; or for merely disagreeing with and challenging them.

Whatever the reasons for the credence given by Freund, Stolten and others to these allegations, this affair highlights an important issue: the manipulative mis-use of referencing (blacklisting some; over-referencing others), which has become an infectious plague in SA historical and social studies. Freund and Stolten would do a useful service if they scrutinised the work of all scholars in this debate more rigorously and even-handedly. They might also consider the implications of the ma-nipulative use of referencing that is widespread in Southern African studies for the value of the "Citation Index", which greatly influences evaluations of academic work and career prospects.[10]

---

8. Greenberg's 1980 book, *Race and Class*, stressed the mutual adaptability, and consequent compatibility, of apartheid and capitalism. But in his later work *Legitimating the Illegiti-mate*, and his chapter in Giliomee and Schlemmer (eds), *Up against the Fences*, there is a marked shift in his analysis towards a striking similarity with the argument set out in my 1980 monograph, in OPTIMA, and in *Capitalism and Apartheid*, about the unworkabil-ity of the labour control system in SA, and the intensity of the conflict between business and the state, and within the state bureaucracy itself. Another striking similarity with my analysis is Greenberg's focus on the bureaucracy and his pattern of interviewing officials in both the Bantu Affairs Labour Control departments and in the private mining sector. It is in connection with these interviews that Greenberg absolved himself from identifying his interviewees because of the need for confidentiality, despite the charges of unprofes-sionalism, on this account, he had made against me and regardless of my own fuller iden-tification of interviewees.

9. The extent to which O'Meara shifted towards the analysis of the liberals he denounced in his 1996 book *Forty Lost Years* is documented in my forthcoming book, *Liberals, Marxists and Nationalists: Competing interpretations of SA history*.

10. An example of the value attached to this is the trouble taken by J. Suckling and L. White to draw to the attention of their readers: "it was notable that no contributor to the York conference found it useful to refer to Merle Lipton's Capitalism and Apartheid" in their Introduction to *After Apartheid*, Currey, 1988.

CHAPTER 16

Afrikaner anti-communist history production in South African historiography

Wessel Visser

In 1958 an American observer travelling through Africa, Edwin S. Munger, made the following comment:

> Communism is a word kicked around in South Africa almost as readily and loosely as communists like to kick 'democracy' and 'liberty' around to score their own goals.[1]

During the 20th century a whole corpus of anti-communist literature was produced, mainly by Afrikaners. And yet, to date apparently no historiographical study on the history of communism in South Africa has been published. One notable exception, though, was Mia Roth's critique of the orthodox versions of the history of the Communist Party of South Africa (CPSA) as portrayed in various so-called pro-communist publications.[2] This chapter attempts to analyse the production and dissemination of 20th century anti-communist literature in South Africa and to investigate the rationale behind it.

Early perceptions of communism

Socialism (as well as its offshoots, such as "Bolshevism" and "communism") was imported mainly from Europe into South Africa.[3] After the discovery of

---

1. E.S. Munger, *African Field Reports*, Cape Town, 1961, p. 645.
2. See M. Roth, "'Eddie, Brian, Jack and Let's Phone Rusty': Is This the History of the Communist Party of South Africa (1921–1950)?", *South African Historical Journal*, Vol. 44, 2001, pp. 191–209.
3. E. Roux, *Time Longer Than Rope. A History of the Black Man's Struggle for Freedom in South Africa*, London, 1948, p. 122. According to Bernard Hessian, "An Investigation into the Causes of the Labour Agitation on the Witwatersrand, January to March 1922", MA thesis, University of the Witwatersrand, 1957, p. 92. The public's percep-

minerals towards the end of the nineteenth century socialism took root on a limited scale via immigrant artisans and, in conjunction with a nascent local labour movement, in the newly emerging South African industrial centres. Various socialist parties and societies, some Marxist orientated, were founded between 1903 and 1909.[4] Apart from press organs established by labour and socialist parties, and a pamphlet by General Smuts in which he asserted that the 1914 general strike was instigated by a so-called "syndicalist conspiracy" (he actually meant by implication a socialist conspiracy)[5], for the greater part of the first two decades of the twentieth century no serious attention was given in South African literature to the phenomenon of socialism or communism.

The first South African reference to communism appeared in July 1910 in the socialist weekly *Voice of Labour* – a paper that was run from 1908 to 1912 by a Scottish socialist immigrant, Archie Crawford, and his Irish-born partner, Mary Fitzgerald. *Voice of Labour* published a learned article by W.H. Harrison (a prominent Cape Town socialist who would become a founding member of the CPSA in 1921) in which the notion of "anarchistic communism", as a socialist school of thought, was discussed.[6]

The Bolshevik Revolution of 1917 in Russia and the general strike of 1922 in South Africa, or the Rand Revolt, generated, however, a new and wider South African interest in communism. Smuts, English mining capital and its media became concerned about the presumed "evils" inherent in communism. In an attempt to de-legitimise the 1922 strikers and their leaders the Smuts government and the media that supported it erroneously depicted the strike as a "Red Revolt", "Red Terror" and a "Red" or "Bolshevist conspiracy". Smuts was concerned about the "danger" if Bolshevism should take

---

tions of concepts such as "socialist", "communist", "Bolshevist" and even "labourer", were mutually linked and sometimes even regarded as synonyms.

4. See D. Ticktin, "The Origins of the South African Labour Party, 1888–1910", PhD thesis, University of Cape Town, 1973, pp. 182,281, 298–299, 305, 328, 362–365, 396; R.K. Cope, *Comrade Bill. The Life and Times of W.H. Andrews, Workers' Leader*, Cape Town, 1943, p. 96; W.H. Harrison, *Memoirs of a Socialist in South Africa*, 1903–1947, Cape Town, 1947, pp. 4–5; H.J. and R.E. Simons, *Class and Colour in South Africa, 1850–1950*, Harmondsworth, 1969, pp. 102–103 and A. Drew, *Discordant Comrades. Identities and Loyalties on the South African Left*, Aldershot, 2000, pp. 8, 25.

5. "Syndicalist Conspiracy in South Africa, a Scathing Indictment", Being General Smuts' Speech in Parliament on the Recent Deportations, Cape Town, 1914.

6. See W.P. Visser, "Die Geskiedenis en Rol van Persorgane in die Politieke en ekonomiese Mobilisasie van die Georganiseerde Arbeiderbeweging in Suid-Afrika, 1908–1924", PhD thesis, University of Stellenbosch, 2001, p. 217.

root among the black population. He contended that what had begun as a purely industrial dispute had deteriorated into something reminiscent of the French revolution. This transformation, according to Smuts, was precipitated by the capture and eventual replacement of the indigenous labour movements by "forces of violence and anarchy" that wished to establish a soviet republic in South Africa. As some Jewish immigrants became involved in local labour organisations, and a small number actively supported the 1922 strike, accusations were also made that the strike was masterminded by "Bolshevik Jews".[7]

In the wake of the 1922 strike Hedley Chilvers, a journalist, published a pamphlet[8] that reiterated many of Smuts's and the mining press's contentions about communism, or "Bolshevism", as it was referred to at that stage. Chilvers begins by painting a terrifying picture of how a "red crime" was committed when the Russian Czar and his whole family were assassinated by Bolsheviks in 1918 and how Bolshevism was ruining Russia. He then proceeds to make white South Africans aware of the "evil" of Russian Bolshevism and "how earnestly the South African 'Reds' are endeavouring [as they did during the 1922 strike]...to reproduce Russian conditions in this country" by, among other things, "red schemes of intrigue among the natives". Chilvers unveils to his readers subversive activities among some of the well-known South African communists of the period, such as David Ivon Jones, Bill Andrews and Sidney Bunting. Therefore he contends "that the 'Red' danger is imminent". Also, in South Africa, local Bolsheviks endeavoured to foment revolution among blacks as part of a "Red world conspiracy".[9]

The Pact government – a political alliance of the Nationalist Party (NP) and Labour Party – also responded to the radicalisation of black and white labour movements in the 1920s. In this period communist influence in the Industrial and Commercial Workers' Union, founded in 1919 for black workers, became stronger.[10]

---

7. W.P. Visser, "Die Geskiedenis en Rol van Persorgane", pp. 368, 442–443; A. Van Deventer and P. Nel, "The State and 'Die Volk' Versus Communism, 1922–1941", *Politikon*, Vol. 17, No. 2, December 1990, pp. 64, 67, 74.

8. "The Menace of Red Misrule", *Facts and Figures for All,* Johannesburg and Germiston, c. 1923.

9. Ibid., pp. 11–19.

10. E. Roux, *Time Longer Than Rope,* pp. 161–175; S. Johns, *Raising the Red Flag. The International Socialist League and the Communist Party of South Africa, 1914–1932,* Bellville, 1995, pp. 95, 168–181.

In the hands of the state, anti-communist measures, according to Van Deventer and Nel, became part of the strategic means through which the working class movements, both black and white, were emasculated in order to provide a pliable source of skilled and unskilled labour for mining and industrial capitalism. The "Communist Peril" was used to justify the imposition of penalties on the "dissemination of foreign ideologies" amongst black workers. Legislation and prosecution in terms of it were employed to drive a wedge between white "leftist" trade unionists and black workers. This was bolstered by a slander campaign against whites who were noticeably members of the CPSA. Anti-communist sentiment was propagated and exploited to provide the state with the necessary means to curtail any perceived threat to white supremacy. For Van Deventer and Nel the origins of anti-communism were therefore coterminous with a comprehensive state strategy to safeguard white interests.[11]

The decision by the CPSA in 1925 to shift its focus and organisational activities from the white to the black proletariat, as well as its 1928 resolution, directed by the Comintern in Moscow, to pursue the goal of establishing a "Native" republic in South Africa, bolstered notions in the white establishment that the communists were fostering a black upheaval against white rule.[12]

Afrikaner nationalism and communism

In South African history the 1930s and 1940s are characterised in particular by the advent of Afrikaner political hegemony. Afrikaner literature of that period also reflects a reaction to the presumed "threats" of communism towards Afrikanerdom.

By the 1930s a fundamental tenet appears in the growing corpus of anti-communist literature produced by Afrikaner intellectuals in particular. Communism was increasingly being seen as a threat to race relations, and especially the continuation of white trusteeship. Blacks themselves were not regarded as the source of a possible disturbance of the paternalistic order of race relations. The real danger lay, so it was believed, with predominantly white communist agitators who could incite blacks against whites. Thus four themes emerged in the development of Afrikaner nationalism's production of anti-communist literature in the 1930s and 1940s. Firstly, the "Red Peril"

---

11. A. Van Deventer and P. Nel, "The State and 'Die Volk'", pp. 65, 78.

12. See S. Johns, *Raising the Red Flag*, pp. 162, 200–201.

was equated with the "Black Peril". Communists were depicted as proponents of racial equality and internationalism, and their principles were regarded as irreconcilable with Christian beliefs. Secondly, there was the danger of divisions among Afrikaner workers if some adhered to communism. Thirdly, given the role of a few prominent Jews within the CPSA and in labour organisations, the "Red Peril" and the "Black Peril" were also equated with the "Jewish Peril". Lastly, in their turn all these "perils" were equated with the danger of Soviet world domination.[13]

These themes were reflected in a concerted attempt of the NP and other Afrikaner nationalist organisations after 1936 to present a unified conception of the "communist menace" to the Afrikaner people and to *volkseenheid* (people's unity), and to attack communism's influence in the white labour movement. The background to this initiative was the formation of the South African Trades and Labour Council (SAT&LC), a trade union federation to which such important trade unions as the Mine Workers' Union (MWU) and the Garment Workers' Union (GWU) were affiliated. The SAT&LC facilitated the exposure of white trade unionists, including Afrikaners, to militant socialist ideas. Some of these Afrikaner workers were even sent to the Soviet Union in order to experience the benefits of a workers' state for themselves. Encouraged by the Comintern, left-wing labour organisations such as the SAT&LC were by the mid-1930s supporting the formation of the United People's Front (UPF) against Fascism, which was to include all members of the working class. This movement actively propagated the breaking down of racial barriers among the working class and promoted the inclusion of Afrikaans-speaking workers in the Front.

Given the prejudice of some Afrikaner intellectuals against the "threat" of non-racialism propagated by the communists, the events related above provided a trigger for the formation of Christian-nationalist alternatives to "communist" trade unions. Leading young Afrikaner cultural entrepreneurs such as Piet Meyer, Nico Diederichs, Eric Louw and Albert Hertzog – all members of the NP and the elitist Afrikaner Broederbond (Brotherhood) (AB) – returned from extensive stays in Europe and America, where they were exposed to extreme forms of anti-Bolshevik and anti-Semitic sentiments. They became the leading proponents of the idea that Afrikaner workers should be protected against the "threats" of liberal-capitalism and communism. Under

---

13. A. Van Deventer and P. Nel, "The State and 'Die Volk'", pp. 65, 70–71. For a detailed study of these arguments see A. Van Deventer, "Afrikaner Nationalist Politics and Anti-Communism, 1937–1945", MA thesis, University of Stellenbosch, 1991.

the guidance of Hertzog the Nasionale Raad van Trustees (National Council of Trustees) (NRT) was created in an effort to purify unions such as the MWU and the GWU of their "communistically inclined" Jewish leadership and to "save" Afrikaner workers from the "baneful influence" of communism and non-racialism.[14]

Consequently, anti-communist literature was produced to support these endeavours. A.J.G. Oosthuizen, a minister of the Nederduits Hervormde Kerk (NHK), wrote a booklet entitled *Kommunisme en die Vakunies* in support of the NRT's initiatives.[15] Oosthuizen wrote of the "dangerous ideology" of "Russian godlessness". The aim of the booklet was "to make our people [Afrikaners] aware of a great [communist] danger threatening us". Therefore the NRT's struggle against the GWU and its general secretary, Solly Sachs, a "communist Jew", was supported by the NHK. Oosthuizen inveighed against *Die Klerewerker*, the organ of the GWU, for inciting a class struggle between (Afrikaner) employees and employers. The Soviet Union was the centre of the "evil of communism" from where a world revolution against the existing (white) order, directed by the "Red Army", would be instigated.

In South Africa the communists, it was claimed, aimed at destroying religion, confiscating private property, overthrowing the state and creating a black republic where blacks and Coloureds "would be boss and govern". The danger lay particularly in "communist" trade union federations such as the SAT&LC and in its affiliated unions for miners, garment workers and builders that represented many Afrikaner workers. In conjunction with the CPSA these organisations tried to bring about equality between black and white. To fight communism a classless *volksosialisme*, which was "inherent in the character of the Afrikaner people", should replace the "evil" of exploitative capitalism. Therefore *volkseie* (people's own) Afrikaner trade unions, such as

---

14. A. Van Deventer and P. Nel, "The State and 'Die Volk'", pp. 71–73. Regarding the NRT's efforts to Afrikanerise the MWU and to fight the leadership of the GWU, see e.g. S. Sachs, *Rebels' Daughters*, Manchester, 1957; L. Naudé, *Dr. A. Hertzog, die Nasionale Party en die Mynwerker*, Pretoria, 1969; L. De Kock, "Die Stryd van die Afrikaner in die Suid-Afrikaanse Mynwerkersunie aan die Witwatersrand, 1936–1948", MA thesis, Rand Afrikaans University, 1983 and D. O'Meara, *Volkskapitalisme. Class, Capital and Ideology in the Development of Afrikaner Nationalism, 1934–1948*, Johannesburg, 1983. Regarding Hertzog's views on communism, and how these views equated with the "Red", "Black" and "Jewish Perils", see also A. Hertzog, "Toesprake van Dr. Albert Hertzog tussen die Jare 1930–1948", unpublished typescript.

15. Heidelberg, c. 1938.

those propagated by the NRT, should be established to counter all the above-mentioned evils.[16]

For Nico Diederichs, political science professor at the University of the Free State and future NP Minister of Finance, communism also implied the annihilation of the existing (capitalist) world order and represented an urge to destroy human institutions such as patriotism, privacy, the family and religion. To him it was clear that the spirit of the communists was the spirit of "Lucifer". According to Diederichs, many individuals, "mostly from the lower and illiterate classes", were already leavened with communist ideas – probably without knowing it. This state of affairs was encouraged by "agitators" who propagated the spread of "communist poison" among black and white.[17] Chapters of Diederichs's book were also published in *Die Huisgenoot*, a popular Afrikaans magazine. In the 1930s the literary contents of this weekly made it a highly esteemed publication as it was regarded as maintaining sound intellectual and academic standards, and in some Afrikaner circles it was even regarded as the "poor man's university".[18]

The "Red" and "Black Peril" themes repeatedly surfaced in the anti-communist publications of the period. F.J. van Rensburg, the leader of the Ossewa-Brandwag (Oxwagon Sentinel) (OB), a fascist Afrikaner cultural movement that gained short-lived popularity among Afrikaners in the 1930s and 1940s, emphasized that the OB, with its authoritarian ideology, offered the Afrikaner an alternative to the policies of racial equality espoused by communist ideology.[19]

By 1944 Piet Meyer, secretary of the NRT who was in later years to become the president of the AB and board chairman of the state-sponsored South African Broadcasting Corporation, toyed with the idea of a distinct form of Afrikaner socialism as an effective counter to the threat of communism.[20]

The NP also often linked the "Red Menace" and the "Black Peril". Early in 1943 Eric Louw wrote a pamphlet entitled *The Communist Danger in South*

---

16. A.J.G. Oosthuizen, *Kommunisme en die Vakunies,* pp. 1–22.

17. N. Diederichs, *Die Kommunisme. Sy Teorie en Taktiek,* Bloemfontein, 1938, pp. 150–153, 172–173.

18. See C.F.J. Muller, *Sonop in die Suide. Geboorte en Groei van die Nasionale Pers 1915–1948,* Cape Town, 1990, pp. 563–572.

19. J.F. van Rensburg, *Die Ossewa-Brandwag en die Kommunisme,* Johannesburg, 1943, pp. 15, 20.

20. See *Die Stryd van die Afrikanerwerker. Die Vooraand van ons Sosiale Vrywording,* Pro Ecclesia, Stellenbosch, 1944.

Africa. In this document Louw set out the party's objections to communist ideology. Communists believed in racial equality and miscegenation. Moreover, they were atheists and were spreading their propaganda among blacks. Thus communists were a threat to the survival of both white civilisation and Christianity in South Africa.[21] The NP premises were put into practice after the party came to power in 1948. Louw, who became South Africa's Foreign Minister in 1948, was instrumental in the closing of the Soviet consulates (established in 1942) in Pretoria and Cape Town, and in unilaterally severing diplomatic relations with the Soviet Union. According to Philip Nel, the "Black Peril" thus finally fused with the "Red Peril" in official thinking.[22]

The accounts of the role of prominent leaders of the CPSA in the freedom struggle that appeared in published biographies and reminiscences from the 1940s onwards also strengthened anti-communist perceptions of communist subversion and agitation intended to foment revolt among blacks against white rule.[23]

An interesting effort to counter the Afrikaner anti-communist rhetoric was a CPSA pamphlet by an Afrikaner communist, Danie Du Plessis.[24] Du Plessis was the secretary of the Paper Workers' Union and the organiser of the Building Workers' Union. Because of the widespread unemployment during the Great Depression of the early 1930s he became disillusioned with capitalism. For Du Plessis capitalism's only intention was to exploit black and white workers and to prevent worker solidarity through racial segregation. In order to generate maximum profits industrial capitalism introduced poll and hut taxes in the black reserves, which had the effect of forcing rural blacks to seek employment in the cities as "cheap slave labour" under the oppressive pass laws. Therefore black workers were not the white workers' enemies but rather their allies. According to Du Plessis, the Afrikaner's religion was not threatened by communism as the church "still existed" under communist rule in Soviet Russia. Afrikaners would only be able to maintain and strengthen

---

21. Quoted by N.M. Stultz, *Afrikaner Politics in South Africa, 1934–1948,* Berkeley, 1974, p. 122.
22. P. Nel, *A Soviet Embassy in Pretoria? The Changing Soviet Approach to South Africa,* Cape Town, 1990, p. 2–3.
23. See e.g. R.K. Cope, *Comrade Bill;* E. Roux, *S.P. Bunting: A Political Biography,* Cape Town, 1944; W.H. Harrison, *Memoirs of a Socialist in South Africa, 1903–1947;* and E. Roux, *Time Longer Than Rope.*
24. *Waarom Ek 'n Kommunis Is,* Cape Town, c. 1940.

their language and culture by forming a non-racial working class in South Africa.[25]

Afrikaner churches and communism

The avowed atheism of international communism understandably touched a raw nerve in the Christian-nationalist ethos of the traditional Afrikaner churches, which in turn stimulated a plethora of studies on communism from an ecclesiastical perspective. These studies reveal the construction of a "volkslaer" discourse. The church would act as a vanguard to shield the Afrikaner people from the "Red Peril" and its offshoots.

Afrikaner cultural entrepreneurs who endeavoured to Afrikanerise certain trade unions and purify them from "communist" influences found staunch allies in the traditional Afrikaner churches. In May 1937 the NHK appointed a special commission of inquiry to report on communism and its activities in the South African trade unions. Eventually Dr H.P. Wolmarans, an ordained clergyman of the church and Professor of Theology at the University of Pretoria, compiled a brochure on the findings of the commission of inquiry, entitled *Kommunisme en die Suid-Afrikaanse Vakunies*.[26] Wolmarans came to similar conclusions on the trade unions as Reverend Oosthuizen had done in *Kommunisme en die Vakunies*. The SAT&LC connived with the "Moscow-ordained" UPF to promote communism and these "pro-soviet" organisations planned to deliver the South African people to Russia. Affiliation to the SAT&LC would imply very negative consequences for the interests of Afrikaner workers, "all" of whom were members of the Afrikaner Protestant churches. Wolmarans's publication was very defamatory about Solly Sachs of the GWU. Sachs was accused of being the main instigator of the SAT&LC and the pro-Soviet front in South Africa, as well as of manipulating and alienating Afrikaner female members of the GWU from their people.[27] Sachs, however, sued Wolmarans for slander and the latter settled out of court for £300 damages.[28]

---

25. D. Du Plessis, *Waarom Ek 'n Kommunis Is*, pp. 1–15.
26. Johannesburg, 1939. See also E.S. Sachs, *The Choice Before South Africa,* London, 1952, pp. 58–59, 173–174.
27. H.P. Wolmarans, *Kommunisme en die Suid-Afrikaanse Vakunies*, p. 2, et seq.
28. E.S. Sachs, *The Choice Before South Africa*, pp. 59, 174; E.S. Sachs, *Rebels' Daughters*, pp. 141–142.

In a booklet dedicated to female social workers of the Dutch Reformed Church (DRC) Norval Geldenhuys revisited the history of the destruction of Russian Christianity under communism, also briefly dealt with in the writings of authors such as Chilvers, Oosthuizen and Diederichs.[29] For Geldenhuys the two "most explosive danger points" in the existence of the Afrikaner people were the poor white problem and the "native problem". The church had a duty to carry out the social upliftment of the Afrikaner poor. Neglect of this duty had already resulted in many female Afrikaner workers joining the ranks of the "communist" GWU. Geldenhuys was also of the opinion that the church and the Afrikaner people should "convince" the black population that the whites' policy of trusteeship and racial segregation "honestly" catered for their social needs. If the church failed in this mission, "unscrupulous communist agitators" would succeed in turning black against white.[30]

From the 1940s onwards the Afrikaner churches – the DRC, the NHK and the Hervormde Kerk – would organise a flurry of anti-communist conferences and symposia to try and investigate the perceived threat of communism to Christianity in South Africa and to find ways to combat this. In October 1946 the Anti-kommunistiese Aksiekommissie (Anti-communist Action Committee), or Antikom, was founded at an ecclesiastical congress on communism held in Pretoria under the auspices of the DRC. Apparently this initiative was conceived within the ranks of the NRT. Some of the most prominent and influential Afrikaner political, cultural, intellectual and church leaders would serve on Antikom. The constitution of Antikom entailed the following, among other things: combating the communist way of life; the promotion of Christian-nationalist trade unionism among the white workers of South Africa; and influencing the black population in the religious, social, educational, economic and other spheres of life in order to woo them to the Christian-nationalist viewpoint on racial apartheid and to combat ideologies opposing such views.[31]

In April 1964 Antikom organised a *Volkskongres* (People's Congress) in Pretoria, attended by 2428 delegates, on the theme "Christianity against Communism". The object of the *Volkskongres* was to alert all whites, not just Afrikaners, to the alleged perils of communist subversion in South Africa.

---

29. *Die Kommunistiese Aanslag teen die Kerk*, Christen-Studentevereniging van Suid-Afrika, Stellenbosch, 1947, p. 1, et seq.

30. N. Geldenhuys, *Die Kommunistiese Aanslag teen die Kerk*, pp. 59, 67–69, 77–79.

31. S.J. Botha, et al., *Bewaar Jou Erfenis. Simposium oor Kommunisme,* Antikom, Port Elizabeth, 1968, pp. 11–15.

The 1964 *Volkskongres* established a standing body, the National Council Against Communism. In 1966 the National Council sponsored an "International Symposium on Communism", held in Pretoria. The chairman was the Reverend J.D. Vorster, the Moderator of the DRC and brother of B.J. Vorster, who would succeed H.F. Verwoerd as Prime Minister of South Africa. The main speaker was Major Edgar Bundy, executive secretary of the Anti-Communist Church League of America. Another Antikom symposium on communism was held in Port Elizabeth in 1968. Antikom also regarded its calling in combating communism to be educational. Therefore published conference proceedings and other works were commissioned for public dissemination. In this way the "Red Peril" theme was kept alive.[32]

The 1964 congress sported a very striking emblem – a hand grasping a dagger (representing the Volkskongres) stabbing a red hammer and sickle octopus draped over South Africa. Even before the congress started fierce polemics broke out in both the English and Afrikaans press as to whether the event, which was referred to by some papers as "religious McCarthyism", should be held at all. In an effort to demonise communism speakers at the congress concentrated on a theological analysis of the "lies" of communism, communist "brain-washing", the "communist onslaught" on the church and how communism was "devouring" and "enslaving" free nations on a worldwide scale. In South Africa the "danger" of communism was not the intention to destroy the church, but rather to infiltrate it and other institutions in the broader society, as well as the youth and the education system in order to transform them into "tools of the communist revolutionary programme". An "onslaught" was directed especially against Afrikaner churches, which represented the majority of South African whites, in order to render them "defenceless" against "liberal" and "communist indoctrination". South Africa was therefore caught up in a "death struggle" against communism and it was the task of the congress to find a "remedy" against it. In reaction to the critique in the liberal press – namely, that the congress would be the prelude to a witch-hunt of communists – some speakers retorted that such a critique showed that the communists were leading the press by the nose.[33]

32. See S.J Botha, et al., *Volkskongres oor Kommunisme,* Pretoria, 1964, pp. 5, 271–272; S.J. Botha, et al., *Bewaar Jou Erfenis,* pp. 7, 16; N.M. Stultz, *Afrikaner Politics in South Africa,* pp. 178–179 and C. Dalcanton, *The Afrikaners of South Africa: A Case Study of Identity Formation and Change,* Pittsburgh, 1973, p. 239.

33. See S.J. Botha, et al., *Volkskongres oor Kommunisme,* Pretoria, 1964.

As mentioned above, the 1966 symposium concentrated on communism in an international context. Speakers came from France, Hungary, Cuba and the USA, among other places. Three major themes were discussed. Firstly, the African National Congress (ANC) and the South African Communist Party's (SACP) insurgence and sabotage activities to overthrow the white government were dealt with by Major-General H.J. van den Bergh, Chief of the South African Security Police. A second theme dealt with methods, strategies and actions by Soviet Russia to take over countries such as Hungary and Cuba.

Thirdly, the 1960s were the heyday of *verkramptheid* (arch-conservatism) in Afrikaner politics. Within this context, as in 1964, the Reverend J.D. Vorster repeated his attacks on liberalism for its "tolerance" of communism. Liberalism was pointed out as a so-called "Fifth Column" of communism. In addition, Vorster attacked what he called "decadent art" and castigated new progressive developments in Afrikaans literature. These liberal tendencies should all be combated, Vorster emphasised, because they undermined moral values that would make the Afrikaner people susceptible to communism.[34]

Vorster was also the keynote speaker at the 1968 Antikom symposium on communism. He asserted that the church was "sentenced to death" by this ideology. Vorster again fulminated against liberalism for doing "valuable pre-labour" on behalf of communism. He even reproached the South African Academy for Science and Arts – the elite academic institution of the Afrikaner establishment – for awarding literary prizes to liberal Afrikaner writers whose work "softened" Afrikaners towards communism.[35] Other papers dealt with how communism subtly attempted to infiltrate areas such as labour movements, education and the media. Conference resolutions were adopted, *inter alia,* to support the underground church behind the Iron Curtain and to request the government to promulgate legislation against multiracial trade unions.[36]

Other Antikom publications followed in similar vein. In the 1950s Piet Meyer published a pamphlet containing a concise history of communist ac-

---

34. See J.D. Vorster, et al., *Oorlog om die Volksiel. Referate gelewer by die Internasionale Simposium oor Kommunisme*, Pretoria, 1966. The CPSA was banned in 1950. After its reconstitution in 1953 it became known as the South African Communist Party (SACP). With regard to the "danger" of liberalism for Afrikanerdom, as it would promote the communist cause, see G.D. Scholtz, *Die Bedreiging van die Liberalisme*, Johannesburg, 1966.

35. See S.J. Botha, et al., *Bewaar Jou Erfenis*, pp. 8, 20–23.

36. Ibid., pp. 35–161.

tivities in South Africa. The cover page displayed the ominous spectre of a Bolshevist looming like a giant over a Christian city in South Africa. Wielding a hammer and a sickle the giant went about destroying the city. Meyer illustrated how the SACP's policy was repeatedly defined and dictated by Moscow. According to Meyer, the Russian consulate, established in Pretoria in the 1940s, was undoubtedly the centre of "a communist campaign in the Union [of South Africa]".[37]

In the spirit of the resolve of organisations such as Antikom to inform and educate especially Afrikaners on the "communist threat" to South Africa, Fred Schwarz's popular book, *You Can Trust a Communist (to be Communist)*, was also translated into Afrikaans by Timo Kriel.[38] Schwarz's work was originally published by the Christian Anti-Communist Crusade in America.[39]

During the 1970s Antikom's publications also started to concentrate on the "Yellow Peril", or Chinese communism, in Africa. At the time 15.000 Chinese "communists" were constructing the Tanzam railway line between Tanzania and Zambia and "tried to control black African states". By means of material assistance and military aid communist countries in Europe and Asia were systematically attempting to influence African countries north of the Limpopo in the direction of communism. White South Africa was the ultimate goal of this Soviet-led communist world strategy. Therefore it was the "responsibility" of Christians in South Africa to combat the threat of this "communist onslaught". On behalf of all the people of Africa communism was to be prevented from controlling southern Africa and therefore also the Atlantic and Indian Oceans and South Africa's mineral wealth.[40]

By this time the Theological Seminary of the DRC at the University of Stellenbosch and that of the NHK at the Potchefstroom University for Christian Higher Education had started to produce brochures of lecture series to theology students and church ministers on Marxism and Soviet-communism.[41]

37. *Die Hand van Moskou in Suid-Afrika. 'n Sonderlinge Geskiedenis van Ongelooflike Gebeurtenisse,* Pretoria, c. 1950, pp. 3–30.
38. The Afrikaans translation was entitled *Jy Kan Die Kommuniste Vertrou (..om presies te doen wat hulle sê!),* Roodepoort, 1962.
39. See H.R. Pike, *A History of Communism in South Africa,* p. 568.
40. P.J. Meyer, et al., *Die Rooi Gevaar is Hier. Kommunistiese Aanslag op ons Land en Gees,* Pretoria, c. 1971, pp. 5, 7–25, 61–65. See also J. Du Plessis, *Kommunisitese Vrede of Christelike Stryd,* Bloemfontein, 1978.
41. See D.J. Kotzé, et al., *Kommunisme. Die Stryd om die Mens,* Cape Town, 1978 and J.A. Du Plessis, *Die Filosofie van die Grafskrif! 'n Inleiding tot die Verstaan van die*

At times Afrikaner churches went to absurd lengths in their quest to demonise communism by means of the public dissemination of anti-communist literature. In 1983 Biblecor, a subsidiary of the DRC, published a Bible correspondence course compiled by P.J. Rossouw. This 68-page booklet purported to present to correspondents a "survey of communism, its doctrine, aims and how it functioned in everyday life". However, its contents reflected superficial and random information on Karl Marx, Lenin, communist ideology, Soviet economic policy and the SACP, and was a very poor attempt to diffuse instant knowledge on communism. Interspersed with biblical texts and references, as well as photos of Marx, Lenin, Stalin, a general meeting of the Russian Communist Party and even of a Russian anti-ballistic missile paraded on Red Square in Moscow, the purpose of this reader was to guide correspondents to the inevitable conclusion that "atheist communism" should be combated as there could be no peace between the latter and Christianity. It was also based on the contentious supposition that, having completed the course, correspondents would have "a [reasonable] knowledge of communist ideology and policies in Russia and South Africa" and be able "to unmask the lies of communism". Correspondents would also be able to "explain the calling of the church regarding communism and its breeding-ground in South Africa and how to contain it".[42]

The publication of ecclesiastical anti-communist rhetoric probably culminated in Henry Pike's *A History of Communism in South Africa* published by Christian Mission International of South Africa.[43] The narrative of this comprehensive 601-page study, illustrated with more than 400 photos, is marred time and again, however, by Pike's subjective anti-communist remarks and commentary that reduce the academic merit of the book to a large extent. The text is also interspersed with biblical texts and references. The central theme of Pike's rhetoric is that the international community at large, liberals, international finance and the United Nations plotted with "Marxist-inspired" organisations such as the SACP, the ANC, etc. to weaken an anti-communist South Africa against a communist "Red onslaught".[44]

Indeed, Pike, a conservative American Baptist missionary who had lived in South Africa for ten years, states emphatically on the dust cover and in his introduction that he was "totally opposed to the left…and every shape, form

---

Sowjet-Kommunisme, Potchefstroom, c. 1970.

42. See *Die Christen en Kommunisme*, Wellington, 1983.

43. Germiston, 1985.

44. H.R. Pike, *A History of Communism*, pp. 548–553.

and fashion of Marxism-Leninism". He categorically declares that it was impossible to write about South African communism from an objective point of view as the "hellish anti-God philosophy" of communism "is inimical to all forms of decent human society". He makes no apologies for these statements, Pike continues, and only regrets that more of the Bible's message of hope could not have been woven into the narrative. The book was intended "primarily for purposes of instruction and education regarding the subject of communism in South Africa and related events". It did not purport to be a definitive, scientific analysis of the South African communist movement. Therefore the book would be "a pure delight to the conservative Christian". Pike also declared that to "seek communism as the answer to the system of apartheid is to slide from the smoke and pain of the mythical purgatory to the fires and damnation of Hell".[45]

South Africa and the internationalisation of Soviet-communism

From the 1950s onwards, as the Cold War became hotter, anti-communist rhetoric in the South African historiography gradually shifted from an internal focus on the danger of the "Red Peril" to Afrikaner and white interests towards the threat posed by international Soviet communism in Africa on a global scale and South Africa in a regional context. As in the case of the ecclesiastical publications, anti-communist history production also began to refer to the "Yellow Peril" that posed a threat to Africa and to South Africa in particular. Soviet Russia, however, remained the central focus of the international approach to communism.[46]

In his 1954 publication on the future of the Afrikaner the renowned Afrikaner historian and journalist, G.D. Scholtz, pointed out that international Soviet policy posed "a danger of Communism in Africa sweeping from Cape Town to the Mediterranean".[47] In this context Russia also presented a "great threat" to Western Europe. In any conflict between democratic and communist powers Africa maintained a strategically important flank position on behalf of the democratic powers in Europe. The Afrikaner's fatherland was an

45. Ibid., pp. xvi-xviii, p. 527.
46. See for instance C. Dalcanton, *The Afrikaners of South Africa*, p. 242 and *Report of the Select Committee on Suppression of Communism Act Enquiry*, Parow, 1953, pp. 150,170–171, 193–194.
47. G.D. Scholtz, *Het Die Afrikaanse Volk 'n Toekoms?*, Johannesburg, 1954.

"outpost" of Western civilisation in Africa. As such the future might demand from Afrikaners that they fight Russian communists side by side with Western Europeans in order to protect their European heritage in Africa.[48]

Scholtz was fascinated with the power of the Soviet Union and the worldwide expansion of the communist ideology that diametrically opposed the Afrikaners' nationalist and apartheid ideology. Following on from *Het Die Afrikaanse Volk 'n Toekoms?* he published a comprehensive 561-page book entitled *Die Stryd om die Wêreld*.[49] The book expounds on the struggle for world domination between East and West in which, according to Scholtz, the fate of the Afrikaner was intimately involved. Scholtz pitches Soviet communism against non-communist countries in Africa, Asia and Europe, and states that the non-communist countries under the leadership of America should make an all-out effort to check the advance of communism.[50]

The 1960s was a productive period for "Red Peril" and "Total Onslaught" historiography. Christian-nationalist-orientated publications by academic pedagogues, intended to inform and educate Afrikaners about "unmasking the falseness of communism" and to prepare them for the "struggle" against this ideology, were still being produced.[51] Likewise anti-communist rhetoric from a Christian-nationalist pedagogical perspective was produced in dissertations at Afrikaans-speaking universities;[52] in extreme cases these studies sometimes bordered on absurdity. For instance, the Faculty of Education at the University of Stellenbosch produced an MA thesis on Marxism and South African school cadets.[53]

In 1967 the security police succeeded in the sensational capture of Yuriy Loginov, a Soviet KGB agent.[54] W.G. Pretorius's study devoted a chapter to

---

48. Ibid., pp. 21, 37, 42–43 ,56, 59. See also F.A. Van Jaarsveld, "G.D. Scholtz se Oordeel oor die Toekoms van die Afrikaner teen die Agtergrond van Wêreldgebeure", *Historia*, Vol. 38, No. 2, November 1993, p. 7.

49. Johannesburg, 1962.

50. F. A. Van Jaarsveld, "G.D. Scholtz se Oordeel", *Historia*, Vol. 38, No. 2, November 1993, p. 8; T.S. van Rooyen, "Boekbespreking: 'Scholtz, G.D.: Die Stryd om die Wêreld'", *Historia*, Vol. 7, No. 4, December 1962, pp. 284–287.

51. See e.g. W.G. Pretorius, *Die Kommunisme. Fabel en Feit,* Johannesburg, 1968 and G. Cronjé (ed.), *Kommunisme: Teorie en Praktyk,* Pretoria, 1969.

52. See e.g. G.E.P. Nel, "Kommunistiese Infiltrasie: 'n Ontleding van die Taktiek in Teorie en Praktyk", MA thesis, University of Pretoria, 1973.

53. J.H. Du Plessis, "Marxisme en Skoolkadette in Suid Afrikaanse Konteks. 'n Studie in die Fundamentele Opvoedkunde", 1988.

54. H.R. Pike, *A History of Communism in South Africa*, pp. 464–467. In January 1981 another KGB agent, Major Alexsei Kozlov was captured in Johannesburg, P.

the training and *modus operandi* of the *Red [Russian] Spy* and to the inner workings of the KGB.[55] The central motive behind these works seemed to be to demonise organisations in the armed struggle against apartheid, especially the ANC, and to portray them as puppets directed by the initiatives and tactics of the SACP.

In his book *The Red Trap. Communism and Violence in South Africa* (appropriately provided with a red cover to illustrate the point)[56] Chris Vermaak, a South African Security Police officer, asserted that a Soviet-inspired communist plot was being hatched to foster anti-apartheid sabotage, subversion and revolution in South Africa. Agents of the CPSA infiltrated organisations such as the National Union of South African Students, the South African Indian Congress, the ANC, *Umkhonto we Sizwe*, the PAC, the anti-apartheid Congress of Democrats (COD), the South African Congress of Trade Unions and even the South African Jewish Board of Deputies.

The objectives of the Freedom Charter, drawn up at Kliptown south of Johannesburg in 1955 by the so-called Congress of the People – a gathering of anti-apartheid organisations – carried "the unmistakable stamp of Communism" as the SACP acted in "international cohesion with Russia". According to Vermaak, the communists instigated the 1946 strike of the African Mine Workers' Union and the 1952 Defiance Campaign against apartheid. They also tried to incite the Bantustans against white authority. And at the 1956 Treason Trials Bram Fischer, in accordance with his communist convictions, succeeded in obtaining acquittals for the defendants.[57] A security police document also maintained that liberation movements such as the ANC were controlled by the SACP, but emphasised that the latter was "subservient to international [meaning Russian] communism".[58]

An interesting "Red plot" revelation was Gerard Ludi's *Operation Q-18*.[59] Ludi was a South African Secret Service agent who had infiltrated the SACP

Nel, *A Soviet Embassy in Pretoria?*, p. 27 and in 1983 a senior South African Navy officer, Commodore Dieter Gerhardt, and his wife, Ruth, were arrested and convicted for passing South African military secrets via the KGB to the Soviet Union, Pike, pp. 524–525. Translated KGB means "Committee for State Security".

55. See W.G. Pretorius, *Die Kommunisme. Fabel en Feit*, pp. 332–376.
56. Johannesburg, 1966.
57. C. Vermaak, *The Red Trap*, p. 14, et seq.
58. See J.J.P. Brümmer, "The Communist Party of South Africa", unpublished typescript, 1967.
59. Cape Town, 1969.

and even managed to visit the Soviet Union to attend the Moscow Peace Congress in 1962. He was also one of the key witnesses who unmasked Bram Fischer as a communist, which led to the latter's successful conviction. According to Ludi, the ANC was "Moscow run", while *Poqo*, the military wing of the PAC, operated "under the aegis of Peking" (the capital of communist China).[60]

The focus of anti-communist literature was adjusted once again in the post-1960s era. From the 1970s onwards many senior South African security and military officers underwent training in strategic studies at military institutions in Western countries such as Britain. From a military point of view South Africa was now being perceived from its strategic global position *vis-à-vis* Soviet and Chinese strategic intentions.[61]

The military assessment of South Africa's changing strategic position in relation to communist intentions also permeated "civilian" anti-communist literature in the 1970s, as was already evident from Antikom's publications in that period. South Africa's control of the Cape sea route was regarded as "of the utmost importance" to her Western European trading partners. The country was portrayed as an anti-communist bastion of democracy in Southern Africa which was feeling the pinch of the "approaching" communist influence. Therefore the discourse of the anti-communist publications of this period shifted accordingly from the "Red Peril" inside South Africa to the "Soviet" and "Red Chinese Menace" and expansionism in African states bordering white South Africa.[62]

---

60. Ibid., p. 6, et seq. For arguments similar to those of Vermaak and Ludi on the relationship between the communists and the liberation movements, see e.g. E. S. Munger, *African Field Reports*, pp. 645–686; G. Ludi and B. Grobbelaar, *The Amazing Mr Fischer*, Cape Town, 1966, p. 29, et seq; N. Weyl, *Traitors' End. The Rise and Fall of the Communist Movement in Southern Africa*, Cape Town, 1970, p. 96, et seq; J.D. Koster, "Die Invloed van die Suid-Afrikaanse Kommunistiese Party (SAKP) op die Rewolusionêre Strategie van die African National Congress (ANC)", MA thesis, Rand Afrikaans University, 1983, pp. 105–138; and Bureau for Information, *Talking with the ANC*, Pretoria, 1986.

61. Communiqué from Professor Philip Nel, former Director of the Institute for Soviet Studies. See also G. Cronjé (ed.), *Kommunisme: Teorie en Praktyk*, pp. 150–201.

62. See e.g. F.R. Metrowich, *Africa and Communism. A Study of Successes, Set-Backs and Stooge States*, Johannesburg, 1967, pp. 9–33, 58 et seq; G. Ludi, *Operation Q-018*, pp. 217–218; N. Weyl, *Traitors' End*, pp. 29–40, 170–187; H.A. Wessels, "Die Stryd van die Republiek van Suid-Afrika teen 'Kommunistiese' Imperialisme – 'n Staatsfilosofiese Studie", PhD thesis, University of the Orange Free State, 1972; C.F. de Villiers, et al., *Die Kommunisme in Aksie*, Cape Town, 1975, pp. 12–13, 64–108, 133–136; I. Greig, *The Communist Challenge to Africa. An Analysis of Contemporary Soviet,*

The anti-communist point of view claimed that apart from physical aggression, international communism also "threatened" South Africa by means of a "psychological onslaught". In an effort to "undermine" South Africa and bring her to her knees, the country's racial problems were internationalised by communists via the media in order to influence world opinion negatively.[63] Against the background of the fall of the Portuguese colonies in Angola and Mozambique in 1974, Zimbabwe's independence in 1980 and increasing black unrest and ANC acts of sabotage inside South Africa afterwards, P.W. Botha's NP government thus became convinced that an internationally co-ordinated "total onslaught" was being directed against the country on all fronts: politically, economically and militarily.[64]

From the mid-1980s South African historiography showed a marked deviation from the anti-communist rhetoric of the previous decades and from the attempts to demonise organisations such as the SACP and the ANC. Academics began to analyse the policies and relationships between the SACP and the ANC in a more sober and objective manner in terms of the historical realities of South Africa. Soviet intentions towards South Africa were treated more realistically as support, via the SACP, for the black population's legitimate struggle against racial discrimination and political oppression, rather than as an aggressive "Red Menace" poised to force the country into a communist empire. Likewise the ANC was portrayed as a national liberation movement in its own right rather than as a puppet of the SACP.[65]

It is interesting to note that throughout the 1960s, 1970s, 1980s and even into the 1990s a fair number of pro-communist publications appeared, ranging from biographies on prominent South African communists to histories and published documents of the SACP, almost as if to counter the continual production of anti-communist rhetoric in the corresponding period.[66]

Chinese and Cuban Policies, Sandton, 1977; C. Groenewald, *Kommunisme in Afrika*, c. 1979, pp. 1–2, 12–40.

63. C.F. de Villiers, et al., *Die Kommunisme in Aksie*, pp. 116–121.

64. *The Citizen*, 22 March 1980, p. 8; *The Citizen*, 22 August 1980, p. 6; P. Nel, *A Soviet Embassy in Pretoria?* pp. 8, 16, 6–47, 96–97, 131.

65. See D.J. Kotzé II, "'n Analise van die Ideologie van die Suid-Afrikaanse Kommunistiese Party, 1950–1984", MA thesis, University of Stellenbosch, 1985, pp. 339–347, 516–521; P. Nel, *A Soviet Embassy in Pretoria?*, p. 8 et seq; W. Esterhuyse en P. Nel (eds), *Die ANC*, Cape Town, 1990, p. 25 et seq.

66. See e.g. H.J. and R.E. Simons, *Class and Colour in South Africa, 1850–1950;* E&W Roux, *Rebel Pity. The Life of Eddie Roux,* London, 1970; A. Lerumo, *Fifty Fighting Years. The Communist Party of South Africa 1921–1971,* London, 1971; B. Bunting,

The University of Stellenbosch and the Institute for the Study of Marxism

Given the South African fascination with communism over such a long period, it follows that this phenomenon would eventually also attract serious attention from academic historians. As early as the 1964 *Volkskongres* on communism A.M. van Schoor, editor of *Die Vaderland*, an Afrikaans daily, already advocated the establishment of chairs at (Afrikaans-speaking) universities "to study world politics with special reference to Communism".[67]

From 1976 Dirk Kotzé, history professor at the University of Stellenbosch, began to lobby for the establishment of an "Institute for the Study of Marxism". At that stage, Kotzé argued, communism was an extremely topical issue for South Africa. In order to "combat" it effectively, a "thorough knowledge of communist theory and tactics" by way of a scientific approach was essential. At the time no institute existed in South Africa where material on communism could be collected and studied in a systematic and comprehensive manner. According to Kotzé, the Department of History at Stellenbosch was at that stage the only academic institution of its kind in South Africa to offer extensive courses, at both under-graduate and post-graduate level, on communism and on the histories of the Soviet Union and Red China. In addition, the departments of Philosophy, Political Science, Economics, Theology, African Studies and Sociology also dealt with aspects of communist ideology in their syllabi. For Kotzé, therefore, the University of Stellenbosch was the most suitable academic institution in South Africa to launch the proposed institute.[68]

Moses Kotane. *South African Revolutionary,* London, 1975; B. Bunting (ed.), *South African Communists Speak. Documents from the History of the South African Communist Party 1915–1980,* London, 1981; S. Forman & A. Odendaal (eds), *A Trumpet from the Rooftops. The Selected Writings of Lionel Forman,* London, 1992; B. Hirson & G.A. Williams, *The Delegate for Africa. David Ivon Jones, 1883–1924,* London, 1995 and B. Bunting (ed.), *Letters to Rebecca. South African Communist Leader SP Bunting to his Wife 1917–1934,* Bellville, 1996. Although not strictly falling into the pro-communist category the 1995 publication of Sheridan Johns's 1965 PhD thesis on the history of South African socialism and communism to 1932, *Raising the Red Flag,* as well as the MA thesis of Alan Brooks, "From Class Struggle to National Liberation: The Communist Party of South Africa, 1940 to 1950", University of Sussex, 1967, should also be mentioned here.

67. S.J. Botha, et al., *Volkskongres oor Kommunisme,* p. 217.

68. Institute for Soviet Studies University of Stellenbosch (hereafter ISSUS) Ms 368, File "Stigting": D.J. Kotzé-Registrateur Akademies, 11.8.1978, p. 2; Ibid., D.J. Kotzé-F. Davin, 4.5.1979; Ibid., Memorandum oor die Skepping van 'n Instituut vir die Studie

Dirk Kotzé was probably the most prolific South African historian on the subject of communism. From 1954 to 1956 he studied communism and nationalism as forces shaping history at the Vrije and Gemeentelijke Universities of Amsterdam under the renowned Dutch Marxist historian Jan Romein. He also studied at the Universities of Bonn and West Berlin, and in 1964 he studied Marxism and socialism at the Institute for Social History in Amsterdam.[69] In *Die Kommunisme Deel 1: Die Klassieke Marxisme* Kotzé wrote biographies on Karl Marx and Friedrich Engels and explained classic Marxist philosophy.[70] In 1970 Kotzé published his third volume on nationalism as a historical factor, entitled *Nasionalisme en Kommunisme*. In this book he explains how nationalism was "used" by communism to advance its own cause in Soviet Russia, Yugoslavia and Red China.[71] This was followed by a booklet, *Soeklig op die Kommunisme,* which focused on the origins of Marxism, the basic principles of communism, Soviet and Chinese communism, and Soviet interest in South Africa, and provided a concise history of communism in South Africa.[72]

Kotzé also wrote a two-part series on the history of communism in South Africa for the journal of the South African Academy for Science and Arts.[73] In 1979 Kotzé produced *Communism and South Africa,* which was an augmented version of his 1977 Afrikaans publication *Kommunisme Vandag.*[74] Here Kotzé discusses the nature of communism, orthodox Marxism, Lenin-

van die Marxisme, pp. 3–5; Ibid., Memorandun Insake die Stigting vir die Studie van Marxisme, Julie 1979; *Eikestadnuus,* 7.9.1979, pp. 1, 4.

69. F.A. Van Jaarsveld, "Obituary: Dirk Jacobus Kotzé (1927–1992)", *Historia*, Vol. 37, No. 2, November 1992, pp. 1–2; P.H. Kapp, "Verantwoorde Verlede. 'n Historiografiese Studie: Die Verhaal van die Studie van Geskiedenis aan die Universiteit Stellenbosch, 1866–2000", Unpublished monograph, 2004, pp. 89–94.

70. Cape Town , 1965.

71. Cape Town, 1970.

72. Cape Town, 1972.

73. D.J. Kotzé, "Die Kommunisme in Suid-Afrika: Verlede, Hede en Toekoms. Deel I: Die Verlede en die Hede", *Tydskrif vir Geesteswetenskappe*, Vol. 16, Issue 2, 1976, pp. 65–76 and D.J. Kotzé, "Die Kommunisme in Suid-Afrika: Verlede, Hede en toekoms. II. Die Toekoms, met besondere verwysing na die Bantoegebiede", *Tydskrif vir Geesteswetenskappe*, Vol. 16, Issue 3, 1976, pp. 119–125. G.A. Rauche published an article on the phenomenon of world communism in the same journal but regarded Chinese communism to be a greater "threat" to South Africa than Soviet communism. See "Die Verskynsel van die Wêreldkommunisme", *Tydskrif vir Geesteswetenskappe*, Vol. 14, Issue 1, 1974, pp. 3–15.

74. Cape Town 1979 and 1977, respectively.

ism, Stalinism, Trotskyism, Maoism, neo-Marxism, the relations between the Soviet Union and Red China as well as communism's attitude to war and peace, religion, nationalism and Pan-Africanism.[75]

On 1 April 1980 the Institute for the Study of Marxism at the University of Stellenbosch (ISMUS) was officially launched. Professor D. J. Kotzé was its first Director.

According to its introductory brochure, ISMUS intended, inter alia, "to stimulate systematic, interdisciplinary research". Its aims were related:

> ... to the conviction that in the academic community in South Africa in general there is a lack of reliable, non-partisan research on Marxism and its relevance for the South African situation.[76]

ISMUS's objectives, among others, were to collect source material on Marxism and communism in general; in depth research of communism in Southern Africa through interdisciplinary research projects and to serve the state and approved institutions in supplying scientifically controlled information on communist theory, strategy and tactics.[77]

Although ISMUS claimed to have a neutral approach towards the study of communism, some members of the multi-discipline Board of Control[78] still adhered to the stereotyped anti-communist paradigm. Kotzé, for instance, regarded Soviet and Red Chinese expansionism in Africa and influence among liberation movements in Mozambique, Angola and Zambia as a prelude to world domination. Therefore communism presented "essentially a national danger" to South Africa.[79] According to Kotzé communism could effectively be combated by means of a counter-campaign involving a national security strategy. Knowledge of the aims, strategies and characteristics of communism was the key to combating this ideology. The forces of all South African population groups "fundamentally opposed to communism" should be mustered and the non-communist world should be approached to prevent the total international isolation of South Africa.

---

75. See D.J. Kotzé, *Communism and South Africa*, p. 1, et seq. Kotzé also wrote numerous press articles and gave several public and radio talks on communism.

76. ISSUS Ms 368, File "Bekendstelling": Brochure – Introducing the Institute for the Study of Marxism.

77. Ibid., Notules 1979–82: Constitution of the Institute for the Study of Marxism.

78. See Ibid., File "Jaarverslag aan Donateurs": Jaarverslag 1980, p. 1.

79. Ibid., File "Stigting": Memorandum oor die Skepping van 'n Instituut vir die Studie van die Marxisme; Ibid., Notules 1979–82: D.J. Kotzé-President RGN, 5.2.1978, p. 2.

Kotzé was also of the opinion that the state had to take a firm stand against communist activities, for instance, by disrupting communist organisations and front organisations by prohibiting the dissemination of communist propaganda and by taking action "against those who incite others to revolt against the laws of the country". There should be more sincere and responsible contact with, interest in, education for, and assistance to "those who usually take their refuge in communism". Kotzé, who belonged to a newer generation of so-called *verligte* (enlightened) Nationalists, suggested that the white government should acknowledge and readily accede to the just demands of (black) nationalistic groups. This would do much to "vitiate the communist onslaught". Black leaders should be well informed on the facts of communism. They should be made aware of the fact that "communist theory cannot stand up to the test of scientific examination and that history has proved it false". Lastly, blacks should be encouraged to value principles that communists regarded as "major obstacles to their cause": individuality and personal freedom, religion and the Church, nationalism and a strong country with loyal citizens.[80]

The Faculty of Education's representative on ISMUS's Board of Control, Dr A.J. Basson, published a Christian-nationalist perspective on the "degenerate" influence of communism on learners and school education.[81] During the 1980s this publication was a compulsory textbook for students at the University of Stellenbosch's Faculty of Education. According to Basson, there were "theoretical similarities" between liberalism and communism. Liberalism and communism were "allies" in the sense that both ideologies contained anti-religious and egalitarian tendencies and were "subversive" with respect to discipline. Therefore educators should be wary of the "pernicious" influence on children of communism via liberalism, as they would become "victims" in the hands of a communist. Knowledge, religion, nationalism and democracy were the educator's "weapons" to combat the influence of communism on education.[82]

In pursuance of its stated objections ISMUS also launched a number of major research projects. The first project, sponsored by the Human Science

80. D.J. Kotzé, *Communism and South Africa*, pp. 195–203. In the 1960s and 1970s Afrikaner politics were characterised by a fierce debate between *verkramptes* (arch-conservatives) and *verligtes* (enlightened Afrikaners).

81. *Kommunisme en Opvoeding*, Durban, 1981. Basson was also the supervisor for J.H. Du Plessis's MA thesis on Marxism and school cadets.

82. A.J. Basson, *Kommunisme en Opvoeding*, pp. 85–106.

Research Council (HSRC), entailed a survey of sources on communism in South Africa by Elizabeth Böhmer. The aim of the project was to compile a research aid on communist sources for academic scholars.[83] In 1984 Böhmer, a temporary researcher at ISMUS, submitted her thesis. This voluminous 1250-page thesis included approximately 8000 references to books, pamphlets, articles, court records, and local and foreign dissertations on communism.[84]

After its inception ISMUS's library vigorously began to collect and purchase literature and source material on communism and Soviet Russia.[85] Among these was the remaining portion of the SACP's former library in Cape Town, which was donated to ISMUS by the South African Public Library.[86]

Another major ISMUS research project was the history of the communist movement in South Africa. Launched in 1982, this project initially received a substantial grant from the HSRC.[87] Eventually, in 1987, Kotzé produced a two-volume report on the history of the communist movement in South Africa to 1921.[88] However, as an academic research publication it had serious shortcomings. The title was misleading in the sense that Kotzé concentrated rather on the history of the South African labour and socialist movement prior to the founding of the CPSA. Basically the report was an uncritical rewrite of existing narratives on South African labour and socialist history. Overall the narrative lacked proper synthesis and it seems clear that it was completed under great pressure.[89] In all fairness it should, however, be emphasised that

83. ISSUS Ms 368, File "Jaarverslag aan Donateurs": Jaarverslag 1980, pp. 3–4 and Jaarverslag 1981, p. 1.

84. "A Bibliographical and Historical Study of Left Radical Movements and Some Alleged Left Radical Movements in South Africa and Namibia, 1900–1981", Master of Library Science thesis, University of Stellenbosch, 1984.

85. ISSUS Ms 368, File "Jaarverslag aan Donateurs": Jaarverslag 1988, pp. 4–5.

86. Ibid., Jaarverslag 1984, p. 3; Ibid., Notules 1983–86: D.J. Kotzé – Voorsitter ISMUS Beheerkomitee, 30.5.1984; Ibid., File "Memorandum i.v.m. ISMUS": D.J. Kotzé – ISMUS Vyf Jaar Oud. ISMUS also received acquisitions of material relating to communism from the South African Security Police.

87. Ibid., File "Jaarverslag aan Donateurs": Jaarverslae 1981–1986.

88. "Die Kommunistiese Beweging in Suid-Afrika tot die Stigting van die Kommunistiese Party van Suid-Afrika in 1921", unpublished typescript.

89. See also F.A. Van Jaarsveld's trenchant criticism of Kotzé's history writing in *Die Afrikaners se Groot Trek na die Stede en ander Opstelle*, Johannesburg, 1982, p. 285. According to Van Jaarsveld Kotzé's extra-mural activities and commitments affected his historical production negatively.

by this time Kotzé had become the victim of Alzheimer's disease of which he died in 1992.[90]

Given the particular and emotional interest in the phenomenon of communism, the Afrikaner churches became intimately involved with the activities of ISMUS right from the beginning. Apart from a few individuals and other organisations, these churches and ecclesiastical institutions such as Antikom became ISMUS's major and most consistent financial donors. In particular, various DRC structures such as congregations, the Theological Seminary at Stellenbosch, the Sinodale Kommissie vir Sending onder die Kommuniste and the Sinodale Kommissie vir Leer en Aktuele Sake sponsored ISMUS with substantial amounts on an annual basis.[91]

The DRC's intimate involvement with ISMUS was also reflected in the request by one of its synods that the church's representation on the Board of Control be increased from one (the Theological Seminary) to two persons. Kotzé, when he was still Director, diplomatically turned down the request by stating that "almost all" members of the Board were also members of the DRC or would be "religiously acceptable" to the DRC.[92]

In another instance members of the Board of Control raised their concerns over the relationship between ISMUS and Antikom, whose outspoken and conservative anti-communist rhetoric could become an embarrassment to the former. It was therefore decided that the Director of ISMUS would clearly communicate to Antikom that acceptance of its annual donations should under no circumstances be interpreted as an ISMUS association with the objectives of Antikom.[93] Similarly, Philip Nel, the Institute's senior researcher,

---

90. See D.J. van Zyl en G.S. Hofmeyr, "D.J. Kotzé (1927–1992): Afrikanerhistorikus en Kultuur- en Bewaringsleier", *South African Historical Journal,* Vol. 31, November 1994, p. 219.

91. See e.g. ISSUS Ms 368, Notules 1979–82: Notule van die Derde Vergadering van die Beheerkomitee, 16.5.1980, p. 1 and Finansiële Staat – Bylaag tot Jaarverslag 1980; Ibid., H.J. Vorster – Direkteur vir Marxistiese Studies, 21.10.1980; Ibid., File "Donasies NG Kerk Oos-Kaapland": Correspondence; Ibid., File "Kommissie vir Sending Onder Kommuniste": Correspondence; Ibid., File "Kommissie vir Leer en Aktuele Sake": Correspondence; Ibid., File "Donateurs Algemeen": Correspondence; Ibid., File "Kuratorium – Donasies en Korrespondensie".

92. ISSUS Ms 368, Notules 1979–82: Notule van die Vierde Vergadering van die Beheerkomitee, 5.12.1980.; Notules 1983–86: Jaarverslag aan Navorsingskomitee 1983, pp. 5–6 and Aanhangsel III, p. 3; File "Korrespondensie Instituut vir die Studie van Marxisme": D.J. Kotzé – Scriba NGK in SWA, 18.6.1980.

93. Ibid., Notules 1983–86: Notule van die Eerste Vergadering van die Beheerkomitee, 3.3.1983, p. 3.

refused to associate ISMUS's name with the contentious Biblecor publication *Die Christen en Kommunisme* because of its factual errors, misinterpretation and misrepresentation of communist ideology.[94]

Until 1984 a historical focus predominated in ISMUS's research priorities.[95] At that stage, however, Nel was already convinced that the real motives behind Soviet involvement in Southern Africa were completely obscured by prominent South African political and cultural leaders as well as the media's simplistic utterances on the so-called "Soviet onslaught" against South Africa. The increased Soviet involvement in Southern Africa after 1975 became a "handy tool" to explain South Africa's internal problems. Such overestimation of the "Soviet threat", together with the "total onslaught" rhetoric, created a "dangerous illusion" that South Africa's socio-political problems were directly caused by the Soviet Union.

In a scathing accusation Nel also criticised the Afrikaans-speaking academic community for having "disgracefully failed" to generate a corpus of expertise on the Soviet Union that could evaluate Soviet capabilities, restrictions and aims in a more balanced way.[96]

In 1986 ISMUS's name change to the Institute for Soviet Studies at the University of Stellenbosch (ISSUS) was ratified by the university authorities.[97] In the same year Nel was promoted to Director of the Institute.[98] In 1985 ISSUS launched the *Soviet Revue*, a bi-monthly current report on Soviet trends in policy towards Africa and elsewhere.[99] The old ISMUS publication, *Studies in Marxism*, was closed down at the end of 1986.[100]

---

94. Ibid., File "Kontrakwerk – Buite Instansies en Korrespondensie": P.R. Nel – F.M. Gaum, 31.8.1982 and P.R. Nel – F.M. Gaum, 2.3.1983. See also footnote 40. p. 11.

95. Ibid., Notules 1983–86: Notule van die Derde Vergadering van die Beheerkomitee, 17.9.1984, p. 1.

96. See Ibid., Notules 1983–86: P. Nel – Voorstelle i.v.m. die loods van 'n Sowjet Studies Program, 9.8.1984, pp. 1–22; *Ibid.*, File "Memorandum i.v.m. ISMUS": K.M. Campbell – Memorandum concerning evaluation of centre and project description, 1.8.1986, pp. 1–6 and P.R. Nel – Memorandum rondom Voorgestelde Verandering van die Benaming van die Instituut vir die Studie van Marxisme, 5.8.1986, pp. 1–5.

97. Ibid., Notules 1983–86: Notule van die Tweede Beheerkomiteevergadering, 29.9.1986, p. 1.

98. Ibid., Notules 1983–86: Notule van die Eerste Beheerkomiteevergadering, 28.2.1986, p. 2.

99. Ibid., File "Jaarverslag aan Donateurs": Jaarverslag 1984, p. 3.

100.Ibid., Notules 1983–86: Notule van die Tweede Beheerkomiteevergadering, 29.2.1986, p. 2.

However, severe cuts in government subsidies to tertiary institutions towards the end of the 1980s prompted a reconsideration of the continuation of all institutes at the University of Stellenbosch and the university authorities contemplated the closure of ISSUS.[101] Finally it was decided to scale ISSUS down to the Unit for Soviet Studies within the Centre for International and Comparative Politics at the Department of Political Science from the beginning of 1990.[102]

Conclusion

Philip Nel offers a possible rationale for what he calls the "excessive pre-occupation with a presumed Soviet onslaught". Due to a prolonged period of international isolation during the 20th century, white South Africans became used to worn-out stereotypes and propaganda about the Soviet Union. The apartheid regime's lack of legitimacy and its growing feeling of insecurity gave rise to the perception that South Africa's beleaguered position in the international community and the spreading of internal resistance to the apartheid system could be ascribed to a co-ordinated international communist onslaught. The result was that the average white South African, especially during the period 1974–84, was imbued with the psychosis of a fear of a world-wide communist threat.[103]

It is relevant to pose the question whether anti-communism has really come to an end in South Africa. For the renowned South African Marxist historian, Martin Legassick, the arguments between pro-worker groups such as the SACP and the Congress of South African Trade Unions on the one hand, and the ANC government on the other, about the pros and cons of the latter's neo-liberal economic policies, could mark the beginning of a new Marxist versus anti-Marxist debate. Legassick notes that works in the revisionist tradition, on elite transformation and on a critique of neo-liberalism, have been published in recent years.[104]

---

101. Ibid., File "Navorsingsfonds Toekennings": Correspondence, P.M. Compion – Direkteur ISSUS, 24.1.1989; P.R. Nel – Voorsitter Navorsingskomitee, 17.5.1989; D.M. Conradie – Rektor, 9.6.1989 and E.P. Wittle – S. Kritzinger, 25.4.1990.

102. US Senaatsnotules, October 1989: Aanbevelingsrapport van die Navorsingskomitee, 19.9.1989, pp. 1–2; Ibid., December 1989: Mededelingsrapport van die Fakulteitsraad Lettere en Wysbegeerte, 15.11.1989, p. 2; Communiqué from Philip Nel.

103. P. Nel, *A Soviet Embassy in Pretoria?*, pp. 6–7, 96; ISSUS Ms 368, File "Kommissie vir Sending onder Kommuniste": Correspondence, P.R. Nel – P.W. de Wet, 12.6.1987.

104. A. Lichtenstein, "The Past and Present of Marxist Historiography in South Africa",

However, in the wake of the collapse of the Iron Curtain and the retreat of communism since 1989 there has been, at least, a drastic down-scaling of the emotional rhetoric on this ideology in South Africa. Unbanned after 1990, the previously demonised SACP and ANC were no longer the distant and almost "mythical" enemies of the previous political dispensation. Consequently, the Afrikaner anti-communist history production in South African historiography also seems to have come to an abrupt halt.

Radical History Review, Vol. 82, 2002, pp. 124–125. Legassick referred to the publications of D. McKinley, *The ANC and the Liberation Struggle: A Critical Political Biography*, London, 1997; H. Marais, *South Africa, Limits of Change: The Political Economy of Transformation*, Cape Town, 1998; P. Bond, *Elite Transition: From Apartheid to Neoliberalism in South Africa*, London, 2000.

CHAPTER 17

"1922 and all that":

Facts and the writing of South African political history [1]

Allison Drew

How does an event become accepted or rejected by historians as a historical fact? What about cases of highly politicized societies like South Africa, whose past has been characterized by massive oppression and suffering and whose history has been contested at the most basic levels? Since the transition to democracy in 1994, South Africa's past has been subjected to an intense public scrutiny, and public intellectuals contest competing versions of the South African past.

But the past is not history, even though the terms are often used interchangeably. André Brink, for instance, writes that: "We now accept that history 'as such' is simply...inaccessible: our only grasp of Waterloo is attained through what has been written about it."[2] It is the past, however, rather than history, that is inaccessible through direct contact. We can only know Waterloo indirectly – normally, through reading histories produced by historians. Nor is history simply a narrative, even if it is frequently written in narrative form, nor a story; nor can it be reduced to public memory, even if histories may shape public memory. Rather, history is an interpretative or explanatory construction of the past that can be assessed through publicly available standards and criteria.

In one form or another, however obliquely, historians of South Africa have been forced by pressure of events to take a stance on the politics of the day. These political imperatives, which reflected developments such as the resurgence of popular struggles in the 1970s, overshadowed pressures by historians themselves for commitment to the standards of their intellectual craft.

---

1. Edward Roux, "1922 and all that", *Trek*, 11 February 1944, p. 12.

2. André Brink, "Stories of History: Reimagining the Past in Post-Apartheid Narrative", in Sarah Nuttall and Carli Coetzee, (eds), *Negotiating the Past: The Making of Memory in South Africa*, Oxford, Oxford University, 1998, pp. 29–42, 32.

The work of many historians was greatly enriched by the demand to respond to this struggle, even though it often came with a price – a concern to avoid criticism of powerful political interests. However, intellectual autonomy and the development of history as an intellectual craft were often secondary to the overwhelming needs of the anti-apartheid struggle. Along with pressures precluding historians from writing about certain historical episodes and events, at times a lack of concern with accountability to the standards of the craft meant a failure to fully interrogate political verdicts on historical episodes.

As a point of departure in exploring these issues, I would like to begin with an example of a frequently made claim about the past that carries a political significance. This concerns the 1922 Rand Revolt and, specifically, the role of the Communist Party of South Africa (CPSA) in that revolt.[3] This claim attributes the notorious slogan "Workers of the World Fight and Unite for a White S.A." to the Communist Party of South Africa (CPSA). What became known as the Rand Revolt began in January 1922 as a strike of white mine workers in response to a threat by the Chamber of Mines to repudiate an agreement stipulating the numbers of white workers and the ratio of black to white workers on the mines. Wages of white mineworkers were protected by a colour bar restricting higher-paid skilled work to whites only. White trade union leaders saw the threat as a prelude to either driving down white wages to the level of lower-paid black workers or eliminating the higher paid white workers from the mines altogether. The South African Mine Workers' Union and the South African Industrial Federation made it clear that

---

3. See, *inter alia*, S.P. Bunting, *"Red Revolt": The Rand Strike, January-March,* 1922, Johannesburg: Communist Party (S.A.), 1922; W.M. MacMillan, "The Truth about the Strike on the Rand", *The New Statesman*, 19, 474, 13 May 1922, pp. 145–6; Edward Roux, *Time Longer than Rope: The Black Man's Struggle for Freedom in South Africa* [1948], 2nd edition, Madison, University of Wisconsin, 1964, pp. 143–52; Jack Simons and Ray Simons, *Class and Colour in South Africa,* 1850–1950, 1968, International Defence and Aid Fund for Southern Africa, 1983, pp. 271–99; Robert Davies, "The 1922 Strike on the Rand: White Labor and the Political Economy of South Africa", in Peter Gutkind, R. Cohen and J. Copans (eds), *African Labour History*, Beverly Hills and London, Sage, 1978, pp. 80–108; Baruch Hirson, "The General Strike of 1922", *Searchlight South Africa*, Vol. 3, No. 3, October 1993, pp. 63–94; Sheridan Johns, *Raising the Red Flag: The International Socialist League and the Communist Party of South Africa,* 1914–1932, Bellville, Mayibuye, 1995, pp. 128–45; Jeremy Krikler, "Women, Violence and the Rand Revolt of 1922", *Journal of Southern African Studies*, Vol. 22, No. 3, September 1996, pp. 349–72; and Jeremy Krikler, "The Commandos: The Army of White Labour in South Africa", *Past and Present*, Vol. 163, Issue 3, 1999, pp. 202–44.

their struggle was "to protect the White race", "to maintain a White standard of living", and "to preserve White South Africa".[4] The strike culminated in March in an armed revolt of several white working-class communities that was brutally squashed by the state. During this period the slogan "Workers of the World Fight and Unite for a White S.A.", was seen on a banner carried by white men and women.[5]

To the best of my knowledge, there is no historical evidence on which to ground the claim that the CPSA or some of its members authored or endorsed this slogan. To the contrary, all evidence suggests that the CPSA was not responsible for this slogan. Why then, has this slogan been attributed to the CPSA or to individual Communists without evidence? The *Illustrated Dictionary of South African History*, for example, states that the CPSA played a leading role in the Rand Revolt and urged "Workers of the World" to "Unite and Fight for a White South Africa" [sic].[6] Similarly, in *South Africa: A Modern History*, Davenport and Saunders write that:

> Communist leaders of the strike justified the slogan carried by the Fordsburg commando – 'Workers of the World Unite, and Fight for a White South Africa' [sic] – with the suspect plea that the struggle would build up class-consciousness among the white workers, opening the way for the disappearance of the colour bar at a later date.[7]

Another example is the account found in the *Historical Dictionary of South Africa*. The entry on the CPSA states:

> During the Rand Revolt … some of its members attempted to combine radicalism and racialism, their slogan in support of the strikers being, 'Workers of the world, unite and fight for a white South Africa' [sic].[8]

4. Simons and Simons, *Class and Colour*, p. 278.

5. See *Through the Red Revolt on the Rand: A Pictorial Review of Events, January, February, March, 1922*, compiled from photographs taken by representatives of *The Star*, Johannesburg: Central News Agency, 1922, 1st, and 2nd editions.

6. Christopher C. Saunders (ed.), *An Illustrated Dictionary of South African History*, Sandton, Ibis Books and Editorial Services, 1994, p. 223.

7. T.R.H. Davenport and Christopher Saunders, *South Africa: A Modern History*, 5th edition, 2000, p. 296.

8. Christopher Saunders and Nicholas Southey (eds), *Historical Dictionary of South Africa*, 2nd edition, Lanham, MD and London, Scarecrow, 2000, pp. 68–9.

Perhaps these claims indicate a reliance on the account of the Rand Revolt in Jack Simons and Ray Simons's massive study, *Class and Colour in South Africa, 1850–1950.* The Simonses claim that Communists gave "unqualified approval for the oldest and most significant colour bar on the mines" and that this "revealed the decision of the communists to back the white worker against the Chamber [of Mines] in all circumstances". They also state that Communists gave "unqualified support for the strike" and "even justified" the notorious slogan.[9] Yet the evidence they provide – detailed accounts of Communist statements – does not support their own judgments. The Simonses note that Communists opposed the colour bar in principle and believed that abolition of the colour bar, by driving down white wages, would lead white workers to recognize the need for working-class unity. Yet, Communists' belief that white workers were justified in defending their conditions and wages hardly indicates unqualified support for the strike. It would have been utopian for Communists to ask white workers to accept pay cuts and retrenchments; the workers went on strike precisely to prevent such an attack. We may know with hindsight that white worker racism increased after the strike; there was no way that Communists of the day could have predicted that. Communists may have used a tortuous logic to explain their support for the strikers. But the Simonses' judgments cannot be accepted at face value.

The onus on historians who make such claims is to make available the evidence upon which they are basing their assertions; the onus on historians using secondary literature as a basis for such claims is to use it with care. Yet, all the archival evidence that I have seen suggests that the CPSA as an organization did not author or, contrary to the verdict of the *Illustrated Dictionary*, support the slogan. And while it is in principle possible that individual Communists supported this slogan, as the *Historical Dictionary* claims, I certainly have never come across any evidence to suggest this. How, in the absence of evidence in the public domain, do we explain why the view that the CPSA or some of its members authored or upheld this slogan has become conventional? Why do standards of evidence and of historical debate in South African historiography facilitate the repetition of such an error? More generally, how does such an inaccuracy reflect on the state of political history within South African historiography?

---

9. Simons and Simons, *Class and Colour*, pp. 276, 285.

What is a historical fact?

Discussion of this problem necessarily raises the question of what constitutes a historical fact. Answers to the question reflect a range of perspectives on the philosophy of history. E.H. Carr, for example, places great emphasis on the role of the historian as interpreter of the past. Influenced by the work of Oakeshott and Collingwood, for Carr historical facts are constituted by theory and interpretation and do not exist independently of the historian; past events, which are the raw material out of which facts are constructed, become historical facts when accepted as such by historians. Carr argues that since we discover history through the historian's words, we need first and foremost to understand the historian. While we can only understand the past from our own vantage point in the present, historians, nonetheless, must have an "imaginative understanding" of the minds of the people about whom they are writing. Carr is aware of the limitations of such a perspective: too much emphasis on the role of the historian can lead to complete subjectivity. Such subjectivity can also lead to what I call a utility trap: taken to its extreme, the criterion for assessing the validity of a particular interpretation is its utility for the present.[10]

By contrast, Richard Evans presents a more positivist perspective, drawing on the work of Sir Geoffrey Elton, who argued, against Carr, that a fact is something that happened in the past that has left traces in documents that historians can use to reconstruct that fact in the present. Theory, in Elton's opinion, was a barrier to historians' knowledge of historical facts, because it obliged them to tailor their evidence accordingly. Evans argues that historical facts, of which events are one type, are phenomena that have occurred in the past and that can be verified with or are at least compatible with traces. Historical facts, in other words, exist independently of the historian. But, unlike Elton, Evans accords theory a role in our understanding and interpretation of historical facts, arguing that facts, once interpreted, can be used as evidence to substantiate broader historical claims.[11]

I stand somewhere between Carr and Evans. I certainly agree that we can only understand the past from our own vantage point in the present, and that to bridge the distance between the present and the past historians need an "imaginative understanding" of those they are writing about. They must seek

---

10. E.H. Carr, *What Is History*, 2nd editon, London, Penguin, 1987, pp. 7–30, esp. 21–30.

11. Richard J. Evans, *In Defence of History*, London, Granta, 1997, pp. 75–102, esp. 75–9.

to understand how people of an earlier period perceived their own societies, the choices available to them and the constraints under which they operated. I also agree that we typically come to an understanding of the past through the words of historians. But while it is important to understand the historian, this is not in itself either the first or the last point in evaluating a work of history. Whether or not a fact happened at time T is not dependent on the historian's knowledge. But we can only suggest that X happened at time T because of interpretations of traces made by historians at time T + 1. Historical works can be and must be evaluated by criteria that exist independently of the specific historian, such as the quality of the evidence and the intelligibility of the interpretation. Such criteria must be publicly available. Their standards and applicability in particular cases may be contestable, and such criteria are always subject to revision; they provide the ground rules for historiographical debate. Historical facts constitute the historian's most important material constraints. However, historians can only know them subjectively once they find traces to verify their occurrence. The subjective and objective elements of history co-exist in a relationship of mutual dependency.

Facts and evidence

Returning to 1922 and the slogan "Workers of the World Fight and Unite for a White S.A.", I would argue that there are traces and, on that basis, facts that can be interpreted as evidence to support the claim that the CPSA did not author or endorse this slogan. By contrast, there are, to my knowledge, no known traces or facts that can be used as evidence to support the thesis that the slogan was that of the CPSA or that Communists supported it; if such traces or facts become known, they will hopefully be brought into the public domain. The traces one can find on this event are mainly documentary and archival. These include the CPSA's organ, the *International*, and CPSA publications and internal documents available in libraries and archives.[12]

These traces must necessarily be assessed; the consequential facts must be interpreted, a process that begins when the historian poses questions about

---

12. For example, the Jack Simons Collection, Manuscripts and Archives Department, University of Cape Town; W. H. Andrews Diary, Mayibuye Archives, University of the Western Cape; S.P. Bunting Papers, Department of Historical Papers, University of the Witwatersrand Library; Communist International Archives, Russian State Archive of Socio-Political History (RGASPI), Moscow; Communist Party of South Africa Collection, Hoover Institution Archives, Stanford; and police reports in the National Archives of South Africa, Pretoria.

the traces and facts and about the types of evidence needed to sustain a claim about Communist activity or policy. For example, to support the argument that this slogan was CPSA policy, a historian would need to point to evidence, such as minutes of committee meetings in which the slogan was discussed or public policy statements by the Party.

The CPSA was a minute organization in 1922 – possibly numbering about two hundred out of a population of at least seven million – and in composition it was overwhelmingly white. Most CPSA members would have been sporadic supporters of the Communist cause, occasionally attending meetings and possibly paying their dues. Very few in 1922 could be counted on for practical work. Contrary to the claim made in the *Illustrated Dictionary*, the Party did not have the resources to get involved in any significant capacity in the Rand Revolt, even if most members were inspired by the revolt's militancy. In 1922 the Party still saw white unionized urban workers as the potential working-class vanguard. Most Communists supported the white workers' struggle against wage cuts and retrenchments.[13] But, significantly, a handful of Communist activists tried to convince white workers to support the needs of black workers and to refrain from attacking black people.

"The white miners are perfectly justified in fighting to keep up the numbers and pay of holders of blasting certificates", claimed Communist trade unionist Bill Andrews:

> They would get native support ... if they also insisted on higher pay and better treatment of the blacks ... For a section which poses at the same time as both masters and workers must sooner or later collapse.[14]

The slogan "Workers of the world unite" became popularized through the *Communist Manifesto*, which by the late nineteenth century had been widely translated, and also through a broader sense of working-class internationalism. In the first few decades of the twentieth century it was frequently seen at trade union rallies around the world, upheld by trade unionists, syndicalists and diverse socialists. The slogan of "white South Africa", espoused broadly by white workers of the day, had a double meaning.[15] Those who espoused it

---

13. Allison Drew, *Discordant Comrades: Identities and Loyalties on the South African Left*, Pretoria, Unisa Press, 2002, pp. 63–4.

14. Quoted in D.I. Jones, *Re General Strike in South Africa*, n.d., RGASPI, 495.64.9; Johns, *Raising the Red Flag*, pp. 135–6, 140.

15. The idea of a white standard had very different meanings in South Africa, where whites were in a minority, and in Australia, with its history of genocide of the indig-

wanted a living wage. But this living wage, historical evidence suggests, was achieved at the price of underpaying black labour so that capital could keep up its profits. White workers, imbued with the racial ideology of the day, overwhelmingly saw cheap black labour as a threat to their own standard of living, which from their point of view was a "civilized" standard. "White South Africa," or "the maintenance of the colour bar, has ... been accepted by the white workers as the prime 'motif' in this strike", acknowledged an article in the CPSA's organ, the *International*. But, the writer continued:

> There is not and never was a white South Africa .... Capitalism, whose first principle all over the world is cheap labour; capitalism, whose profits can be made only at the workers' expense, is responsible for the black man doing the bulk of the work in this country ... Natives at starvation wages, that is the thing to attack: that is what ruins the white standard.

The writer tried to appeal to white workers using their own discourse, here using the slogan "white South Africa" to mean a living wage or a "civilized" standard that should be available to all:

> Communism alone can make South Africa a white man's country, in the sense that Communism alone can secure to every worker – whatever his colour – the full product of his labour.[16]

A CPSA manifesto issued to the striking workers on 30 January stated that:

> ... without necessarily identifying itself with every slogan heard in the strike, the Communist Party of South Africa gladly offers its assistance ... convinced that essentially this is a fight against the rule of the capitalist class .... To maintain the 'white standard' to build a 'white South Africa', is impossible under capitalism, whose nature is to degrade every class it employs.[17]

---

enous people and where exclusion was a feasible policy.

16. "'White South Africa.' Two Voices," *The International*, 27 January 1922 in Allison Drew (ed.), *South Africa's Radical Tradition: A Documentary History*, Vol. 1, Cape Town, University of Cape Town, Buchu and Mayibuye, 1996, pp. 48–50.

17. "The Fight to a Finish", Manifesto issued by the Communist Party to the Striking Workers of the Witwatersrand on January 30, 1922, in Brian Bunting (ed.), *South African Communists Speak: Documents from the History of the South African Communist Party*, 1915–1980, London, Inkululeko, 1981, pp. 68–9.

Typically, in any mass demonstration, many flags will be flying. Not every participant in a demonstration supports every single slogan espoused by other participants.

In the absence of any historical traces or facts that can be used as evidence to argue that either individual Communists or the CPSA produced or endorsed this slogan, I find Edward Roux's assessment in *S.P. Bunting* the most convincing of the other secondary accounts. Fearful that their wages would be pushed down by the availability of cheap black labour, a group of white miners and their supporters – whom Roux described as "Marxist socialists" – took an old banner bearing the slogan "Workers of the world unite" and "modernised" it to demand what they saw as a fair living standard – with the racism that this entailed – expressed in the phrase a "white South Africa".[18]

Communists and labour activists of the day interpreted strikes through a particular conceptual model: they believed that strikes were a learning process that would lead to radicalization of workers' consciousness. Hence, Communists like Bill Andrews and Sidney Bunting hoped that white workers would learn a lesson through their divisive refusal to consider the needs of black workers. Although Davenport and Saunders interpret this hope as "suspect", there was nothing unique in the expectations of those early South African Communists. Historically, we know, this did not happen; nor, history tells us, do workers generally learn lessons about solidarity from strikes. Any statement by historians concerning specific organizations necessarily should be tested by the standards of the profession – and this means being able to scrutinize and ask carefully formulated questions about the historical traces and facts that form the evidence upon which historical claims are based. The conventional view that the CPSA was responsible for the slogan in question has rested on an absence of evidence. It has assumed a particular interpretation of a slogan that was probably made up on the spur of the moment and may well have had different meanings for those marching under it. The conventional view should be challenged.

Perceptions and misperceptions about history

It is easy to suggest that the tendency to skip too rapidly over the relationship of facts, evidence and arguments in discussions of South Africa's Rand Revolt is a legacy of the ideological biases that have hampered the serious study of

---

18. Edward Roux, *S.P. Bunting: A Political Biography* [1944], Bellville, Mayibuye, 1993, pp. 91–2.

Communist history in any country. But the problem in this case is complicated by South Africa's protracted liberation struggle, which overshadowed intellectual work throughout the twentieth century. One impact of this for history as a discipline or a craft is the very polarized range of views concerning the relationship of facts and theory and the aim and meaning of history.

Along one axis, views about historiography oscillate between what could be called a fetishism of facts and a fetishism of grand theories. The fetishism of facts takes a number of forms. One example is seen in the statement that "all the facts about X are known". In a country such as South Africa, where black existence was rendered invisible in the public sphere by white authorities for much of the twentieth century and where much of the century's political activity was subjected to acute repression and forced into illegality, where political documentation had to be destroyed to protect individuals against state repression, it is doubtful indeed that "all the facts about X are known" – whatever X may be.

A second example of this fetishism of facts is seen in the view: "Historian Y does not present new facts". One can point to Colin Bundy's claim, when reviewing the 1993 edition of Roux's biography of *S.P. Bunting*, that the book's contents were so well known that they no longer offered any surprises.[19] Yet the text is significant not only for what it tells us about Bunting the subject or about Roux the author, but for what we can learn about others through their reactions to it.[20] New insights can be gained by reading the same text through different lenses, and facts can be subject to reinterpretation.

An extension of this fetishism of facts is seen in Stephen Ellis's contention that "history-writing involves assembling masses of verifiable facts and arranging them in a series, generally a chronological one, or a set of such series". It also involves, Ellis continues,

> ... the effort to penetrate the thinking of those who were implicated in the past. Arranging the data in a sequence and attempting to re-think the thoughts of those involved create a narrative...[21]

19. Colin Bundy, "Bunting and Basner", *Southern African Review of Books*, Vol. 5, No. 6, November-December 1993, pp. 16–17.

20. Premesh Lalu, "Lived Texts, Written Texts and Contexts: Eddie Roux and the Making of the South African Past", MA, University of the Western Cape, 1994, pp. 84–5.

21. Stephen Ellis, "Writing Histories of Contemporary Africa", *Journal of African History*, Vol. 43, 2002, pp. 1–26, 2–3.

Are there any historians who think that their work consists in "assembling masses of verifiable facts and arranging them in a series"? I can write out a chronological series of facts right now, and I can also try to "re-think" the thoughts of the allegedly relevant actors; this would not constitute a history. Those activities might be steps in the writing of a history, but Ellis leaves out the crucial ingredients of intellectual creativity and theoretical work. Facts need to be interpreted to provide an explanation of the past that can stand up to scrutiny based on recognized standards.

In contrast to the fetishism of facts, is a fetishism of grand theories. This is the view that what counts are grand sociological statements that one can either agree or disagree with. In this perspective, books that contain large amounts of empirical material, especially that derived through historical research, are merely "descriptive". They are presumed to be empirical rather than analytical or theoretical; indeed, "empirical" and "analytical" are seen as polarized types. This perspective reflects, very likely, the legacies of the 1970s radical revisionist school, some of which was theoretically inspired by the structural Marxism of Althusser and Poulantzas. It indicates a lack of understanding about historical facts and their relationship to the writing of history; hence, the very sharp and polarized distinction between what is presumed to be "empirical history" and what is presumed to be "analysis" and "theory". Yet, against this dichotomy, historians present their analysis through the empirical evidence. But theory is also fundamental to historians' selection and interpretation of facts, which are used as evidence to produce historical arguments.

Along another axis, are views about history that range from utilitarian to teleological. Constructions of South Africa's past have frequently been justified or evaluated in terms of their use for the present, whether by historians trying to justify apartheid or by historians trying to justify the liberation movement. One example of the latter might be seen in debates about people's history in the 1980s, in which historians sought to commend their work by its relevance to the national liberation struggle. Today, the view that history's role is to promote heritage culture, which can be marketed by the tourist industry, is one type of utilitarianism that reflects the wave of economic liberalization that has swept across South Africa. Another expression of utilitarianism is seen in the efforts of political parties to promote accounts of the past that legitimate their present political successes. Such accounts might be both utilitarian and teleological.

Teleology involves the explanation of the past by reference to a future outcome that occurs independently of the historical actors' intentions. An example of this is found in the Simonses' work. Although characterized by a very high degree of scholarly research and historical accuracy, in their account Communists were pushed inexorably to merge their own struggle with the national liberation struggle. Thus, they conclude that with the CPSA's

> dissolution as a legal party, the communists could claim the achievement of an objective that had been central to their purpose since 1928. The class struggle had merged with the struggle for national liberation.[22]

The Simonses use facts as evidence to sustain the argument that the merger of the class and national struggles, in the early years of apartheid, was not only inevitable but was the best of all conceivable outcomes. In making this argument, the Simonses have to stretch certain facts and downplay others. For example, the formation of the CPSA is presented as a sharp break in the development of the South African socialist movement. This characterization is exaggerated. A reading of the early socialist press before the foundation of the CPSA, when syndicalist influences on socialist thought were relatively strong, indicates that the colour bar was discussed more often and more critically by these early syndicalists and socialists than the Simonses suggest. By the same token, the Simonses also paint too sharp a break between the CPSA of the 1940s and the subsequent activities of Communists in the underground phase. Historically, there is no reason for us to assume that the particular relationship that developed between the underground SACP and the ANC was inevitable; many permutations could have been possible. Their treatment of the Rand Revolt conforms with this broader vision, dovetailing neatly with the thesis that the early CPSA was essentially a radical party of white labour, that over the next two decades it "cooperated or competed with the liberation movement" and that only after its disbanding could it really give primacy to the struggle for national liberation.[23]

Finally, many discussions of South African history are characterized by an overemphasis on the values or identity of the historian. This is not surprising in a highly politicized society such as South Africa, where labels were not only placed on the population through state fiat but where different political groups and tendencies used labels to categorize each other. But the assump-

---

22. Simons and Simons, *Class and Colour*, p. 609.
23. Simons and Simons, *Class and Colour*, p. 620.

tion that a characterization of a historian's political preferences can serve as a basis for evaluating their work is not tenable. Even if an understanding of historians' political perspectives might provide insights into their work, the quality of any historical work can only be assessed by standards that are publicly debatable and independent of any particular historian. These standards relate to questions of historical facts and factual accuracy, and to the credibility of interpretations of such facts for use as evidence in arguments.

South African historiography
– the limits of classification

All of these problems, in one way or other, can be traced back to the question of what constitutes a historical fact, and how historians relate facts to interpretation, evidence and argument. In their South African manifestations, these problems are, no doubt, a legacy of the traumas of the past century.

The conventional categories used to describe South African historiography may offer convenient ways of organizing material but they can also blind us to other ways of understanding historical trends. South African historiography has been broadly grouped into four main categories, "conservative history", "liberal history", "radical revisionism" and "social history".[24] But even at first glance, it is evident that these are not parallel categories. The categories of "conservative history" and "liberal history", for instance, suggest ideological or political perspectives, while "radical revisionism" can be construed either in political or methodological terms. The category of "social history", by contrast, is generally understood as a particular branch of history, on a par with economic history, political history or cultural history.

These categories reflect the perceptions of succeeding generations of South Africanist historians seeking to distinguish themselves from the preceding generations. Thus, while the conservative history of the late nineteenth and early twentieth centuries saw South African development through the dynamics of white settler interactions, the liberal history of the inter-war and early post-war years saw racial ideology and discrimination as antipathetic to capitalist development. In the 1970s, rejecting what they saw as the pro-settler

---

24. Alan Cobley, "Does Social History Have a Future? The Ending of Apartheid and Recent Trends in South African Historiography", *Journal of Southern African Studies*, Vol. 27, No. 3, September 2001, pp. 613–25 and Neville Alexander, *An Ordinary Country: Issues in the Transition from Apartheid to Democracy in South Africa*, Pietermaritzburg, University of Natal, 2002, pp. 9–27.

tradition but also critical of what they called the liberal tradition, a new generation of historians and social scientists styled themselves broadly as radical revisionists. This move was both ideological and methodological: many radical revisionists, critics of capitalism, used a Marxist methodology that emphasized political economy. But all categories are to some degree arbitrary. According to Alan Cobley, for instance, the pro-settler tradition can be seen today in school books, "portraying white-black relationships as a struggle between the forces of 'civilisation' and 'savagery'". And in the liberal tradition, Cobley writes, "clashes between settlers and Africans were portrayed as a tragic confrontation between modernity and irrationality".[25] But these descriptions do not clearly delineate two historical schools or two methodological approaches.

To take another example, W. M. MacMillan is described by Cobley as a "powerful voice" of the liberal school, whose "hallmark became the manner in which the analysis of the South African past was mediated by humanitarian concern for the victims". Yet, a particularly striking aspect of MacMillan's work is his understanding of capitalist penetration and development in rural South Africa.[26] Were I to put a label on him, I would call him an economic historian – a characterization outside the dominant categories. And one can think of many historians of South Africa – of varying political and intellectual hues – who would consider their work as mediated and motivated by humanitarian concern for the oppressed population. My point here is that labels are rigid; they become conventions that offer partial and often misleading understanding. It is time to stand back and take a fresh look at the state of South African historiography and to reconsider these labels.

Radical revisionists who focused on political economy played an important role in interpreting facts to use as evidence for their arguments about the link between capitalism and the racial system. However, their highly structural conception of political economy marginalized human agency and, consequently, important aspects of causality and change. Social historians responded by highlighting the centrality of agency, especially black and African agency; this, too, reflected both methodological and ideological considerations. South Africanist social historians by and large have focused on com-

---

25. Cobley, "Does Social History Have a Future?", pp. 613–14.

26. W.M. MacMillan, *The South African Agrarian Problem and Its Historical Development*, Johannesburg: Council of Education, Witwatersrand, 1919; W.M. MacMillan, *Africa Emergent: A Survey of Social, Political and Economic Trends in British Africa*, Harmondsworth, Middlesex, Penguin, 1949.

munity issues and struggles rather than their workplace equivalents, which, for the most part, have been the province of sociologists and thus have been contemporary rather than historical. Nor, with some important exceptions, have social historians focused on political history.[27] Thus, despite valuable and at times path-breaking works produced within these schools and fruitful debates amongst them, important issues and problems concerning South Africa's past have not been addressed by these approaches. Indeed, those whose work does not fit the categories may find themselves invisible. These categories were coined and applied in a particular historical context by particular historians. They have become a barrier to the way in which South African historiography is viewed – so much so that some of its most significant and problematic characteristics are not seen. It is time to move beyond them.

Looking to the future of South African history

Although the teaching of history in South African schools, colleges and universities certainly faces obstacles and challenges, warnings of a crisis about history as a craft are overstated.[28] However, the transition to democracy in South Africa has led to a new relationship between state and society, which necessarily means that intellectuals need to rethink their relationship with the state. The challenge in the post-apartheid era is to develop an intellectually autonomous practice of history that asks critical questions about the relationship of facts, evidence and argument that critically interrogates hypotheses and, by doing so, avoids becoming the mouthpiece of any particular political organization.

There is a wealth of archival material available for research on South African political history – and on working-class and socialist history. Much of this material has been under-utilized. But documentary traces are often inadequate, given that South African blacks were typically written out of history during the previous racial order. Oral history has expanded the traces that enable us to discover previously lost, hidden or unknown aspects of black South African lives.[29]

---

27. Notable exceptions include Tom Lodge, *Black Politics in South Africa since 1945*, London and New York, Longman, 1983 and Shula Marks, *The Ambiguities of Dependence in South Africa: Class, Nationalism and the State in Twentieth-Century* Natal, Johannesburg, Ravan, 1986.

28. Cobley, "Does Social History Have a Future?", pp. 617–20.

29. As a seminal example, see Charles Van Onselen, *The Seed Is Mine: The Life of Kas*

Historians often focus on formal institutions, neglecting that which is not readily visible or audible. Yet absences are crucially important. A striking absence in South African history is the study of why certain popular movements, political organizations and ideologies became dominant at particular moments, while others were marginalized.[30] Indeed, it is amazing that in a country that has witnessed such phenomenal political shifts, there is such a striking lack of political history. The problem is so acute that one cannot be certain that our contemporary impressions about political organizations reflect the actual status of those organizations in their day rather than historians' presentations of or neglect of them.

One way to begin investigating these problems is to examine key episodes where decisions were taken – or avoided – leading either to a turning point in policy or to continuity, which is not as unproblematic as hindsight would suggest. This would combine a recognition of the constraints (both socioeconomic and organizational) under which actors operate with a concern for agency, which can be broadly interpreted to include personality, perceptions and misperceptions of actors, political preferences and choices. The Industrial and Commercial Workers' Union was a tremendously important organization in South African history. Its history poses a range of questions about political alliances, relationships between national headquarters and regional offices and about rank and file members and their leaders, amongst many other things. Yet, it has been the subject of very few books.[31] The history of the left and of workers' movements in the early twentieth century remains in many respects a blank slate; the lives of black labour activists such as William Thibedi and Gana Makabeni merit investigation. Political movements and rural struggles need further research; women's movements are neglected across the entire century. Charlotte Maxeke, Minah Soga, Fanny Klenerman and Josie Mpama organized women, yet they have received only passing references in histories – which portray South African politics as a predominantly male domain.

The concept of "space" – whether geographic, political or civic and cultural – is one that can help us to understand that which is not readily cap-

---

Maine, a South African Sharecropper, 1894–1985, Cape Town, David Philip, 1996.

30. The historical silence about the Non-European Unity Movement is a notable example.

31. P.L. Wickens, The Industrial and Commercial Workers' Union of Africa, Cape Town, Oxford University, 1978; Helen Bradford, A Taste of Freedom: The ICU in Rural South Africa, 1924–1930, New Haven and London, Yale, 1987.

tured in conventional studies. Corinne Sandwith has pointed to the use of public space by radical women: often excluded from or marginalized within hierarchical political organizations, these women operated in the public space through writing and other political-cultural activities. Olive Schreiner, Dora Taylor and Ruth First are notable examples of women who shaped South African politics through their writing. The socialist and feminist tradition that Olive Schreiner represented became marginalized after her death, particularly with the rise of Bolshevik politics and its gendered model of left-wing revolutionaries. The paradigm of a male revolutionary in a small, closed and hierarchical organization has generally been accepted without acknowledgement in historical and political thinking; it certainly has not been subjected to serious scrutiny or challenge in the historiography. In South Africa, debates about socialism have been invariably economic; there is a striking absence in left discourse to this day of discussions about culture, gender and ethics. In approaching any topic historians need to think carefully about what types of traces to look for, what types of facts to select and how to transform facts into evidence that sustains arguments about the past.

CHAPTER 18

A useable past:
The search for "history in chords"

Catherine Burns

Introduction

This article is a critical engagement with assertions that South African history research, teaching, writing, and the development of South Africanist historiography, is dying or suffering from a terminal "post" malaise. While it is true that the post-anti-apartheid era is over, of course the changing shape and form of South African life, and the study of this life, continue to be engaged dialogically with material, cosmological, mythical, iconographical, emotional, cultural, spacial, and physiological connections to the past. The question for many historians inside the country and historians of this country abroad–as indicated by a body of recent conference papers, a number of publications, e-mail debates, and several papers for the Copenhagen gathering–echoes the one framed in the title of the 1997 University of the Western Cape History Conference of that name: "The Future of the Past?".[1]

This chapter is partly a tale of how the discipline of history in a post-anti-apartheid South African University is in dialogue–through its teaching, research, and historiographical grapplings–with South African history and its discontents. We believe we are having an impact, however small, on the regional and national choreography that is "history today". I write from the position of an institution on the eastern seaboard of South Africa where I have been based since 1995 when I joined a Department of History, now morphed into a Historical Studies Programme. I have also spent time and energy in these years as a member of a small team of academics on our campus frequently called upon by the university to address schools and teacher gatherings across the region as part of the university's publicity and recruit-

---

1. University of the Western Cape Conference, 1997, "The Future of the Past?". Papers of Minkley and Rassool; Legassick; Freund.

ment drives, and in this capacity I have attended dozens of open days at schools and many more smaller focus groups. The data gathered in question sessions and through questionnaires about the views that young women and men and their parents hold concerning liberal arts undergraduate degrees in general, and about History in particular, has been instructive. In Durban, at the previously white, and still and English-language dominated university on the city's southern hills, we have built a small, diverse, excellent, and very active history programme. History at UND is alive partly because of the willingness of its members to engage across disciplinary boundaries and teach and write, often in teams, with people from inside and outside the academy. .That this engagement brings challenges of its own, and is not always successful, does not undermine the optimism and in particular the graduate student interest and enrolment that we have generated since 1994/5.

Most historical scholarship on South Africa is written by people outside the country and many of these people were born, and partially, trained, in this region. This is even truer for the sciences–especially biomedicine–and a few other key fields. Very often colleagues from abroad comment on the impossibility of moving to South Africa, or remaining here if they are leaving, as the chances for serious historical work, as they see it, are diminishing. I disagree. The departure of these trained historians in great numbers, young and seasoned, in the post-anti-Apartheid era is qualitatively different to their exile or "interested and committed" outsider positions of the 1970s and 1980s. It adds a special tension to the impact of history-making on the university and school communities in which we work, and by whom we are worked upon. It must also impact upon the way the history of this region is understood and written in the rest of the world: in the 1980s, for example, there was always the presumption (perhaps it was a pretension) in the work of radical, liberal and Africanist scholarship–and most work was a melange of these–that the audience for this new writing and work was the "one day to be free" citizenry of South Africa, as much as it was addressing an audience of the world. What has happened to that imagined audience? The audience imagined by the historian of South Africa, based in South Africa today, might be even more complex to create, sustain, or call forth.

The dreaded past?

South Africa remains apart from and inside of the broader modernist narratives of humanity's last 300 years: of pre-industrial and post-industrial; colonial and anti-colonial, and yet we are not yet in any clear or simple way post-colonial. South African historians can safely claim, I think, only this: South Africa is a post-anti-apartheid society. The South African specificity – the force and shape and particularity of the apartheid state system – is even under challenge, in works as wide ranging as Mamdani's widely read study linking South African post-1940s experiences with the wider African colonial and anti-colonial histories, and the work of Americanists and others who find "apartheids" in their own national or regional history settings.[2]

This is not a post-historical society. None of the complex social groupings in our national borders, or our diasporic pods, articulates a Fukuyaman position: that the forces shaping our destinies have been largely fulfilled.[3] We are not a post-apartheid society either. The return of Sarah Baartmann's remains in 2002 (timed to take advantage of the National Women's Day and International Indigenous People's Day) sparked off a host of newspaper, radio and television short pieces and sound bites containing popular and academic commentaries on the history of biomedical and western science's elaboration of – some argued creation of – racism from the late 18th century on.[4] The impact of, and the connection between, these histories of oppression and the colonial violence against southern African women and black people stretching back into the 17th century and forward into the 21st century, was a central motif. The fragility and brittleness of popular memorialisations (stimulated in this case by both academic and state-sponsored historical research) and the publications addressed and audiences called forth since then around the Bartmann memorialisation in particular, seem to me to be occasioned not by the fact that South African society is in danger of forgetting what the then Deputy President, and now President, Thabo Mbeki once referred to as "the

2. Mahmood Mamdani, *Citizen and Subject: Contemporary Africa and the legacy of late colonialism*, Kampala, Fountain, 1995.

3. Francis Fukuyama, *The end of history and the last man*, London, Hamish Hamilton, 1992; also his book on the USSR, F. Fukuyama and Korbonski, Andrzej (eds), *The Soviet Union and the Third World: The last three decades*, Cornell University Press, 1987.

4. There are many recent sources on S. Baartmann and the debate around her return. An excellent summation is contained in *Sunday Times* of 11 August 2002, by Charlotte Bauer entitled "Battle for Sarah Baartmann". In it she includes interviews with Prof. Philip Tobais (tasked with negotiating with his French counterparts in Paris), Brigitte Mabandla (Deputy Minister of Arts and Culture); Prof. Henry Bredekamp (Director of the Institute for Historical Research, University of the Western Cape and Patron of the National Khoi-San Consultative Conference); and Dr Yvette Abrahams and a host of people involved in the return and memorialisation.

dreaded past"[5]. Rather, it seems to me, the brittleness and fragility of historical consciousness thus evoked is thematised at the expense of periodisation
and a rigorous investigation of cause and its complexities, and effect and its
multi-dimensions. It is as if aesthetic and artistic methodologies overtake analytical and historical ones. Bartmann's aesthetic memorialisation – already
achieved on a smaller scale by artists such as Penny Siopis and Willie Bester
– lives far more in this pageantry than through the words of the historian
Yvette Abrahams, whose detailed PhD on Bartmann informed the behind-
the-scenes negotiations with the French state and museum community, but
was never present in other settings, and the care, detail, and full implication
of that account were absent from public insight and scrutiny.

Why is this important? Because it is clear that everywhere South African
historians are at work, and all sorts of layers of society depend upon their
interventions. The evidence they provide, the detail, the rich arguments, and
the mass of connections with local and international literatures that they
have established and continue to establish, are key threads in wider webs and
social dynamics. But like the spiders that this image evokes, their identity is
often hidden in crannies and under rocks: it crawls out into view at the start
and conclusion of news and other reports, activist broadsheets, state and official occasions of every sort, school syllabi, and into the framing of major
speeches, and state as well as civil society texts.[6] To succeed in a quest to
make critical and difficult debates and arguments of historical work part of
the anticipated theme, if not playing the lead role, of academic, school and
educational settings, and at least a complicating factor in many of the issues
addressed by popular discourses in South Africa, is a demanding but not impossible task. Think of the way, for example, that debates around biomedicine
have–despite, and maybe because of–widespread dissemination and public
debate–maintained a certain gravitas and built-in restraint or pause, before
too easy conclusions. I write "maybe because of" as the level of public knowledge generated through the debate around the biochemical work of patho-
gens such as the HIV virus, and the social and economics might and agendas
and internal debates within biomedical institutions, associated research in
medical schools and pharmaceutical company laboratories, is at an unprec-

---

5. Thabo Mbeki, *Speeches Collected*, 1997.

6. This, we believe, is in the process of shifting as the former Minister of Education's,
   (Kadar Asmal's) Ministerial Task Team on History redraws sections of the relevant
   "learning area" in the school syllabus and rethinks history's place in social science,
   ethical and humanistic education nationally.

edented level across the region. And this in a generally scientifically illiterate society. The discipline of History well tackled is hard work. And if the goal posts for good historical writing and argument and teaching are moved we will certainly lose not gain an audience in this region and indeed in the rest of the world. We are already in danger of this happening as History is seen as a "do it yourself" operation with half empty work boxes full of relativistic sub-clauses (on the one hand) and sherry quaffing absent minded professors mumbling dates (on the other).

History in chords

Why can't we do both? I want to be an historian and a public health expert. I told them, "Listen, the two are connected and I will do both.[7]

In April of 2001 an outstanding history student at the University of Natal in Durban was interviewed by a Selection Committee making decisions about the awarding of prestigious international scholarships for study in the USA. The Committee, drawn almost entirely from the ranks of distinguished South Africans, all with tertiary qualifications, was evidently impressed by this student's academic record. In short she was an ideal scholarship candidate in any setting, but her gender and race classification (still maintained, with little challenge, in South African university settings as part of the Equity and Affirmative Action drives, and broader commitments within the educational sector in general) also counted in her favour. The Committee had evidently decided to interview her despite their anxiety, voiced early in the interview, concerning her future plan: to undertake a PhD in Public Health. How on earth could her past degrees equip her for this future path, they asked? How could someone evidently passionate and informed about history–the history of Southern Africa; the history of medicine and epidemics; the history of women and gender relations–how could such as person be a serious contender for a position as a PhD candidate in a School of Public Health. Ultimately the candidate managed to convince the Committee, in the hour or so when she met them face to face, and by reference to several other aspects of her submission that this was a possible and worthy career and study plan, and they awarded her a scholarship.

---

7. Personal e-mail communication, August 2001, with author and an MA student, in the Historical Studies Programme, at the University of Natal, Durban.

At about the same time that this graduate student, at the start of her academic career was defending the link between the serious study of history and
the work of applied public health policy-evaluation and research, a highly
respected, widely published, and decorated figure in Southern African historical scholarship, Shula Marks, was giving her plenary talk at the University
of the Witwatersrand Conference AIDS in Context. Marks opened her session by asking: "What can an historian say about the AIDS pandemic?" She
continued with a 10 page address structured around responding to that very
question.[8]

Her paper, and the papers collected in the first of several forthcoming
books and volumes emerging from the Conference, all evince what the historian, Peter Delius, and the historical sociologist, Liz Walker, describe in their
Introduction as the crucial work of historians and other social researchers.
This new wave of research has arisen late in the epidemic's research process,
and its foundation is the ethnographic work of the 1900s to 1950s anthropological researchers, as well as the revisionist historians of the 1970s and 1980s.
Delius and Walker point to what any reader on South African life knows: the
epidemic is high on South Africa's political agenda. Neither a day nor week
passes without HIV/AIDS related civic action, government or cabinet level
comment, organized labour or business action or reaction. Yet, the authors
argue:

> The epidemic has not, however, enjoyed equal prominence in social scientific
> research ... while there are important social scientific research projects under
> way, we have a limited understanding of the social factors that have fuelled the
> especially rapid expansion of AIDS in the region. All too often the discussion of
> causes does not proceed beyond invoking a crude and undifferentiated role for
> poverty and/or migrancy. Much work remains to be done on the specific interac-
> tion of the historical, social, political and cultural factors that have shaped the
> epidemic.

Walker and Delius do not explain the cause for this late start, except for pin-
pointing the sense of urgency in non-governmental and certain state sectors
around the epidemic after 1994 and especially after 1997, which animated
emergency-style focus on rapidly executed projects set up with the promise or

---

8. Shula Marks, "An Epidemic Waiting to Happen? The Spread of HIV/AIDS in South
   Africa in Social and Historical Perspective", *African Studies*, Vol. 61, No. 1, 2002,
   pp. 12–13.

hope of immediate and maximum clinical and behavioural benefits.[9] The implication is that this pressure could have contributed to the "on the side lines" response from researchers of language and literature, music and cultural life, deep political and sociological analyses, and responses from within the ranks of historical researchers.

Of course there are historians working at the very coal-face of HIV/ AIDS-related activist and research circles, but they sometimes have to be found under the rocks of these individuals more public identities! Zackie Achmat, possibly the most important figure to emerge in the civic life of this new society, as head of the Treatment Action Campaign (TAC), is the pre-eminent example, but he is not alone.[10] Several screenings on SABCTV and E-TV, of a biographical documentary, which includes details of his present life as a sufferer from AIDS, have animated national interest around him, with talk-shows and other radio shows. This has been cemented recently by public references to his courage and the national need to support the cause for which TAC stands in speeches and addresses by former president, Nelson R. Mandela.[11]

---

9. Peter Delius and Liz Walker, "Introduction: Aids in Context", *African Studies*, Vol. 61, No. 1, 2002, p. 5.

10. Biographical information on Zackie Achmat is taken from a decade long association with him personally and professionally and from published sources: his official CV (as submitted to the University of Natal FORUM lecture planning committee; a summary of his non-academic credentials widely reported in major newspapers at the time of his award-presentation to the United Nations and major newspaper articles on him including B. Berisford's in *Mail & Guardian* from 2000 to 2002; published articles he has written such as Z. Achmat, "It is not just lives that are at risk: The political manipulation of the Medicines Control Council is a threat to our democracy" *Sunday Times*, 11 August 2002; his own address to the UN: Z. Achmat, "Realising the right to health: Access to HIV/AIDS-related medication: The role of civil society in South Africa" to the 58th Session of the UN Commission on Human Rights, April 3 2002 and the excellent summary and analysis of his work and that of his associates in M. Mbali, "A History of AIDS policy-making in South Africa", Unpublished Dissertation, Durban, University of Natal, Historical Studies Honours, 2001 as well as M. Mbali, "Mbeki's Denialism" in *Mail & Guardian*, April 2002.

11. SABC showed "Special Assignment" in November 2001 and again in 2002. The documentary showed, "Its My Life", is an incredible documentary film about him and the political struggle of the Treatment Action Campaign and his refusal to take anti-retroviral medicines until they are made available by the government in public hospitals and clinics. For more information: http://frif.com/new2002/mlife.html. Also June and July speeches by Mandela as reported in the *Business Day* and *Sunday Times* as well as *Mail & Guardian*.

Achmat is a trained historian who has, since his late teens, twinned a deep commitment to political activist work with a thirst for structured reading and research into the past, where the twisted roots of causes and deep structures nourish present society. Enriched, he argues, by his jail experiences, he saw no necessary distinction between work in film making and film distribution (which led to award winning films such as *Die Duiwel Maak My Hart So Seer*) and activist work; between this work and his scholarship around sexual identity (which fed into the arguments for the South African precedent internationally: the passage into law of an "equality of sexual identity" section in the Bill of Rights, and thus the new Constitution); and between his work on sexuality and disease and his current TAC leadership role. His first graduate thesis and MA work undertaken at UCT, as well as published historical papers, have all played a key role in his thinking and strategy in the TAC.[12] He and other members of South Africa's activist and civil service based intelligentsia have drawn a direct link between the crisis in HIV/AIDS now and the apartheid era, and have repeatedly stressed the need for detailed historical connections between the past and present.

In his addresses and speeches Edwin Cameron (Justice of the Supreme Court of Appeal, author of leading papers and texts on labour history and labour law, as well as a key late apartheid advocate in trials defending activists charged with labour law and political crimes, and more recently known for his public announcements about his HIV/AIDS positive status and his work supporting the TAC), captured this mood:

> ... the denial of AIDS represents the ultimate relic of apartheid's racially imposed consciousness, and the deniers achieve the ultimate victory of the apartheid mindset. [13]

Neither Achmat nor Cameron are practising historians in the sense that either holds posts in academic departments or programmes of history, but their writing is shot through with references to historical argument and they are *au fait* with the past 20 years of historical scholarship on this region.

---

12. Z. Achmat's UWC Honours and MA citation; his 1992/3 *Social Dynamics* paper as well as references to his work in Mark Gevisser and Edwin Cameron, *Defiant Desire: Gay and Lesbian Lives in South Africa*, Johannesburg, Ravan Press, 1994.

13. Judge Edwin Cameron's speech delivered at the launch of Gideon Mendel's book, *A Broken Landscape*, in the South African National Gallery, Cape Town on 13 April 2002. Online website for SA National Gallery.

In 2000 Justice Cameron was awarded an honorary degree by the UND Faculty of Law. I was honoured to give the oration before his award. I spent some time explaining to him how the course myself and members of my Department teach annually, "Law and Society", is run specifically for law students. This is a history course in every way but name and yet we have only managed to get law students through the door by seeing South African history through the thresholds of world experience. And we have only been able to draw out first rate historical oral debate, research, and written papers by immersing the student intake in legal cases and examples. We also offer courses at Edgewood College (the last remains of the college level system for school teacher training in the province, now part of the university) and the Medical School campus. At both these campuses students enrolled in courses without "history" flagged in the title find themselves in history courses. In these courses we engage students in reflections and readings about the difficulties, posturings, power plays, classist, gendered, raced and other evidently and less obviously position-based truth claims of this history profession, and the longing for, the doubt within, the human search for evidence and counter evidence, certainty and objectivity. In short, we teach history through many back doors at UND.

In a 2001 edition (also available online) of the University of Natal's in-house magazine, NUFOCUS, journalist Kathy Waddington, wrote a piece that conveyed some of the energy and enthusiasm with which our small group has gone about addressing itself to this set of complications in our imagined and created History audience:

> Leading the way ... is the Historical Studies Programme at Natal University's Human Sciences Faculty in Durban. Five years ago the number of history students declined dramatically – mostly as a result of the national Education Department's withdrawal of grants and bursaries for student teachers – and appeared to signal the demise of the department. Overnight, it seemed, from an overflowing department, with seven staff battling to cope with some 400 students, the lecture rooms had emptied and the remaining four staff tried to attract enough first year students to justify their existence. 'We refused to give up,' said Dr Catherine Burns. 'We had never believed that history was only for history teachers. But we had to do something to replace the vocational driving force that had been teaching, and it had to be something measurable.' A way was sought to convince employers that history students learned skills far beyond being able to teach history in schools.

The solution came with a force that has outstripped their expectations. The thriving programme will soon be back to its staff strength of seven and once again the corridors are bustling with students ... For the skills that underpin history scholars are fundamental to virtually all professional areas – the skills of logical debate, analysis, critical reasoning, detecting bias and contextualizing and evaluating evidence.[14]

During 1998 the students began publishing their own web pages and, in a pilot project with Emory University in Atlanta, where students were involved in a similar assignment on American culture and history, they used satellite hook-ups to inform and evaluate each other's work. At the end of that year, the students emerged with real experience in online archival evaluations.

By the year 2000 the third year students who had "guinea-pigged" the first courses created full online portfolios including essays, oral history projects, examinations and work done with different archives. Several students of the first group secured jobs soon after – one as a researcher in the corporate sector, others at news organisations, and national heritage and museum sites such as the Robben Island Museum. The coming years will see the programme reaching out to schools and industry, communicating this new area of knowledge and packaging the "new history" skills.

History Departments and programmes at several other South African universities are responding with hard work and similar creativity to these challenges, but many are not, and they are in a bad state of repair. Examining the demands and expectations being placed on history specialists by biomedical researchers; gender activists; educationalists; ethicists; legal scholars; development specialists; economists and others, historians are being called on with just as much urgency as in the 1980s, but to answer very different questions about the new South African social and political order, and indeed this region's place on planet earth. While, as we have seen, few historians are taking up this challenge, fewer still may be around in the future to prefer debates and policies outside of academic historiography. The reasons for this are complex: partly, as I have indicated, because many historians of Southern Africa live abroad; partly because the funding for teacher training dried up in the late 90s; partly because the take-up of history as a career by black intellectuals has been so limited, it appears as if "history" as a genre of human

---

14. www.nu.ac.za/focus/text/vol12no2/cyberspace.txt. Also see UND Historical Studies Site at www.history.und.ac.za/courses for links to staff and their research interests, recent publications, and courses. Also www.expertise.und.ac.za.

thought production, is under siege. But this appearance disguises key openings and potentials.

The case of the expansion of medical and health history (and its connections to the history of gender relations; sexuality; the family; and the complex inter-twinings of biomedical and indigenous knowledge systems and practices), or what I call the study of "desire, disease, delight and death", our common conditions, could provide, and to some degree are providing, new ground for history research, writing and teaching.

As this paper has implicitly argued, no theoretical paradigm is useful or interesting when it is so self-conscious it renders the study of past an unusable part of the dialogical material of human persuasion, with no different constraints or purposes than works of the imagination; or when the purpose of history is to score victories for new groups or classes of people against others. Young people today, as in all days, want to believe that they can communicate with others, be understood by different people, and so change themselves, that their lives have more meaning than their given positionalities. History as a discipline has the great capacity to be dialogical in its self-organization and methodology and in its impact and purpose. The rather late move towards the reading of post-structuralist theory and engaging with stand-point and extreme relativist writing, on the part of the academy of historians in South Africa, rendered many vulnerable to complete dismissal of the work of the past 20 years in particular. This also contributed to the weakness of History's response to the young students and new audiences for South African post-1994 histories. In turn, this is one reason among many for the popularity and inclusion of autobiographical works in the corpus of school, institutional, and private libraries.[15] While few lively minds approach an autobiography with complete naïveté (knowing there is purpose and intent in the work beyond the words on a page) readers of these texts perceive a head-on engagement with the past, a willingness to take responsibility for arguments and views and actions that seems to disappear mirage-like in new history writing. In school texts and in several curricula designed to "boil down" these critiques of master narratives of the past, an unpalatable concentrate was poured off into the school curriculum and undergraduate teaching. This was often as off-putting to curious minds as National Party Official School History.

To think of a way out of this, and to make critical and difficult debates and arguments of historical work part of the chorus of South African life, will require some new fingerwork and maybe even new instruments. We need to

---

15. M. Daymond; J. Hyslop; Catherine Burns; S. Nuttal.

consider the possibility of a national professional body, which accredits historians recognized by their educators and peers. This is turn will have to be debated at great length with a rage of history-engaged groupings: the emerging
and flourishing heritage community and associated tourism, museum and archive associations; with bodies of historians globally and with education and
other institutions. Such a suggestion (the need to create academically based
criteria for a category of work called "historical research") will have to be
carefully distinguished from politically conservative or socially elitist moves
which have sought, and could again seek, to isolate or undermine the goals
and values of the democratising of history writing and reception that the History Workshop Project, the New Nation publications, the "Write Your Own
History" and the many local based often oral and visual history projects have
evinced since their inception in the late 1980s and 1990s.

This new, and tentatively suggested direction, will itself require working closely with historians outside universities and research settings–ranging
from trained historians now in journalism, legal, public sector, commercial,
creative and other fields, as well as organic, self-trained and motivated historians who have other day jobs and work on history as they work on family,
memory and life. This body of professionally trained and engaged historians–an academy–will have to engage every day with researching, teaching,
public addressing, writing, and publishing. Their working "in chords" may
become vital for the next generation of South African historians, even more
than it was for the last. But what seems clear is that without any academic
set of commonly accepted frames for what constitutes professional rigorous
historical research and writing history will face emptier concert halls and
thinner school based audiences. But, if this is a solution, this scenario will
take a long time to develop. In the meantime, there is work to be done.

Young women and men across the world today, as well as young South
Africans, face a world of complexity and multiple layers of causation, culpa-
bility, compromise, contradiction, and contentedness. Many young women
and men are right to be bored and contemptuous of much of what passes for
history in schools and in the public domain. Histories, which address and
animate the pasts of these complex presents, have a thirsty audience, even if
that means that for the foreseeable future history will have to wear disguises
and sleep under rocks in the light of the southern sun.

GARY BAINES is a Senior Lecturer in the History Department, Rhodes University, Grahamstown, South Africa. He holds an MA from Rhodes University and a Doctorate from the University of Cape Town. His areas of research include South African urban history and culture, especially film and music. He has published a monograph and numerous articles on the history of Port Elizabeth where he lived for a decade.

ANNA BOHLIN graduated from the School of Oriental and African Studies in 1994 with a BA (Hon) in Social Anthropology and Politics. She completed her doctoral dissertation, "In the Eyes of the Sea: Memories of Place and Displacement in a South African Fishing Town" in 2001 at the Department of Anthropology, Gothenburg University, Sweden, and is currently working on a Sida-financed anthropological project entitled Land Restitution and Local Citizenship in South Africa: Place, Memory and Democratisation. Among her publications is "The Politics of Locality: Remembering District Six in Cape Town" in Lovell (ed.) *Locality and Belonging*, London: Routledge Press, 1998.

COLIN BUNDY is Professor, Director, and Principal at the School of Oriental and African Studies, University of London. He studied at the University of Natal and the University of the Witwatersrand, got his MPhil in American History and a DPhil in South African Rural History from Oxford University. Colin Bundy held teaching and research positions at the University of Oxford before returning to South Africa in 1985 as Professor in History at the University of Cape Town. In 1987, he had a joint appointment as Professor of History at both UCT and the University of the Western Cape, before moving full-time to UWC in 1991. In 1994, he moved into university administration and served as Vice-Rector at UWC before moving to the University of the Witwatersrand, Johannesburg in 1997, where he served as Principal and Vice-Chancellor. Colin Bundy was an influential member of a generation of historians who, in the 1970s and 1980s, contributed to the reinterpretation of South African history. Best known for his *The Rise and Fall of a South African Peasantry*, he also co-authored *Hidden Struggles in Rural South Africa* and wrote *Remaking the Past: New Perspectives in South African History*. He has written more than 40 scholarly articles and chapters on South African history and politics, and over a hundred reviews and shorter articles. He has been

Editor of the *Journal of Southern African Studies*. In South Africa, Professor Bundy chaired the UNESCO National Commission, was a member of the Board of the Human Sciences Research Council, and the Council of the Robben Island Museum.

CATHERINE BURNS is a Senior Lecturer in History at the University of Natal in Durban. She obtained her BA Honours in History at the University of the Witwatersrand, an MA in History from Johns Hopkins University, and she did her PhD on "Reproductive Labours: The Politics of Women's Health in South Africa: 1900 to 1960" at Northwestern University. Burns is currently involved in research on the social history of biomedicine in South Africa, which focuses on the history of western biomedicine in Southern Africa. The field of research includes women's health, indigenous health and healing systems, and the history of women and past and present gender identities in Southern Africa. Part of this research focuses on the work of nurses and their historical roles, as well as women's letter writing 1920s to 1940s. She has published widely on these themes.

ALLISON DREW teaches Politics at the University of York. Her research has focused on South African politics and history, especially the relationship between socialist organizations and the national liberation movement. She has published *Discordant Comrades: Identities and Loyalties on the South African Left*, 2000, 2002, *South Africa's Radical Tradition: A Documentary History*, 2 vols., 1996–97, and numerous articles. Her biography of South African Communist Sidney Bunting, Between Empire and Revolution: A Life of Sidney Bunting, 1873–1936, will appear in 2007. She is currently engaged in comparative research on Communism in South Africa and Algeria.

SAUL DUBOW was educated at the universities of Cape Town and Oxford and received his PhD from St. Antony's College. He has been at Sussex University since 1989 where he has been working as Professor and Chair of History at the School of African and Asian Studies. His teaching and research concentrates on the history of modern South Africa from the mid-nineteenth century to the present. His work has focused on the development of racial segregation and apartheid in all its aspects: political, ideological and intellectual. He has special interests in the history of race and national identity, as well as the nature of imperialism and of colonial science. He is currently the holder of a British Academy Research Readership and is completing a book on *The Commonwealth of Knowledge*. Dubow's principal publications include *Racial Segregation and the Origins of Apartheid in Twentieth Century South*

Africa, 1919–36, 1989, *Scientific Racism in Modern South Africa,* 1995, and *The African National Congress,* 2000. He is on the editorial board of the *Journal of Southern African Studies* and is director of the Southern African Research Centre.

ALBERT GRUNDLINGH is Professor and Head of the History Department at the University of Stellenbosch. Before taking up the position as Head of the History Department at Stellenbosch in 2001, he headed the History Department at the University of South Africa (Unisa). Professor Grundlingh has published monographs on collaborators in Boer society during the South African War of 1899–1902 and South African black people and the First World War. Among his publications are "Sosiale geskiedenis en die dilemma in afrikanergeskiedskrywing", *South African Historical Journal,* 19, 1987 and *Writing a Wider War: Rethinking Gender, Race, and Identity in the South African War, 1899–1902,* Ohio University Press, 2002 (together with Greg Cuthbertson and Mary-Lynn Suttie).

MARTIN LEGASSICK is Professor in the History Department at the University of the Western Cape. He holds a MA from Oxford University and a PhD from the University of California, LA. He also worked at the University of Warwick. Legassick has written on many aspects of South African history and society, from pre-colonial times to the present day. His current research focus is on the Northern Cape. He has directed several projects for the Commission on Restitution of Land Rights concerning forced removals in the Northern and Western Cape. He is also involved in the Presidential SADET project, researching the history of the struggle for democracy in South Africa between 1960 and 1994. Through the South African Historical Society, he has examined the teaching of history under Curriculum 2005. He is the author of works like: "The frontier tradition in South African historiography", *Collected Seminar Papers on the Societies of Southern Africa,* Vol. II, Institute of Commonwealth Studies, 1971; "The making of South African 'Native Policy' 1913–23: The origins of segregation", Institute of Commonwealth Studies Postgraduate Seminar, 5/2–1972; "Legislation, Ideology and Economy in Post-1948 South Africa in Martin Murray (ed.), *South African Capitalism and Black Political Opposition,* Cambridge, Massachusetts, 1982.

MERLE LIPTON is a Senior Research Fellow at the School of African and Asian Studies, Sussex University. She has also worked at John Hopkins University, Yale University, at Chatham House, and the Centre for International Studies at the London School of Economics. Merle Lipton's current research area is "The role of economic factors in eroding apartheid: Revisiting the debate about South Africa". This research, which will focus on the role of business and of economic sanctions, is funded by the UK's Economic and Social Research Council. Her publications include *Capitalism and Apartheid: South Africa 1910–86*, Gower, 1986, *Sanctions and South Africa*, London School of Economics, 1991, *State and Market in Post-Apartheid South Africa*, Witwatersrand University Press, 1993, "White Liberals, the 'Left' and the New Africanist Elite in South Africa", in *International Affairs*, January 2000, and "The Role of Business in South Africa: Confronting a Painful Past: Contributing to a Challenging Future", *Research Report*, Afras, Sussex University, 2001.

BERNHARD MAKHOSEZWE MAGUBANE is Professor of Sociology and Director for the South African Democracy Education Trust. He holds an BA and an MA from the University of Natal, Durban, an MA in Sociology, and PhD in Anthropology from the University of California, L.A. Magubane returned to South Africa after working for many years at the University of Connecticut. He went to the United States in 1961 to campaign for an end to apartheid. He has held teaching positions at the University of Zambia, UCLA and at SUNI in Birmingham. He has also worked at the Monthly Review Press. After returning to South Africa, Professor Magubane joined the Human Sciences Research Council as a Chief Research Specialist. He has published extensively, and his most widely read works include *The Political Economy of Race and Class in South Africa*, Monthly Review Press, New York, 1979/1990 (edited with Nzongola-Ntalaja), *Proletarianisation and Class Struggle in Africa*, Synthesis Publications 1983 (edited with Ibbo Mandaza), *Whither South Africa?*, Africa World Press, 1988, *The Making of a Racist State: British Imperialism and the Union of South Africa, 1875–1910*, Africa World Press, 1996.

MARTIN J. MURRAY works as Professor at the Department of Sociology, the State University of New York at Binghamton. He holds a BA in Philosophy from the University of San Francisco, an MA in Philosophy, and a PhD in Sociology from the University of Texas in Austin. Professor Murray has worked at the Department of Sociology, the University of the Witwatersrand, at the University of Cape Town, and at the Department of Sociology, the University of Missouri, Kansas City. His books include *Visions of the New South Africa: Myth and Memory after Apartheid*, London/New York, Verso, 2000. *The Revolution Deferred: The Painful Birth of Post-Apartheid South Africa*, London, 1994, "Building Fires on the Prairie," in *South Africa: Time* *of Agony, Time of Destiny*, London, 1987, several chapters in *South African Capitalism and Black Political Opposition*, Boston, 1980, he has also published numerous others articles and papers.

THIVEN REDDY is a Senior Lecturer in the Department of Political Studies at the University of Cape Town. He completed his Bachelor of Social Science Honours degree at the University of Natal in Durban and his Masters and PhD in Political Science at the University of Washington in Seattle. His areas of specialisation are Comparative Politics including Contemporary South African Politics and Political Theory including Marxism and Post-Colonial Theory. His book *Hegemony and Resistance: Contesting Identities in South Africa*, London, 2000, draws on the writings of Gramsci and Foucault to theorise the construction of identity in South Africa. He has published articles on political theory, South Africa's democratic transition, and contemporary South African politics. He was awarded a Commonwealth Fellowship to Bristol University in 2001 and the Harvard/Mandela Fellowship in 2003.

CHRISTOPHER SAUNDERS is Professor in History at the University of Cape Town. His doctorate from Oxford University dealt with the history of the Transkei. Since then, he has been one of the most productive South African historians. He has written widely on various aspects of Cape and South African history. Prof. Saunders' main research interests are in the areas of Cape history, South African historiography, recent Namibian history, education policy and nation-building. He is the author of numerous books on aspects of South African history and of many articles especially in the *South African Historical Journal*. Among his best known publications are *Historical Dictionary of South Africa*, London, 1983/2000; *The Making of the South African Past: Major Historians on Race and Class*, 1988, and *South Africa. A Modern History*, Fifth Edition, 2000 (together with Rodney Davenport).

HANS ERIK STOLTEN is a historian from the University of Copenhagen, where he works as a lecturer and researcher at the Centre of African Studies. He has also been working with the Great Danish Encyclopaedia as author and reader on Southern African topics. He has a history in the Danish anti-apartheid movement and in international solidarity work. He has written articles, reviews and reports on South African matters for several periodicals and he was editor of two books on the anti-apartheid movement. His MA examined the history of the South African trade union movement and his PhD dealt with the writing of history in South Africa. He worked as Research

Fellow for Denmark at the Nordic Africa Institute in Uppsala, Sweden from 1999 until 2002.

ELAINE UNTERHALTER is Senior Lecturer in Education and International Development at the Institute of Education, the University of London. Her early academic training was as a historian and she studied at the University of the Witwatersrand and at Cambridge University. She completed her PhD at the School of Oriental and African Studies in London. This was a social history of the Nqutu District of Zululand in the late 19th century. Her later work has focused on the sociology of gender and education. She has written on international organisations, and on gender and development issues in South Africa, India and Bangladesh. Her main research interests focus on the education of women and girls with particular focus on Southern Africa. Her current funded research project is on the National Qualifications Framework in South Africa and its impact on women and she is doing collaborative research together with the Education Policy Unit at the University of the Witwatersrand, Johannesburg.

GEORGI VERBEECK is currently Associate Professor of History at the universities of Maastricht in the Netherlands and Leuven in Belgium. His recent publications concentrate on the historiography and politics of memory in Germany and South Africa. His publications include "Een nieuw verleden voor een nieuw natie. Een Duits model voor Zuid-Afrika?", in Jo Tollebeek, Georgi Verbeeck and Tom Verschaffel (eds), *De lectuur van het verleden. Opstellen over de geschiedenis van geschiedschrijving aangeboden aan Reginald der Schryver*, Louvain, 1998 and "A New Past for a New Nation? Historiography and Politics in South Africa. A Comparative Approach", in *Historia*, 45, 2, 2000.

WESSEL VISSER has been a Lecturer in South African history at the University of Stellenbosch since 1988. He completed his PhD in 2001 and was promoted to senior lecturer ad hominem in 2003. His research specialization is the history of the South African labour movement, trade unions, labour, socialist and communist press. His current research project deals with the history of the South African Mine Workers' Union. His PhD dealt with the role of the press during trade union organising.

AAM	Anti-Apartheid Movement
AB	Afrikaner Broederbond/Broederbond
ANC/SANNC	African National Congress/South African Native National Congress)
Antikom	Anti-kommunistiese Aksiekommissie
AWB	Afrikaaner Weerstandsbeweging
BC/BCM/BCMA	Black Consciousness Movement of South Africa
BL	British Library, London
CAHAC	Cape Areas Housing Action Committee
CAS	Centre of African Studies, Copenhagen
Codesa	Convention for a Democratic South Africa
COSATU	Congress of South African Trade Unions
CPSA/SACP	Communist Party of South Africa/South African Communist Party
CRLR	Commission on Restitution of Land Rights (Land Commission)
DACST	Department of Arts, Culture, Science and Technology
DANIDA	Danish International Development Assistance
DoE	Department of Education
FET	Further Education and Training (Curriculum)
GAA	Group Areas Act
GEAR	Growth, Employment and Redistribution Strategy
GET	General Education and Training (Curriculum)
GNU	Government of National Unity
HARME	The History and Archaeology Report to the Minister of Education
HBU	Historically black universities
HEG	History Education Group
HRC/SAHRC	South African Human Rights Commission
ICS	Institute of Commonwealth Studies, University of London
ICU	Industrial and Commercial Workers Union
IDS	Institute of Development Studies, University of Sussex

IFP	Inkatha Freedom Party
ISMUS	Institute for the Study of Marxism, University of Stellenbosch
JSAS	Journal of Southern African Studies
MCH	Ministerial Committee on History
MDM	Mass Democratic Movement
NAI	Nordiska Afrikainstitutet/Nordic Africa Institute, Uppsala, Sweden
NGK/DRC	Nederduitse Gereformeerde Kerk/Dutch Reformed Church
NGOs	Non-government organisations
NP	National Party
OBE	Outcomes-based education
OFS	Orange Free State
OH	Oxford History (eds Wilson and Thompson 1969/71)
RDP	Reconstruction and Development Programme
SACOB	South African Chamber of Commerce
SADET	South African Democracy Education Trust
SAHP	South African History Project
SAHRA	South African Heritage Resources Agency
SAM	South African Museum
SATLC/SAT&LC	South African Trade and Labour Council
SOAS	School of Asian and African Studies, University of London
SOMAFCO	Solomon Mahlangu Freedom College in Tanzania
TAC	Treatment Action Campaign
TRC	Truth and Reconciliation Commission
UDF	United Democratic Front
Unisa	University of South Africa, Pretoria
UWC	University of the Western Cape
V&AW	Victoria & Alfred Waterfront
WITS	University of the Witwatersrand

More abbreviations can be found on a website, together with a chronological list of events in South African history, references to literature on South African historiography, etc.: http://www.jakobsgaardstolten.dk/ Choose the path: Databases, Queries.